The testimonials below are from individuals who have used the strategies in this book to achieve great results, but they do not necessarily represent the opinion of the organization he or she is affiliated with. Keep in mind that your results will vary and depend on a variety of factors, such as your work experience and skill in applying the strategies in this book, as well as the prevailing job market and wage conditions in which employment is being sought.

From Job Seekers . . .

These strategies have worked for me twice. I sent out two resumes, landed two interviews, and accepted a $30,000 position with a $2,000 sign-on bonus. And, I was a new graduate! In my next move, I used the same resume to apply and be hired for a position with a major international avionics company that started at $37,000. Within two years my salary has grown to $50,000. The Proven Resumes System really does result in great resumes that can help you land a job you love!

—*Dawn Mitchell, Field Engineer*

After reading Regina's book and writing a resume that highlighted my sales achievements, I applied for an internal position. My supervisors complimented me extensively on my resume and promoted me from sales rep to sales manager—with a fifty percent salary increase! I would have never achieved such a promotion without the strategies I learned in Regina's book. Several years later, I'm still referring to her materials to update my resume, and each time I find something new to improve. The most recent promotion I received resulted in a salary package increase of nearly twenty-three percent! Thanks again!

—*Darla J. Piercy, Sales Manager*

In one day of flooding the net with my new and improved resume, I got offered forty-five dollars an hour in Atlanta, fifty dollars an hour in Tulsa, and sixty dollars an hour in New Jersey. The offer I took was less, but it's less than two miles from my home. After being on the job ten months, my employer dusted off my resume and offered me another position at a twenty-nine percent pay increase! . . . [T]he money I spent on your book has easily returned a thousandfold. Smartest money I ever invested!

—*Al White, Programmer/Software Tester*

Using the resume and cover letter styles you recommend in your book, I generated over a fifty percent request for interviews. I then landed a position with GTE, which provided an opportunity to make $10,000 more annually. Thanks so much!

—*Michelle VanWinkle, Account Executive*

I hadn't been getting responses, then I rewrote my cover letter following Regina's system, which includes using skill-based paragraph headings, and I immediately got a hit. I did another letter highlighting in bold the key words that I had picked out of the ad, and got a hit with that also. Now I'm rewriting my resume. This system really works!

—*Mark W. Rosenquist, MSBA*

I landed my current position as a computer/network specialist, which increased my salary by ten percent after using these strategies. Prior to reading Regina's book, I had sent out numerous resumes and cover letters with little response. After I used her techniques, I received three responses within a week and several more after I landed my job. Regina's book made resume writing enjoyable, and that's pretty amazing!

—*David Brendible, Computer/Network Specialist*

I used my new resume for application to a very competitive graduate program for nurse practitioners. Well, my application was accepted! Since that time I've also used your strategies to write my resume and be hired as a nurse practitioner. Thanks for helping me achieve my career goals!

—*Barbara Ann Boslaugh Haner, MN, ARNP, Certified Family Nurse Practitioner*

. . . I applied for two positions . . . and got called for interviews for both. Today I was hired on the spot for the second one. I knew that if I could just get in for an interview I could get the job. I wouldn't have gotten the interview if not for the strategies presented in your book! You provide an invaluable service and I, for one, am most appreciative.

—*Karen Brady Smith*

I printed off my new resume, faxed it to three companies, and had callback messages within three hours for all three companies. It's too late in the day to call today, but I'm right there first thing in the morning. Thanks again.

—*John Franklin, Senior Safety Manager/Fire Warden*

From Career Professionals . . .

I provide placement service and help job seekers write resumes. Over the last three years I have had over 12,000 client visits. I have many books in my office but use yours exclusively. Many clients weren't generating interviews, but by following the examples in your book they immediately began landing interviews and higher salary offers. Keep up the good work!

—*Bob Middlebrook, Executive Director, Sound Words Job Center*

I have increased revenues 400 percent in the last two years due to my ability to recruit and hire exemplary employees. The strategies in Regina's book have aided me in assisting my field employees in creating powerful resumes and presenting themselves in an effective way. This has resulted in better jobs and higher salaries leading to future growth in a world-leading industry. I recommend this book to anyone who is unemployed or looking for a better job!

—*Linda Philp, CTS, CPC, Onsite Staffing Specialist*

Following a successful formula creates a resume that works. I have used Regina's book to assist over 700 customers to produce concise and informative resumes that result in employment. That's as good as it gets!

—*J. Rellis, Program Specialist*

This book is the best out there in the Career Development field. It has assisted literally thousands of Shoreline Community College students yearly in launching careers at top salaries!

—*Berta Lloyd, Director Professional/Technical Programs and Career/Employment Services, Shoreline Community College*

This book really motivates job seekers. One of my students piped up in class and said, "I bought the book two weeks ago and have already read it. It is wonderful. I was feeling bummed out, couldn't find a job, and felt like I didn't have any skills. Then I started reading this book and couldn't put it down." It's getting started that's so hard for job seekers but this book makes it easy. The questions and examples really help people pull out and identify their best skills and this builds confidence and motivation . . . plus it lands jobs!

—*Gina Meyers, Counselor/Instructor*

This is the only resume book I've found that addresses self-confidence issues and that's critical to achieving maximum job search success. I've used Regina's strategies with hundreds of job seekers, and learning how to control your image really does increase your confidence, land more interviews, and results in higher salary offers.

—*Angela Picardo, Job Search Instructor*

After a presentation on Regina's methods, a student came back so excited. Not only had she written a great resume and been offered a new job, but she had also helped her friend rewrite his resume and he got a great new job. Regina's method is graspable and successful!

—*Julia Buchholz, Career Counselor*

This is the most outstanding resume book I have used in three decades of work with thousands of university graduates and students seeking jobs. They feel stronger and are hired after using Regina's powerful strategies. A must for all job seekers, career classes, and counselors.

—*Kathleen Bernhard, Ph.D., Director, Counseling and Student Activities, University of Washington, Bothell*

This is the best resume book I've read in fourteen years of education experience. Our staff used the book for three months and significantly increased student placement.

—*Ed Tarry, Past V.P. of Operations, a Northwest Technical College*

As a Business Communications professor, I've seen scores of books on resume writing. This book is truly vastly superior in its emphasis on the visual and psychological framing of the resume and its suggestions about how to target market experience to achieve maximum results—and salary increases! The Before and After examples are excellent!

—*Anne Illinitch, Assistant Professor, Business Administration*

Using Regina's book, a job seeker wrote her resumes to match the descriptions of three job announcements. She sent out three resumes, each of which led to an interview. All three employers extended job offers and she was able to choose the one that was best for her. A hundred percent success rate!

—*Nancy Kolosseus, Career Center Consultant*

PROVEN RESUMES

PROVEN RESUMES

*Strategies That Have Increased Salaries
and Changed Lives*

REGINA PONTOW

Ten Speed Press
Berkeley   Toronto

Proven Resumes: Strategies That Have Increased Salaries and Changed Lives is a derivative work of *Proven Resumes and Confidence Builders* by Regina Pontow, copyright © 1992, 1994, 1995, 1996, 1997, 1998.

Names of individuals, employer and personal information, and product references used in the resumes and cover letters throughout this book have been changed to fictitious information to maintain confidentiality. Any resemblance to a particular individual or job situation is purely coincidental.

Publisher's Note: This publication is designed to provide accurate and authoritative information in regard to the subject matter covered. It is sold with the understanding that the publisher and author are not engaged in rendering professional career services. If expert assistance is required, the service of an appropriate professional should be sought. If legal advice regarding employment issues is required, the advice of an attorney should be sought.

Ten Speed Press
PO Box 7123
Berkeley, California 94707
www.tenspeed.com

Distributed in Australia by Simon and Schuster Australia, in Canada by Ten Speed Press Canada, in New Zealand by Southern Publishers Group, in South Africa by Real Books, in Southeast Asia by Berkeley Books, and in the United Kingdom and Europe by Airlift Books.

Text Design by Lisa Patrizio
Cover Design by Jennifer Crook

Library of Congress Cataloging-in-Publication Data

Pontow, Regina.
        Proven resumes : strategies that have increased salaries and changed lives / Regina Pontow.
                        p   cm.
        Includes index.
        ISBN 1-58008-080-4 (pbk.)
        1. Résumés (Employment) 2. Job hunting. 3. Applications for positions. I. Title.
HF5383.P652 1999
808'.06665—dc21   99-030493 CIP

First printing, 1999
Printed in Canada

1 2 3 4 5 6 7 8 9 10 — 03 02 01 00 99

CONTENTS

Acknowledgments . . . . *vi*

Preface . . . . *vii*

Introduction *1*

1 Image Control: The Key to Higher Salary Offers 9

2 Maximize Your Accomplishments 19

3 Choosing the Best Resume Format 27

4 Create a Powerful Resume in Six Steps 35

5 Skill Lists and Sample Sentences 65

6 Twelve Questions to Shape and
   Control Your Image 89

7 Strengthening Your Resume Content 103

8 Creating Powerful Objective Statements 109

9 What You Should and Shouldn't Tell Employers 119

10 Designing and Printing Your Final Resume 135

11 Sample Resumes That Will Blow Away
    Your Competition 139

12 Cover Letters That Increase Salaries and
    Land More Interviews 203

13 Electronic Resumes and Internet Job Search
    Strategies 227

14 How to Find and Land the Job You Want 245

15 Winning Interview Strategies 275

Conclusion *313*

Appendix *314*

Index *317*

ACKNOWLEDGMENTS

Scores of individuals have contributed to the success of this book and my thanks go to the following: the job seekers I have been privileged to work with and who ultimately laid the foundation for all of the strategies shared herein; those individuals who provided testimonials about the success they or their organizations achieved when using my materials; the many instructors who have used my materials in their classes; Sheryl Fullerton, my agent, for believing in this work and representing it when the market for resume books was already overflowing; Holly Taines White, my editor, for her expertise in shaping the logical flow of ideas so that the book is highly accessible to readers; and my daughter, Melissa, for working with me side by side in preparing the manuscript and in managing the ProvenResumes.com website.

PREFACE

Hundreds of worker assistance and college programs, career centers, schools, and municipal, military, and corporate outplacing departments throughout the United States use my materials. Based on the volume of clients these organizations counsel, I estimate that the strategies presented in this book have been used to teach effective resume and job search strategies to well over one million job seekers. To reach this point, my career has taken many turns.

In the early 1980s I started a resume writing business and within two years had written over 1,500 resumes. The first clients I worked with saw an immediate jump in their interview rates and the number of job offers they received. Seeing such successes, I knew that the system I was developing was unique and consistently positioned job seekers as top candidates. Wanting to expand my experience in the career field, I closed my resume business and became a personnel coordinator with a national employment agency. In that position I gained experience interviewing and placing hundreds of employees with major employers.

My next career move was to become an outside sales representative for a national temporary placement agency and develop experience placing employees in the high-tech industry. Having learned the ins and outs of the personnel business, I then opened and managed my own placement agency. Loving to teach and counsel job seekers, I found I needed a change from the constant demand of marketing my agency and became a career development instructor for a leading business college. Around this time I also finished my first book, *Proven Resumes and Confidence Builders*, and became a job placement specialist with the University of Washington, Bothell.

At UW Bothell, I taught job search classes and helped four-year students and master's degree graduates write their resumes. After hearing from a substantial number of students regarding their successes, the dean of the nursing program and an associate business professor asked me to give in-class lectures on resume development. Many UW Bothell students came to me for assistance in creating resumes as part of their application packages to graduate schools. My resume-writing strategies also proved successful in this arena as students using them began being accepted into highly competitive programs.

While at UW Bothell, I was asked to provide resume and job search training seminars to placement and instructional staff at other colleges. As word spread, a handful of state employment offices and worker assistance programs purchased my book and instruction materials. This quickly grew to more than forty offices. As a result of counselors in worker assistance programs seeing my strategies work with their own clients, I was asked to provide presentations to regional offices.

Needing more time to market my materials, I left UW Bothell and over the last ten years have written more than 4,000 resumes and spent well over 10,000 hours counseling job seekers in all areas of resume writing and job search strategies. In 1997 I launched my first website, ProvenResumes.com, which has been reviewed and listed in the career sections of major websites such as Yahoo! and AltaVista. A large portion of my time is now spent writing new resume materials and launching career-specific websites.

My initial desire to write resume and career books came about because so many of my clients experienced the same fears and feelings of self-doubt I did when changing jobs. I had felt that I must be the only one who had such feelings, but as I spent thousands of hours counseling job seekers I found that such feelings are universal and have a dramatic impact on our success and our self-esteem. Realizing this, I set out to create a system that would address and integrate these issues with proven resume writing, advertising, and marketing secrets. The outcome has been a program that increases job seeker confidence and self-esteem as an end result of writing a great resume or landing a better job.

Once you've completed this book, you too will experience increased self-esteem and confidence in your job skills. This is truly more important than better jobs or increased salaries, although they contribute much toward raising our standard of living and providing for our families.

However, this book does provide many testimonials about significant salary increases that job seekers have received; therefore, I believe it's important to remind readers that the results each person achieves in using this book will vary and may be different from those described in the testimonials. All readers should keep in mind that a variety of factors will determine each job seeker's success. These include, but are not limited to, each person's skill in applying the strategies in this book, looking for a job, and interviewing, as well as the prevailing wage and labor market conditions in which he or she is seeking employment. It has been my experience and the experience of those individuals providing testimonials that the strategies in this book do have a proven history of increasing job seeker salaries, but such results are not guaranteed. Job seekers can expect to learn a wealth of information that will enable them to create powerful resumes and apply proven strategies to advance their careers.

Many of the testimonials are from readers, instructors, or agency directors who used the first version of this book and the accompanying instructor set, which have been incorporated into this book. I have received permission to cite the organizations provided in the testimonials, but the testimonials do not necessarily represent the opinion of such agencies.

To protect the confidentiality of my clients, the names, addresses, employers, dates of employment, and other information have been altered in the resume examples shared in this book. Only the testimonials provide each person's actual name and job title. This has been done to prevent any person, business, or other entity from being recognized. Any similarity to an individual, business, organization, product, or any other detail mentioned is purely unintentional and any assumption of intentionality would be unfounded. Likewise, statistical or numerical information used in each resume is only provided to illustrate the principle of creating an excellent resume and has been changed to conceal each person's background. Although these changes have altered the resume examples from their original form, they still convey the principles of creating highly effective resumes for each targeted job objective.

Throughout this book I tell stories of job seekers that I have counseled or who have used my materials. Such anecdotes reflect my own experience in hiring job applicants along with feedback I've received from employers as to why they hired or did not hire someone. The examples I provide are based on these factors and do not represent the views of all employers or all job seekers.

I believe it's also important that job seekers use their own judgment in deciding when and how to apply the strategies presented throughout this book. If something does not apply to their situation or isn't an appropriate option for them, they should adapt what they learn to fit their own unique situation. If legal advice regarding employment issues is needed, then the advice of an attorney should be sought.

With all this said, my hope is that every reader will leave this book having acquired a tremendous amount of knowledge that results in a true sense of excitement and motivation in writing a powerful resume and carrying out an effective job search. Thanks to all the readers who use the proven strategies in this book. My best wishes in your journey!

Are Resumes Really That Important?

The strategies in this book form a comprehensive resume and job search program. They integrate the best of what I've learned as a resume writer, personnel agency owner, career instructor, and master trainer and have been proven effective by hundreds of career professionals who coach job seekers. By faithfully applying these strategies, you will not only write a resume that lands you more interviews and better job offers, you will also learn how to actively market yourself and project an image that makes employers take note of your accomplishments—and this leads to long-term career success.

Resumes have a tremendous impact on the number and quality of the interviews, job offers, and salaries we receive. Throughout this book you'll read the success stories of real people who have used their resumes as powerful career tools. Step by step, you'll discover how job seekers with incomes ranging from $20,000 to $200,000 have consistently

- Taken a zero to ten percent interview rate up to a thirty, fifty, or seventy-five percent rate . . . with some achieving 100 percent interview rates
- Received salary increases ranging from several hundred dollars more per month . . . up to as much as $20,000, $30,000, or more per year.

While these success rates may sound hard to believe, the system you'll learn in this book will transform your resume into one that grabs an employer's attention, sells your top qualifications in seconds, and creates an impressive image of you in an employer's mind. These key strategies will result in more interviews and higher salary offers for you.

A Strong Resume Conveys Your Image to Employers

On the basis of your resume, a prospective employer forms an impression of you before you even walk in the door for an interview. That's why strong resumes are so important. Most of us do not have the confidence or verbal skills to take our image from a low point and elevate it substantially during an interview. Many job seekers do not understand this critical point. They land interviews but don't get a job. So they flounder around trying to improve their interviewing skills. Yet, what they really need to do is step back and take another look at the image of themselves they have created in their resumes. Setting a strong and appropriate image is important for anyone, whether for a senior executive or for an entry-level worker.

To illustrate how important image is, we'll review several real-life examples. We'll start with Scott, who had landed nine interviews plus several second and third interviews. Yet he never received a job offer for the permanent teaching position he sought. His family was pushing him to take a training job with a bank but he didn't look happy telling me this. With tears in his eyes Scott said, "I've spent the last six years completing a master's degree in education because I love teaching children. It really hurts to think I'm not going to make it, but we can't keep going on like this financially." Knowing that teaching was really Scott's dream—not working for a bank—I reviewed his resume. Take a look at a section from Scott's first resume. It is very apparent why his interviews were going so poorly.

Substitute Teacher, Winston Elementary 8/98 to 12/98

1st Grade Student Teacher, Peter Frank Elementary 9/96 to 4/97

Church School Teacher, Hermitage Christian School 12/94 to 6/95

School Custodian, Lake Washington School District 10/93 to Present

Lab Technician, Western Photographics 6/92 to 8/93

Office Assistant, Radix Group International 6/91 to 5/92

Since Scott was landing interviews, he thought there wasn't any real problem with his resume. In reality, it was causing him many problems. For one, it set an image of him as having only taught first graders and Sunday School classes, and it presented an image of his longest employment as being a custodian. He hadn't provided descriptions of his teaching experience.

Scott's history of landing second and third interviews, but no job offers, proved that he, like most job seekers, was unable to overcome these problems and turn a weak image into a strong image during his interviews. Scott's resume needed a complete overhaul in order to present him as being well qualified. Take a look at this condensed section from Scott's After resume.

AFTER

1st, 2nd, 4th, and 5th Grade Substitute Teacher
- Taught students of varied academic, socioeconomic, cultural, and age levels. Substituted for classes of up to 60 students, adapting to a variety of teaching situations on short notice.

1st Grade—Primary Teacher
- Developed an innovative literature-based/Whole Language reading program that gave students of all reading abilities relevant choices of reading material and projects.
- Taught math using manipulatives, focusing on problem solving, computation, and math awareness in everyday life. Teamed with teachers to develop curriculum and share materials.

1st and 2nd Grade Student Teacher
- Used multiage and cooperative learning techniques to integrate two grade levels.
- Integrated computers into the curriculum using Jostens/MECC, introduced students to Windows and word processing, and started a class computer lab using surplus computers.

3rd Grade Instructional Practicum
- Tutored students one-on-one in math and observed a Spalding demonstration classroom.
- Oversaw students during recess.

6th Grade—Church School Teacher
- Taught small groups of up to 12, on a weekly basis.

Scott's new resume paved the way for interview success by emphasizing that he was an elementary teacher with experience in all grade levels. As Scott's new resume demonstrates, the layers of information that Scott needed to share about his teaching abilities were much too complex for him to communicate effectively in a short interview. Yet, within seconds, Scott's new resume conveys the depth of his experience. In only three weeks Scott landed a permanent teaching position and his dream finally came true.

Employers Look for Growth and Promotion Potential

Resumes are also important because they form the initial opinions employers have of our growth and promotion potential. Beyond the initial position we are hired for, many employers want to know that we can take on additional responsibility. A weak resume causes employers to have a narrow view of our promotion or growth potential. For example, if you compare Robert's vacuum parts manager description to his division manager description (see page 6), which one presents him as having greater growth potential? Which one makes Robert seem like a better long-term investment?

Always Lower the Employer's Risk

Employers are always at risk any time they make a hiring decision. Hiring an employee that does not work out can cost tens of thousands of dollars. Therefore, your resume should convince employers that they have little or no risk in hiring you. The After example we reviewed eliminated or substantially reduced the risk employers perceived in hiring each applicant. Throughout this book, you too will learn step-by-step strategies that control your image and help managers feel more comfortable about your present and future skills.

Getting Past Employer Screening

To achieve high interview rates, you must understand how resumes are screened. Many employers receive 100 to 400 resumes for each position they advertise, but select only five to fifteen people to interview. With competition like this, your resume must stand out and get an employer's attention. It must highlight skills an employer is looking for and be arranged in a style or format that makes these skills easy to spot. Your resume presents a written picture of you and must make an employer want to meet you in person.

Employers who receive hundreds of resumes must sort them quickly. Spending only thirty seconds to glance at each resume, employers take more than an hour and a half to screen 200 resumes. Most hiring officials have many other responsibilities and often view resume screening as an interruption in their workday. Therefore, your resume must attract and hold an employer's attention before he or she moves on to other tasks.

> *Studies show that employers spend as little as five to ten seconds glancing at resumes before discarding them or saving them to look at further.*

As employers find resumes that match their needs, they put them in a stack to be examined further. After all resumes have been screened, an employer then has a smaller stack of twenty to thirty resumes to review more thoroughly. This final screening narrows the last group to approximately five to fifteen resumes. These are the individuals who will be called for an interview. Therefore, your goal is to create a resume that "passes inspection" and lands, time after time, in that last pile of resumes that get interviews. If you are not getting enough interviews, then you know that your resume is not passing inspection and you need to rewrite it. You'll know you've done this successfully when you do land interviews for the jobs you want.

Writing a Resume Is Great Preparation for an Interview

Writing a resume makes you identify and verbalize your strongest skills and helps you be aware of your weaknesses. This is great preparation for an interview, since most employers ask you to describe both your strengths and weaknesses. Getting your skills on paper and presenting them in an effective eye-catching format also increase your confidence. Organizing your thoughts makes you better prepared to discuss how your skills match the position you are interviewing for.

Because most interviews only last fifteen to thirty minutes, you must be familiar with your qualifications before each interview begins. You must be prepared to sell yourself. You won't have time in an interview to assess your abilities or fumble around trying to express them. Most interviewers don't have the time or the skill to identify and pull this information from you. Your resume must do this for them, quickly and efficiently. A strong resume will also guide the interviewer as she or he asks you questions. After initial introductions, most employers will read your resume while you sit at their desks. Many will refer back to your resume in order to ask you questions about your work history and experience. In this way, a strong resume continually reinforces your best qualifications throughout the interview.

If you have a weak resume, the interviewer will ask you questions based on weak information. If you have a strong resume, the interviewer will ask you questions based on your greatest strengths. This automatically elevates your interviews, making you one of the strongest candidates, because the majority of applicants have very weak resumes.

Who Gets Hired?

It's often not the best technically qualified applicant who receives a job offer. It's the person who develops an effective resume and interviews well, thereby convincing an employer that he or she is the most qualified. I'm sure that of the nine interviews that Scott received, he was better qualified than several of the candidates who were hired. Yet they had probably created resumes that presented a broader range of skills than Scott's first resume had. On paper his competitors looked more qualified and were hired instead of Scott. The U.S. Census Bureau conducted a survey of ten million job seekers in order to identify successful job hunting tactics. It concluded: "The skills that make a person employable are not so much the ones needed on the job as the ones needed to get the job, skills like the ability to find a job opening, complete an application, prepare a resume, and survive an interview."

Just like Scott, many qualified job seekers apply for jobs but don't get hired. The real problem is that most people don't know how to market themselves effectively. Highly qualified applicants often lose job opportunities to lesser-qualified applicants because the lesser-qualified applicants know how to write effective resumes and market themselves.

You Must Market the Full Range of Your Skills

As you write your resume, it is very important that you market the full range of skills you possess that match the jobs you want. Many people have tunnel vision when it comes to their skills. They are used to describing their experience with terminology used only in their industry. This often limits their ability to see how these skills can be transferred or applied in other jobs or careers. For example, Todd was a construction worker who wanted to move into an office setting. He felt stumped every time he tried to describe his experience in such a way that he sounded qualified for an office position. Here's his first attempt:

CONSTRUCTION LABORER

- Completed labor projects on-site including concrete pouring and laying of foundations, digging of ditches, and laying of drainage pipes. Understand a wide range of construction terms and building requirements.

To begin the revision, Todd told me a little about his responsibility as a construction laborer. Each morning his supervisor came to the work site for about thirty minutes and gave Todd instructions for daily projects. His supervisor then returned late each day and inspected Todd's work. If anything was to be changed, he gave Todd instructions on what to do and inspected it again the next morning. To capitalize on Todd's experience completing projects, we substituted a skill heading for his job title, and avoided labor- and construction-oriented descriptions. Here's what we came up with:

PROJECT IMPLEMENTATION

Completed projects on properties valued to $ $3/4$ million, working independently over 90% of the time.

- Followed superintendent's work orders to meet contract specifications.
- Worked as part of a 4-person team completing rush projects.
- Position required attention to detail, accurate completion of work orders, and governmental reporting forms.

As you can see, Todd's experience does match that of many office workers who work independently, follow the instructions of others, process detailed paperwork, and serve as a team member who completes projects. Compare Todd's old description to the one you just read. Which one creates an image in your mind of someone who would fit into an office environment? This is another good example of how important it is to develop an image that matches the jobs you want and to set an appropriate image with employers.

Why couldn't Todd come up with the second description on his own? Because he got stuck, like many people do, viewing his job as he had always heard and seen it described. This also happens because we may experience negative feelings about ourselves and our jobs as we try to describe them. Todd really saw himself as a laborer on a construction site, and even though he wanted an office position he doubted his ability make such a career move. These feelings kept him from being able to see the value in what he had to offer employers. Just like Todd, many job seekers don't realize how many marketable and transferable skills they possess, regardless of the level of position they hold or the salary they make. Yet, when they are shown resumes describing similar skills to the ones they possess they say things like

> *"Hey, this resume could be mine!"*
> *"I didn't know the work I did was this important."*
> *"I'd never have thought to describe it that way."*
> *"Gee, I already feel better."*
> *"I guess I've got more skills and experience than I thought!"*

Robert experienced similar feelings of being unsure of his transferable skills. As a manager, he oversaw a division that manufactured vacuum-formed parts. Robert found it hard to move beyond his title of vacuum parts manager. Because most of us have no idea what a vacuum parts manager does, Robert had to make sure that anyone reading his resume would understand the full range of his skills. Compare these examples:

BEFORE **VACUUM PARTS MANAGER**
- Oversaw vacuum parts production. Maintained inventory and schedules.
- Supervised warehouse and production employees.

AFTER **DIVISION MANAGER**
- Managed manufacturing division generating production of $24 million annually.
- Oversaw 25 employees, successfully leading the department to meet or exceed all quotas.
- Maintained an in-house inventory of $1.5 million.
- Coordinated and expedited delivery schedules with the engineering department for 2,000 accounts.
- Administered all departmental activities including controlling a $ 3/4 million budget, overseeing payroll approval, issuing purchase orders, and verifying invoicing, production, and shipping logs.

Since Robert's goal was to move into a higher paying position in the $75,000 to $100,000 range, which description creates a strong and appropriate image? As you can see, Robert's After resume presents him as a person with much more impressive skills and responsibilities, deserving of a much higher salary.

Robert was thrilled with his new resume. It gave him a new way of viewing his experience and how his skills were transferable to higher-level positions. His new resume worked very well, and within a month he was hired to manage a new manufacturing division and received a fifteen percent salary increase.

People Put Little Effort into Creating Their Resumes

Consider that people spend two to four years, or more, of their lives completing a college education in order to land better jobs, pursue a particular career path, or improve their standard of living. Yet when it comes time to make these years of hard work pay off by applying for and landing a great job, most college graduates spend less than four hours writing a resume.

Compare the time spent writing a resume to the time spent in college classes. Most bachelor programs require more than 4,000 hours of class time, including time spent on research, internships, or doing homework. We all know that the process of obtaining an education is serious business. So why do people treat the process of marketing such an education insignificantly? Just as Scott's example proves, having an education does not guarantee career success. Knowing how to market your education and experience is often the critical point that determines career success.

It has never made sense to me that college programs don't treat resume and job search classes just as seriously as any other discipline. Scott put much more time and effort into researching and writing his master's thesis than he put into job hunting. This lack of effort almost caused him to waste years of education that he had worked so hard to obtain.

Outside of academia, consider people who have spent five to ten years of their lives shaping a career, fighting for promotions and higher salaries. Then it comes time to look for another job and these people are also willing to risk many years of hard work with a resume that they've spent just a few hours creating. Many people have probably spent more time writing an expense or sales report than writing their resumes.

I feel very strongly about this because I have helped thousands of job seekers who were ready to give up their career dreams, just like Scott was. Most job seekers or recent college graduates who get a poor response to their resumes think they are the reason they are not hired. Yet when they create resumes that market the full range of their skills, they get hired. So put forth the effort to create an excellent resume whether you are a seasoned professional or a college graduate!

It Takes Time to Create a Great Resume

You may feel impatient putting a resume together, perhaps taking only an hour or two to complete it. However, it takes time to evaluate the skills and abilities that you have developed over your years of employment. You may not remember some of your most important achievements until a day or so after beginning your resume. If you've already prepared your resume, you may be tempted to leave out any new information you remember. But this could be what catches an employer's eye and gets you an interview.

It often takes my clients several hours before they remember some of their significant achievements. For example, I worked with Sandra for about two hours, and we were almost done when I asked her if she received compliments on the job. She said, "Yes, I'm complimented all the time on how quickly I serve customers and how well I know their accounts." So I asked Sandra what her responsibility was in handling the accounts. She said, "Well, I deal with about fifty key accounts each day. In fact, I once reviewed the charge account for a major client and caught a $4,500 error. We should have charged the customer $5,000 but a typo was made and he was only charged $500. I went to my boss and let him know about the mistake. That's when he promoted me to oversee client accounts in our front office."

Before this discussion, Sandra had a self-image of being "merely a secretary." This new information presented her as an account manager, which is something entirely different. As we talked, I asked Sandra how she liked this type of duty. She said she loved dealing with customers and processing their accounts. As a result, we emphasized these skills in her resume. About five weeks later Sandra dropped in to tell me about her new account representative position. She was no longer a secretary and had made an impressive career move. Sandra beamed as she gave me her business card, pointed to her new title, and said, "I can't believe I just accepted a position that pays $800 more per month!" This story is just one more example that shows how important it is to take the time to thoroughly explore your skills and abilities in order to create a strong resume.

Your Resume Is a Powerful Career Tool

A resume that effectively matches your top skills to the jobs you want can accelerate your career and salary growth whether it's for an internal promotion or with a new employer. For example, Gina had been a sales representative working for a national hotel chain and wanted to move into a sales manager position and then be promoted to regional manager.

However, a large portion of her first resume was devoted to describing her prior experience as a front desk clerk, culinary hostess, and sales assistant. After applying the strategies in this book, Gina realized that her resume must emphasize the sales achievements most relevant to being a sales manager. After analyzing the sales manager job description, Gina focused her new resume entirely on her sales accomplishments under the headings of "Outside Sales," "Territory Development," and "Key Account Management." Under these headings she detailed the fact that she had increased sales to her base of 150 accounts by more than twenty-one percent, had consistently exceeded her quota by bringing in $500,000 in new sales per month, and had eliminated the need for an assistant, which cut labor costs by more than $25,000 annually.

Gina's new resume elevated her image by several employment levels, allowing her to be promoted to sales manager, with more than a fifty percent annual salary increase. By carefully analyzing the career growth she wanted to achieve and structuring her resume to market her most relevant skills, Gina made a very impressive career move.

As Gina's story, and dozens of others in this book, illustrates, you too will learn how to advance your career and create a resume that

- Controls and elevates your image
- Sells your top skills in seconds and matches them to the jobs you want
- Gets you screened in—not screened out
- Generates more interviews and higher salary offers
- Lays the foundation for stronger interviews
- Puts you ahead of your competition and positions you as a top candidate
- Makes your career dreams come true
- Increases your confidence
- Changes your life.

1 Image Control: The Key to Higher Salary Offers

There's probably nothing harder or more stressful than looking for a job. Whether you're just beginning or have already been looking for a job unsuccessfully, you may feel overwhelmed and not know what to do. If so, do any of these problems describe your job search and maybe your resume?

- I've been getting interviews and job offers, but terrible salary offers.
- I get into the second and third interviews, but don't get hired.
- I'm making a career change; I have a lot of great skills but I'm not getting interviews.
- I need a higher salary but my titles don't sound like the jobs I want so I'm not getting interviews.
- I want a management job, but employers aren't calling because I haven't had the title of manager.
- I'm an executive and the jobs I can apply for are limited so I haven't gotten any interviews.
- I'm a recent college graduate, but the interviews I get are unrelated to my education.
- I have the skills for a better job but keep getting offered entry-level jobs.
- I want a technical management job, but I'm offered jobs that are strictly technical.
- I'm older; when employers see my extensive work history they say I'm overqualified.
- I haven't worked in several years and I'm not getting a response to my resume.
- I've never written a resume before, and I don't know where to start.

You may be reading this book because you're dealing with one or several of these situations. If so, you may feel confused or discouraged. You may be running out of financial resources and beginning to believe that you'll never land a job you want. Or you may want to make sure that you avoid such problems. Be reassured, this book provides a rational process for creating powerful resumes that will get the results you want.

Ineffective resumes cause many of the problems described above because most of us don't understand how to control the image of ourselves we present in resumes. Employers look at the majority of resumes and think, "This resume doesn't list the skills or experience I need, so there's no reason to interview this person." To maximize job search success, we must learn how to identify what employers need and to tailor our resumes to match those needs. For example, let's say that Rhonda wants a position that will pay her $12,000 more as an assistant to the V.P. of a major *Fortune* 500 corporation, but her resume contains titles like front office secretary. An employer reading that title won't form a mental image of someone who's used to dealing with senior executives. What the resume doesn't show is that Rhonda currently works as an assistant to the V.P. of marketing for a firm with sales of $150 million and that Rhonda oversees all front office operations.

A resume that uses a heading like "Executive Assistant to V.P. of Marketing" will generate more interviews and higher salary offers because it creates the correct image. Rhonda goes from looking unqualified to looking qualified—and substantially increases her job search success.

Controlling Your Image, Step by Step

Creating a powerful resume begins with learning how to control and elevate your image. This process makes many people feel uncomfortable, even though they see that it's needed. If you feel this way, like many job seekers do, remember that the stories you read in this book are from real people who also felt this way, yet succeeded. *Proven Resumes* will guide you step by step in identifying and marketing the best of your skills. Learning how to control the image you present is essential, whether you're creating a chronological or a skill-based resume, or whether you're in the $12,000 or the $100,000+ salary range. Most of us have a very narrow view of our skills and abilities, and in turn we present this narrow view to employers—no matter how broad our skills really are. You must learn how to expand and broaden your own view of your skills and abilities so that you can convey an accurate image to employers. This chapter includes strategies that will help you develop a deeper, more well-rounded image in order to land more interviews and higher salary offers. If you feel anxious about your job search, like many job seekers do, Chapter 2 is devoted to confidence building and provides success stories that will inspire and encourage you.

Boost Your Response Rate

Many job seekers continue to use ineffective resumes for long periods of time, even though they aren't receiving interviews. To improve resume effectiveness, it makes sense to keep track of how many resumes you send out along with how many requests for interviews they generate. If you don't receive enough interviews—I like to see at least a twenty to thirty percent response rate—then your resume needs to be rewritten! That means you should receive four to six calls for interviews from every twenty resumes you send out. My optimum goal, for those who faithfully follow the *Proven Resumes* system, is a thirty to fifty percent response rate. Many stories in this book are from job seekers who received anywhere from a fifty to a one hundred percent response rate.

Some people will say that these figures are out of line and that I am building your hopes too high. If you were being encouraged to use an average resume and conduct an average job search, that might be true. But as you will see from the examples on the next few pages, these response rates aren't too high to expect. By learning how to control your image and how employers respond to job titles, main headings, and content within resumes, you can dramatically improve yours. It's not a mysterious or difficult process, but it does take advantage of proven advertising and resume writing secrets. Once you understand these secrets you'll not only write a better resume for yourself, you'll probably help all your friends and relatives write better resumes.

I met Fran while teaching a workforce training workshop. She was upset because she had applied for more than twenty customer service positions but hadn't landed even one interview. In one of the positions—which had a two-page job description—Fran had every one of the skills described, but still didn't get an interview. She was really frustrated. I could see that she was worried that her entire job search was going to be like this. Using the strategies you'll learn in this book, Fran rewrote her resume. In only a week she was telling me a very different story. She had faxed two resumes on a Friday, and on Monday had already gotten calls for interviews from both employers. Fran had taken her response rate from zero to one hundred percent. What was so different about her new resume? You'll see as you review Fran's Before and After resumes on pages 12 and 13.

Advertising Secrets: Who Is Your Audience and What Do They Want to Hear?

Fran's first step in creating a new resume was to do the first thing that advertisers do: understand the audience. Advertisers always study who their audience is, what that audience wants to hear, and what they need to tell their audience in order to generate sales. To create an effective resume, Fran also had to apply these strategies. Since Fran wanted a corporate customer service representative position, she needed to think about the type of environment she would be working in and what type of skills corporate employers need in staff performing this work. Then she could understand how to present her skills so that they match these needs.

To begin, Fran thought about the requirements that employers have for corporate customer service staff. She realized that corporate customer service staff need to project a professional image and often deal with large numbers of customers. They often work as part of a team, resolving customer problems in order to maintain strong customer relationships that result in repeat business and sales. Once Fran had identified the skills and image that corporate employers want, she realized that her Before resume had missed the mark. To understand why Fran's Before resume didn't work, we'll graph it.

Graph of Fran's Before Resume

As you'll see, graphing is a quick way to understand how employers will respond to the job titles, skill headings, and content you use in your resume. On the basis of this information they will decide whether or not they think you are qualified for the job. Let's look at a graph of Fran's Before resume. Keep in mind that Fran wants a corporate customer service representative position in the $33,000 range, so we've put that in the top left-hand corner of the graph. Her resume should create an image that matches that position in our minds and in employers' minds—so that's how we'll judge whether Fran's resume does the job. Let's think of Fran's work history in terms of how well each job title she's held in the past relates to the position she's seeking.

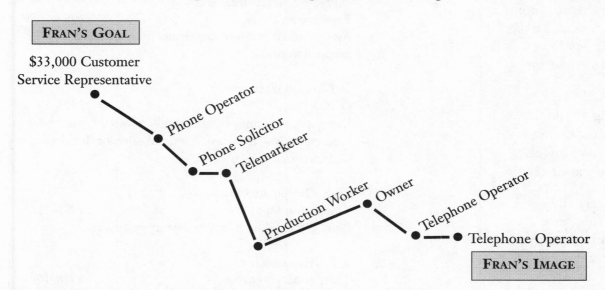

Fran's most recent job title was phone operator. Does this title match your image of a $33,000-per-year customer service position? Does someone who is a phone operator sound like they're qualified for this salary? No, so let's graph it below Fran's goal. Fran's second and third most recent job titles were phone solicitor and telemarketer. Do these titles make Fran's image go up or down? Most people would graph these titles much lower than directory operator.

What's wrong with Fran's Before resume?

- When you glance at Fran's Before resume, where does your eye go first, second, then third?

- What headings and job titles grab your attention?

- Does this information create an image of Fran's skills that make her sound qualified for a corporate customer service position?

- On the basis of the image this resume creates, what salary range does Fran look qualified for?

- Fran had been making $33,000 per year and wanted a customer service position at or above that level.

- Does this resume match that salary level?

Fran DelVecchio
555 55th Avenue
Fremont, MD 83945
(555) 555-5555

OBJECTIVE: An interesting position with growth company using customer service skills.

EXPERIENCE:

Pacific Northwest Telephone Company
Phone Operator 1995–1999
Provided directory assistance to customers.

Marketing Research Inc.
Phone Solicitor 1990–1994
Scheduled customer appointments for this condominium time-share company to receive gifts and on-site sales presentations.

You've Got It Maid
Telemarketer 1989–1990
Scheduled house cleaning appointments.

Widget Manufacturing Inc.
Production Worker 1989–1990
Assembled electronic components on high-speed production lines.

DelVecchio Fireworks
Owner 1985–1989
Developed customer accounts and increased repeat business each year owned. Managed sales for distribution of fireworks products.

Skagit Telephone Company
Telephone Operator 1981–1985
Long distance and marine directory assistance.

U.S. Telephone Inc.
Telephone Operator 1978–1981
Centrex and long distance directory assistance.

Fran DelVecchio
555 55th Avenue
Fremont, MD 83945
(555) 555-5555

Seek a position utilizing my
Customer Service, Management, and Administrative experience.

CUSTOMER SERVICE REPRESENTATIVE

- Dealt with up to 1,200 residential, business and governmental requests for telephone and operator assistance for a 5-state region.
- Received Departmental Achievement Award for assisting in design of programs that increased productivity 55% within 18 months.
- One of two representatives selected to service government officials in the capitol and hundreds of Northwest agencies.
- Served on a 4-person team, analyzing and developing training systems used by over 2,000 employees in 15 branch locations.
- Trained over 50 customer service representatives in directory assistance and handling of emergency situations.
- Commended by management for consistently meeting and exceeding departmental quotas and quality control requirements.
- Performed the duties of a Customer Service Representative throughout 10 years experience as a Directory Operator.

MARKETING & ADMINISTRATIVE MANAGEMENT

- Managed start-up business to development of over 50 accounts.
- Within 8 months took firm from debt to profit by analyzing and implementing effective sales and bookkeeping systems.
- Coordinated and negotiated with vendors, set up new customer accounts, approved credit, and purchased new computer system.
- Hired and trained staff in sales, customer service, and production.
- Developed strong repeat and referral business during 5 years of management.
- Sold business at a profit 4 times my initial investment.

Work History

Customer Service Representative (Phone Operator), PTC 1995–99
Marketing Representative, Marketing Research 1990–94
Business Manager, DelVecchio Fireworks 1985–89
Customer Service Representative (Telephone Operator), STC and UST Inc. 1978–85

What's different about Fran's After resume?

- Glancing at this resume, where did your eye go first, second, then third?

- How do the headings in Fran's After resume do a better job of marketing her for a $33,000 customer service position?

- Read the content Fran has written in the second and third sections of her After resume.

- Now read the content or descriptions of each of Fran's jobs in her Before resume.

- Which resume presents an in-depth picture of Fran's skills and experience?

- Result? This resume took Fran's response rate from zero to one hundred percent.

What happens with the next title of production worker? Does Fran's image become more or less impressive? Most people say Fran's image drops dramatically. How about the title of owner? Up or down? Most people say up slightly—but they don't know how "owner" relates to customer service, so this title doesn't have much impact. Then we see Fran's oldest job titles are telephone operator. Most people say these titles bring Fran's image back down.

Looking at the graph of Fran's titles, it's obvious that the Before resume created an image of her that wasn't even close to her goal. And that's exactly why Fran didn't receive any interviews. Even though Fran had all the skills required for the position she wanted, her resume caused employers to perceive her as underqualified.

Graph of Fran's After Resume

Fran's new resume used a stronger job title and a stronger skill heading: "Customer Service Representative" and "Marketing & Administrative Management." Does the title of "Customer Service Representative" match Fran's salary goal of $33,000? Does her image go up, down, or match her goal as you read this title? As the graph below illustrates, most people would say that the title customer service representative is appropriate to Fran's goal of a $33,000 position. Does the skill heading of "Marketing & Administrative Management" match Fran's goal? Does her image go up, down, or match her goal as you read this skill heading? Again, most people would graph their response to this heading on the same level as Fran's goal. Fran's new title and skill heading matched what employers want to hear and motivated them to call Fran for an interview.

Use Graphing to Control Your Image

The graphs of Fran's Before and After resumes make it very clear why most resumes don't work. They reveal a mismatch between the job titles and skill headings we use in our resumes compared to the demands of the position we're applying for. Once you've finished your resume, graph it and ask others to graph their response to your resume based on the type of job and salary you want. If their graphs of the titles and skill headings used in your resume don't match the level of jobs and salary you want, change your resume!

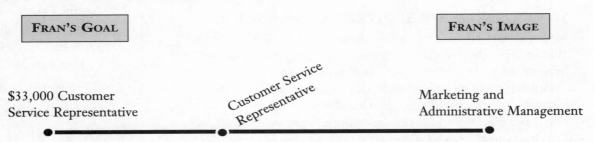

FRAN'S GOAL

FRAN'S IMAGE

$33,000 Customer Service Representative

Customer Service Representative

Marketing and Administrative Management

Another Success Story: Tammy's Before and After Resumes

Tammy and I became friends while working at a personnel agency. She was in sales but needed a position paying substantially more. Over a month's time her first resume didn't land her any interviews. Using the strategies you're learning, we created a new resume. Tammy then applied for two positions, landed interviews for both, and achieved a dramatic salary increase. What caused this to happen? You'll see as you review Tammy's resumes on pages 16 and 17. Once you've reviewed them, return to the top of the facing page and we'll graph Tammy's resumes.

Graph of Tammy's Before Resume

The ad for the $40,000 position (which Tammy was offered and accepted) asked for someone with outside sales and credit approval experience to market credit reporting systems. So, those are the criteria that should be used to judge the effectiveness of Tammy's Before and After resumes.

Tammy's Before resume used the titles of personnel recruiter, placement specialist, and customer service associate/credit approval. Below, we've graphed her recent job title of personnel recruiter. Does your image of Tammy go up or down when you read this job title? Does this title match your image of the $40,000 outside sales position? Does it match the requirement for credit approval experience? As the graph illustrates, most people would graph personnel recruiter much lower than Tammy's goal.

Tammy's second most recent job title was placement specialist. Does this job title make Tammy's image go up or down? Is it stronger or weaker? Most people would say weaker, even lower than they graphed personnel recruiter. Tammy's oldest job title was customer service associate/credit approval. How well does this title match your image of the $40,000 position? Most people say this heading elevates Tammy's image somewhat because it matches the requirement for credit approval experience, but they also think that customer service associate sounds more like a clerk making $18,000. So this title graphs only slightly higher than placement specialist. In the end Tammy's image is still way below her goal; her Before resume presents her in the $18,000 to $20,000 salary range. And that's not the result she wanted.

TAMMY'S GOAL

$40,000 Outside Sales
Position Marketing Credit
Reporting Systems

Personnel Recruiter

Placement Specialist

TAMMY'S IMAGE

Customer Service Associate
Credit Approval

Tammy's After resume uses two job titles: outside sales representative and credit representative. It also uses the skill heading "Key Account Management." (In a moment we'll discuss why and how we replaced Tammy's old job titles with these new titles and this skill heading.)

We've graphed Tammy's After resume on page 18. Does the first title of outside sales representative match your image of a $40,000 outside sales position? Most people graph this title as matching Tammy's goal of the outside sales position. Does the skill heading of "Key Account Management" match Tammy's goal? Most people also graph this skill heading even with Tammy's goal.

Does Tammy's last title of credit representative match her goal? Again, most people graph this title even with Tammy's goal. As you can see, these titles and this skill heading present Tammy as well qualified for the $40,000 outside sales position. That's why Tammy landed interviews for both of the positions she applied for and accepted one that took her salary from $20,000 to $40,000 in one job move.

How effective is this resume at marketing Tammy's outside sales skills?

◆ When you glance at Tammy's Before resume, where does your eye go first, then second, then third?

◆ Is your attention drawn to the under-lined headings, then to the dates, then to the bolded company names and job titles?

◆ Does this informa-tion create an image of Tammy as having strong outside sales experience?

◆ What salary range do you think Tammy was in, based on the image this resume pre-sents?

Tammy Millett
P.O. Box 7777
Seattle, WA 98118
(555) 555-5555

Objective: To secure a stable sales position.

Education: Bachelor of Arts, University of Washington

Employment History:

1993–Present   **Advantage Personnel, Seattle, WA**
Personnel Recruiter

Call on accounts and develop proposals. Maintain a tele-marketing/tracking system for all contacts and follow-up needed. Interview and place temporary personnel. Instruct clerical staff regarding client reports and sales contracts. Conduct on-site workplace evaluations.

1991–1993   **AccuTemps, Seattle, WA**
Placement Specialist

Marketed placement services to accounts. Trained person-nel in sales procedures. Telemarketed services and set appointments. Developed a major account with sales of $50,000 annually. Revised the filing and sales order pro-cessing systems.

1989–1991   **Frederick & Nelson, Bellevue, WA**
Customer Service Associate/Credit Approval

Met with customers, ran credit checks, and approved new accounts. Served on credit committee. Trained employees, revised filing systems.

References: Available Upon Request.

Tammy Millett   P.O. Box 7777
(555) 555-5555   Seattle, WA 98118

Seek an Account Representative position
utilizing the following experience:

- Increasing Northwest Territory sales by 200% within 6 months.
- Approving $1.2 million in consumer credit annually.
- B.A. Degree, University of Washington.

Outside Sales Representative, Advantage Personnel 1993–Present

Develop and maintain key accounts such as ATL, Washington Natural
Gas, CX Corporation, and Leviton Telecom.

- Increased sales from $62,000 to $132,000 per month in first 5 months.
- Increased hourly gross margin approximately 20%.
- Maintained weekly quota of 60 cold calls and 30 maintenance calls.
- Implemented 1999 marketing plan; currently on track to meet projected goals.
- Developed written sales proposals, contracts, bill and pay rates.
- Hired and assigned employees; resolved personnel service problems.
- Performed duties as an Outside Sales Representative while employed as a
  Personnel Recruiter.

Key Account Management, AccuTemps 1991–1993

Pioneered Seattle territory, exceeding 2nd year sales goals in 18 months.
Developed major accounts such as IBM, US Bank, and National Frozen Foods.

- Received 2 National Awards for outstanding achievement.
- Successfully negotiated fees ranging up to $12,000.
- Negotiated placements with top executives and personnel managers.
- Developed extensive telemarketing skills with ability to set
  appointments and generate orders by phone.
- Conducted confidential staff searches. Recruited and qualified
  applicants.

Credit Representative, Frederick & Nelson 1989–1991

Approved up to $1.2 million in consumer credit annually. Gathered
credit and salary information from customers by phone, analyzed credit
reports, and authorized new accounts and credit extensions.

- Awarded merit raise for Outstanding Credit Achievement.
- Served on Credit Action Group.
- Created an 80-page credit authorization procedures manual.
- Resolved billing disputes and negotiated overdue account payments.
- Performed the duties of a Credit Representative, working under the title
  of Customer Service Associate, in the Credit Approval Department.

Why is Tammy's After resume better?

- ◆ Looking at Tammy's After resume, where did your eye go first, then second, then third?

- ◆ Do Tammy's job titles make it clear to employers that she has outside sales experience that matches their needs? Will employers be more likely to call her for an interview?

- ◆ Compare the objective statements in each resume. Does the After resume present a much more dynamic image of Tammy's skills and abilities? The result? Tammy landed a job that increased her salary by $20,000!

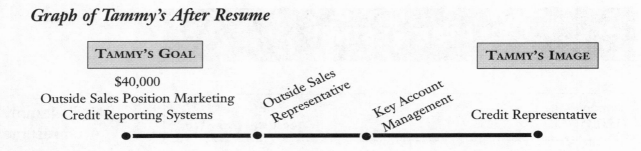

Graph of Tammy's After Resume

The Art and Science of Skill Headings and Job Titles

If you are like many job seekers, the idea of replacing your actual job titles with more impressive job titles or skill headings, as we did for Fran and Tammy, may scare you. You may feel like you are exaggerating and worry that you'll get caught lying when employers check your references. A useful rule of thumb when replacing job titles is to make sure the new title is interchangeable with the old title. For example, Tammy began employment as a personnel recruiter. She was then given responsibility for outside sales fifty percent of the time but was never given a new job title. In her case, she was truly performing work as an outside sales representative.

If you review Tammy's After resume, you'll see that the last statement says, "Performed duties as an Outside Sales Representative while employed as a Personnel Recruiter." This provides Tammy's actual job title and explains to potential employers how she gained this experience. When Tammy's references are checked, the information provided in her resume will match information prospective employers may be told, such as her actual job title and the duties she performed. If you modify one of your job titles with a truthful and more appropriate title, insert a similar statement at the end of that job description, as well as in your employment history section, as shown in Tammy's After resume. You'll learn other ways to insert such details in the next chapter.

Whenever possible, choose job titles (rather than skill headings) that are a direct match to your job objective. This is important because job titles usually present a stronger image than skill headings. For example, which sounds stronger: "Office Manager" or "Office Management"? In this instance, the title of office manager sounds stronger.

On the other hand, if a job title weakens your image, it is very important that you replace it with a stronger title or skill heading that matches the job you want. For example, Tom is a receptionist with responsibility for managing front office functions under the direction of an office manager. In this instance, office manager would not be a truthful job title for Tom to use. But the skill heading of front office management is a truthful and accurate description of Tom's responsibilities because he really did manage front office functions. In this instance, the skill heading of front office management is stronger than Tom's title of receptionist.

Job seekers often feel anxious or uncomfortable as they consider changing and elevating their image. In many instances, people let such feelings control what they're willing—and frequently not willing—to put in their resumes. Just like Fran's resume, this often results in resumes that are substantially weaker than the person's real skill level. This is a very important issue, since weak resumes generate fewer interviews and substantially lower salary offers. The next chapter discusses this issue in detail and provides many stories about job seekers who felt uncomfortable elevating their image yet realized what they were saying was entirely true and then reaped the rewards of landing better jobs and higher salaries. It's imperative that job seekers learn to adapt a broader, truthful, and more realistic view of their skills before moving into the process of actually writing their resume in Chapter 3.

2 Maximize Your Accomplishments

You've been learning how important it is to control and elevate your image in order to create a powerful resume. If you are like many job seekers, you may feel a little intimidated by this process. I've found that even though most people say they want to create a strong resume they frequently create resumes that de-emphasize their top achievements. This results in resumes that market them thousands of dollars beneath their goals and significantly hampers career growth. Some job seekers say they want to land a better job but don't even apply for jobs that pay more even though they are well qualified. Or in some cases, job seekers may put off working on their resumes for months or years because they doubt their ability to make a successful career change.

Such responses often stem from the fact that many of us feel uncomfortable tooting our own horn. Or it may be that our accomplishments, or true level of job responsibilities, have been discounted by our employers. In turn, this can then lead us to discount our skills and question their value. We might also respond like this if our self-confidence is at a low point. Being aware of and reversing such feelings is critical before we can begin the process of writing a resume. Such awareness is important because our feelings control, to a great extent, what we are willing and not willing to say about ourselves.

How Fran's Feelings Contributed to a Weak Resume

You may remember Fran, with whom I had worked during a resume writing workshop. Her goal had been to land a $33,000-per-year customer service representative position. Fran had spent about ten minutes giving me and a class of about twenty other job seekers an overview of her work history. We then developed the skill headings in the left column below. That evening Fran wrote her resume at home. I was quite surprised when I made a transparency of it to share with the class the next day. Fran had replaced the headings we had created in class with the headings in the right column.

Customer Service Representative	Customer Service
Marketing & Administrative Management	Administrative

Take a moment and review both columns. Would a higher salary range fit the person in the left column or the person in the right column? Most people will say the left column is a good match for a position in the $30,000 to $33,000 range, which matched Fran's goal. But people will say the right column sounds more like someone making $24,000, which is $9,000 lower than Fran's goal.

When Fran replaced the stronger headings in the left column with the weaker ones, she was merely responding to her feelings, with what felt the most comfortable to her. However, she did not understand or assess the negative consequences of weakening her resume and how this would impact her salary offers.

Negative Situations Can Cause You to Discount Your Skills

Some job seekers experience feelings similar to Fran's because they've had a bad experience with an employer and this has caused them to question their skills. This had happened to John. He managed a branch sales office, yet his boss treated him with little respect. John handled all customer complaints, sales processing, and emergency problem solving. He literally ran the office because the staff were in the field ninety-five percent of the time. When I recommended he label his experience as branch management and customer service administration, he felt very uncomfortable. John said his boss never acknowledged that he performed work at that level and treated him as if his work was menial. He said, "Oh, I can't say branch management or customer service administration. My boss would never say I was the branch manager or customer service manager. He always referred to me as an inside sales person. In fact, when I asked for a raise last year he denied it because I hadn't taken on any new responsibilities. In his mind I was still just a clerk."

I told John we wouldn't say he was a branch manager or a customer service manager. We would instead substitute skill headings to describe his experience. Even if his boss told a prospective employer he hadn't managed the branch office, John had every right to accurately describe his responsibilities in his resume. To help John maximize his experience and feel he was being truthful, we noted that his job included inside sales at the end of his job description. Here's what it looked like:

BRANCH MANAGEMENT CUSTOMER SERVICE ADMINISTRATION

Managed all branch and customer service administration functions, including the following:

Sales quoting, order processing, and problem solving to support a staff of 10 Sales Representatives (Inside Sales for XYZ Company).

Reading the sample above, John said, "Written that way, it sounds great. If they call my employer they'll see I was also performing inside sales and I'm being truthful. Let's do it!" I have helped many people who perform work beyond their job titles to describe their experience in stronger ways. Situations such as John's cause people to doubt their abilities and feel they are lying even when they truthfully describe their job duties.

If John had written his resume without a pep talk, how do you think it would have turned out? If you have had a negative on-the-job experience like John's, it's easy to understand the mixed emotions you may feel as you write your resume. Feelings of self-doubt and memories of an employer's negative attitude can cloud your judgment and result in a weak resume.

Accurately Describing the Work You Do

If you feel like Fran or John and are concerned about replacing your job titles, here are three very good reasons to upgrade your titles so that they market you more effectively.

Many Titles Have Little Meaning

The first reason is that many people are given job titles that have little meaning outside of the industry, company, or department they work for. Brian's job title of returns merchandise authorization clerk is a good example of this. This title makes me think of someone working in the retail industry processing items being returned for a refund. No one outside of Brian's company would have any idea that he is actually an electronics test technician. When applying for electronic technician positions, Brian would have received a very poor response if the first job title an employer had seen on his resume was "Returns Merchandise Authorization Clerk." But the title of test technician accurately describes Brian's job duties and will generate more interviews.

Weak Titles Control Salary Levels

A second reason to replace weak titles is that many employers purposely create titles that under-represent the work that their employees perform. Such employers know that they can pay less money to someone who has a weak job title. This happened when I worked in a union office and took over the responsibility of researching and resolving member benefit claims. I then asked for a new title of benefits coordinator. The president of our union negotiated our contract and was very resistant to giving me a new title. He said, "I can't be giving you a new title because next year you'll just use it as a way to negotiate for more money." The union reps didn't want to handle benefit claims, so they rallied round and helped me get my new title. Sure enough, my salary increased fifty percent that year and another thirty percent the following year. Obviously, the union president was a skilled negotiator and knew the power of job titles.

Employers Are More Interested in Skills than Titles

A third reason to replace weak titles is that employers really are much more interested in your skills and what you can do for them, than what your actual title has been. Marcia, the human resources director for one of Seattle's largest law firms, sat through my presentation at a community college. During her presentation, Marcia reemphasized the points I've made above.

She said that she is so busy during the day that she usually takes resumes home to screen them. She told the audience to imagine her at home at 8:00 P.M. Her eyes are tired and she's faced with a five-inch stack of resumes to sort through. Marcia then described how she spends about five seconds glancing at each resume. Those resumes that make it easy for her to see job titles or skills that match the legal jobs she has open receive a closer look; those that don't are put aside.

Marcia stressed that she doesn't have the patience or the time to look at unrelated job titles and try to decipher if the person had gained skills that relate to legal positions. She gave the example of an executive secretary she had hired. She said this person's title didn't hook her, but the subheadings of "Legal Research," "Contract Administration," and "Word Processing of Legal Documents" grabbed her attention. These headings made it clear that the executive secretary had many of the legal skills she needed, so she interviewed and then hired her.

Take to heart the importance of the work you do. If your job title is weak in comparison to your job duties, give yourself a stronger, interchangeable title or skill heading that is truthful and matches the job you want. Then insert your actual title in your work history and write a short statement at the end of your title or skill heading section that describes how you gained that experience. Refer to Fran's and Tammy's resumes on pages 13 and 17 for examples.

Writing a Resume Is Difficult

I've found that job seekers at all income levels often question their abilities as they write a resume. Ted is a good example. He was qualified for a six-figure salary, yet felt compelled to minimize his top achievements. As I worked with him, Ted let me know that he had patented a product that had generated more than four million dollars for his company. He also managed major accounts with annual sales of fifty million dollars, which was very impressive. When I asked him what salary he would negotiate for, he said, "Somewhere between $100,000 to $125,000." But when we completed his resume, Ted said, "This sounds great, but I don't know, what if an employer expects me to be able to do all these things? It's kind of scary."

When I told Linda, a personnel manager, about Ted, she said, "I can't believe he'd have any trouble looking for a job." On the flip side, many of us think Linda should have no problem writing a resume because she's a personnel manager. She admitted, though, that "I write resumes for all my friends and employees but I can't write one for myself. Here I am managing personnel operations for a staff of 250 with a salary of $45,000. It's embarrassing that I can't write my own resume." When Ted returned to pick up his resume, he mentioned how glad he was to have it completed. He felt silly that he had so much trouble putting it together. So I told him Linda's story. He couldn't believe that even a personnel manager would find writing her resume difficult. The point is, we all tend to doubt or minimize our abilities when writing a resume. Don't let such feelings lead you to create a weak resume that undersells you and ultimately limits your job possibilities.

Becoming Comfortable with Your New Resume

Remember Ted's first reaction? He said, "This really sounds great, but what if an employer expects me to do all this? It's kind of scary." Clearly, he felt out of his comfort zone. He worried about whether he could live up to his resume. What made Ted doubt his abilities? I believe he felt that way because his new resume focused on his strongest accomplishments. These were not tasks that he did every day with ease. Obtaining the patent had been hard work, and it turned out that he had often doubted himself during the process.

Ted also discounted the skills he used to manage his accounts. He saw himself as merely someone dealing with friends and helping them solve their problems. He had never estimated the sales from his accounts. The fact that he managed key accounts with annual revenues of $50 million was more impressive than the image he had of himself.

Describing the money his patent had generated along with the million-dollar accounts he managed pushed Ted way out of his comfort zone. These statements made him feel like he was exaggerating and being phony. His feelings prompted him to minimize his accomplishments and exclude dollar figures from his resume. Just like Fran, Ted knew this would make him feel more comfortable.

To help Ted realize that he should put this information in his resume, I asked him, "Did you really do these things? Can you do them again? And are the figures you've given me correct?" His answer to each question was "Yes!" By proving to Ted that the statements on his resume were accurate and not exaggerated, I helped him realize that he was being truthful. He then chose to include the information about his patent and the revenues generated from his accounts. He realized these accomplishments would help him obtain a higher position with an increased income and better advancement opportunities. Once Ted sorted out his feelings and understood them, he felt comfortable with his new resume. And in the end it helped to increase his salary by $29,000!

If you still feel a little uncomfortable at the prospect of creating a stronger image of your skills, then ask yourself these questions:

- Did I perform this task—even if my job title doesn't sound like it?
- Could I do this again on another job?
- Are the estimates of my achievements accurate?

If your answers are all "yes," you are not overstating your skills and you should describe them as strongly as possible.

Accepting Your Top Skills Increases Confidence

Pam also experienced similar feelings, although her salary was barely more than $13,000 per year. Pam had seven years of experience in reception, general office, and customer service work but felt that her experience wasn't important. She said, "I'm really a hard worker and have accomplished any task I've been given, but I can't write a resume that shows my capabilities. The more I read about resume writing, the more confused I become. Every book recommends something different. It's been at least two months since I even worked on my resume and I need a new job now!" Her voice revealed the self-doubt and fear she was experiencing. I asked her to describe her work history and what she had been responsible for. Once I got a good idea of her background, I told her she had very good skills and could make at least four hundred dollars more per month. She said, "Boy, I don't know, it seems like I don't have that level of skills. My salary has only been $1,100 a month."

By summarizing her strongest skills, I knew her resume would convince employers to interview her and would result in higher salary offers. It was obvious she doubted what I was saying. To her surprise, Pam's confidence increased as she read her new resume. She said, "I can hardly believe it's me. I would have never described my background like this. I really thought a lot of these things were too trivial to mention."

About two weeks later, Pam dropped into my office to say she had just accepted a job starting at $1,500 a month. She said the person who had hired her had kept nodding his head "yes" as he read her resume. Then she said, "He thinks I can do a lot. I'm scared, but I'm really glad I changed my resume! I can't believe I just increased my salary by almost forty percent."

Do You Feel You're Worth a Higher-Paying Position or a Promotion?

Sometimes our feelings can also prompt us to avoid applying for higher-paying positions or promotions. This was the situation Penny faced. As an office manager she had developed a history of accepting jobs where she was required to work twelve-hour days at a salary of $7.50 an hour. She was extremely overworked and underpaid, but her skill level had grown by leaps and bounds. While writing her resume, Penny saw that she had developed extensive experience in full-charge bookkeeping, branch management, and the supervision of administrative staff. In reality she was well qualified for a position in the $28,000 to $35,000 range.

I was intrigued by Penny's case and wanted to see what types of positions she would be qualified for. Looking through my newspaper's help-wanted section, I found several ads for positions that listed every skill we had put into Penny's resume.

Thinking she'd be thrilled, I pulled them out and shared them with her when she came to pick up her resume. I was quite surprised when she said, "Oh, I can't apply for those jobs. I've only made $7.50 an hour, and those jobs pay, oh my gosh, $12 an hour, and wow, the other one pays almost $17 an hour. Who's going to give me $5 more per hour, let alone almost $10 more an hour? Those jobs are out of my league."

As with Ted, I went through the process of asking her if what we had said in her resume was accurate. She answered, "Yes," but I couldn't convince her to apply for these jobs. She just didn't believe that she was worth $28,000 to $35,000. To my surprise, she applied for another job at $7.50 an hour and of course the employer snapped her up! Thinking she just wasn't ready to make a move up, I put her situation out of my mind. Then about three months later she called to say that she had gotten fed up with the job she had taken—same old story of being overworked and underpaid—and had quit. Overjoyed, she said she had just been hired for a new job making $11.75 an hour.

Evidently Penny had just needed some time to adjust, question, and then accept the value of her skills. I'm happy to say that even though it's taken three years since we created her resume, she's now making $36,000 per year and working fewer hours!

I've seen other people turn down promotions that they were well qualified for. I saw this happen to Dale several times. He always gave logical-sounding reasons as to why he couldn't accept a promotion, like "Oh, that will interfere with taking my kids to their Little League games," or "That's too much responsibility," or "I'm just not the supervisor type." Yet the real reason, he confided much later, was that he doubted his ability to succeed in the new position. Rather than trying the new job on for size and testing himself, he said he had felt safer staying in a job he knew he could do and do well.

I bring up issues like the ones Penny and Dale faced because achieving maximum success with your new resume often goes hand in hand with applying for higher-paying positions or promotions. If you have feelings similar to Penny's or Dale's, those feelings could keep you from accelerating your career growth. But becoming aware of them paves the way to increased success.

Don't Question or Diminish Your Value

When they are making career changes, I find that many people say things to themselves like "I've never worked in that kind of job before. Of course they'll have better qualified applicants so I won't have a chance. Why bother applying?" Such assumptions are often not accurate, and as a result some job seekers severely limit their opportunities. I almost made this mistake. After deciding to leave my job as a career development instructor, I found an ad for a position with the University of Washington, Bothell. It required teaching resume and job search classes and helping students write resumes. It was a great fit for me. However, as I read the ad I felt quite anxious. The first thought that went through my mind was "Oh, why would they want me to counsel their students, who are completing four-year and master's degree programs? I only have a two-year degree. There's no way they'll think I'm qualified." Questioning my response I then thought, "Well, hey, it won't hurt to apply, and being hired by the University of Washington would be great for my resume." I applied and ended up being hired, beating out sixty-five other applicants—most of whom had degrees in career counseling and even master's degrees. Many job seekers changing jobs or careers have similar feelings when they read ads or job openings. The majority let such feelings keep them from applying for jobs, and they lose out on a wider range of opportunities.

Apply Even If You Don't Have Every Skill

Job seekers also limit their job possibilities because they think that they have to have every skill requested in an ad or job description in order to be considered for it. This is a fallacy. When employers write ads or job opening descriptions, they throw in every important skill they can think of. Sure, they'd like to hire someone with each and every requirement they list, but they know it's not likely that will happen. Knowing this, employers look for candidates who have some portion or combination of the required skills that will enable that person to do the job effectively. For example, you might find an ad you would like to respond to that requests eight important skills, two or three of which you possess. Like many people you may automatically assume there's no way you would even be considered for such a job. However, you never know the level of skills your competition possesses.

During some hiring seasons you might be competing against many highly qualified candidates, but at other times you may have very little competition. And with little competition, you may appear to be an excellent candidate and land an interview. Another factor to consider is that most people write and submit extremely weak and misdirected resumes. By submitting a resume that markets even a few skills that match the job you want, you can look well qualified and land interviews.

How Employers Make Hiring Decisions

Here's an example of someone who was hired that appeared unqualified but was selected over someone who possessed every skill the employer had wanted. At the time, my job was interviewing and placing temps for a national employment agency. Ann, our permanent placement specialist, came to me and said that Vicky, one of my employees, would be a perfect match for her biggest client. I read a page of job requirements that the employer was requesting and thought it was pretty overwhelming. Among the desired skills were typing eighty-plus words per minute, a legal secretarial background, and experience using WordPerfect and Lotus 1-2-3. I went back and reviewed Vicky's application and resume. She typed sixty words per minute and had worked in a legal office as a receptionist but not as a legal secretary. While Vicky had WordPerfect experience, she didn't have Lotus experience.

When I told Ann this, she said, "Oh, yeah, I know. But you can see how bright and bubbly she is. My client is going to love her personality. I know she'll fit right in with the staff he already has. Once she's typing all the time, her speed will go up. She's had secretarial training, which included legal terminology. She can learn to be a legal secretary. I'm sure he'll hire her!" I was not so convinced, and felt that Ann was going to pull the wool over her client's eyes. I thought there was no way he would be interested in Vicky, especially since Ann was sending him another candidate with all the skills he had requested.

The client and several other of his staff members interviewed both of the applicants. Surprisingly, he hired Vicky. He liked her personality and felt she was very trainable. The person with all of the hard skills just didn't seem like a good fit to them. They felt she would want to have things done her way rather than the firm's way. On the other hand, they felt Vicky had an excellent personality because she was outgoing and eager to learn. I had only been in personnel for a month when this happened, and it opened my eyes to what employers really look for when interviewing candidates. It's most often intangible factors—like personality and willingness to learn—*combined* with some quantifiable skills that actually motivate employers to hire someone.

I recommend that you apply for any position that you are interested in and have some qualifications for. You may not always get your foot in the door, but many times you will. You'll then have a chance to sell yourself and your personality. If you skip over jobs you think you're not qualified for, you will eliminate a huge segment of the job market. If you're interested—apply!

Resumes Are Only Part of Your Job Search Package

I often see job seekers hold resumes responsible for the ultimate success they achieve in landing a better job. Mitchell's story is one example of this. He had found an open international manufacturing management position at Microsoft and applied for it.

Out of 400 applicants, he ended up being one of only three people called for an interview. Hearing this, most job seekers say, "Wow." Then they ask if Mitchell got the job. When I tell them he didn't, I can see that they immediately think, "Oh, then the resume didn't work." No one has ever asked, "Well, how good were his interviewing skills?" or "Did he not hit it off with the interviewer?"

It's important to stress that no component of the job search process can be discounted. Interviewing skills are extremely important, yet I find that people don't consider them when they try to figure out why they're not landing job offers. Taking the time to find quality job openings or to cultivate those that don't yet exist is just as important as resume writing and interviewing skills. Or writing powerful cover letters. Or developing a phone script so that you market yourself verbally with the same power that your resume does in written form. Or sending thank you letters and following up after interviews. Any one of these could be the key that makes the difference to your being hired for the job you want. So none can be overlooked or diminished in importance. All the secrets you'll learn about controlling and elevating your image in a resume must be carried into each component of your job search to achieve maximum success. This is what makes the *Proven Resumes* system an integrated job search program from start to finish.

Now You're Ready to Write Your Resume!

Understanding how your feelings can control what you are willing to put in your resume, the salary level you think you're worth, and the types of jobs you're willing to apply for paves the way to greater job search success. With an awareness of these underlying issues you're now ready to begin writing your resume. In the next chapter you'll begin by finding out which type of resume format is best for you. Then you'll be guided through a step-by-step process to create a powerful resume that get the results you want and that you will be proud of.

3 Choosing the Best Resume Format

The first step in creating a powerful resume is to select a resume format that highlights the best of what you have to offer while minimizing your weaknesses. In this chapter you'll determine if a skill-based resume or a chronological resume is best for you. A skill-based resume focuses on the skills you've acquired, while a chronological resume focuses on the sequence of jobs you have held. How do you figure out which one will market you most effectively?

When Is a Skill-Based Resume Better?

As Fran's case will illustrate, a skill-based resume is appropriate if your skills are more impressive than your job titles. It can also highlight older work experience while de-emphasizing dates of employment by using a condensed work history at the bottom of the resume. This format is also a good choice if you've gained significant skills from a position that lasted a short period of time. It lets you devote a large portion of your resume to these skills while de-emphasizing length of employment.

Think back to how we graphed Fran's chronological resume on page 11. While graphing our response to Fran's series of positions, we saw that the job titles in it didn't match Fran's goal of landing a $33,000-per-year customer service representative position. That was a clue that a skill-based resume might be better.

To determine what format was best for Fran, we analyzed her resume using the three-part form on the next page. On the left we listed her job titles. In the middle we created stronger job titles or skill headings. For example, "Customer Service Representative" was stronger than her original "Phone Operator" title. This new title was truthful because Fran functioned as a customer service representative when she worked as a directory operator. However, Fran didn't serve as a customer service representative in two of her jobs as a phone solicitor and telemarketer. In these positions, she merely scheduled customer sales appointments, so we labeled both of these positions with the skill heading of "Customer Service." As a production worker, Fran's job was even further away from customer service. In that job she read blueprints to assemble electronic units, so we merely relabeled it "Electronic Assembly." Finally, Fran had owned a business selling and distributing fireworks with responsibility for marketing, office, and bookkeeping functions, so we replaced the title of "Owner" with "Marketing & Administrative Management" because these skills are required in customer service positions.

With these new job titles and skill headings in the middle column, we graphed them again to determine whether Fran's image would become stronger or weaker. Most people say that "Customer Service" and "Electronic Assembly" are very weak and would cause Fran's image to drop significantly. Now, compare the middle column to the right-hand column of selected skill headings. Does the middle or the right-hand column create the best image of Fran's skills for the $33,000 position? The middle column makes it clear that trying to stick with a chronological resume wouldn't work. Fran would be much better off with a skill-based resume that uses the job title and skill heading shown in the right-hand column.

Job Titles	Stronger Job Titles and Skill Headings	Best Job Titles and Skill Headings
Phone Operator	Customer Service Representative	Customer Service Representative
Phone Solicitor	Customer Service	
Telemarketer	Customer Service	
Production Worker	Electronic Assembly	
Owner	Marketing & Administrative Management	Marketing & Administrative Management
Telephone Operator	Customer Service Representative	
Telephone Operator	Customer Service Representative	Marketing & Administrative Management

There are no real disadvantages to a skill-based format that includes a condensed work history. Providing a condensed work history keeps employers from feeling that you are hiding something about past employment but still creates the impression you wish. A skill-based resume is the most appropriate format for about eighty-five percent of job seekers.

Here's an example of the condensed work history section from Fran's After resume. Notice that it de-emphasizes where Fran worked and keeps the employer focused on her skills.

Customer Service Representative (Directory Operator), PTC 1995–99
Customer Service, Marketing Research 1990–94
Marketing & Administrative Management, DelVecchio Fireworks 1985–89
Customer Service Representative (Telephone Operator), STC and UST, Inc. 1978–85

When Is a Chronological Resume Better?

Chronological resumes can be an excellent choice for job seekers with stable work histories and experience that matches the jobs they're seeking. Chronological resumes start with your current position and go backward, listing each position you have held. This format is most widely used because employers are more familiar with it than any other style; it provides dates of employment, which many employers like to see; and it is the easiest to prepare since it requires less creativity than a skill-based resume.

Because the chronological format includes dates of employment, it can also emphasize many years of employment in a desired field and can draw positive attention to advancement from one position to the next. By stacking job titles or skill headings that are supportive of the job objective, it can present a strong image of one's experience.

The chronological resume has several disadvantages for someone with an erratic, short, unrelated, or older work history. Because the dates are prominently displayed, employers can see gaps in employment within seconds, even before glancing at skill or experience sections. As a result, many chronological resumes are passed over. This format can also be redundant if you have had the same job title in several different jobs you've held; this can make your experience look limited.

If you look again at Tammy's resume on page 17, you can begin to determine if a chronological resume is best for you. Tammy was a good candidate for a chronological resume because she has a stable work history, but the job titles in her Before resume didn't match her job objective. We strengthened Tammy's chronological resume by replacing weak titles with stronger ones. We replaced "Personnel Recruiter" with "Outside Sales Representative" because Tammy had been responsible for outside sales. Then we replaced "Placement Specialist" with the skill heading of "Key Account Management." We used this heading because Tammy had been responsible for placing staff with key accounts such as IBM, US Bank, and National Frozen Foods. Once an employee was hired, Tammy was responsible for managing these accounts to ensure that each employer was satisfied with the hiring decision and that new employees were performing up to expectations.

We also replaced "Customer Service/Credit Approval" with the title of "Credit Representative." When Tammy worked for Frederick & Nelson, she met with customers, reviewed credit applications, and had the authority to approve credit. As a result, she performed work as a credit representative. The analysis below shows that merely changing Tammy's titles took her from looking unqualified to qualified. These headings resulted in the best of both worlds— Tammy created a strong image based on all of her skills but was able to stay within the framework of a chronological resume.

Job Titles	Stronger Job Titles and Skill Headings
Personnel Recruiter	Outside Sales Representative
Placement Specialist	Key Account Management
Customer Service Associate/Credit Approval	Credit Representative

Many job seekers who have a stable work history jump to the conclusion that a traditional chronological resume will work the best for them. But they are often disappointed when their chronological resumes result in few interviews or low salary offers. This happened with Tammy. Her chronological resume didn't generate any interviews because her titles were weak. If you believe you are a good candidate for a chronological resume, use the graphing techniques in the first chapter to analyze the image your job titles create. If your titles create a weak image, then relabel them with equivalent, but truthful, job titles or skill headings that do match your goal. Then follow Fran's and Tammy's resume examples on pages 13 and 17 to insert but de-emphasize your actual job title. Making these changes will turn weak chronological resumes into powerful ones.

Three Steps to Selecting the Right Resume Format

Step 1: List Your Job Titles

Using the worksheet on the following page, write the title or type of job you want along with the salary you desire. In the first column on the left, write down the job titles you have been given in each job you've held. Keeping your job and salary objectives in mind, review your job titles. If they are a great match for your job objective and create an image of you as a well-qualified applicant, use these titles to create a chronological resume. If any of your titles weaken your image, go on to Step 2.

Step 2: Replace Weak Job Titles

If any of the job titles you listed in the left column cause your image to drop significantly, replace them with stronger but truthful job titles or skill headings. (You'll learn how to do this in a moment.) Write these new job titles or skill headings in the middle column. If some of your job titles are a direct match to your job objective, transfer those titles to the middle column. Then review all of the job titles and skill headings you have listed in the middle column. If this list presents a strong image of your skills, then use these job titles and skill headings to create a chronological resume. If any of the titles or skill headings you listed in the middle column weaken your image, follow the guidelines below, then go on to Step 3.

A WORD ABOUT REPLACING JOB TITLES

It's easy to say "replace those weak job titles." You may be wondering how you could possibly do that—isn't that what professional resume writers do? The fact is, it's not as hard as it may seem. To make this process easy for you, I've included skill lists for more than forty-five industries beginning on page 67. These lists contain many of the skill headings I've used successfully with thousands of clients. We'll use Tim as an example to show you how to use the lists. Tim has been a lead assembler on a high-speed production line, an assistant restaurant manager, and an accounting clerk. Reviewing these titles, Tim realized he needed to replace them because none of them creates an image that matches the position or higher salary he hopes to get as a production supervisor.

CHOOSING A RESUME FORMAT WORKSHEET

Job You Want: _____   Salary You Want: _____

Chronological Resume	Skill-Based Resume

Step 1	**Step 2**	**Step 3**
List Your Job Titles Starting with Your Most Recent Job	Use New Job Titles or Skill Headings to Replace Weak Job Titles	Will Fewer Job Titles or Skill Headings Present a Stronger Image of Your Skills?
_____	_____	_____
_____	_____	_____
_____	_____	_____
_____	_____	_____
_____	_____	_____
_____	_____	_____
_____	_____	_____
_____	_____	_____

To begin, Tim turned to the Assembly/Production list on page 68 and read the columns of skills at the top of that page. Reviewing this list, Tim checked off skills that he developed as an assembly lead, which he will also use as a production supervisor. Below are six of the skill headings that Tim selected. Of these six skill headings, Tim chose "Production Management" to replace his title of "Assembly Lead." Tim chose this skill heading because it matches the image of a production supervisor, yet is truthful because Tim managed an assembly production line.

Title: ~~Assembly Lead~~
New Skill Heading: **Production Management**

Computerized Inventory Control	Quality Control/Inspection	High Volume Production Control
✔ Production Management	Staff Supervision/Training	Workstation Management

Next, Tim needed to replace his title of assistant restaurant manager. So he turned to the Restaurant/Food Service skill list on page 83. He then checked off the restaurant management skills he has developed that he will also use as a production supervisor. Below, you'll see the six skill headings that Tim selected. Tim replaced his title of assistant restaurant manager with "Staff Supervision/Training" because this skill heading matches our image of a production supervisor, which we assume oversees and trains staff. In contrast, the title of assistant restaurant manager causes us to imagine Tim in a food service environment, supervising cooks preparing food and waitstaff serving customers. A heading of "Staff Supervision/Training" will generate the best response because it conveys the image that Tim's restaurant skills will be transferable to a production environment.

Title: ~~Assistant Restaurant Manager~~
New Skill Heading: **Staff Supervision/Training**

Departmental Management	Operations Management	Shift Management
Floor/Shift Setup	Quality Control	✔ Staff Supervision/Training

Tim then needed to replace his last job title of accounting clerk. So he turned to the Accounting/Bookkeeping list on page 67 and checked off the accounting skills he has developed that he will also use as a production supervisor. At the top of the next page are six of the skill headings that Tim selected. Tim combined "Inventory Control/Tracking" with "Job Costing/ Control" to create "Job Costing/Inventory Control." He created this heading because he will be responsible for job costing and inventory control as a production supervisor. This heading markets the specific accounting skills Tim gained as an accounting clerk that are a direct match to the job he wants.

Title: ~~Accounting Clerk~~

New Skill Heading: **Job Costing/Inventory Control**

Computerized Accounting Applications	✔ Inventory Control/Tracking	✔ Job Costing/Control
Time Card Tracking	Purchase Order Management	Contract Administration

When we compare the first column of Tim's job titles below to the second column of skill headings, it's clear that Tim's new skill headings pull together his most impressive skills as a production supervisor.

Job Titles	Skill Headings Used to Replace Job Titles
Assembly Lead	Production Management
Assistant Restaurant Manager	Staff Supervision/Training
Accounting Clerk	Job Costing/Inventory Control

AVOID REPETITIVE JOB TITLES

This process can also be used to diversify repetitive titles, which often present a narrow image of your skills. For example, consider if you had been given the title of regional manager in three of your jobs but now you want a higher-paying position as a national accounts manager. You've been responsible for managing national accounts, new branch set-up, budgets, and branch auditing but the title of regional manager doesn't reflect this experience. Expanding repetitive titles, as the example below illustrates, broadens your experience at a glance—and makes you look more qualified.

Job Titles	Job Titles Expanded with Skill Headings
Regional Manager	National Account Management/Regional Manager
Regional Manager	Branch Development & Administration/Regional Manager
Regional Manager	Budget Control—Unit Auditing/Regional Manager

Step 3: Select Titles and Skill Headings that Control Your Image

Review the job titles or skill headings that you listed in the middle column on page 30. With what you've just learned, can you strengthen them? If so, do it and then review the titles and headings that you've listed in the middle column. Do any of the titles or skill headings still create a weak image? If so, write only those job titles and skill headings that create the strongest image of your skills in the right-hand column of the worksheet on page 30. Then compare the middle and right-hand columns. Which list markets you the best? If the middle column of job titles and skill headings works best, then create a chronological resume. If the third column of job titles and skill headings works best, then create a skill-based resume.

Summary: Check Which Format Is Best for You

The worksheet you completed on page 30 should make it clear which resume format is best for you. To confirm the choice, read each of the lists below and put check marks next to those statements that match your background. Whichever list you give the most checks to is probably the best resume format for you, and should coincide with the format you've already selected. When you're finished go on to Chapter 4, which will guide you step by step in completing your resume.

REMEMBER, CREATE A SKILL-BASED RESUME IF . . .

__ You have held many jobs. A chronological resume will be too long.

__ You have minor gaps in employment. A chronological resume will draw attention to this weakness.

__ You have gaps in employment of more than two years. You need to use a condensed work history.

__ You are reentering the job market after a prolonged absence. A chronological resume will make it very apparent that you have not worked in recent years. You may want to omit the condensed employment history.

__ Your past work history and job titles aren't related to your job objective. You must market your skills rather than your titles in order to look qualified for the job you want.

__ You have experience that relates to your job objective but your job titles are weak. You must market your skills in order to look qualified for the level of job you want.

__ Your most current employment doesn't relate to or support your job objective. Starting your resume with this position will make you look unqualified for your job objective.

__ Several of your job titles are the same. A chronological resume would be redundant. Use skill headings or modify your job titles so that you look better qualified.

__ You have little or no work experience. You must focus your resume on skills and training.

__ You have no paid work experience. You must focus on skills gained from volunteer work and home management, or self-taught skills.

CREATE A CHRONOLOGICAL RESUME IF . . .

__ You have a strong work history. You have worked for two or more years in each position. You have gaps of only a few months between each job you've held.

__ Your job titles create an image that matches the skills required for the job you want.

__ Your job titles create an image that matches the salary level of the job you want.

__ Your work history is strong but you have weak job titles. If you replace your job titles with skill headings or strengthen them, are you able to create an image that matches the position and salary you want? If so, you may still be a good candidate for a chronological resume.

4 Create a Powerful Resume in Six Steps

In the last chapter you completed worksheets to determine whether a skill-based or a chronological resume is best for you. Choosing the correct format is absolutely critical. So if you didn't complete the worksheets, go back and work on them before you read further. This chapter will take you step by step through the process of creating a rough draft of your resume. You'll learn how to identify and list your skills, strengthen weak job titles and skill headings, analyze employers' ads, match your skills and job titles to the ads, describe each job title or skill heading more effectively, and create the objective, education, and employment sections of your resume.

As you complete these steps, you'll be referred to Chapters 5 through 10. Chapter 5 provides more than 1,400 keywords and sample resume statements that will help you identify your skills. Chapter 6 will walk you through a series of questions to help you describe each skill. Chapter 7 will show you how to edit and strengthen the content in your resume. In Chapter 8 you'll learn how to write strong objective statements. Chapter 9 will help you finalize your resume by showing you how to minimize weaknesses and maximize strengths in your education and employment history. And Chapter 10 will teach you how to design and print your final resume. The Six Steps Worksheets in this chapter will guide you every step of the way toward creating a resume that effectively markets *you*—whether you're at an entry or executive level.

Now it's time to begin your resume! If a skill-based resume is the best format for you, look below and you'll be taken through the six steps. If a chronological resume is the best format for you, turn to page 50 and you'll be guided through the six steps there. Several of the steps are the same for either type of resume, but it's less confusing if each format is addressed separately.

The Six Steps of Creating a Skill-Based Resume

To illustrate how to develop a skill-based resume, we'll use Terry as an example. Terry wants to move into a retail management position, increasing her salary of $18,000 to $26,000 or higher. Even though Terry's jobs as a production lead, a head cashier, and a head waitress don't sound like management positions, she has successfully carried out many management responsibilities. Terry's therefore a good candidate for a skill-based resume because skill headings will sell her background more effectively than her job titles. Take a moment to review Terry's Before and After resumes on pages 36 and 37, then continue reading to see how Terry followed each of the Six Steps to create her resume.

The Six Steps of a Skill-Based Resume at a Glance

1. List all skills for each position you've held.
2. Relabel skills with skill headings.
3. Analyze a want ad or job posting to understand required skills.
4. Select skill headings that match the ad or job opening.
5. Describe each skill heading.
6. Create the objective, education, and employment history sections.

◆ Read Terry's objective statement in her Before resume. Then compare it to the first section in her After resume. Does the After resume look and sound like it describes the same person?

◆ Do the job titles in Terry's Before resume present her as a strong candidate for a retail management position?

◆ What salary level do these job titles cause you to think Terry is qualified for?

◆ Do they present an image that matches her current salary goal of $26,000?

◆ As you can see, it will be much harder for Terry to land interviews for retail management positions using the Before resume.

Terry Calhoon
890 Route 30
Billington, Oregon 98383
(555) 555-5555

Objective:

Seeking a Retail Management position utilizing over 10 years retail cashiering and lead experience.

Head Cashier, Kids "R" Us 1990–Present
- Supervised and trained staff to perform a variety of sales and cashiering duties.
- Oversaw daily opening and closing operations for new facility including cash reports.
- Coordinated performance evaluations with management.
- Managed my workstation in addition to 5 other stations.
- Communicated with various departments—returns, product departments, electronics, stocking, receiving, and maintenance.
- Provided service for high volume of daily customers.
- Increased sales by promoting add-on products.
- Communicated with other stores to coordinate customer orders.

Production Lead, Unique Used Salvage 1987–90
- Trained 10 production staff to pull salvaged building goods such as doors, windows, toilets, and plumbing to fill orders.
- Received and processed customer orders.
- Verified shipment and packing slips against P.O.s.
- Assisted customers by phone to research and ship orders.
- Performed data entry to pull parts and maintain inventory.

Head Waitress, Ghorm's Drive-In 1984–87
- Trained and supervised 8 waitresses.
- Each shift kept an eye on open orders and monitored completion times.
- Took daily and weekly inventory.
- Assisted in bringing computerized system into the store.

Computer Skills
- Trained to use Peachtree Accounting System.
- Learned to input and track customer orders, inventory, sales, and limited accounts receivable and payable.
- Trained waitresses to use the computer to input inventory.

Terry Calhoon
(555) 555-5555

890 Route 30
Billington, Oregon 98383

<u>Seek a Retail Management position utilizing</u> the following experience:

- Overseeing retail sales and customer service procedures for up to 600 customers daily, processing sales in excess of $2 million annually.
- Supervising and training over 40 managers and customer service staff in sales, cashiering, problem solving, inventory control, and schematics.
- Implementing computerized bookkeeping systems for retail operations.

Retail Sales Management

Staff Supervision / Training
Supervised and trained over 40 managers and customer service staff in sales, cashiering, and inventory control.
Oversaw operations for new facility, audit, and daily cash reports.
Coordinated performance evaluations with regional managers.

Departmental Coordination
Coordinated customer service with 8 departments—returns, product departments, electronics, stocking, receiving, and maintenance.
Managed my own station in addition to staff at 5 other stations, providing service to 600 customers with sales of up to $21,000 daily.

Customer Service / Staff Training

Workflow Coordination
Supervised and coordinated workflow of 8 staff serving up to 200 customers per shift, with sales of $60,000 per month.
Instrumental in implementation of computerized systems.

Operations Management

Customer Service / Order Administration
Managed order processing, opening and closing operations for department completing over $ 1/4 million in customer orders per month.
Dealt directly with key accounts to expedite shipments.
Analyzed product requirements for fulfillment of orders and delegated production activities to staff of 10.

Retail—Computerized Applications

- Implemented Peachtree Accounting System to input and track customer orders, inventory, sales, accounts receivable and payable.
- Trained service staff in use of system to input on-hand inventory statistics.

Work History
Retail Sales Management (head cashier), Kids "R" Us 1990–Present
Operations Management (lead), Unique Used Salvage 1987–90
Customer Service / Staff Training (head waitress), Ghorm's Drive-In 1984–87

Like many people, Terry had initially created a weak resume for several reasons.

- **Many industries tend to give employees job titles that are beneath the level of duties they perform. This had happened in Terry's situation with all three jobs she had held. Even though her actual titles were head cashier, production lead, and head waitress, she had been given management responsibilities in each position.**

- **Do the skill headings in Terry's After resume do a better job of marketing her for a retail management position than the job titles do in the Before resume?**

- **Even though this resume presents a much stronger image of Terry's skills, it is entirely true.**

Step 1: List All Skills for Each Position You've Held

Using the skill lists in Chapter 5 (on pages 67, 70, 83 and 88), Terry identified and listed many of the skills she had gained at her previous jobs. She also added many skills she had developed that weren't in these lists. The list of skills Terry compiled in Step 1 is below.

STEP 1: TERRY'S SKILL LIST

Kids "R" Us: Head Cashier

Manage Workstations and Balancing of Tills
Train and Oversee Retail Sales Cashiers
Operate Register, Greet and Assist Customers
Completed Sales Reports/Safe Drops/Deposits
Stocking/Inventory
Coordinate with Various Departments
Increase Revenues with Add-On Sales
Supervise Opening & Closing
Audit Procedures
Display Merchandise Following Schematics
Employee Orientations
Problem Solving/Dealing with Irate Customers
Handle Multi-Line Phones

Unique Used Salvage: Production Lead

Trained and Supervised Production Staff
Received and Processed Customer Orders
Dealt with Key Accounts Expediting Orders
Assigned Daily Work Duties
Compiled Sales and Order Reports
Utilized Computer to Input/Pull Stock
Researched Late Shipments
Oversaw Daily Production Activities
Planned Weekly Production Requirements
Issued P.O.s for Production Materials

Ghorm's Drive-In: Head Waitress

Trained Waitresses Filling Customer Orders
Coordinated and Monitored Customer Orders
Supervised and Delegated Workflow
Maintained Computerized Inventory
Coordinated with Suppliers
Streamlined Workstation Layout
Coached Employees to Improve Performance
Served as Team Leader
Interfaced with Staff and Management
Assisted with Computer Implementation
Peachtree Accounting Software
MS Word and Excel

STEP 2: TERRY'S RELABELED TITLES AND SKILLS

Job Title: Head Cashier

Retail Sales Management
Staff Supervision/Training
Customer Service
Sales/Cash Accountability
Inventory Control/Tracking
Departmental Coordination
History of Increased Sales
Opening & Closing Operations
Retail Auditing Procedures
Schematics/Merchandising
Retail Staff Orientations
Customer Service/Problem Solving
Branch Reception

Job Title: Production Lead

Operations Management
Customer Service/Order Administration
Key Accounts/Order Expediting
Workflow Delegation
Sales & Customer Order Reports
Computerized Parts Tracking
Shipment Research/Expediting
Production Management
Production Planning/Control
Materials Purchasing/Requisitions

Job Title: Head Waitress

Customer Service/Staff Training
Order Coordination/Administration
Workflow Coordination
Retail—Computerized Applications
Vendor Coordination
Workflow Design
Performance Coaching
Team Leader
Staff & Management Liaison
Retail—Computerized Applications
Computerized Accounting Applications
Word Processing/Spreadsheet Applications

Step 2: Relabel Skills with Skill Headings

In Step 1, under "Kids 'R' Us: Head Cashier," Terry wrote "Manage Workstations and Balancing of Tills." In Step 2 she relabeled this with the skill heading of "Retail Sales Management" using the skill list on page 70. Terry chose this heading because it matches her goal of becoming a retail sales manager. In Step 2, Terry used new skill headings to relabel her skills. If you compare Terry's titles to her skill headings, it's clear that Terry's skills—not her job titles—are stronger. This shows why it is often better to use skill headings rather than job titles in many resumes.

Step 3: Analyze a Want Ad or Job Posting to List the Required Skills

To make sure Terry fully understands what skills employers require for the job she wants, she found and analyzed an ad for a retail management position. Notice that she underlined the skills requested in the ad.

Retail Management

The Limited needs <u>outgoing, customer-oriented</u> sales staff for management positions. Must have <u>professional appearance</u> with at least <u>12 months retail supervisory experience.</u> Qualified applicants will have <u>experience managing all areas of customer service, overseeing multiple cashiering/workstations, opening and closing procedures,</u> possess knowledge of <u>retail accounting/inventory tracking systems.</u> <u>Detail oriented</u> with <u>ability to maximize profits</u> and prepare <u>sales reports, deposits, and staff schedules.</u> Please send resume to: The Limited, P.O. Box 209, Bellevue, WA 98007

Terry also categorized the skills requested as "hard" or "soft" skills, then she listed them below. She used this list of skills to create and select skill headings for her resume. Hard skills are those skills you can see someone perform, like using a computer. Soft skills are skills you can't really see someone perform, like prioritizing or problem solving. When you encounter soft skills like "Team Player," use a heading that shows exactly what you mean. For example, being a team player should occur in any job or setting. Therefore, the heading of "Team Player" doesn't have a lot of meaning. Compare it to "Departmental/Team Coordination." Which is better?

Hard Skills

12 Months Supervisory Experience
Managing Customer Service
Overseeing Multiple Cashiering/Workstations
Opening and Closing Procedures
Retail Accounting/Inventory Tracking Systems
Able to Maximize Profits
Prepare Sales Reports, Deposits, and Staff Schedules

Soft Skills

Outgoing, Customer-Oriented
Professional Appearance
Detail-Oriented

As you analyze ads or job openings, you will find that employers often request a combination of both hard and soft skills. To look highly qualified, you'll want to include a blend of both hard and soft skills in your resume and cover letters. The skill lists on pages 67 to 88 will help you create such skill headings. They also contain many of the key skills and phrases employers look for when screening resumes.

If you are unsure about the exact position you want, read through the Sunday newspaper's help-wanted section. It will be easy for you to decide what types of jobs you don't want. Then as you find jobs and ads that list skills you have and would like to use, make a list of these skills. Use this list to guide you in creating skill headings for your resume. Then when you've compiled a strong list of skill headings, find positions that use these skills.

Step 4: Select Skill Headings That Match the Ad or Job Opening

Once Terry had analyzed the ad and made a list of all the skills required, she reviewed the skill headings she had listed in Step 2. They are shown below. Terry then put check marks next to those skill headings that most closely matched the ad. Reviewing the skill headings she had checked, Terry realized the skill headings were much stronger than her titles so she crossed out all three of her job titles:

~~Job Title: Head Cashier~~	~~Job Title: Production Lead~~	~~Job Title: Head Waitress~~
✔ Retail Sales Management	✔ Operations Management	✔ Customer Service/Staff Training
✔ Staff Supervision/Training	✔ Customer Service/Order Administration	Order Coordination/Administration
Customer Service	Key Accounts/Order Expediting	✔ Workflow Coordination
Sales/Cash Accountability	Workflow Delegation	Vendor Coordination
Inventory Control/Tracking	Sales and Customer Order Reports	Workflow Design
✔ Departmental Coordination	Computerized Parts Tracking	Performance Coaching
History of Increased Sales	Shipment Research/Expediting	Team Leader
Opening & Closing Operations	Production Management	Staff and Management Liaison
Retail Auditing Procedures	Production Planning/Control	✔ Retail—Computerized Applications
Schematics/Merchandising	Materials Purchasing/Requisitions	Computerized Accounting Applications
Retail Staff Orientations		Word Processing/Spreadsheets
Customer Service/Problem Solving		
Branch Reception		

To describe her job as a head cashier, Terry chose "Retail Sales Management" as a main heading because it matches the title of the position she was applying for. Terry chose "Staff Supervision/Training" as a subheading because the ad asked for twelve months of supervisory experience. Terry chose "Departmental Coordination" as a second subheading because it matches the requirement for experience "overseeing multiple cashiering/workstations," which often requires coordinating with several different departments.

To describe her job as a production lead, Terry chose "Operations Management" as a main heading because the ad asked for experience opening and closing the store, which had been Terry's responsibility. Terry chose "Customer Service/Order Administration" as a subheading because the ad asked for experience preparing sales reports and deposits.

To describe her job as a head waitress, Terry chose "Customer Service/Staff Training" as a main heading and "Workflow Coordination" as a subheading because the ad asked for experience managing customer service. This requires training and supervising staff and delegating duties to them, which Terry did extensively as a head waitress. The last skill heading Terry chose was "Retail—Computerized Applications" because this sounds much stronger than "Computer Skills" and because the ad asked for retail accounting/inventory tracking systems experience.

There is no right or wrong way to create or select skill headings for your resume, so don't worry that your headings have to be perfect. If they are a close match to the ads you respond to, you'll look more qualified than the majority of applicants, because most people do not show how their skills match an employer's needs. As you move through this and the rest of the chapters in the book, you'll continue to gain insights that will help you shape your skill headings even further. Relax, and have fun elevating and perfecting the image your resume communicates. This process will benefit you not only in your current job search but as you continue to market yourself in all areas of your career.

Step 5: Describe Each Skill Heading

The eight skill headings Terry selected in the previous step are too many for a one-page resume, so she decided to use four main headings with four subheadings, as shown below. While Terry could have used the four main headings alone, the subheadings show the depth of her experience at a glance. The number of headings and subheadings you can use varies; just be sure to keep your resume streamlined and easy to look at.

Section from Terry's After Resume

Retail Sales Management

Staff Supervision / Training

Supervised and trained over 40 managers and customer service staff in
   sales, cashiering, and inventory control as a head cashier.
Oversaw operations for new facility, audit, and daily cash reports.
Coordinated performance evaluations with regional managers.

Departmental Coordination

Coordinated customer service with 8 departments—returns, product
   departments, electronics, stocking, receiving, and maintenance.
Managed my own station in addition to staff at 5 other stations, providing
   service to 600 customers with sales of up to $21,000 daily.

Customer Service / Staff Training

Workflow Coordination

Supervised and coordinated workflow of 8 staff serving up to 200
   customers per shift, with sales of $60,000 per month.
Instrumental in implementation of computerized systems.

Operations Management

Customer Service / Order Administration

Managed order processing, opening and closing operations for department
   completing over $ 1/4 million in customer orders per month.
Dealt directly with key accounts to expedite shipments.
Analyzed product requirements for fulfillment of orders and delegated
   production activities to staff of 10.

Retail—Computerized Applications

• Implemented Peachtree Accounting System to input and track customer
   orders, inventory, sales, accounts receivable and payable.
• Trained service staff in use of system to input on-hand inventory statistics.

To describe each skill heading, Terry checked off many of the sample sentences in the skill lists on pages 67, 70, 83, and 88. The lists are a great starting point. Just as they did for Terry, they'll get you to remember your skills. To beef up and strengthen the sample sentences, it's important that you then answer the Twelve Questions on the next page. These questions are critical because they show you how to control and elevate the image you present in the text of your resume.

Detailed examples of how to use and answer each question are provided in Chapter 6. For now, we'll merely show you how Terry answered the questions to describe her first set of skill and subheadings. On the next page, we listed Terry's main skill heading of "Retail Sales Management," along with its two subheadings, "Staff Supervision/Training" and "Departmental Coordination." Read the answers Terry wrote to the questions. Then read the "Retail Sales Management" section above to see where she placed her answers. This illustrates how you can use the Twelve Questions to create powerful content for your resume.

Headings in First Section of Terry's After Resume

Skill Heading: *Retail Sales Management*
Subheading: *Staff Supervision / Training*
Subheading: *Departmental Coordination*

THE TWELVE QUESTIONS

Question 1: Whom did you work for or with? Will mentioning them strengthen your image?
Answer : *Coordinated customer service with 8 departments including returns, product departments, electronics, stocking, receiving, and maintenance.*

Question 2: Will describing the size of the department you worked for strengthen your image?
Answer: *Managed my own station in addition to staff at 5 other stations, providing service to 600 customers with sales of up to $21,000 daily.*

Question 3: Will using numbers to describe your responsibilities strengthen your image?
Answer : *Accounted for cash in 6 tills and completed balance sheets.*

Question 4: Did you create, reorganize, conceive, or establish any procedures or systems?
Answer : *Not here but implemented computer system at another job.*

Question 5: Have you increased productivity, saved money, or reduced labor?
Answer : *Not really.*

Question 6: Did you have responsibility for special projects? If so, how large were they?
Answer : *Oversaw operations for new facility, audit, and daily cash reports. Coordinated performance evaluations with regional managers.*

Question 7: Have you been complimented for special talents?
Answer : *Yes, by customers for being very cordial.*

Question 8: Do you have technical or special skills relevant to your objective?
Answer : *Yes, computerized accounting systems but put answer in that section.*

Question 9: Do you have experience training or supervising staff? If so, how many?
Answer : *Supervised and trained over 40 managers and customer service staff in sales, cashiering, and inventory control.*

Question 10: Have you received promotions that demonstrate achievement?
Answer : *Not promoted, but given additional duties as subheadings show.*

Question 11: Have you received any awards or certificates that relate to your job objective?
Answer : *No.*

Question 12: Have you identified the top five skill requirements for the position you want?
Answer : *Yes, the top skills are addressed in my headings and subheadings.*

Step 6: Create Objective, Education, and Employment History Sections

These sections of your resume also offer great opportunities to present your qualifications and further enhance your attractiveness to an employer.

OBJECTIVE STATEMENTS

In the objective statement section of her resume below, Terry listed the type of position she wants, along with three of her strongest qualifications. This is the most powerful way to create an objective statement section, because employers want to know the type of position you are seeking and what you can do for them. This format answers these questions immediately and clearly. The Six Steps Worksheets will help you create this type of objective statement. Refer to Chapter 8 for detailed examples of how to prepare this and other types of objective statements.

**Seek a Retail Management position utilizing
the following experience:**

- Overseeing retail sales and customer service procedures for up to 600 customers daily, processing sales in excess of $2 million annually.
- Supervising and training over 40 managers and customer service staff in sales, cashiering, problem solving, inventory control, and schematics.
- Implementing computerized bookkeeping systems for retail operations.

EDUCATION

Terry had not attended college, so she didn't include an education section in her resume. If Terry had attended college and completed a degree, she could have created an education section like the example below. Refer to Chapter 9 for in-depth discussions about how to describe education with or without a degree, when to include your GPA, and the dates you attended college.

Education
B.A. Degree, University of Wisconsin   1991

EMPLOYMENT HISTORY

Since the body of Terry's resume doesn't include the names of the companies she worked for, or dates of employment, she used a condensed work history to list that information at the bottom of her resume. Notice that Terry used the main headings from the body of her resume, followed by her actual titles, then listed the company she worked for, followed by the dates of employment.

Work History
Retail Sales Management (head cashier), Kids "R" Us   1990–Present
Operations Management (production lead), Unique Used Salvage   1987–90
Customer Service / Staff Training (head waitress), Ghorm's Drive-In   1984–87

Listing her skill headings in this way keeps the employer's focus on the best of what she has to offer. It also explains where Terry gained her retail sales management, operations management, and customer service/staff training experience. If Terry had merely listed her titles (which aren't included in the body of her resume), employers wouldn't understand where Terry had gained these skills.

Refer to Chapter 9 to discover ways to emphasize a strong work history or to minimize work history problems such as gaps in employment or experience in unrelated career fields.

WORKSHEETS FOR CREATING SKILL-BASED RESUMES

Step 1: List All Skills for Each Position You've Held

To help you describe your work experience, use the skill lists for the forty-five different career fields found on pages 67 to 87. As you read through the lists and find skills that match your background, put checks next to them, and then write them below.

If you need help identifying more of your skills, analyze help wanted ads or job postings as shown in Step 3. The *Dictionary of Occupational Titles* also provides thousands of job descriptions that can be used to identify more of your skills. Answering the Twelve Questions on page 42 will also help you to identify and describe more of your skills.

Step 2: Label Groups of Skills with Skill Headings

Now that you've listed your skills, you're ready to label each one with a skill heading, as Terry did. Or you may find it easier to group similar skills together and then label that group of skills with a skill heading. Use the skill lists on pages 67 to 87 to select skill headings that match your job objective. Feel free to edit or change the headings in order to create skill headings that match the level of the job you want and present you as strongly qualified for your job objective.

This process makes many people uncomfortable, especially if they are relabeling their skills with headings that sound more important than their job titles. If you experience these feelings, take time to review Chapter 2.

First Job Title: _____

List Skills Used in This Job:

_____

_____

_____

_____

_____

_____

_____

_____

_____

_____

_____

_____

_____

_____

_____

First Job Title: _____

Relabel Skills with Skill Headings:

_____

_____

_____

_____

_____

_____

_____

_____

_____

_____

_____

_____

_____

_____

_____

Second Job Title: _____

List Skills Used in This Job:

_____
_____
_____
_____
_____
_____
_____
_____
_____
_____
_____
_____
_____
_____
_____
_____
_____

Second Job Title: _____

Relabel Skills with Skill Headings:

_____
_____
_____
_____
_____
_____
_____
_____
_____
_____
_____
_____
_____
_____
_____
_____
_____

Third Job Title: _____

List Skills Used in This Job:

_____
_____
_____
_____
_____
_____
_____
_____
_____
_____
_____
_____
_____
_____
_____
_____

Third Job Title: _____

Relabel Skills with Skill Headings:

_____
_____
_____
_____
_____
_____
_____
_____
_____
_____
_____
_____
_____
_____
_____
_____

Step 3: Analyze a Want Ad or Job Opening and List the Required Skills

Find several want ads or job postings for the type of positions you want and paste them below. Next to each ad or job posting, list the skills requested.

Step 4: Select Titles and Skill Headings That Match the Ad or Opening

Using the skills requested in the ads or job postings you just analyzed, select headings from your lists on pages 44 and 45 that are a good match for your job objective. Then write them below.

Paste Ads Here:

List Skills Requested:

_____

_____

_____

_____

_____

_____

_____

_____

_____

_____

_____

_____

_____

_____

_____

_____

_____

_____

_____

_____

_____

Best Titles and Skill Headings from Step 2:

_____

_____

_____

_____

_____

_____

_____

_____

_____

_____

_____

_____

_____

_____

_____

_____

_____

_____

_____

_____

_____

Step 5: Describe Each Title or Skill Heading

Now that you've selected the titles and skill headings you'd like to use in the body of your resume, transfer them to the worksheet below. Once you've written down your titles and headings, read through the skill lists on pages 67 to 88 that match your background. Select any sentences that match your background and write them beneath the appropriate title or heading.

Then answer the Twelve Questions on page 42 for each title or skill heading you've written below. For example, the first question is "Whom did you work for or with? Will mentioning them strengthen your image?" Terry's first subheading was "Staff Supervision/Training." So Terry asked herself, "When I performed staff supervision and training, whom did I work for or with?" It is impressive that Terry supervised and trained more than forty managers and customer service staff. This answer elevates her image. Terry's second subheading was "Departmental Coordination." So Terry asked herself, "When I coordinated departmental functions, whom did I work for or with?" It is impressive that Terry coordinated customer service with eight departments—this answer also expands and elevates her image. As you go through each question, ask yourself how that particular question relates to the title or skill heading you wish to describe. Then answer accordingly.

When you've finished both steps, you will have many statements to use in your resume. Review and prioritize them. Then select the strongest ones for your resume. Use an additional piece of paper if you run out of space on the worksheets. Once you've completed all Six Steps, refer to Chapter 7 for an in-depth discussion about how to edit and strengthen your statements.

First Title or Skill Heading: _____

Optional Subheading: _____

_____

_____

Optional Subheading: _____

_____

_____

Second Title or Skill Heading: _____

Optional Subheading: _____

_____

_____

Optional Subheading: _____

_____

_____

Third Title or Skill Heading: _____

Optional Subheading: _____

_____

_____

Optional Subheading: _____

_____

_____

Step 6: Create Your Objective, Education, and Employment History Sections

While these are short sections in your resume, they provide an employer with important information and can affect hiring decisions. So put as much effort into them as the rest of your resume.

YOUR OBJECTIVE STATEMENT

Employers want to know what you can do for them and if you have the skills they need. A formula that works well is to name the position you want and then list two to four of your strongest skills related to the position. For example, Terry's After resume on page 37 combined the objective statement with several qualifications statements. Monty's After resume on page 53 lists his objective as "Seek a position utilizing my Assistant to Controller, Corporate Accountant, and Project Accountant experience." It's simple but effective. You can create both types of objective statements by completing the worksheet below, then select the strongest one for your resume. Refer to Chapter 8 for in-depth details and worksheets that illustrate how to create a powerful qualifications statement.

Seeking a _____ position utilizing my _____,

_____, and _____ experience.

Seeking a _____ position utilizing the following experience:

- _____
- _____
- _____

YOUR EDUCATION

If you have more than one college degree, list the degree that is most relevant to your job objective first. If you don't have a college degree but would like to list your coursework, label the coursework you've taken with a heading that supports your job objective. If your college education is one of your strongest selling points, consider listing the most important courses in columns as the form below provides. Refer to Chapter 9 for examples of how to list and describe your education.

_____,	_____,	_____
Degree	College Attended	Date of Completion
_____	_____	_____
_____	_____	_____

YOUR CONDENSED EMPLOYMENT HISTORY

Take a look at the employment history section in Terry's resume on page 37. Notice that each line includes a skill heading followed by job title, company worked for, and dates of employment. Write your work history below. Refer to Chapter 9 for in-depth examples of how to list and describe your employment history.

_____,	_____,	_____
Title or Skill Heading	Company	Dates of Employment
_____,	_____,	_____
Title or Skill Heading	Company	Dates of Employment
_____,	_____,	_____
Title or Skill Heading	Company	Dates of Employment

TEMPLATE TO CREATE A SKILL-BASED RESUME

Use this template as a guide to create a skill-based resume like the one on page 37.

_____   _____

_____   _____

Seeking a _____ **position utilizing the following experience:**

- _____
- _____
- _____

First Title or Skill Heading: _____

Optional Subheading: _____

_____

_____

Optional Subheading: _____

_____

_____

Second Title or Skill Heading: _____

Optional Subheading: _____

_____

_____

Optional Subheading: _____

_____

_____

Third Title or Skill Heading: _____

Optional Subheading: _____

_____

_____

Optional Subheading: _____

_____

_____

Education _____, _____ _____

Work History

_____

_____

The Six Steps of Creating a Chronological Resume

As with a skill-based resume, you'll need to have completed the worksheets in Chapter 3 to make sure that a chronological resume is the best choice for you. If you haven't completed the worksheets, go back and complete them before you proceed. Selecting the correct resume format is crucial to creating a powerful resume.

Many people who have a stable work history jump to the conclusion that a chronological resume will market them effectively. However, many job seekers find that they receive a poor response when using chronological resumes. This happens because most chronological resumes are a mixture of jobs and job titles from diverse fields that do not match the applicant's current job objective. Such resumes can be strengthened by replacing job titles that don't match the job objective with job titles or skill headings that do match.

The process of modifying or replacing weak job titles often worries job seekers and makes them feel uncomfortable. However, employers are much more interested in your skills and if your skills match their needs than they are in knowing your actual job title. This is because many job titles have little meaning outside of the company assigning that title. Here is a title that has little meaning: "Clerk Specialist III." Do you have any clue as to what this job entails? "Clerk Specialist III" was a title given by a city department for a person processing warrants in a court. If this person wanted to apply for a job in another court, a title such as "Court Warrant Processor" or a skill heading of "Court Warrant Processing" is much more effective. When you use titles or skill headings that are truthful and accurate, employers are appreciative because it helps them see that you have skills that match their needs. If you modify or replace a job title with a stronger but truthful title, insert a statement at the end of that job description that explains how you gained the experience you describe. Using the previous example of clerk specialist III, a statement could be inserted like this:

> Performed work as a Court Warrant Processor while employed as a Clerk Specialist III with Tarrant County Courthouse.

As you work on your resume, ask yourself if each of your job titles is a strong match for the job you want. If a title isn't, then replace it or strengthen it.

To begin, we'll look at how Monty dealt with this problem. Monty was a good candidate for a chronological resume because he had a stable work history, but his title as an accounting supervisor didn't match his goal of becoming an assistant controller at a large hospital. As Monty worked through the Six Steps, he realized he could strengthen his resume by replacing one of his job titles with a skill heading. Take a few moments to read Monty's resumes on pages 52 and 53. Then we'll review each of the Six Steps Monty followed to create his chronological resume.

Step 1: List All Skills for Each Position You've Held

Using the skill lists on pages 67, 79, 81, and 88, Monty was able to identify and list many of the skills he had gained while working at his previous jobs. He also added any skills he had developed that weren't in these lists. You'll see the list of skills Monty compiled in Step 1, below.

STEP 1: MONTY'S SKILLS LIST

Southwest Oil: Accounting Supervisor

Supervised Accounting/Administrative Staff
Assisted Controller
Assisted in Managing 12 Divisions
Managed Multiple Sets of Books
Organized/Supervised Special Projects
Implemented New Computer System
Oversaw Manual Conversions
Client and Vendor Communication/Contracts
Oversaw A/R and A/P Accounts

Bernstad Homes: Project Accountant

Managed Asset Portfolio
Managed Accounting for Construction Projects
Analyzed Depreciation and Tax Expenditures
Job Costing, Bid Development
Materials Requisition and Vendor Negotiation
Budget Development and Control

Pembroke Aerospace: Accountant

Managed Multiple Accounting Divisions
Set Up Accounting Procedures and Controls
Supervised G/L and Journal Maintenance
Supervised Assistant Accountants
Managed Remote Accounting Locations

STEP 2: MONTY'S RELABELED TITLES AND SKILLS

Job Title: Accounting Supervisor

Corporate Accounting Supervisor
Assistant to Controller
Regional Accounting Management
Division and Regional Accounting Systems
Project Management
Information System Implementation
Computerized Conversions
Client Relations/Contract Administration
A/R and A/P Management

Job Title: Project Accountant

Asset Management
Cost Accounting
Depreciation/Tax Expenditure Reduction
Project Job Costing/Bidding
MRP and Vendor Negotiation
Budget Control/Long-Range Planning

Job Title: Accountant

Regional Management
Accounting Controls
General Ledger/Subsidiary Journals
General Accounting Supervisor
Off-Site Accounting Management

Step 2: Relabel Titles and Skills

Notice that in Step 1 under "Southwest Oil: Accounting Supervisor," Monty wrote "Supervised Accounting/Administrative Staff" and "Assisted Controller." In Step 2, he relabeled both sets of skills with the titles of corporate accounting supervisor and assistant to controller. Both of these titles are truthful, and both elevate Monty's image.

In Step 1 under "Bernstad Homes: Project Accountant," Monty wrote "Managed Asset Portfolio" and "Managed Accounting for Construction Projects." In Step 2, he relabeled these skills with the skill headings of "Asset Management" and "Cost Accounting." He developed these headings by using the skill list on page 67. Turn to that page and in the first column of skills you'll see "Asset Management" and in the second column you'll see "Cost Accounting." Monty chose these headings because many assistant controllers are responsible for both duties. He used "Cost Accounting" instead of "Managed Accounting for Construction Projects" because he had performed cost accounting for construction projects but wanted to change fields and work for a major hospital. So a heading of "Cost Accounting" with no reference to the construction industry worked much better.

In this step, you'll begin the process of deciding if job titles or skill headings will work the best in your chronological resume. In Monty's case, the title of assistant to controller starts his resume off as a strong match for assistant controller positions. Then his second and third titles combined with the subheadings he chose create a well-rounded picture of his skills.

At a glance, which of these resumes sells Monty the best as an assistant controller?

◆ Read the experience section of Monty's Before resume. In this description, does Monty sound more like an accounts payables/receivables clerk or an assistant controller?

◆ On the the basis of the image that this section creates, what salary range do you think Monty was at? $18,000, $24,000, or $36,000?

◆ Now find Monty's job titles in the employment history section of his Before resume. Do these job titles present Monty at a higher salary level? Just as Monty had done here, people often bury important job titles. Make sure that job titles that do match your job objective stand out. Replace or strengthen those that don't support your goal.

Monty V. Herring
263 South Oregon Street
Vermont, Texas 78393
(555) 555-5555

EXPERIENCE

- **Nine years of experience in these responsibilities:**
  Accounts payable, accounts receivable, purchase order, general ledger, and customer service.
- **Five years:**
  Federal/state/local taxes, job costing, and journal entries.
- **Three years:**
  Bank reconciliation, supervision, and training of 2 to 6 people, fixed assets, inventory control, office management, and payroll data entry.
- **Additional Experience:**
  Organizing and managing special projects, helping to implement new or updated software, chart of account maintenance and design, establishing and maintaining accounting procedures, and assisting the controller.

EMPLOYMENT HISTORY

Southwest Oil, Accounting Supervisor, Petroleum Industry 1994–99
Bernstad Homes, Project Accountant, Construction Industry 1990–94
Pembroke Aerospace, Accountant, Aerospace Industry 1987–90
Marshall's Exchange, A/R and Customer Service Clerk, Fur Industry 1985–87
Baker Construction, A/R Clerk, Construction Industry 1983–85

MILITARY EXPERIENCE

1980–82, U.S. Army, Military Police, Germany, Honorable Discharge

EDUCATION

Completed undergraduate courses in Literature, Drama, Science, and Music toward B.A. Degree with Major in Accounting, Troy University GPA 3.94
A.A. Degree in Accounting and Business Administration, Alabama College

SOFTWARE AND COMPUTERS

IBM PC, Unisys, MAS90, 10-Key, WordPerfect, Lotus, Windows, Excel, Word, Tvalue, ProcomPlus, Formtool.

Monty V. Herring
(555) 555-5555

263 South Oregon Street
Vermont, TX 78393

Seek a position utilizing my
Assistant to the Controller, Corporate Accountant,
and Project Accountant experience.

ASSISTANT TO CONTROLLER, Southwest Oil 1994–99

Corporate Accounting Supervisor
Managed 3 sets of books, working directly with Controller to oversee
12 divisions for firm with annual revenues in excess of $125 million.
Supervised staff of 10 bookkeepers, clerks, and administrative staff.

Project Management
Organized and supervised special projects such as implementation of
$2 million computer system utilized by 200 employees.
Oversaw conversion, auditing, and streamlining of manual records to
computerized system, which cut costs by $125,000 annually.

Client Relations and Contract Administration
Managed key accounts such as Lockheed Aircraft and IBM.
Controlled 2,000 accounts receivable and 200 vendor
contracts and accounts payable.

PROJECT ACCOUNTANT, Bernstad Homes 1990–94

Asset Management
Managed portfolio of corporate assets exceeding $50 million.
Analyzed asset depreciation and made recommendations, which cut
tax expenditures over 12% annually.

Cost Accounting
Managed accounting for up to 300 annual construction projects
with revenues exceeding $12 million annually.
Gained extensive experience in job costing, bid development, contract
administration, materials requisition, and vendor negotiation.
Recognized for maximizing profits by thoroughly analyzing each
contract and job costs, and by controlling project budgets.

ACCOUNTANT, Pembroke Aerospace 1987–90

Regional Management
Managed internal accounting division with revenues of $25 million
annually, overseeing general ledger and subsidiary journals.

General Accounting Supervisor
Supervised 6 assistant accountants as well as accounting performed in
5 remote locations preparing A/R, A/P, payroll, and inventory reports.

Education
Accounting Major, Troy University—Completing B.A. Degree (GPA 3.94)
A.A. Degree, Accounting & Business Administration, Alabama College

---

Does Monty's After resume do a better job of marketing him in the $36,000 range?

◆ Monty had been an assistant to the controller but his actual job title was accounting supervisor. This title is too weak for assistant controller positions because many accounting supervisors are only responsible for daily accounting functions.

◆ As an assistant to the controller, Monty had been given additional responsibility for staff completing multiple sets of books, auditing procedures, and special projects.

◆ We replaced the title of accounting supervisor with assistant to controller because this made Monty's resume a much stronger match for assistant controller positions. This title is truthful as Monty worked directly with the controller, assisting him in all areas of accounting management for twelve divisions.

Step 3: Analyze a Want Ad or Job Opening and List the Required Skills

To make sure he fully understands what skills employers require for assistant controller positions, Monty found and analyzed this ad. Notice that he underlined the skills requested in the ad.

Assistant Controller

Fast growing manufacturer seeks an accounting professional to <u>assist Controller</u> who is responsible for ensuring <u>accurate accounting processes,</u> <u>controls,</u> <u>reporting,</u> and for <u>analysis of key financial indicators.</u> Candidate should possess <u>4 years of supervisory operations accounting,</u> <u>cost accounting,</u> <u>contract administration,</u> and <u>asset management experience.</u> <u>Implementation of computerized information systems</u> preferred. Candidate must be a <u>team player,</u> able to <u>handle crises</u> and <u>solve problems.</u> Resume to: P.O. Box 492, Vermont, TX 78393.

You'll notice that Monty underlined the skills requested in the ad and identified them as "hard" or "soft" skills. Remember, hard skills are those quantifiable skills you can see someone perform, like using a computer. Soft skills are skills you can't really see someone perform, like prioritizing or problem solving. When you use soft skills like "Team Player," make sure your heading shows exactly what you mean. For example, being a team player should occur in any job or setting. Therefore, the heading "Team Player" doesn't have a lot of meaning. Compare it to "Departmental/Team Coordination." Which makes you sound more qualified?

Hard Skills	**Soft Skills**
Assist Controller	Team Player
Ensure Accurate Accounting Processes	Handle Crises
Controls, Reporting	Solve Problems
Analysis of Key Financial Indicators	
4 Years Supervisory Accounting Experience	
Cost Accounting	
Contract Administration	
Asset Management	
Information Systems Implementation	

As you analyze ads or job openings, you'll find that employers often request a combination of both hard and soft skills. To look well qualified, you'll want to include a blend of both types of skills. The skill lists on pages 67 to 88 will help you develop and select such skill headings. They also contain many of the key skills and phrases employers look for when screening resumes.

If you are unsure about the exact position you want, read through the Sunday newspaper's help-wanted section. It will be easy for you to decide what types of jobs you don't want. Then as you find jobs and ads that list skills you have and would like to use, make a list of these skills. Use this list to guide you in creating skill headings for your resume. Then when you've compiled a strong list of skill headings, find positions that use these skills.

Step 4: Select Skill Headings That Match the Ad or Job Opening

Once Monty had analyzed the ad and made a list of all the skills required for the position, he reviewed the job titles and skill headings he had listed in Step 2. Monty then put check marks next to those job titles and skill headings that most closely matched the ad, as shown below.

~~Job Title: Accounting Supervisor~~
- ✔ Corporate Accounting Supervisor
- ✔ Assistant to Controller
  Regional Accounting Management
  Division and Regional Accounting Systems
- ✔ Project Management
  Information System Implementation
  Computerized Conversions
- ✔ Client Relations/Contract Administration
  A/R and A/P Management

✔ Job Title: Project Accountant
- ✔ Asset Management
- ✔ Cost Accounting
  Depreciation/Tax Expenditure Reduction
  Project Job Costing/Bidding
  MRP and Vendor Negotiation
  Budget Control/Long Range Planning

✔ Job Title: Accountant
- ✔ Regional Management
  Accounting Controls
  General Ledger/Subsidiary Journals
- ✔ General Accounting Supervisor
  Off-Site Accounting Management

Doing this, Monty realized that his job title of accounting supervisor created a weaker image than the title of assistant to controller. So he crossed out "Accounting Supervisor" and put a check next to "Assistant to Controller." Monty wanted to maximize his accounting supervisor title so he strengthened it by relabeling it "Corporate Accounting Supervisor." He then put a check next to that title along with the skill headings of "Project Management" and "Client Relations/Contract Administration" because he knew that assistant controller positions often require this experience. Monty felt that his second title of project accountant was a good supportive title to "Assistant to Controller" so he put a check next to that title without changing it. He then checked "Asset Management" and "Cost Accounting" to use as subheadings beneath his title of project accountant. Monty also felt that his title of accountant was a good supportive title so he didn't change it and put a check next to it. He then checked "Regional Management" and "General Accounting Supervisor" to use as subheadings beneath that title.

All together Monty selected three job titles and seven skill headings for his resume. In Step 5, we'll look at how Monty used them in his new resume.

Step 5: Describe Each Job Title or Skill Heading

In the previous step, Monty put check marks next to three job titles and seven skill headings. This is too many main sections for a one-page resume, so Monty used the seven skill headings as subheadings beneath his job titles. While Monty could have used the titles alone, the subheadings show the depth of his experience at a glance. This makes him look more qualified than if he had only used his titles. The number of titles and subheadings you can use varies; just be sure to keep your resume streamlined and easy to read.

ASSISTANT TO CONTROLLER, Southwest Oil 1994–99

Corporate Accounting Supervisor
Managed 3 sets of books, working directly with Controller to oversee
12 divisions for firm with annual revenues in excess of $125 million.
Supervised staff of 10 bookkeepers, clerks, and administrative staff.

Project Management
Organized and supervised special projects such as implementation of
$2 million computer system utilized by 200 employees.
Oversaw conversion, auditing, and streamlining of manual records to
computerized system, which cut costs by $125,000 annually.

Client Relations and Contract Administration
Managed key accounts such as Lockheed Aircraft and IBM.
Controlled 2,000 accounts receivable and 200 vendor contracts and accounts payable.

PROJECT ACCOUNTANT, Bernstad Homes 1990–94

Asset Management
Managed portfolio of corporate assets exceeding $50 million.
Analyzed asset depreciation and made recommendations, which cut
tax expenditures over 12% annually.

Cost Accounting
Managed accounting for up to 300 annual construction projects with
revenues exceeding $12 million annually.
Gained extensive experience in job costing, bid development, contract
administration, materials requisition, and vendor negotiation.
Recognized for maximizing profits by thoroughly analyzing each
contract and job costs, and controlling project budgets.

ACCOUNTANT, Pembroke Aerospace 1987–90

Regional Management
Managed internal accounting division with revenues of $25 million
annually overseeing general ledger and subsidiary journals.

General Accounting Supervisor
Supervised 6 assistant accountants as well as accounting performed in
5 remote locations preparing A/R, A/P, payroll, and inventory reports.

To describe each job title and skill heading, Monty checked off many of the sample sentences on pages 67, 79, 81, and 88. The lists are a great starting point. Just as they did for Monty, they'll get you to remember your skills. To beef up and strengthen the sample sentences, you must then answer the Twelve Questions on the facing page. These questions are critical because they show you how to control and elevate the image you present in your resume.

Detailed examples of how to use and answer each question are provided in Chapter 6. For now, we'll merely show you how Monty answered the questions to describe his first job. On the facing page, you'll notice the title "Assistant to Controller" followed by three subheadings. Read the answers Monty wrote to the questions. Then read the "Assistant to Controller" section above to see where he placed his answers. This illustrates how you can use the Twelve Questions to create powerful content for your resume.

Headings in First Section of Monty's After Resume

Job Title:	*Assistant to Controller*
Subheading:	*Corporate Accounting Supervisor*
Subheading:	*Project Management*
Subheading:	*Client Relations and Contract Administration*

THE TWELVE QUESTIONS

Question 1: Whom did you work for or with? Will mentioning them strengthen your image?

Answer: *Managed 3 sets of books, working directly with Controller to oversee 12 divisions for firm with annual revenues in excess of $125 million. Managed key accounts such as Lockheed Aircraft and IBM.*

Question 2: Will describing the size of the department you worked for strengthen your image?

Answer: *Firm with annual revenues in excess of $125 million (in sentence above).*

Question 3: Will using numbers to describe your responsibilities strengthen your image?

Answer: *Managed 3 sets of books (in sentence above).*

Question 4: Did you create, reorganize, conceive, or establish any procedures or systems?

Answer: *Organized and supervised special projects such as implementation of $2 million computer system utilized by 200 employees.*

Question 5: Have you increased productivity, saved money, or reduced labor?

Answer: *Oversaw conversion, auditing, and streamlining of manual records to computerized system, which cut costs by $125,000 annually.*

Question 6: Did you have responsibility for special projects? If so, how large were they?

Answer: *Answered in question 4.*

Question 7: Have you been complimented for special talents?

Answer: *Yes, for my ability to meet deadlines and solve problems.*

Question 8: Do you have technical or special skills relevant to your objective?

Answer: *Am showing "accounting technical skills" with my subheadings.*

Question 9: Do you have experience training or supervising staff? If so, how many?

Answer: *Supervised staff of 10 bookkeepers, clerks, and administrative staff.*

Question 10: Have you received promotions that demonstrate achievement?

Answer: *Not promoted, but given additional duties as subheadings show.*

Question 11: Have you received any awards or certificates that relate to your job objective?

Answer: *No.*

Question 12: Have you identified the top five skill requirements for the position you want?

Answer: *Yes, top skills are reflected in titles and subheadings.*

Step 6: Create Objective, Education, and Employment History Sections

These sections of your resume offer great opportunities to present your qualifications and further enhance your attractiveness to an employer.

OBJECTIVE STATEMENTS

In the objective statement of his resume below, Monty listed three areas of expertise that qualify him for an assistant controller position. Remember that employers want to know what skills and experience you have to offer. Monty's objective statement is simple but effective. The Six Steps Worksheets will guide you as you create this type of objective statement, as well as one that combines your objective with several qualification statements. Prepare each type of objective statement and then select the strongest one for your resume. Refer to Chapter 8 for detailed examples and worksheets that will help you craft powerful objective statements.

> **Seek a position utilizing my Assistant to the Controller,
> Corporate Accountant, and Project Accountant experience.**

EDUCATION

Below, you'll see how Monty had originally prepared the education section of his resume. The Before example has several weaknesses. It's not beneficial for Monty to point out that he has only completed two quarters of his B.A. degree. Like many people, Monty is better off omitting classes in literature, science, drama, and music from his education section because they don't relate to his job objective. In contrast, the After example emphasizes that Monty is pursuing an accounting major at Troy University with a current GPA of 3.94. This statement is strengthened by listing Monty's A.A. degree. As you can see, the After example sells the best that Monty has to offer. Marketing his education in this way and combining it with the strength of the titles and subheadings in his resume will allow Monty to compete very effectively with other applicants. Many employers will consider a combination of experience and partial education as equivalent to a bachelor's or master's degree. Refer to Chapter 9 for in-depth details on how to describe and list your education.

BEFORE   **Education**
Completed undergraduate courses in Literature, Drama, Science, and Music
toward B.A. Degree with Major in Accounting, Troy University GPA 3.94
A.A. Degree in Accounting and Business Administration Alabama College

AFTER   **Education**
Accounting Major, Troy University—Completing B.A. Degree (GPA 3.94)
A.A. Degree, Accounting & Business Administration, Alabama College

EMPLOYMENT HISTORY

Monty's employment history was included in the body of his resume. Monty used the new title of assistant to controller but also included his actual job title of corporate accounting supervisor along with a description of his job duties. In this way, Monty explains to employers how he gained the assistant to controller experience and is truthful about it. If you take a look at his resume on page 53, you'll notice that he lists each of his titles, followed by the name of the company where he worked along with dates of employment all on one line. This approach saves space and keeps your resume looking streamlined. The Six Steps Worksheets will guide you in using this one-line approach. Refer to Chapter 9 for in-depth details about how to emphasize a strong work history or to minimize work history problems.

WORKSHEETS FOR CREATING CHRONOLOGICAL RESUMES

Step 1: List All Skills for Each Position You've Held

To help you describe your work experience, use the skill lists for the career fields listed on pages 67 to 87. As you read through the lists and find skills that match your background, put checks next to them and then write them below.

If you need help identifying more of your skills, analyze help wanted ads or job postings as shown in Step 3. *The Dictionary of Occupational Titles* also provides thousands of job descriptions that can be used to identify more of your skills. Answering the Twelve Questions on page 57 will also help you to identify and describe more of your skills.

Step 2: Relabel Titles and Skills

Now that you've listed your titles and skills, you're ready to decide if any of your titles need to be strengthened. If so, relabel them with stronger titles or skill headings and list them below. Relabel your skills, or groups of skills, with skill headings to see if they are stronger than your titles or if you can use them as subheadings to strengthen your resume.

Use the skill lists on pages 67 to 87 to select titles or skill headings that are a better match for your job objective. Feel free to edit or change the headings in order to create skill headings that match the level of job you want and present you as well qualified for your job objective.

First Job Title: _____

List Skills Used in This Job:

_____

_____

_____

_____

_____

_____

_____

_____

_____

_____

_____

_____

_____

_____

_____

_____

_____

_____

_____

_____

First Job Title: _____

New Titles and Skill Headings:

_____

_____

_____

_____

_____

_____

_____

_____

_____

_____

_____

_____

_____

_____

_____

_____

_____

_____

_____

_____

Second Job Title: _____

List Skills Used in This Job:

_____

_____

_____

_____

_____

_____

_____

_____

_____

_____

_____

_____

_____

_____

_____

_____

Second Job Title: _____

New Titles and Skill Headings:

_____

_____

_____

_____

_____

_____

_____

_____

_____

_____

_____

_____

_____

_____

_____

_____

Third Job Title: _____

List Skills Used in This Job:

_____

_____

_____

_____

_____

_____

_____

_____

_____

_____

_____

_____

_____

_____

_____

Third Job Title _____

New Titles and Skill Headings:

_____

_____

_____

_____

_____

_____

_____

_____

_____

_____

_____

_____

_____

_____

_____

Step 3: Analyze a Want Ad or Job Opening and List the Required Skills

Find several want ads or job postings for the type of positions you want and paste them below. Next to each ad or job posting, list the skills requested.

Step 4: Select Titles and Skill Headings That Match the Ad or Opening

Using the skills requested in the ads or job postings you just analyzed, select titles and skill headings from your lists on pages 59 and 60 that are a good match for your job objective. Then write them below.

Paste Ads Here:

List Skills Requested:

Best Titles and Skill Headings from Step 2:

Step 5: Describe Each Title or Skill Heading

Now that you've selected the titles and skill headings you'd like to use in the body of your resume, transfer them to the worksheet below. Once you've written down your titles and headings, read through the sample sentence lists on pages 67 to 88 that match your background. Select any sentences that match your background and write them beneath the appropriate title or skill heading.

Then answer the Twelve Questions on page 57 for each title or skill heading that you've written below. For example, the first question is "Whom did you work for or with? Will mentioning them strengthen your image?" Monty's first title was followed by the subheading of corporate accounting supervisor. So Monty asked himself, "As a corporate accounting supervisor, whom did I work for or with?" It is impressive that Monty worked directly with the controller to oversee twelve divisions for a firm with annual revenues of $125 million. This answer expands and elevates his image. As you go through each question, ask yourself how that particular question relates to the title or skill heading you wish to describe. Then answer accordingly.

When you've finished these steps, you will have many statements to use in your resume. Review and prioritize them. Then select the strongest ones for your resume. Use an additional piece of paper if you run out of space on the worksheets. Once you've completed all Six Steps, refer to Chapter 7 for in-depth examples of how to edit and strengthen your statements.

First Title or Skill Heading: _____

Optional Subheading: _____

_____

_____

Optional Subheading: _____

_____

_____

Second Title or Skill Heading: _____

Optional Subheading: _____

_____

_____

Optional Subheading: _____

_____

_____

Third Title or Skill Heading: _____

Optional Subheading: _____

_____

_____

Optional Subheading: _____

_____

_____

Step 6: Create Your Objective, Education, and Employment History Sections

While these are short sections in your resume, they provide an employer with important information and can affect hiring decisions. So put as much effort into them as the rest of your resume.

YOUR OBJECTIVE STATEMENT

Employers want to know what skills and experience you have to offer. A formula that works well is to name three of your strongest skills or areas of experience for the position. For example, in Monty's After resume on page 53, he listed his objective as "Seek a position utilizing my Assistant to Controller, Corporate Accountant, and Project Accountant experience." It's simple but effective. Terry's After resume on page 37 combined the objective statement with several qualifications statements. You can create both types of objective statements by completing the worksheet below, then selecting the strongest one for your resume. Refer to Chapter 8 for in-depth details and worksheets that illustrate how to create a powerful qualifications statement.

Seek a _____ position utilizing my _____

_____, and _____ experience.

Seeking a _____ position utilizing the following experience:

- _____
- _____
- _____

YOUR EDUCATION

If you have more than one college degree, list the degree that is most relevant to your job objective first. If you don't have a college degree but would like to list your coursework, label the coursework you've taken with a heading that supports your job objective. If your college education is one of your strongest selling points, consider listing the most important courses in columns as the form below provides. Refer to Chapter 9 for examples of how to list and describe your education.

_____, _____, _____
Degree   College Attended   Date of Completion

_____   _____   _____

_____   _____   _____

LISTING EMPLOYMENT INFORMATION

Since you are creating a chronological resume, your employment history is provided in the body of your resume. If you take a look at Monty's resume on page 53, you'll see that he listed his title followed by the name of the company he worked for along with his dates of employment. This one-line approach saves space and keeps your resume streamlined. Refer to Chapter 8 for in-depth examples of how to list and describe your employment history.

_____, _____, _____
Title or Skill Heading   Company   Dates of Employment

_____, _____, _____
Title or Skill Heading   Company   Dates of Employment

_____, _____, _____
Title or Skill Heading   Company   Dates of Employment

TEMPLATE TO CREATE A CHRONOLOGICAL RESUME

Use this template as a guide to create a chronological resume like the one on page 53.

_____   _____

_____   _____

Seek a _____ **position utilizing my**
_____, _____, **and** _____ **experience.**

First Title or Skill Heading: _____

Optional Subheading: _____

_____

_____

Optional Subheading: _____

_____

_____

Second Title or Skill Heading: _____

Optional Subheading: _____

_____

_____

Optional Subheading: _____

_____

_____

Third Title or Skill Heading: _____

Optional Subheading: _____

_____

_____

Optional Subheading: _____

_____

_____

Education _____, _____ _____

5 Skill Lists and Sample Sentences

To help you brainstorm, read the index below to find skill lists and sample sentences that match your background. Go to those pages and check off any skills or sentences that describe your experience. Once you've finished reading the lists, transfer the skills and sentences you have checked off to the worksheets on pages 44 to 45 or 59 to 60.

INDEX OF SKILL LISTS AND SAMPLE SENTENCES   **PAGE NUMBER**

Accounting/Bookkeeping	67
Assembly/Production	68
Automotive/Machine Shop/Mechanic/Industrial Maintenance	69
Cashiering/Customer Service/Retail Sales	70
Computer Programs/Equipment	71
Computer System Administration/Technical Support	72
Construction/General Labor	73
Driving/Shipping/Warehouse	74
Engineering/Drafting	75
Executive Secretary/Office Management	76
Facilities Maintenance/Janitorial	77
Healthcare	78
Human Resources Management/Recruitment/Training	79
Inside/Outside Sales	80
Management and Supervision	81
Reception/General Office	82
Restaurant/Food Service	83
Self-Employed/Consultants	84
Social/Human Services	85
Teaching/Education	86
Writer/Reporter/Copywriter	87
Transferable Skills	88

As you read these lists, you may recall other skills or responsibilities that are not listed. Add any skills you think of that are not included in the skill lists to your worksheets on pages 44 to 45 or 59 to 60. You may be surprised to find that you have skills listed in an entirely different skill category than the one you originally looked for. For example, a nurse would use the Healthcare list but will also find he has many skills listed in the Management, Human Resources, and Social/Human Services lists. Since these lists cover a broad range of jobs and industries, they can help almost every job seeker describe work experience within a variety of fields.

These lists are by no means exhaustive. They are meant to assist you in compiling your skills rather than being the only source for creating your resume. Be sure to answer the Twelve Questions on pages 91 to 102. These questions are extremely important in helping you to control your image.

Chapter 7 also provides tips on how to prioritize and use power verbs so that the sentences or statements you use in your resume have maximum impact.

To create the skill lists and sample sentences, I read hundreds of help-wanted ads and job descriptions. Most want ads and job descriptions were very specific in describing the skills required for each industry. Many industry-specific, hard skills are not as transferable as soft skills. For example, consider the case of a battalion commander who plans to leave the military and use his skills to manage a department and its inventory. Below, we crossed out the title of battalion commander because it does not match our image of a department manager in a civilian job. We replaced "Battalion Commander" with the skill heading of "Staff Supervision/Departmental Management." We also crossed out "Maintaining Combat Weapons" and replaced it with "Equipment Maintenance." "Inventory Control" is clearly transferable, so this skill heading is used as is and didn't need to be changed or replaced. If you are making a career change, list all your skills or the duties for which you were responsible. Describe them using language standard for your industry. Then, keeping your objective in mind, review your skills and cross out words, phrases, or duties that are not transferable to the job you want. Replace them with words or phrases that match your job objective, as this example illustrates:

~~Battalion Commander~~	Staff Supervision/Departmental Management
~~Maintenance of Combat Weapons~~	Equipment Maintenance
Inventory Control	Inventory Control

The Power of Transferable Skills

In contrast to hard skills, soft skills are transferable to all industries. For example, strong time management and organizational skills are important in most positions. The ability to prioritize projects and meet deadlines is also an important skill in any position or industry. Take a moment and review the sample sentences on page 88 that describe transferable skills used in all jobs and industries. Ask yourself how you've used these skills in each of your jobs and mark those that match your experience.

Carmen wants to use her experience as a banquet manager for a major hotel chain to apply for a project management position with a city's customer service department. The ad for the position also emphasized the need for strong leadership skills. Here's how we described her background:

PROJECT MANAGEMENT / TEAM LEADERSHIP

- Managed projects generating up to $752,000 annually, coordinating customer requirements with 5 departments and 43 staff.
- Expedited projects with short lead times and demonstrated strong team leadership and motivational skills.

Notice that we labeled Carmen's experience to match the position requirements. We omitted Carmen's title of banquet manager and labeled this experience "Project Management." We also used "Team Leadership" because it is stronger than the word "Leadership" alone. This communicates that Carmen's skills are transferable to a city department.

Always keep in mind the image that you want to project with your resume. Describe your background so that it matches the transferable skills employers want. By doing so, you will dramatically increase the success of your resume and your job search.

ACCOUNTING/BOOKKEEPING

These Skills May Also Be Used as Skill Headings

___ Accounts Payable/Receivable	___ Corporate Audit Procedures	___ Integrated Accounting Software	___ Profit Sharing Records
___ Asset Management	___ Corporate Bank Accounts	___ Interest Calculations	___ Purchase Order Management
___ Assistant to Controller	___ Cost Accounting	___ Internal Finance Controls	___ Purchasing/Buying
___ Bad Debt Management/Tracking	___ Credit Management	___ Inventory Control/Tracking	___ Quarterly Taxes
___ Balance Sheets	___ Departmental Coordination	___ Inventory Valuation Methods	___ Sales Journals
___ Bank Deposits/Reconciliations	___ Departmental Liaison	___ Invoice Verification	___ Staff Supervision/Training
___ Benefits Administration	___ Depreciation Reports	___ Job Costing/Control	___ State and Federal Taxes
___ Budgets and Forecasting	___ Employee Orientations	___ Loan Applications	___ Subsidiary Ledgers
___ Business Plans	___ Expense Allocations	___ Office Management	___ Supervision—Accounting Staff
___ Cash Accountability	___ Expense Journals	___ Operations Management	___ Supervision of Clerical Staff
___ Cash Disbursements	___ Financial Analysis/Forecasting	___ Payment Negotiation	___ Supply Budgeting
___ Cash Management	___ Financial Statements	___ Payroll Preparation and Taxes	___ Tax Analysis and Control
___ Computerized Accounting Applications	___ Fiscal Management/Control	___ Performance Evaluations	___ Tenant Accounts
___ Computerized Billing	___ Full Charge Bookkeeping	___ Personnel Administration	___ Time Card Tracking
___ Contract Administration	___ General Ledgers	___ Petty Cash Management	___ Trial Balance
___ Conversion to Automated Systems	___ Gross Margin Analysis	___ Portfolio Management	___ Trust Accounts
___ Corporate Accounting	___ Insurance Administration	___ P&L Responsibility	___ Vendor Contact Management

Sample Sentences Using Some of the Skills Listed Above

___ Managed manual to computerized system conversion.

___ Utilized Lotus and Excel to prepare financial documents.

___ Worked with state auditors to review accounting records.

___ Coordinated with ___ divisions to track billing/invoicing.

___ Worked directly with President and ___ managers.

___ Consulted ___ management staff in financial forecasting.

___ Prepared salary and benefit reports for ___ employees.

___ Set up new accounting and records control systems.

___ Trained ___ staff in use of invoicing and billing systems.

___ Served as lead, resolving problems for ___ key accounts.

___ Controlled $___ in inventory and supplies.

___ Issued up to ___ purchase orders annually.

___ Managed front office functions to support staff of ___.

___ Researched and selected phone system valued to $___.

___ Selected computer systems valued to $___.

___ Maintained files and documents to support ___ staff.

___ Scheduled conferences and appointments for ___ staff.

___ Managed corporate accounting for ___ departments.

___ Supervised daily accounting operations including ___.

___ Prepared contracts and correspondence for ___ staff.

___ Managed bookkeeping, office and reception functions to support staff of ___.

___ Managed general ledger and journals for firm with sales of $___ annually.

___ Oversaw all bookkeeping functions through financial statements.

___ Tracked cash disbursements for corporation with sales of $___ annually.

___ Maintained A/R, A/P, and billing for over ___ accounts.

___ Processed payroll and calculated sales commissions for staff of ___.

___ Consulted management in budgeting, portfolio, and fixed asset analysis.

___ Prepared and filed quarterly reports, state and federal taxes.

___ Worked with auditors verifying all accounting records.

___ Purchased $___ annually in capital equipment and inventory.

___ Negotiated and managed purchase agreements valued up to $___ per contract.

___ Developed and maintained database for over ___ vendors.

___ Tracked purchase orders for department with sales of $___ annually.

___ Approved invoicing for ___ departments with sales in excess of $___ monthly.

___ Managed credit application and approval for client base of over ___ customers.

___ Authorized to set up new accounts or extend credit to $___.

___ Increased bad debt collection by $___ annually.

___ Oversaw billing for ___ accounts with sales in excess of $___ annually.

___ Supervised and trained staff of ___ accounting and clerical personnel.

___ Coordinated workflow for ___ departments composed of ___ employees.

Skill Lists and Sample Sentences for

ASSEMBLY/PRODUCTION

These Skills May Also Be Used as Skill Headings

___ Assembly/Inspection	___ Employee Scheduling/Training	___ Parts Kit Preparation	___ Project Management
___ Assembly Drawings	___ Equipment/Instrument Calibration	___ Parts Processing	___ Quality Control/Inspection
___ Assembly Lead	___ Equipment/Product Testing	___ Parts Purchasing/Requisition	___ Record of Low Rejection Rates
___ Assembly Schematics	___ File & Records Control	___ Pneumatic Ladders	___ Safety Regulations
___ Blueprints/Drawings	___ Forklift/Pallet Jack Operation	___ Precision Instruments	___ Shift Scheduling/Tracking
___ Certified Forklift Operator	___ Hazardous Materials Management	___ Product Inspection	___ Shipping/Receiving
___ Close Tolerance Soldering	___ High Productivity Record	___ Product Packaging/Assembly	___ Staff Supervision/Training
___ Computerized Inventory Control	___ High Volume Production Control	___ Product Testing	___ Team Coordination/Leader
___ Computerized Parts Tracking	___ Inventory Control	___ Production Control	___ Tooling Setup
___ Crew Supervision	___ Invoice Verification	___ Production Line Coordination	___ Vacuum Formers/Sealers
___ Customer Service	___ Machining	___ Production Line Troubleshooting	___ Vendor Contact/Coordination
___ Daily Work Delegation	___ Material Forecasting	___ Production Management	___ Visual Inspection Techniques
___ Data Entry/Parts Control	___ Material Handling	___ Production Planning	___ Warehousing Procedures
___ Departmental Coordination	___ Material Planning	___ Production Scheduling	___ Workflow Improvement
___ Dies/Fabrication Equipment	___ Mechanical Maintenance	___ Production Space Design	___ Workflow Management
___ Document Control	___ Order Expediting	___ Production Speed & Accuracy	___ Work Prioritization
___ Electronic Assembly	___ Order Processing	___ Project Coordination	___ Workstation Management

Sample Sentences Using Some of the Skills Listed Above

___ Trained ____ employees in all production procedures.

___ Controlled quality of ____ products assembled per month.

___ Read blueprints/drawings to insure quality control.

___ Maintained contact with approximately ____ vendors.

___ Served as Assembly Lead supervising ____ employees.

___ Tested over ____ products valued up to $____.

___ Supervised crew of ____ in ____ departments.

___ Completed defective parts reports for up to ____ items.

___ Delegated daily work duties for ____ production lines.

___ Scheduled ____ rotating shifts for ____ employees.

___ Controlled and tracked an in-house inventory of $____.

___ Verified invoicing for $____ worth of monthly shipments.

___ Trained ____ employees in material handling procedures.

___ Pulled parts and prepared kits for ____ orders monthly.

___ Managed workstation producing ____ parts per month.

___ Worked independently assembling over ____ items daily.

___ Maintained a ____% rejection rate.

___ Praised for consistently meeting all assembly quotas.

___ Set up and maintained equipment valued at $____.

___ Selected as Crew Lead in absence of manager.

___ Assembled ____ items to produce over ____ products daily.

___ Evaluated performance of ____ employees to maximize production.

___ Coordinated with ____ supervisors in production of ____ parts or units.

___ Managed assembly of over ____ products, consistently meeting deadlines.

___ Assisted in preparation and distribution of ____ assembly drawings.

___ Coordinated with ____ shipping and receiving departments.

___ Forklift Certified: ____ years experience with excellent safety record.

___ Utilized computerized parts tracking system to verify $____ in inventory.

___ Met all production/quality control quotas, producing over ____ units per day.

___ Coordinated with ____ staff to insure assembly and supply deadlines were met.

___ Consulted with department manager to forecast weekly production quotas.

___ Cross-trained ____ staff in assembly, quality and document control procedures.

___ Coordinated with ____ departments to resolve problems and expedite orders.

___ Processed over ____ inventory parts utilizing computerized tracking system.

___ Managed ____, ____, and ____ projects for a $____ department.

___ Performed visual inspection of ____ assembly parts to maintain quality control.

___ Operated and maintained ____, ____, and ____ production equipment.

___ Maintained documentation for up to ____ products valued in excess of $____.

___ Maintained over ____ files and production documents utilizing ____ program.

___ Prioritized and assigned workload for ____ staff in ____ departments.

AUTOMOTIVE/MACHINE SHOP/MECHANIC/INDUSTRIAL MTC

These Skills May Also Be Used as Skill Headings

___ 3-, 4-, 5-Axis Machines	___ Double Action Press	___ Lathe/Mill Operation	___ Reading of Blueprints/Schematics
___ Advanced Engine Control	___ Electrical/Boiler/Plumbing	___ Loaders, Trucks, Towers	___ Refrigeration Systems
___ ASE Certifications	___ Engine Systems & Repair	___ Machine/Department Setup	___ Repair of Electrical Panels
___ Automotive Electronics/AC Systems	___ Engineering Liaison	___ Materials Requisition Planning	___ Sheet Metal Fabrication
___ Automotive Repair	___ Extrusion Methods	___ Mechanical, HVAC	___ Shop Management/Scheduling
___ Benchwork	___ Facilities Management	___ Movers, Shovels, Forklifts	___ Shop Supervisor
___ Bid Development/Repair Estimating	___ Fadal, Fanuc, Haas Controllers	___ Precision Diagnostic Equipment	___ Staff Supervision/Training
___ Brake/ABS Systems	___ Faulty Processes Detection	___ Precision Machining	___ Subcontractor Coordination
___ Budget/Expense Control	___ Field Technician/Repair	___ Preventive Maintenance	___ Suspension/Steering Systems
___ CAD/CAM Programming	___ Finish Applications	___ Process Inspection	___ Thin Gauge Welding
___ Close Tolerance Specifications	___ Fleet Maintenance	___ Production Management	___ TIG Welding
___ CNC Machinist	___ Foreign/Domestic Vehicles	___ Programmable Controllers	___ Trades Supervision
___ Computerized Control Systems	___ Heavy Equipment Mechanic	___ Project Planning/Scheduling	___ Transmission/Transaxle
___ Computerized Parts Control	___ Hydraulic, Pneumatic Systems	___ Punch, Router, Shaper, Saws	___ Trim Shop Operations
___ Crew Lead	___ Industrial Maintenance	___ Purchasing/Inventory Control	___ Tune-Up/Engine Performance
___ Departmental Coordination	___ Install, Troubleshoot, Repair	___ QA ISO9002/DI9000A	___ Warranty Verification
___ Diesel/Hydraulics/Pneumatics	___ Instrument Calibration	___ QC/Parts Buy-Off	___ Workflow Delegation

Sample Sentences Using Some of the Skills Listed Above

___ Set up equipment and stock for daily production runs.

___ Purchased and managed $____ of in-house inventory.

___ Inspected parts with final buy-off approval or rejection.

___ Read blueprints and schematics to produce ____ parts.

___ Used ____ and ____ to fabricate sheet metal products.

___ Performed close-tolerance TIG welding to produce ____.

___ Hired and coordinated subcontractors to produce ____.

___ Supervised ____ shifts of ____ staff as Shop Supervisor.

___ Managed shop operations including ____ and ____.

___ Hired, trained, and supervised ____, ____, and ____ staff.

___ Supervised workers performing ____, ____, and ____.

___ Verified warranty expiration and coverage for ____.

___ Delegated and coordinated workflow for ____ staff.

___ Provided repair estimates as Service Advisor for ____.

___ Certified in ____, ____, ____, and ____.

___ Hold licenses in ____, ____, ____, and ____.

___ Experienced in CNC operation and programming.

___ Own ____, ____, ____, and ____ tools.

___ Skilled in heavy equipment and forklift operation.

___ Trained over ____ mechanics and technicians in ____.

___ Developed bids for projects with sales of up to $____ per contract.

___ Served as lead for ____ crew members producing ____ and ____ products.

___ Managed contract budgets and expenses for the ____ department.

___ Manufactured close tolerance parts, achieving a ____% rejection rate.

___ Utilized computerized inventory system to maintain inventory valued at $____.

___ Coordinated engineering changes and delivery schedules with ____ departments.

___ Performed precision calibration utilizing ____, ____, and ____ instruments.

___ Managed facilities maintenance including ____, ____, and ____ systems.

___ Served as field technician providing repair services for ____ locations.

___ Oversaw fleet maintenance for ____ vehicles including ____, ____, and ____.

___ Served as Engineering Liaison, interfacing with manufacturing and customers.

___ Maintained ____, ____, and ____ as a Heavy Equipment Mechanic.

___ Performed industrial maintenance for ____ buildings totaling ____ square feet.

___ Repaired ____, ____, and ____ systems as an Industrial Technician.

___ Set up and calibrated machines for close-tolerance specification manufacturing.

___ Utilized precision diagnostic equipment including ____, ____, and ____.

___ Performed preventive maintenance procedures including ____, ____, and ____.

___ Managed production on ____ machines utilized by ____ machinists.

___ Inspected parts in process to detect production faults and minimize scrap.

___ Planned projects from initial bid to equipment setup through final delivery.

Skill Lists and Sample Sentences for

CASHIERING/CUSTOMER SERVICE/RETAIL SALES

These Skills May Also Be Used as Skill Headings

___ Add-On/Promotional Sales	___ Customer Service/Problem Solving	___ Maximizing Floor Space/Sales	___ Sales Reporting
___ Approval of Checks/Charges	___ Customer Service Administration	___ Opening/Closing Operations	___ Seasonal Sales Promotions
___ Authorization to Keys/Safes	___ Data Entry/10-Key	___ Operations Management	___ Setting Credit Limits
___ Balancing of Daily Receipts	___ Departmental Management	___ Order Expediting	___ Shift Scheduling
___ Balancing of Tills	___ Departmental Support	___ Petty Cash Control	___ Staff Supervision/Training
___ Bank Deposits/Safe Drops	___ Employee Interviewing	___ Posting of Cash Receipts	___ Stock Rotation
___ Branch Management	___ Employee Orientations	___ Price Quoting	___ Stocking/Pricing
___ Branch Reception	___ Employee Scheduling/Training	___ Product Promotions	___ Store Layout/Design
___ Building/Store Security	___ Floor Setup/Displays	___ Project Management	___ Store Management
___ Cash Accountability	___ Front Counter Sales	___ Purchasing/Requisitions	___ Team Coordination
___ Computerized Account Processing	___ High Closing Ratio	___ Quality Control	___ Theft Control
___ Computerized Cashiering Systems	___ Inventory/Merchandise Control	___ Receiving/Invoice Verification	___ Time Card/Payroll Tracking
___ Computerized Retail Applications	___ Inventory Reporting	___ Records Control	___ Vendor Contact/Management
___ Corporate Sales Procedures	___ Key Account Servicing	___ Retail Sales Management	___ Window Displays/Merchandising
___ Credit Card Processing	___ Labor Planning	___ Salary Recommendations	___ Work Coordination/Delegation
___ Crew Lead	___ Lead Trainer	___ Sales Forecasting	___ Workflow Delegation
___ Cross-Training of Staff	___ Market Analysis/Sales Trends	___ Sales Receipt Processing	___ Workstation Management

Sample Sentences Using Some of the Skills Listed Above

___ Increased sales up to ____% through add-on sales.

___ Maintained posting of daily receipts in excess of $____.

___ Approved checks and charges for up to ____ accounts daily.

___ Served as Lead Trainer to crew of ____.

___ Verified and approved invoices for ____ departments.

___ Planned weekly, monthly, and seasonal labor requirements.

___ Greeted ____ customers and promoted ____ product lines.

___ Purchased up to $____ in merchandise on a monthly basis.

___ Served as Crew Lead to a staff of ____ in ____ departments.

___ Accounted for $____ of inventory for a ____ -square-foot store.

___ Provided sales support to ____ departments.

___ Performed employee orientations for ____ departments.

___ Handled up to ____ customer returns and store credits daily.

___ Stocked and priced merchandise valued in excess of $____.

___ Dealt with up to ____ customers, generating $____ in sales.

___ Assisted branch manager in training ____ employees.

___ Processed and recorded ____ inventory transactions monthly.

___ Managed key accounts including ____, ____, and ____.

___ Maintained computer database of ____ customer accounts.

___ Supervised up to ____ workstations employing ___ retail staff.

___ Have over ____ years experience using manual/computerized cashiering systems.

___ Handled up to $____ monthly, consistently balancing tills to the penny.

___ Dealt with up to ____ customers daily, handling over $____ per month.

___ Accounted for up to $____ per day, making safe drops and bank deposits.

___ Approved checks and charges for up to ____ accounts daily.

___ Managed front counter sales, generating sales in excess of $____ annually.

___ Handled multi-line phones, taking and processing ____ orders daily.

___ Managed inventory for ____-square-foot department.

___ Stocked and priced merchandise for ____ departments.

___ Verified and approved invoicing, and signed for orders.

___ Purchased up to $____ in merchandise on a monthly basis.

___ Increased sales approximately $____ by setting up innovative displays.

___ Developed good rapport with approximately ____ vendors.

___ Analyzed marketing trends to purchase $____ in seasonal merchandise.

___ Opened and closed facility with sales in excess of $____.

___ Authorized to carry all keys with access to safes and personnel records.

___ Reduced losses by ____% through implementation of theft control measures.

___ Hired and supervised staff of up to ____ performing ____ and ____ duties.

___ Trained employees in cashiering, customer service, and inventory systems.

___ Coordinated workflow for ____ departments.

Skill Lists and Sample Sentences for

COMPUTER PROGRAMS/EQUIPMENT

These Skills May Also Be Used as Skill Headings

___ Accounting Software
___ Active Server Pages ASP
___ Adabas/Natural, IDX
___ AIX Netview
___ Antivirus Software/Security
___ Blackbox, Whitebox
___ C/MOTIF/Unix
___ CL, OPNQRYF, DL1, IDMS DBA
___ COBOL, CICS, MVS, VSAM
___ Computerized Office Applications
___ Computer Operating Systems
___ Database Management
___ DB/2, IMS, UNIX, C, SQL
___ Desktop Publishing/Presentations
___ DYNIX/PTX, MVS
___ Easytrieve, JCL, Assembler
___ ERD Model Development

___ Ethernet, SNA
___ Excel, Access
___ Focus, ESQL, OLTP
___ FoxPro, Lotus 1-2-3, Paradox
___ FrontPage, PageMill
___ GIF Animation
___ Hardware/Peripherals
___ HTML, JAVA, CGI Scripting
___ Internet Information Server
___ LAN/WAN Administration
___ Laser Printers, Plotters
___ Lotus WordPro
___ Mainframe Systems
___ MFC, SDK, VBA, Superbase
___ Microfocus, Databus, Mapper
___ Modems, Sound Systems
___ MS DOS, OS/2, Sun, Solaris

___ MS Word, MS Works, WordPerfect
___ MYOB, One Write
___ Novell CNE
___ Oracle RDBMS, OMNIS
___ PageMaker, Illustrator, PowerPoint
___ PC/Microcomputers
___ Peachtree, TurboTax
___ Photoshop, Corel Draw, Freehand
___ Programming/Software
 Development
___ Programming/System Management
___ Quick Books, Quicken
___ Robohelp, Framemaker
___ SDLC, Winrunner, TSL
___ Spreadsheet Programs
___ Supertool, Quiz, QTP
___ Sybase, Informix, Powerbuilder

___ TCP/IP, OSPF, Frame Relay
___ Technical Documentation
___ Testing
___ TSO/ISPF, CA7/11, JES, VTAM
___ Turbo Pascal, Paradox, Delphi
___ UI Architect
___ UNIXWARE
___ VAX VMS, HP UX, OLE, VSE
___ VB, C++, RPG 400, GUI
___ VB Script
___ VC++, PERL, Rainman
___ Visual Test
___ Web Page Connectivity
___ Website Design
___ Windows NT, Mac OS, UNIX
___ Word Processing Programs

Sample Sentences Using Some of the Skills Listed Above

___ Trained staff and customers in use of ____ and ____.
___ Set up ____ workstations utilizing a ____ network system.
___ Researched and purchased ____, ____, and ____ programs.
___ Consulted with programmers to implement ____ system.
___ Ran computerized reports with ____ and ____ programs.
___ Maintained a networked system with ____ users.
___ Provided troubleshooting for ____ terminals and users.
___ Consulted management regarding computer system needs.
___ Managed intranet and e-mail systems used by ____ staff.
___ Trained ____ staff in use of computerized systems.
___ Coordinated repair of $____ of computers and peripherals.
___ Oversaw website administration and training of ____ staff.
___ Utilized integrated accounting software for ____ accounts.
___ Served as Liaison to ____ computer vendors and suppliers.
___ Recommended purchase of $____ computer system.
___ Utilized ____ program to track over ____ projects annually.
___ Developed over ____ boilerplate documents.
___ Maintained computer files for ____ users.
___ Managed computer security, backup, and circuitry systems.
___ Coordinated with vendors to purchase ____ equipment.

___ Utilized ____ and ____ programs to process reports and spreadsheets.
___ Skilled in advanced editing, mail merge, and list management applications.
___ Created ____ -page corporate newsletter distributed to ____ employees.
___ Designed flyers, brochures, and company stationery utilizing ____ program.
___ Converted manual system to computerized ____ accounting system.
___ Utilized ____ program to process over ____ A/R and A/P accounts.
___ Processed payroll for over ____ employees using ____ program.
___ Performed statistical analysis of hazardous materials using ____ program.
___ Utilized ____ to produce monthly payroll and time-card tracking system.
___ Prepared annual budget for corporation with sales in excess of $____.
___ Compiled and updated database for over ____ customers and accounts.
___ Produced mailing lists for over ____ accounts utilizing database software.
___ Experienced in basic function of ____ and ____ operating systems.
___ Managed files and hard disk storage utilizing a ____-gigabyte system.
___ Programmed database and accounting software utilizing ____.
___ Over ____ years programming experience includes ____, ____, and ____.
___ Utilized ____, ____, and ____ to prepare documents.
___ Managed backup of ____ -megabyte system processing ____ daily transactions.
___ Utilized ____ and ____ word-processing programs to prepare ____ documents.
___ Prepared legal documents utilizing ____ including ____ and ____ functions.

Skill Lists and Sample Sentences for

COMPUTER SYSTEM ADMINISTRATION/TECHNICAL SUPPORT

These Skills May Also Be Used as Skill Headings

___ Antivirus Security Management
___ Applications Development
___ Automated Attendant Systems
___ Beta Testing
___ Contract Development
___ Customer Service/Technical Support
___ Customer Support Administration
___ Customer Support Liaison
___ Customized Data Analysis
___ Data Planning/Systems Design
___ Departmental Coordination
___ Departmental Support
___ Distributed Computing Systems
___ Document Management
___ Electronic Messaging Systems
___ End User Training
___ Field Service Maintenance

___ Hardware/Peripheral Repair
___ Implementation of Program Changes
___ Infrastructure Development
___ Installation/Testing/MTC
___ Internal Customer Support
___ Interface Design
___ Intranet Development
___ Inventory/Parts Control
___ IT Planning
___ LAN Architecture/Protocols
___ MIS Management
___ MTC Contract Management
___ Multisite System Management
___ Multitask Project Management
___ Multitier Client/Server Systems
___ Network Administration
___ PC/Technical Support

___ Product Development
___ Program Debugging
___ Program Testing/Analysis
___ Project Consultant
___ Project Leader
___ Project Management
___ R&D/Quality Control
___ Resource/Equipment Allocation
___ Service Level Agreements
___ Setup of User Accounts
___ Site Supervision
___ Software Engineering/Design
___ Standards Planning/Compliance
___ Strategic Planning
___ System Backup
___ System Design/Implementation
___ System Security Management

___ System Troubleshooting
___ Team Leadership
___ Technical Manual Writing
___ Telephony Systems
___ User Assessment
___ User/Technical Staff Liaison
___ Technical Presentations
___ Technical Staff Supervision
___ Technical Support
___ Technical Writing
___ UNIX Administration
___ User Support
___ Vendor Management
___ Web Applications
___ Website Content Development
___ Website Management
___ Workstation Support

Sample Sentences Using Some of the Skills Listed Above

___ Managed ____ vendor and subcontractor accounts.

___ Provided workstation support to ____ users.

___ Performed daily backup for a ____ system.

___ Managed system security including ____ and ____.

___ Developed website content and marketing literature.

___ Provided system troubleshooting for ____ and ____.

___ Served as Design Team Leader for staff of ____.

___ Created technical manuals for ____, ____, and ____.

___ Assessed user needs and resolved system problems.

___ Presented contract proposals to ____ corporate accounts.

___ Hired, trained, and supervised ____ technical staff.

___ Provided technical support to ____ staff.

___ Maintained in-house equipment/inventory worth $____.

___ Set up and assigned ____ user accounts.

___ Conducted R&D for ____, ____, and ____ projects.

___ Managed installation of projects with sales of $____.

___ Developed intranet serving ____ divisions and ____ staff.

___ Managed multisite networked system for ____ locations.

___ Tested and debugged programs using ____ and ____.

___ Managed a ____ multitier client/server system.

___ Developed ____ applications utilizing ____, ____, and ____.

___ Managed security for a $____ multisite system used by ____ staff.

___ Conducted beta testing for ____, ____, and ____.

___ Developed software design, hardware installation, and maintenance contracts.

___ Provided customer service and technical support for ____ end users.

___ Managed customer support administration for ____ key accounts.

___ Served as Customer Service Liaison between engineers, clients, and technicians.

___ Assessed client needs and developed ____ customized data analysis programs.

___ Analyzed data requirements, planned and executed projects and schedules.

___ Coordinated with ____ departments to maintain and service $____ system.

___ Supported ____ staff in ____ departments to provide training and PC support.

___ Developed extensive experience in distributed computing environments.

___ Managed document development and control for ____ divisions.

___ Managed electronic messaging system for LAN system serving ____ users.

___ Provided end user training and technical documentation for ____ accounts.

___ Performed field maintenance and repair for systems valued up to $____.

___ Conducted site supervision to ensure QA of installation and maintenance.

___ Led software engineering and design teams of up to ____ staff members.

___ Instituted standards compliance for programming and testing procedures.

___ Spearheaded strategic planning, resource allocation, and staffing requirements.

Skill Lists and Sample Sentences for

CONSTRUCTION/GENERAL LABOR

These Skills May Also Be Used as Skill Headings

___ Account Follow-Up
___ Billing/Invoicing
___ Blueprint Reading/Schematics
___ Bricklaying
___ Budgeting/Expense Control
___ Computerized Office Applications
___ Construction Documentation
___ Construction/Project Planning
___ Construction Supervision
___ Contract Compliance
___ Contract Management/Negotiation
___ Coordination with Building Dept.
___ Coordination with Permit Officials
___ Crew Lead/Project Coordinator
___ Crew Supervision
___ Curbing/Asphalt Repairs
___ Customer Service/Problem Solving

___ Decks/Patios
___ Document/Records Control
___ Electrical/Lighting
___ Employee Orientations
___ Equipment Maintenance
___ Estimating/Bidding
___ Excavation
___ Expediting Orders
___ Finish Work
___ Floor Plans/Design
___ Foundations
___ Heating/Ventilation
___ Heavy Equipment Operation
___ Interior/Exterior Painting
___ Inventory Control
___ Job/Project Cost Control
___ Key Account Servicing

___ Kitchens/Cabinets
___ Knowledge of Trades
___ Landscaping
___ Liaison to Builders/Architects
___ Material Handling
___ On-Site Construction
___ On-Site Inspection
___ Plumbing
___ Preparation of Hand Drawings
___ Price Quoting
___ Production Control
___ Project Documentation
___ Project Management
___ Project Troubleshooting
___ Projects on Time and at Budget
___ Proposal Development
___ Purchasing/Ordering

___ Quality Control
___ Renovations/Remodeling
___ Residential/Commercial Accounts
___ Roofing & Repairs
___ Safety Regulations Compliance
___ Sales/Marketing
___ Sheetrock
___ Shift Scheduling/Tracking
___ Siding Installation
___ Site Lead/Project Supervision
___ Staff Supervision/Training
___ Trades/Subcontractor Management
___ Vendor Coordination/Management
___ Windows/Doors
___ Work Order Changes
___ Work Order Processing
___ Work Prioritization/Delegation

Sample Sentences Using Some of the Skills Listed Above

___ Approved invoices and billing for ____ accounts.

___ Read blueprint and building plans.

___ Completed ____ projects with total sales of $____.

___ Supervised crew of ____ during all phases of construction.

___ Trained ____ crew members in all site operations.

___ Served as Crew Lead supervising up to ____ crew members.

___ Developed good rapport with approximately ____ vendors.

___ Assisted in completion of ____ projects valued to $____.

___ Coordinated with ____ subcontractors and vendors.

___ Own all tools necessary for interior/exterior work as a ____.

___ Delegated daily work duties for ____ projects.

___ Prepared bids and estimates for projects valued to $____.

___ Areas of experience include ____, ____, ____.

___ Managed on-site projects valued to $____.

___ Inspected on-site projects valued to $____.

___ Maintained tools and inventory for up to ____ projects.

___ Processed computerized billing for ____ customers.

___ Completed ____ projects for up to ____ customers monthly.

___ Negotiated with vendors, cutting ____% off inventory costs.

___ Processed over ____ orders for purchasing/account billing.

___ Increased sales ____% by asking for referrals from established accounts.

___ Coordinated with ____ and ____ in completion of ____ projects.

___ Completed over ____ projects, consistently bringing projects in on time.

___ Purchased and ordered over $____ of tools, supplies, and merchandise.

___ Controlled customer service and quality of ____ accounts with sales of $____.

___ Completed ____ projects for residential accounts valued up to $____.

___ Tracked time cards and scheduled ____ rotating shifts for ____ employees.

___ Completed ____ projects for commercial accounts valued up to $____.

___ Background demonstrates strong math and computer skills including ____.

___ Maintained documentation for up to ____ projects in excess of $____.

___ Coordinated with ____ vendors to acquire products for completion of projects.

___ Worked independently completing ____ projects valued up to $____.

___ Coordinated repairs and renovations with subcontractors on ____ projects.

___ Calculated commercial/residential account billings with revenues of $____.

___ Trained ____ employees in proper safety and material handling regulations.

___ Maintained contact with ____ on-site subcontractors and tradespeople.

___ Prepared quotes and estimates for projects worth up to $____.

___ Performed maintenance duties for projects up to ____ square feet.

___ Performed maintenance for over ____ accounts monthly, valued to $____.

___ Coordinated with ____ crew members to expedite and prioritize ____ orders.

Skill Lists and Sample Sentences for

DRIVING/SHIPPING/WAREHOUSE

These Skills May Also Be Used as Skill Headings

___ Account Servicing	___ Departmental Coordination	___ Loading to Maximize Deliveries	___ Security Procedures
___ Account Verification	___ Departmental Management	___ Marketing/Add-On Sales	___ Servicing of Corporate Accounts
___ Airport Deliveries/Procedures	___ Departmental Records Control	___ Material Handling/Safety Precautions	___ Shipment Pick-Ups
___ Approval of Checks/Charges	___ Dock/Delivery Procedures	___ Materials Verification	___ Shipping/Receiving Management
___ Blueprint Reading/Schematics	___ Document/Blueprint Control	___ Operations Management	___ Shipping Records Control
___ Business Math/Calculations	___ Domestic Shipments	___ Order Expediting	___ Staff Supervision/Training
___ Cash Accountability	___ Driving of Trucks [state size]	___ Parts Kit Preparation	___ Territory Development
___ Completion of Billing Records	___ Employee Training	___ Product Demonstrations	___ Territory Management
___ Credit Approval	___ Excellent Driving/Safety Record	___ Product/QC Inspection	___ Theft Control/Prevention
___ Customer Billing	___ Forklift/Pallet Jack Operation	___ Product/Sales Recommendations	___ Traffic/Vehicle Regulations
___ Customer Service	___ International Shipments	___ Project Coordination	___ Vehicle Maintenance
___ Damage Prevention	___ Inventory Control/Requisition	___ Project Management/Troubleshooting	___ Vendor Contact/Negotiation
___ Deadline/Production Quotas	___ Invoice Verification	___ Quality Control	___ Visual Inspection/QC
___ Delivery Documentation	___ Key Account Servicing	___ Route Management	___ Warehouse Administration
___ Delivery/Route Management	___ Knowledge of Delivery Area	___ Route Scheduling/Dispatch Control	___ Warehouse Management
___ Delivery Scheduling	___ Knowledge of Driving Routes	___ Safety Regulations	___ Work Coordination
___ Delivery Van [state size driven]	___ Knowledge of Product Lines	___ Sales/Receipts Documentation	___ Work Order Processing

Sample Sentences Using Some of the Skills Listed Above

___ Increased sales up to ____% through add-on sales.

___ Supervised staff of up to ____ employees.

___ Processed ____ purchase orders and returns monthly.

___ Managed shipping and receiving for ____ orders daily.

___ Maintained posting of $____ in cash receipts.

___ Dispatched ____ deliveries throughout the ____ area.

___ Managed fleet of ____ vehicles and ____ drivers.

___ Serviced ____ customers, accounting for $____ in sales.

___ Maintained over ____ files and shipping documents.

___ Verified invoicing for $____ in monthly shipments.

___ Controlled quality of shipments valued to $____.

___ Scheduled up to ____ deliveries and appointments daily.

___ Processed over ____ orders valued to $____ per day.

___ Trained ____ employees in dock/delivery procedures.

___ Maintained excellent driving and safety record.

___ Managed a ____-square-mile route with ____ accounts.

___ Completed over ____ work orders/billing records daily.

___ Input parts numbers to process ____ daily shipments.

___ Assisted manager in maintenance of ____ departments.

___ Completed international shipping documentation.

___ Coordinated with staff of ____ to meet shipping and delivery deadlines.

___ Coordinated with ____ departments to expedite and prioritize orders.

___ Over ____ years experience operating forklifts and pallet jacks.

___ Prepared ____ domestic/international shipments utilizing UPS/Federal Express.

___ Stocked and inventoried up to ____ products.

___ Managed shipments for ____, ____, and ____ key accounts.

___ Over ____ years experience delivering high-value shipments.

___ Loaded ____ vans to maximize delivery time and prevent product damage.

___ Verified invoices, freight and packing slips for $____ worth of products.

___ Trained ____ employees in proper safety and material handling procedures.

___ Pulled parts and prepared parts kits for ____ orders monthly.

___ Conducted customer product demonstrations increasing sales by ____%.

___ Delivered ____ shipments to appropriate destinations including airports.

___ Implemented security procedures for shipments and deliveries valued over $____.

___ Increased warehouse productivity by implementing ____ and ____ systems.

___ Processed checks and charges for up to ____ shipments and deliveries daily.

___ Delivered ____ orders daily handling over $____ worth of inventory.

___ Worked independently completing ____ shipments valued up to $____.

___ Developed knowledge of ____ product lines including handling regulations.

___ Answered customer questions regarding ____ different products.

Skill Lists and Sample Sentences for

ENGINEERING/DRAFTING

These Skills May Also Be Used as Skill Headings

___ 3-D Drawings	___ Cost Distribution/Estimating	___ Industrial Design	___ Project Management/Planning
___ Architectural Design	___ Departmental Coordination	___ Job Costing/Budgeting	___ Project Scheduling
___ Assembly Drawings	___ Design Methodologies	___ Landscape Design	___ Proposal Development
___ AutoCAD R13	___ Design Team Coordination	___ Layering Standards	___ Script Files with Slide Shows
___ AutoLISP Programs	___ Device Symbols, Block Diagrams	___ Liaison to Architects/Builders	___ Site Plans, Sections, Details
___ Bidding/Estimating	___ Document Control	___ Logic Diagrams	___ Structural Design
___ Building Code Compliance	___ Drawing Layout	___ Machining, Forming Processes	___ Structural, Piping, Civil Drafting
___ Building/Equipment Inspection	___ Electrical/Electronics Design	___ Mechanical Principles	___ Take-Offs/Specifications
___ Civil Engineering	___ Engineering/Design Support	___ Menu Programming	___ Team Coordination
___ Computer-Aided Drafting	___ Engineering/Drafting Fields	___ On-Site Inspection	___ Technical Documentation
___ Construction Management	___ Engineering Systems	___ Paper Space, Model Space, XRefs	___ Technical Staff Supervision
___ Contour Maps, Highway Layout	___ Facilities Management	___ Plot Plans, Foundations	___ Trades Management
___ Contract Administration	___ Floor Plans, Elevations	___ Plumbing Design	___ Traverses/Civil Profiles
___ Contract Enforcement/Compliance	___ Fluid Dynamics	___ Preliminary Drawings	___ Weldments, Threads, Fasteners
___ Contract Management/Negotiation	___ Framing Plans, Load Forces	___ Printed Circuit Board Layout	___ Wiring/Ladder Control Diagrams
___ Contractor Specification	___ Heat Loss/Gain Calculations	___ Project Coordination	___ Workload Prioritization
___ Coordination with Permit Officials	___ HVAC Design	___ Project Execution	___ Work Order Changes

Sample Sentences Using Some of the Skills Listed Above

___ Conducted on-site inspections for ____ projects.

___ Created preliminary drawings for ____ projects.

___ Coordinated ____ and ____ project requirements.

___ Managed all phases of project scheduling and execution.

___ Planned and controlled projects with total fees of $____.

___ Developed and submitted over ____ proposals.

___ Specified and supervised up to ____ trades contractors.

___ Prepared take-offs and specifications for ____ projects.

___ Coordinated design requirements with team of ____.

___ Prepared technical documentation for work order changes.

___ Supervised ____ staff, which included ____, ____, ____.

___ Prepared 3-D drawings utilizing AutoCAD R13.

___ Prioritized workload to support ____ engineers.

___ Managed work order changes for ____ staff.

___ Drafted details for ____, ____, and ____ systems.

___ Updated and corrected plans submitted by architects.

___ Revised up to ____ plans daily during peak periods.

___ Drafted, plotted, and inventoried attributes for ____ projects.

___ Prepared site development plans including ____ and ____.

___ Performed loading, stress, and heat loss calculations.

___ Managed bidding and proposal development for firm with annual sales of $____.

___ Met with architects, builders, and subcontractors to ensure code compliance.

___ Conducted on-site inspections of buildings and equipment for ____ projects.

___ Supported ____ engineering staff as a drafter utilizing AutoCAD R____.

___ Customized CAD environment and programmed with ____, ____, and ____.

___ Have extensive knowledge of AutoCAD ____, ____, and ____ systems.

___ Supervised construction sites with project fees of up to $____ annually.

___ Controlled contract and project scheduling for ____ projects.

___ Oversaw all aspects of contract administration including ____, ____, and ____.

___ Negotiated contract fees, schedules, and equipment specifications with ____.

___ Served as liaison to building permit officials, architects, and contractors.

___ Wrote contract specifications and designated contractors and equipment.

___ Controlled ____ documents for ____ projects.

___ Served as Design Team Leader for group of ____ design engineers and drafters.

___ Have over ____ years CAD experience in the fields of civil and architectural design.

___ Coordinated with ____ departments to complete drafting and change notices.

___ Provided design support to ____ engineers and field supervisors.

___ Supervised facilities construction, redesign, and HVAC equipment maintenance.

___ Managed design projects overseeing ____, ____, and ____.

___ Performed job costing and expense distribution for ____ projects.

EXECUTIVE SECRETARY/OFFICE MANAGEMENT

These Skills May Also Be Used as Skill Headings

___ Accounting Administration
___ Administrative Management
___ Benefits Administration
___ Bid/Proposal Development
___ Board Meeting Transcription
___ Branch Administration
___ Branch Office Management
___ Budget Administration
___ Capital Equipment Purchasing
___ Client/Vendor Liaison
___ Computerized Accounting App.
___ Computerized Office Applications
___ Computerized Spreadsheet App.
___ Computerized System Administration
___ Computerized System Conversions
___ Confidential Records Management
___ Contract Administration

___ Corporate Communications
___ Corporate Policy Development
___ Corporate Secretary
___ Credit Management
___ Customer Service Management
___ Departmental Coordination
___ Departmental Management
___ Departmental Planning
___ Departmental Secretary
___ Departmental Support
___ Division Management
___ Employee Manual Development
___ Employee Orientation
___ Events Planning/Management
___ Executive Assistant
___ Executive Calendar Scheduling
___ Executive Correspondence

___ Executive Itinerary Management
___ Executive Meeting Minutes
___ Executive Presentations
___ Executive Support
___ Executive Team Member
___ Field Support/Administration
___ Financial Administration
___ Front Office Management
___ Hiring/Training of Clerical Staff
___ International Secretary
___ Invoicing/Billing Management
___ Key Account Management
___ Legal Secretary
___ Marketing Administration
___ Multicultural/Bilingual
___ Multisite Branch Management
___ Multitask Project Management

___ Office Administration
___ Office Management
___ Organizational Management
___ Program Management
___ Project Coordination
___ Project/Expense Planning
___ Project Management
___ Project Troubleshooting
___ Purchasing/Inventory Control
___ Records/Document Control
___ Regional Administration
___ Report/Document Writing
___ Senior Management Secretary
___ Staff Recruitment/Screening
___ Staff Supervision
___ Vendor Management
___ Workload Delegation

Sample Sentences Using Some of the Skills Listed Above

___ Attended Executive Board meetings to transcribe minutes.
___ Fast track achiever, was promoted ____ within ____ years.
___ Managed ____ key accounts such as ____, ____, and ____.
___ Served as liaison to ____ client and vendor accounts.
___ Have executive-level multicultural and bilingual expertise.
___ Managed administration for ____ branch locations.
___ Led multitask project teams of up to ____ staff.
___ Recruited, hired, and trained ____ administrative staff.
___ Researched, selected, and hired ____ vendors.
___ Supervised ____ staff performing ____, ____, and ____.
___ Prioritized and delegated weekly and project workloads.
___ Served as Senior Management Secretary to ____.
___ Provided employee orientations to over ____ new staff.
___ Managed front office administration for ____ departments.
___ Maintained general supplies for division with ____ staff.
___ Planned seasonal and annual staffing requirements.
___ Served as International Secretary to ____ accounts.
___ Worked directly with ____ developing corporate policy.
___ Developed corporate communication materials.
___ Managed customer service for ____ national accounts.

___ Supervised accounting and related administration for ____ departments.
___ Provided administrative management to support staff of ____ in ____ offices.
___ Managed benefits administration for ____ employees in ____ departments.
___ Prepared bidding and proposal documents for projects ranging up to $____.
___ Oversaw all branch administration functions including ____, ____, and ____.
___ Controlled and tracked annual budgets and expenses up to $____.
___ Researched and purchased up to $____ annually in capital equipment.
___ Managed computerized accounting functions including ____ and ____.
___ Computerized office applications include ____, ____, and ____.
___ Utilized ____ and ____ spreadsheet programs to create ____ and ____.
___ Managed computer system requirements with technicians and programmers.
___ Directed the conversion of all ____ manual records to computerized system.
___ Controlled confidential records such as employee files, bids, and contracts.
___ Managed all contract administration functions for ____ projects annually.
___ Served as Executive Assistant to staff of ____ including ____, ____, and ____.
___ Provided departmental support to ____ divisions in a ____ state region.
___ Developed employee orientation, corporate policy, and job description manuals.
___ Managed executive calendar for ____, ____, and ____ traveling internationally.
___ Wrote, edited, and prepared executive correspondence including ____ and ____.
___ Provided marketing administration support for staff of ____ sales representatives.

FACILITIES MAINTENANCE/JANITORIAL

These Skills May Also Be Used as Skill Headings

___ Bidding/Repair Estimating

___ Blueprint Reading

___ Building Maintenance

___ Coordination with Building Supervisors

___ Coordination with Work Crews

___ Cost Savings/Expense Control

___ Crew Supervision

___ Customer Service/Problem Solving

___ Departmental Coordination

___ Departmental Management

___ Document Control

___ Employee Counseling

___ Employee Orientation

___ Employee Scheduling

___ Equipment Calibration/Testing

___ Equipment Repair/Maintenance

___ Expediting of Repair Orders

___ Facility Maintenance

___ Facility Security Systems

___ Facility Troubleshooting

___ Floor Maintenance

___ Floor Setup

___ Hazardous Materials Control

___ HVAC, Electrical, Plumbing

___ Inventory/Parts Control

___ Inventory Forecasting

___ Key Account Servicing

___ Knowledge of Building Systems

___ Knowledge of Floor Plans

___ Labor & Cost Projection

___ Laborsaving Procedures

___ Material Handling

___ Opening/Closing Operations

___ Operations Management

___ Organization of Projects/Production

___ Performance Evaluations

___ Product Inspection

___ Project Management

___ Project Scheduling/Control

___ Purchasing

___ Quality Control

___ Recycling Management

___ Safety & Health Regulations

___ Salary Recommendations

___ Scheduling of Shifts

___ Scheduling to Meet Deadlines

___ Servicing of Accounts

___ Shift Documentation

___ Shift Scheduling/Deadlines

___ Staff Orientations

___ Staff Training/Supervision

___ Stock Rotation

___ Stocking/Supply Ordering

___ Subcontractor Management

___ Subcontractor Scheduling

___ System Diagnostics/Repair

___ Team Coordination

___ Theft Control

___ Time/Money Saving Techniques

___ Use of Precision Instruments

___ Vendor Contract Management

___ Vendor Supervision

___ Work Assignment Delegation

___ Work Inspection

___ Work Order Processing

___ Work Prioritization

___ Work Site Inspection

___ Workflow Planning

Sample Sentences Using Some of the Skills Listed Above

___ Supervised up to ____ employees in ____ departments.

___ Assisted in hiring/supervision of crews of ____ employees.

___ Completed over ____ maintenance projects per month.

___ Trained ____ employees in all site operations.

___ Implemented security procedures for ____ -square-foot building.

___ Maintained over ____ files and account documents.

___ Managed on-site accounts valued to $____.

___ Stocked and inventoried $____ of supplies.

___ Scheduled ____ rotating shifts for up to ____ employees.

___ Planned weekly shifts and hours for up to ____ employees.

___ Maintained facilities of over ____ square feet.

___ Delegated maintenance duties to ____ employees.

___ Purchased up to $____ of supplies monthly.

___ Maintained contact with ____ vendors monthly.

___ Operated ____, ____, and ____ equipment.

___ Coordinated service requirements with ____ departments.

___ Prepared maintenance records for ____ accounts.

___ Accounted for $____ of supplies for ____ accounts monthly.

___ Developed good rapport with approximately ____ vendors.

___ Performed maintenance including ____, ____, and ____.

___ Maintained service requirements for ____, ____, and ____ key accounts.

___ Coordinated with ____ departments to meet maintenance requirements.

___ Assisted in performance evaluations of ____ crew members.

___ Coordinated with ____ supervisors to meet facility maintenance requirements.

___ Coordinated repairs and maintenance of ____ accounts.

___ Oversaw account recycling programs implemented in ____ buildings.

___ Performed servicing of ____ accounts, successfully meeting health regulations.

___ Scheduled ____ employees in ____ departments to meet shift deadlines.

___ Hired and trained workers in all areas of ____, ____, and ____.

___ Processed and recorded over ____ maintenance log sheets per month.

___ Completed ____ projects for commercial accounts valued up to $____.

___ Supervised crew of ____ performing required maintenance procedures.

___ Coordinated facility duties with ____ teams in ____ departments.

___ Oversaw theft control procedures, decreasing loss by ____%.

___ Controlled floor setup and organization for ____ -square-foot facility.

___ Continuously met deadlines by utilizing timesaving techniques.

___ Maintained equipment/inventory for up to ____ accounts, valued to $____.

___ Supervised maintenance of building equipment valued in excess of $____.

___ Inspected on-site maintenance procedures for up to ____ accounts monthly.

___ Oversaw customer service and maintenance of ____ -square-foot facility.

HEALTHCARE

These Skills May Also Be Used as Skill Headings

___ Academic Research/Presentations	___ Emergency Room	___ Internal Medicine	___ Patient Education & Intervention
___ Addiction Management	___ EMT	___ Inventory Control/Requisition	___ Pediatrics
___ Adult Medicine	___ ENT	___ Legal Ethical Issues Management	___ Physical Therapy
___ Anesthesiology	___ Family Systems Assessment	___ Medical/Legal Risk Management	___ Physician/Patient Liaison
___ Budget Management/Expense Control	___ Federal Reporting Requirements	___ Medical Protocol Administration	___ Preventive Care Programs
___ Burn Unit	___ Full Range of Treatment Modalities	___ Medical Records Control	___ Program Implementation
___ Cardiology	___ General Practice	___ Medical Team Facilitator	___ Psychology/Counseling
___ Central Supply Experience	___ Geriatrics	___ Med/Surg	___ Radiology
___ Clinic Management	___ Health Program Implementation	___ Multidisciplinary Experience	___ Respiratory Care
___ Community Resource Referral	___ Healthcare Research	___ Neurology	___ Staff Recruitment and Training
___ Comprehensive Primary Care	___ Hospital Regulatory Compliance	___ OB/GYN	___ Staff Supervision/Scheduling
___ Computerized Patient Records	___ In-service Training/Presentations	___ Operating Room	___ Total Patient Care
___ Continuous Quality Improvement	___ Institution of Standards of Care	___ Order/Interpret Diagnostic Studies	___ Tracking/Analysis of Patient Loads
___ Control of Medicines/Narcotics	___ Insurance/Patient Billing	___ Orthopedics	___ Trauma Care
___ Departmental Management	___ Intensive Care Unit	___ Patient Assessment	___ Triage/Initiation of Emergent Care
___ Dermatology	___ Interdisciplinary Cross-Training	___ Patient/Case Management	___ Unit Management
___ Dispensing of Medicines	___ Interdisciplinary Team Member	___ Patient Consent/Disclosure	___ Urology

Sample Sentences Using Some of the Skills Listed Above

___ Conducted academic research/presented findings to ____.

___ Experienced in central supply and med/surg asepsis.

___ Made appropriate community referrals to ____ agencies.

___ Maintained computerized records for ____ -bed unit.

___ Managed addiction/counseling program for ____ patients.

___ Recruited, trained, and supervised ____ medical staff.

___ Ordered and interpreted diagnostic studies for ____.

___ Managed caseload of ____ patients for ____ -bed unit.

___ Informed patients of medical procedures and consent.

___ Provided patient education and intervention.

___ Served as liaison between patients and ____ physicians.

___ Instituted preventive care programs for ____ departments.

___ Supervised and scheduled staff of ____ on ____ shifts.

___ Tracked and analyzed patient loads for ____ -bed unit.

___ Provided triage and instituted emergent care.

___ Managed departmental administration and budgeting.

___ Rotated on the ____, ____, ____, and ____ units.

___ Consulted with staff of ____ physicians regarding patients.

___ Trained ____ residents, nursing, and administrative staff.

___ Coordinated security, equipment, and facility maintenance.

___ Managed departmental budget of $____ annually, cutting expenses by ____%.

___ Supervised clinic serving ____ patients and staff of ____ physicians.

___ Controlled annual budget and expenses in excess of $____ annually.

___ Provided comprehensive primary care as a ____ coordinating with ____ staff.

___ Instituted quality improvement program, which increased revenues by ____%.

___ Controlled medicines and narcotics for a ____ -square-foot facility.

___ Managed department with patient billing exceeding $____ per month.

___ Coordinated with staff of ____ physicians, reading charts and dispensing meds.

___ Conducted family systems assessment in cases of ____ and ____.

___ Supervised records and patient care in compliance with federal requirements.

___ Provided full range of treatment modalities for ____, ____, and ____ patients.

___ Conducted healthcare surveys and research to recommend new patient services.

___ Implemented new healthcare programs and procedures utilized by ____ staff.

___ Served as facilitator to hospital administration and ____ medical staff.

___ Oversaw medical protocol administration and policy implementation.

___ Managed medical records for ____ -bed unit prepared by ____ staff.

___ Coordinated patient care with multidisciplinary staff specializing in ____.

___ Submitted all medical/ethical/legal issues to hospital counsel for review.

___ Received multidisciplinary training, working in the ____, ____, and ____ units.

___ Presented in-service training to ____ staff specializing in ____, ____, and ____.

Skill Lists and Sample Sentences for

HUMAN RESOURCES MANAGEMENT/RECRUITMENT/TRAINING

These Skills May Also Be Used as Skill Headings

___ Budget/Expense Control
___ Classification/Compensation
___ Classified/Professional Staffing
___ Compensation Negotiation
___ Computerized HR Systems
___ Continuous Improvement Plans
___ Corporate Culture Development
___ Corporate Mission Statements
___ Corporate Training Programs
___ Departmental Management
___ Departmental Needs Assessment
___ Departmental Staffing
___ Direct Sourcing Programs
___ EEO/FLSA Laws
___ Employee Discipline Systems
___ Employee/Management Liaison
___ Employee Orientations

___ Employee Performance Counseling
___ Employee Records Control
___ Employee Relations Management
___ Employee Relations Programs
___ Employee Relocation Programs
___ Employee Training Manuals
___ Employment and Labor Law
___ Employment Contract Management
___ Executive Recruitment
___ Exempt/Nonexempt Staffing
___ Exit Interviewing
___ Expansion Management
___ Grievance Processing
___ Health and Safety Administration
___ Hiring/Firing Guidelines
___ Human Resource Allocation
___ Human Resources Generalist

___ HR Reporting Compliance
___ Industrial Safety Guidelines
___ International Recruitment
___ Job Analysis/Descriptions
___ Job Classifications
___ Labor Management Relations
___ Labor Planning/Allocation
___ Labor/Shift Scheduling
___ Merit System Rules
___ Multisite HR Management
___ Organizational Development
___ Organizational Needs Assessment
___ OSHA/WSHA Compliance
___ Performance Evaluations
___ Performance Measurement
___ Policy/Procedures Development
___ Preemployment Testing

___ Professional Staffing
___ Regulatory Compliance
___ Risk Management
___ Retirement/Pension Programs
___ Salary/Benefits Negotiation
___ Salary/Benefit Surveys
___ Senior Team Member
___ Staff Development Programs
___ Strategic Planning
___ Technical Recruitment
___ Temporary Agency Utilization
___ Temporary/Contract Staffing
___ Termination Packages
___ Training Program Development
___ Training Systems Infrastructure
___ Union Contract Negotiation
___ Workers' Comp Analysis

Sample Sentences Using Some of the Skills Listed Above

___ Developed/implemented training systems infrastructure.
___ Analyzed workers' compensation to assign job duties.
___ Conducted preemployment testing for over ___ staff.
___ Developed corporate HR policies and procedures.
___ Trained departmental managers in hiring/firing laws.
___ Determined staffing needs to allocate staff appropriately.
___ Served as HR Generalist overseeing ___ and ___.
___ Developed performance measurements for ___ positions.
___ Provided multisite HR management for $___ firm.
___ Instituted a merit system utilized by ___ departments.
___ Served as Senior Team Member overseeing ___ and ___.
___ Conducted salary and benefit surveys to control expenses.
___ Scheduled labor and rotating shift requirements.
___ Planned and allocated seasonal labor resources.
___ Established industrial safety guidelines such as ___.
___ Ensured compliance with OSHA/WSHA regulations.
___ Developed termination/employee separation documents.
___ Counseled employees regarding attendance/performance.
___ Implemented ___ employee relations programs.
___ Directed employee relocation services for ___ staff.

___ Managed labor and expense budgets of up to $___ annually.
___ Classified positions and assigned compensation guidelines for ___ staff.
___ Directed classified and professional staff for ___ departments with ___ staff.
___ Negotiated compensation packages for staff with salaries ranging up to $___.
___ Administered computerized HR systems including ___, ___, ___, and ___.
___ Developed and implemented continuous improvement plans for ___ locations.
___ Developed corporate mission statements working directly with Board of Directors.
___ Developed/implemented corporate training programs including ___ and ___.
___ Managed HR departmental staffing overseeing generalist and administrative staff.
___ Conducted departmental needs assessment for hiring and training requirements.
___ Developed direct sourcing programs, which cut recruitment time by ___%.
___ Complied with EEO and FLSA laws for major corporations such as ___ and ___.
___ Instituted employee discipline systems including legal documentation.
___ Served as management/employee liaison to ___ staff in ___ divisions.
___ Conducted employee orientations for over ___ staff throughout my career.
___ Developed employee training manuals for ___, ___, and ___ industries.
___ Conducted exit interviews and documentation to minimize legal risk.
___ Directed HR and staffing expansion to accommodate building of new plant.
___ Negotiated union contracts with ___ different unions.
___ Implemented health and safety procedures utilized by ___ employees.

Skill Lists and Sample Sentences for

INSIDE/OUTSIDE SALES

These Skills May Also Be Used as Skill Headings

___ Add-On Sales/Product Up-Selling
___ Bidding/Estimating
___ Billing/Invoice Verification
___ Blueprint Reading
___ Call Center Management
___ Cold Calling/Lead Development
___ Computerized Parts Tracking
___ Contract Management/Negotiation
___ Contract Proposals
___ Coordination with Headquarters
___ Corporate Presentations
___ Corporate Training
___ Creation of Sales Literature
___ Customer Service Administration
___ Customer Service/Troubleshooting
___ Customer Training Seminars
___ Delivery/Shipping Coordination

___ Departmental Liaison/Coordination
___ Design/Sales Management
___ Die/Fabrication Requisition
___ Engineering/Factory Liaison
___ Freight Forwarding Methods
___ Freight Pricing/Calculations
___ High Closing Ratio
___ Inside Sales/Customer Support
___ International Marketing
___ Key Account Management
___ Lead Follow-Up/Generation
___ List Management
___ Maintenance of Key Accounts
___ Manufacturing Liaison
___ Market Expansion Strategies
___ Material Take-Offs
___ Materials Calculation

___ Maximizing Sales/Profits
___ National Marketing
___ Networking for Leads
___ New Account Setup
___ Order Follow-Up
___ Order Processing
___ Parts Requisition
___ Penetration of Key Accounts
___ Price/Delivery Quoting
___ Product Demonstrations
___ Production Planning
___ Profit Margin Analysis
___ Program Implementation
___ Project Management
___ Project Troubleshooting
___ Proposal Development
___ Proposal Submittals

___ Purchase Order Processing
___ Quality Control/Assurance
___ Records/Contract Compliance
___ Regional Sales Representative
___ Regional Sales Support
___ Research and Development
___ Setting/Exceeding Quotas
___ Technical Marketing
___ Technical Servicing
___ Technical Support
___ Territory Development
___ Territory Management/Outside Sales
___ Top Sales Achiever
___ Up-Selling of Key Accounts
___ Value Added Sales
___ Vendor Catalog Management
___ Vendor Contact/Negotiation

Sample Sentences Using Some of the Skills Listed Above

___ Awarded for highest closing ratio competing with ____ staff.
___ Was Sales Trainer for staff of ____ Sales Representatives.
___ "Top Sales Leader" generating $____ in sales.
___ Met and exceeded all quarterly and annual sales quotas.
___ Recognized for excellent territory management skills.
___ Increased sales by monitoring quality control of products.
___ Increased sales by ____% through add-on promotions.
___ Prepared bids for projects valued to $____.
___ Negotiated contracts totaling over $____ annually.
___ Coordinated sales proposals and orders with headquarters.
___ Gave corporate presentations for groups of up to ____.
___ Provided customer support to ____ key accounts.
___ Served as Liaison between customers and engineering.
___ Assisted in design of ____ customer products.
___ Ordered die and fabrication equipment to produce orders.
___ Provided international marketing to ____ accounts.
___ Managed ____ key accounts with sales of $____.
___ Turned ____% of leads into orders.
___ Served as Manufacturing Liaison for ____ accounts.
___ Prepared material take-offs from blueprints and specs.

___ Handled up to ____ calls daily, generating sales of $____ monthly.
___ Managed and developed key accounts including ____, ____, ____, and ____.
___ Negotiated individual sales in excess of $____.
___ Calculated materials requirements and verified delivery for ____ accounts.
___ Expedited orders with ____ manufacturers and ____ production departments.
___ Developed proposals for projects in excess of $____.
___ Processed orders for over ____ monthly sales transactions.
___ Demonstrated strong mathematical, problem solving, and negotiation skills.
___ Utilized extensive knowledge of freight forwarding methods and pricing.
___ Increased sales by ____% by meeting projected cold call quotas.
___ Coordinated order requirements with ____ departments.
___ Maintained current catalog and pricing information from over ____ vendors.
___ Increased repeat sales through creative design and scheduling solutions.
___ Managed projects in excess of $____ annually.
___ Utilized computerized parts tracking system to schedule ____ work orders.
___ Developed ____ territory covering ____ states and generating $____ annually.
___ Developed corporate proposals for individual contracts in excess of $____.
___ Increased sales by ____% by implementing ____, ____, and ____.
___ Developed client list and marketing materials, which increased leads by ____%.
___ Provided technical training to groups of up to ____ customers and vendors.

Skill Lists and Sample Sentences for

MANAGEMENT AND SUPERVISION

These Skills May Also Be Used as Skill Headings

___ Accounting/Fiscal Management
___ Administrative Management
___ Benefits/Insurance Administration
___ Budget and Expense Allocation
___ Branch Management
___ Business Acquisition/Development
___ Capital Asset Management
___ Cash Flow Management & Control
___ Centralization Efficiency Programs
___ Consolidation & Reorganization
___ Continuous Process Improvement
___ Contract Management/Negotiation
___ Corporate Downsizing/Restructuring
___ Corporate Image Building
___ Corporate Infrastructure Design
___ Corporate Mission Planning
___ Cost Reduction/Revenue Generation

___ Credit Administration
___ Crises/Risk Management
___ Customer Service Management
___ Departmental Management
___ District Management
___ Emerging Technology Analysis
___ Equipment Leasing/Acquisition
___ Export/Import Management
___ Facilities Management
___ Fast Track Achievement
___ Federal/Licensing Compliance
___ Financial Management
___ General Management
___ Global Market Planning
___ International Management
___ Key Account Management
___ Legal & Regulatory Compliance

___ Long-Term Strategic Planning
___ Loss to Profit Turnaround
___ Manufacturing Compliance
___ Manufacturing Management
___ Market Analysis & Forecasting
___ Market Positioning/Planning
___ Marketing Implementation
___ Materials Requisition Planning
___ Mature Market Expansion
___ MIS Management
___ National Program Management
___ New Business Start-Up
___ Operations Management
___ P&L Responsibility
___ Performance Analysis/Reporting
___ Policy Development/Writing
___ Portfolio Management

___ Product Integration Programs
___ Program Development
___ Purchasing/Inventory Control
___ Quality Assurance Programs
___ Regional Management
___ Reporting to Board of Directors
___ Sales Acceleration/Expansion
___ Sales Management & Planning
___ Senior Operations Management
___ Staff Development & Training
___ Staff Recruitment Programs
___ Staff Supervision/Management
___ Standardization of Procedures
___ Total Quality Management
___ Vendor Management
___ Venture Capital Acquisition
___ Worldwide Market Development

Sample Sentences Using Some of the Skills Listed Above

___ Managed all administrative functions for ____ divisions.
___ Fast track achiever, was promoted ____ within ____ years.
___ Managed ____ key accounts such as ___, ___, & ___.
___ Analyzed emerging technologies to stay competitive.
___ Managed import/export operations with sales of $___.
___ Complied with federal & regional licensing requirements.
___ Managed ____ -square-foot facility valued at $___.
___ Oversaw general management of ____ departments.
___ Developed and implemented global marketing plans.
___ Managed a $___ international marketing program.
___ Developed and instituted long-term strategic planning.
___ Supervised manufacturing department with staff of ___.
___ Analyzed buying trends to forecast production needs.
___ Managed MIS department of ____ technical staff.
___ Held full P&L responsibility for this $___ corporation.
___ Analyzed and reported on departmental performance.
___ Recruited, supervised, and trained ____ staff.
___ Managed ____ staff performing ____ and ____ functions.
___ Created sales acceleration program for ____ territory.
___ Took division from ____ loss to ____ profit.

___ Oversaw accounting/fiscal management for division with annual sales of $___.
___ Managed benefits and insurance administration with total budget of $___.
___ Controlled annual budget and expenses in excess of $___ annually.
___ Managed branch with ____ staff and revenues of $___ annually.
___ Spearheaded acquisition & development of new division, increasing sales by ____%.
___ Implemented capital asset management program for $___ million firm.
___ Designed centralization and consolidation program, which reduced labor by ____%.
___ Recaptured key account by instituting continuous process improvement program.
___ Negotiated and managed contracts in excess of $___ per year.
___ Implemented successful downsizing and restructuring of ____ branch locations.
___ Created customer relationship building system, which increased revenues by ____%.
___ Instituted redesign of corporate infrastructure, which cut operating costs by ____%.
___ Integrated branch planning in compliance with corporate mission statement.
___ Analyzed and streamlined administrative systems, which cut expenses by $___.
___ Implemented crisis planning/risk management procedures for ____ departments.
___ Managed credit administration for ____ accounts with sales of $___ annually.
___ Supervised customer service administration for ____ national accounts.
___ Managed all departmental operations including ___, ___, ___, and ___.
___ Managed district with ____ branch locations and total revenues of $___.
___ Negotiated equipment leasing and acquisition, which cut expenditures by ____%.

Skill Lists and Sample Sentences for

RECEPTION/GENERAL OFFICE

These Skills May Also Be Used as Skill Headings

___ Administrative Assistant
___ Administrative Support
___ Appointment Scheduling
___ Authorization to Keys/Safes
___ Automated Phone System Admin.
___ Branch Reception
___ Cash Accountability/Light Bkpg.
___ Clerical Staff Supervision/Training
___ Computerized Account Processing
___ Computerized Office Applications
___ Computerized Spreadsheet App.
___ Computerized Word Processing App.
___ Conference/Meeting Coordination
___ Confidential Personnel Files
___ Contract Preparation
___ Control of Office Supplies
___ Copy Center Management

___ Corporate Reception
___ Correspondence/Reports
___ Credit Approval/New Accounts
___ Customer Service
___ Data Entry/10-Key
___ Departmental Administration
___ Departmental Liaison
___ Departmental Reception
___ Departmental Support
___ Document Control
___ Employee Orientation
___ Equipment Purchasing
___ Executive Support
___ Expediting Orders
___ Express Mail Procedures
___ File Maintenance
___ File/Records Control

___ Front Office Administration
___ Front Office Coordination
___ Front Office Support
___ General Office Administration
___ Inventory Control/Tracking
___ Key Account Support
___ Legal Document Preparation
___ Management of Mail Room
___ Message Taking
___ Multiline Phones
___ Newsletter Creation
___ Office Administration
___ Order Administration
___ Order Processing
___ Petty Cash Control
___ Project Organization
___ Project Management/Support

___ Project Prioritization
___ Project Support
___ Project Troubleshooting
___ Purchasing/Inventory Control
___ Scheduling of Clerical Staff
___ Secretarial Support
___ Supervision of Clerical Staff
___ Supervision of Temporary Staff
___ Supply Purchasing
___ Switchboard Management
___ Training of Clerical Staff
___ Training of Temporary Staff
___ Travel Arrangements
___ Typing ___ wpm
___ Vendor Contact/Bid Requests
___ Work Prioritization
___ Writing/Editing

Sample Sentences Using Some of the Skills Listed Above

___ Produced ____ documents for use by ____ staff.

___ Opened and distributed mail to support ____ staff.

___ Managed incoming/outgoing mail for ____ departments.

___ Completed ____ projects for key accounts valued to $____.

___ Operated ____, ____, and ____ office equipment.

___ Inventoried $____ worth of office equipment and supplies.

___ Scheduled conferences/appointments for ____ attendees.

___ Prepared bulk mailings for ____ departments.

___ Accounted for $____ in petty cash fund.

___ Processed computerized billing for ____ customers.

___ Managed distribution of office supplies valued at $____.

___ Dealt with ____ customers daily, in person and by phone.

___ Maintained files/documents to support ____ departments.

___ Conducted employee orientations for ____ departments.

___ Supervised ____ employees in ____ departments.

___ Supervised and delegated workflow to ____ clerical staff.

___ Purchased $____ annually in equipment and supplies.

___ Managed front office administration to support ____ staff.

___ Updated filing and records for up to ____ departments.

___ Provided clerical support for staff of up to ____.

___ Completed marketing and administrative projects to support ____ staff.

___ Provided front office and bookkeeping support for staff of ____.

___ Handled ____-line phone system, transferring calls to ____ extensions.

___ Created ____-page corporate newsletter distributed to ____ employees.

___ Oversaw order administration for department with sales of $____ annually.

___ Utilized ____ and ____ programs to prepare correspondence and reports.

___ Stocked and inventoried office equipment and supplies valued at $____.

___ Maintained ____, ____, and ____ records for up to ____ staff members.

___ Implemented new mail routing procedures for ____ departments.

___ Performed ____ and ____ tasks consistently meeting company guidelines.

___ Oversaw office recycling program implemented in ____ departments.

___ Created interdepartmental memos and letters for up to ____ employees.

___ Authorized to carry keys for ____ departments and access confidential records.

___ Greeted visitors and announced them to ____ departments.

___ Provided executive support to President and staff of ____ sales agents.

___ Compiled and updated database for over ____ customers and accounts.

___ Trained clerical and temporary employees in ____ and ____ procedures.

___ Utilized ____ programs to track and inventory items for ____ departments.

___ Processed work orders for department with sales of $____ annually.

___ Organized company functions for ____ employees in ____ departments.

Skill Lists and Sample Sentences for

RESTAURANT/FOOD SERVICE

These Skills May Also Be Used as Skill Headings

___ Advertising—Newspaper/Radio
___ Authorization to Keys & Safes
___ Balancing of Tills
___ Bank Deposits/Safe Drops
___ Banquet/Bid Quotation
___ Banquet Management
___ Budgeting/Expense Control
___ Building Security
___ Cash Accountability
___ Contract/Sales Management
___ Cost Control
___ Crew Supervision
___ Customer Service
___ Departmental Accounting
___ Departmental Coordination
___ Departmental Cross-Training
___ Departmental Management

___ Departmental Support
___ Document Control
___ Employee Orientations/Training
___ File & Records Control
___ Floor/Shift Setup
___ Health/Safety Regulations
___ Hiring Recommendations
___ Inventory Control
___ Invoice Verification
___ Key Account Servicing
___ Lead Trainer
___ Marketing/Add-On Sales
___ Menu Development
___ Merchandising
___ Multiline Phones
___ Opening/Closing Operations
___ Operations Management

___ Order Expediting
___ Order Follow-Up
___ Order Processing
___ Posting of Daily Receipts
___ Price/Bid Negotiation
___ Price Calculations/Quoting
___ Product Displays/Sales
___ Product Promotions
___ Production Control
___ Production Scheduling
___ Project Management/Troubleshooting
___ Project Organization
___ Purchasing/Ordering
___ Quality Control
___ Restaurant Management
___ Salary Recommendations
___ Sales Forecasting

___ Seasonal Planning
___ Seating/Service Coordination
___ Security Procedures
___ Shift Management
___ Shift Scheduling
___ Staff Hiring/Supervision
___ Staff Scheduling
___ Staff Supervision/Training
___ Stock Rotation
___ Team Coordination
___ Theft Control
___ Vendor Contact/Management
___ Vendor Negotiation
___ Work Coordination
___ Work Prioritization
___ Workflow Delegation
___ Workstation Management

Sample Sentences Using Some of the Skills Listed Above

___ Served as Lead Trainer to crew of ____.
___ Managed key accounts including ____, ____, and ____.
___ Handled $____ monthly, balancing till to the penny.
___ Maximized floor displays increasing sales by ____%.
___ Prepared banquet bids and quotes for up to $____.
___ Opened and closed facility with sales in excess of $____.
___ Supervised crew of ____ employees in ____ departments.
___ Increased sales by up to ____% through add-on promotions.
___ Coordinated service requirements with ____ departments.
___ Prepared orders for ____ customers on a monthly basis.
___ Managed inventory for ____-square-foot department.
___ Prepared over ____ items for setup of next shift.
___ Purchased $____ in merchandise on a monthly basis.
___ Verified and approved invoices for ____ departments.
___ Stocked and priced merchandise for ____ departments.
___ Developed good rapport with approximately ____ vendors.
___ Designed creative menu plans increasing sales by ____%.
___ Scheduled ____ rotating shifts and hours for ____ staff.
___ Processed over $____ daily in credit card accounts.
___ Successfully negotiated up to ____% off major purchases.

___ Input data to create reports to track over $____ of inventory and supplies.
___ Accounted for up to $____ per day, making all safe drops and deposits.
___ Authorized to carry all keys with access to safes in ____ departments.
___ Analyzed sales and marketing trends to purchase up to $____ of inventory.
___ Maintained daily bookkeeping and posting of $____ in cash receipts.
___ Served up to ____ customers daily, with sales in excess of $____ monthly.
___ Conducted performance evaluations for ____ employees.
___ Managed multiline phones, reservations, and seating for ____ customers.
___ Prioritized work projects for ____ staff to meet project requirements.
___ Decreased customer waiting time by ____% by developing a reservations schedule.
___ Controlled customer service and sales for department with revenues of $____.
___ Implemented a theft control program, which decreased losses by ____%.
___ Processed ____ orders for up to ____ staff, handling over $____ monthly.
___ Implemented security procedures for department of ____ square feet.
___ Provided sales and service to ____ customers daily.
___ Accounted for $____ of inventory for a ____-square-foot store.
___ Coordinated repairs and maintenance of ____ departments with ____ vendors.
___ Coordinated workflow for ____ employees in ____ departments.
___ Assisted with inventory audits for ____ departments.
___ Ordered and distributed merchandise worth $____ to ____ departments.

Skill Lists and Sample Sentences for

SELF-EMPLOYED/CONSULTANTS

These Skills May Also Be Used as Skill Headings

___ Account Development	___ Contract Administration	___ Key Account Management	___ Proposal Development
___ Account Management	___ Contract Development	___ Leasing Management	___ Purchasing/Inventory Control
___ Accounting/Fiscal Management	___ Contract Management/Negotiation	___ License/Permit Compliance	___ Quarterly Tax Submittal
___ Advertising Management	___ Corporate Policies/Procedures	___ Management Consulting	___ Receiving/Shipping Management
___ Benefits Administration	___ Corporate Presentations	___ Manufacturing Management	___ Recruitment/Hiring of Staff
___ Bidding/Estimating	___ Cost/Expense Control	___ Market Expansion Strategies	___ Research and Development
___ Budget Management	___ Crew Supervision	___ Market Penetration Strategies	___ Resource/Equipment Allocation
___ Business Development	___ Crisis Management	___ Networking/Lead Development	___ Sales Forecasting
___ Business Funding/Procurement	___ Customer Service Management	___ New Account Setup	___ Sales Presentations
___ Business Management	___ Departmental Management	___ Order Fulfillment	___ Site/Location Selection
___ Business/Market Analysis	___ Design of Business Materials	___ P&L Responsibility	___ Staff Supervision/Training
___ Business Plan Development	___ Direct Marketing/Cold Calling	___ PR/Promotional Campaigns	___ Strategic Planning
___ Capital Equipment Purchasing	___ Expansion/Growth Management	___ Price Quoting	___ Subcontractor/Vendor Management
___ Cash Flow Management/Control	___ Facilities Management	___ Price/Schedule Negotiation	___ Territory Management
___ Client Credit Approval	___ Financial Administration	___ Product Development	___ Venture Capital Acquisition
___ Client Database Management	___ Inside Sales	___ Project Management	___ Workload Delegation
___ Computerized Accounting	___ Invoicing/Billing	___ Project Scheduling	___ Workload Prioritization

Sample Sentences Using Some of the Skills Listed Above

___ Managed multiple tasks and projects as Sole Proprietor.

___ Consulted clients in ___, ___, and ___.

___ Analyzed emerging competitors to stay competitive.

___ Managed import/export operations with sales of $___.

___ Complied with federal & regional licensing requirements.

___ Managed ___ -square-foot facility valued at $___.

___ Oversaw general management of ___ departments.

___ Managed a ___ state territory marketing ___ products.

___ Hired and supervised ___ subcontractors and vendors.

___ Analyzed goals and formulated marketing strategies.

___ Led company to top performance competing with ___.

___ Launched market expansion program including ___.

___ Designed all advertising, business, and accounting forms.

___ Held full P&L responsibility for this $___ corporation.

___ Negotiated individual contracts valued up to $___.

___ Recruited, supervised, and trained ___ staff.

___ Managed ___ staff performing ___ and ___ functions.

___ Created sales acceleration program for ___ territory.

___ Won ___ contracts resulting in over $___ annual sales.

___ Developed ___ accounts within ___ years of business start-up.

___ Managed ___ key accounts including ___, ___, and ___.

___ Maintained accounting/fiscal management for operation with sales of $___.

___ Launched advertising campaign, which included ___, ___, and ___.

___ Administered employee benefits program for ___ staff.

___ Developed bids and estimates for projects valued in excess of $___ annually.

___ Spearheaded business development team, which procured $___ in funds.

___ Managed business from start-up to growth of $___ sales annually.

___ Conducted extensive business/market research before launching ___ program.

___ Created business plan that resulted in bank funding and loans of $___.

___ Researched and purchased over $___ in capital equipment.

___ Managed cash flow and disbursements for business serving ___ accounts.

___ Set up new client accounts, verified and approved credit up to $___.

___ Built database of over ___ key business contacts and customer accounts.

___ Called on selected accounts to market ___ services and ___ products.

___ Supervised and dispatched crews of up to ___ on ___ daily projects.

___ Analyzed and solved crisis situations by effectively prioritizing workloads.

___ Conceived and developed a ___ product line sold at a ___% profit.

___ Negotiated price, production schedules, and delivery with ___ accounts.

___ Managed up to ___ projects daily, while overseeing ___ staff.

___ Reengineered operational systems for ___ departments.

Skill Lists and Sample Sentences for

SOCIAL/HUMAN SERVICES

These Skills May Also Be Used as Skill Headings

___ Addiction Management
___ Adolescent Counseling
___ Adult Counseling
___ Advisory Board Member
___ Agency Administration
___ Agency Performance Reports
___ Anger/Rage Control
___ Bereavement Counseling
___ Budgeting/Financial Planning
___ Budgeting/Staff Planning
___ Career Exploration
___ Case Documentation
___ Case Management
___ Chemical Dependence/Addiction
___ Child Abuse Counseling
___ Chronic Illness
___ Client Education/Skill Development

___ Client Needs Assessment
___ Clinical Counseling
___ Clinical Triage/Counseling
___ Communication Skills
___ Community/Agency Referrals
___ Community Liaison
___ Coping Strategies
___ Couples Counseling
___ Crisis Intervention
___ Cross-Cultural Populations
___ Depression/Medication Control
___ Developmentally Disabled
___ Diagnosis/Prognosis Reporting
___ Diagnostic Evaluation
___ Diagnostic Profiles
___ Effective Parenting Methods
___ Essential Living Skills

___ Family Disorder Counseling
___ Family Planning
___ Family Systems Assessment
___ Fund-Raising Management
___ Goal Setting
___ Grant Writing
___ Group Counseling Facilitator
___ In-service Training/Presentations
___ Intake Interviewing/Assessment
___ Interdisciplinary Team Member
___ Job Placement
___ Legal/Medical Documentation
___ Life Transition Counseling
___ Mediation/Conflict Resolution
___ Multilingual Populations
___ Nonprofit Management
___ Outpatient Counseling/Referral

___ Private Practice Management
___ Program Analysis
___ Program Implementation
___ Program/Project Management
___ Psychosocial Assessment
___ Psychotherapeutic Methods
___ Rape/Physical Abuse Counseling
___ Self-Empowerment
___ Self-Esteem Development
___ Shelter Management
___ Short/Long-Term Care Planning
___ Small/Large Group Counseling
___ Stress Management
___ Suicide Prevention Counseling
___ Treatment/Counseling Categories
___ Treatment Disclosure
___ Treatment Plan Development

Sample Sentences Using Some of the Skills Listed Above

___ Supervised case documentation for base of ____ clients.

___ Counseled clients regarding ____, ____, and ____.

___ Provided treatment for ____, ____, and ____ clients.

___ Recruited, trained, and supervised staff of ____ counselors.

___ Managed private practice serving ____ clients.

___ Provided emergency care to ____ rape relief clients.

___ Spearheaded grant writing team for ____ agencies.

___ Served as counseling facilitator for groups of ____ clients.

___ Provided in-service training for staff of ____.

___ Managed nonprofit agency, overseeing ____ staff.

___ Mediated client and family disputes in volatile situations.

___ Coordinated client scheduling and probation enforcement.

___ Supervised front office and records administration.

___ Controlled client vouchers, petty cash, and disbursements.

___ Facilitated contact with DSHS and ESD offices.

___ Motivated clients to comply with treatment requirements.

___ Directed agency expansion from ____ to ____ clients.

___ Managed ____ staff performing ____ and ____ functions.

___ Coordinated in-home visits, counseling, and client care.

___ Program Administration included ____, ____, and ____.

___ Managed agency serving population of ____ and providing ____ services.

___ Served as Advisory Board Member overseeing ____, ____, and ____.

___ Analyzed biannual performance and prepared reports to maintain funding.

___ Controlled a $____ annual budget for ____ staff and shelter operating expenses.

___ Conducted client needs assessment, intake interviews, and diagnostic profiles.

___ Developed and taught client education classes for ____ clients and ____ staff.

___ Taught clients skills in ____, ____, ____, and ____.

___ Conducted clinical counseling based upon physician and psychiatric diagnoses.

___ Provided clinical and crisis triage and recommended emergent care strategies.

___ Assessed client needs and made agency/physician referrals for ____ clients.

___ Served as liaison between clients, court, and probation officers.

___ Managed a caseload of ____ clients referred from ____ and ____ agencies.

___ Diagnosed physical and mental symptoms and reported prognosis to ____.

___ Conducted diagnostic evaluations for ____ and ____ clients.

___ Implemented crisis planning/risk management procedures for ____ agency.

___ Developed short- and long-term care plans for caseload of ____ clients.

___ Provided voluntary counseling to ____, ____, and ____ clients.

___ Provided involuntary counseling to ____, ____, and ____ clients.

___ Managed a variety of projects including ____, ____, and ____.

___ Implemented a suicide prevention program for ____ agencies.

Skill Lists and Sample Sentences for

TEACHING/EDUCATION

These Skills May Also Be Used as Skill Headings

___ Advanced Teaching Methods	___ Drug Abuse Assessment	___ In-service Training	___ Pilot Program Development
___ Agency Referral/Intervention	___ Educational Units Taught	___ Instructional Program Development	___ Political Science
___ Art/Art Appreciation	___ English/Grammar	___ Interactive Learning Activities	___ Positive Discipline Teaching
___ Business/Marketing	___ ESL	___ Large Group Instruction	___ Pre-Reading
___ Career Development	___ Essential Life Skills	___ Learning Assessment Interpretation	___ Public Speaking
___ Civics/Economics	___ Family Systems Assessment	___ Learning Assessment Tools	___ Science/Biology
___ Classroom Enrichment Activities	___ Field Trip Coordination	___ Learning Center Implementation	___ Self-Esteem Development
___ Classroom Management	___ Foreign Language	___ Learning Needs Assessment	___ Small Group Instruction
___ Class Volunteer Coordination	___ Geography	___ Learning Unit Development	___ Social Skills Development
___ Coaching	___ Gifted Instruction	___ Lesson Plan Development	___ Special Needs Students
___ Computer Technology	___ Goal Setting/Achievement	___ Master Instructor	___ Student/Parent Counseling
___ Conference Presentations	___ Grading/Progress Documentation	___ Mathematics Courses	___ Student Teacher Supervision
___ Conflict Resolution	___ Grant Writing/Fundraising	___ Motor Skill Development	___ Supervision of Instructional Staff
___ Cultural Awareness Programs	___ Group Dynamics	___ Multiage Classroom Instruction	___ Tech Prep Programs
___ Cultural Language Transition	___ Health Education	___ Music/Band	___ Training of Instructional Staff
___ Cultural Transition Activities	___ High-Risk Student Populations	___ Parent/Teacher Consultation	___ Verbal Communication Skills
___ Diverse Student Populations	___ History	___ Physical Education	___ Writing/Journalism

Sample Sentences Using Some of the Skills Listed Above

___ Provided intervention and classroom conflict resolution.

___ Assisted Principal in defining program/educational goals.

___ Implemented positive discipline in challenging classes.

___ Trained and supervised ____ instructional staff.

___ Created pilot ____ program implemented in ____ schools.

___ Served as Master Instructor to ____ staff in ____ subjects.

___ Created learning style units for special needs students.

___ Taught ____ tech prep classes including ____ and ____.

___ Broad-based instruction included ____, ____, and ____.

___ Spearheaded implementation of new ____ program.

___ Redesigned learning center utilized by ____ students.

___ Integrated computer technology into ____ classes.

___ Restructured annual teaching plan following district rules.

___ Increased student attendance/performance by ____.

___ Initiated after-school activities such as ____ and ____.

___ Motivated students through ____, ____, and ____.

___ Recognized by school administration for ____.

___ Fostered a ____ environment that resulted in ____.

___ Created gifted and advanced units for ____ students.

___ Served on ____ board, with responsibility for ____.

___ Taught mixed-age groups of ____ students utilizing advanced teaching methods.

___ Developed and integrated classroom enrichment activities into ____ classes.

___ Managed classrooms with up to ____ ESL and multicultural students.

___ Assessed student and parent needs and made appropriate agency referrals.

___ Recruited/coordinated ____ adult and high school volunteers for reading classes.

___ Coached over ____ students in ____, ____, and ____ activities.

___ Organized parent/teacher conferences and PTA activities for ____ members.

___ Instituted cultural awareness program adopted districtwide in ____ schools.

___ Counseled students and parents in cultural and language transition.

___ Developed curriculum for ____ classes utilized by staff of ____ teachers.

___ Assessed potential drug abuse and student addiction for referral to counselors.

___ Taught over ____ years of ____, ____, and ____ classes to ____ students.

___ Conducted family assessments in cases where student performance was failing.

___ Coordinated parental permission and field trips for up to ____ students.

___ Maintained grading, progress reports, and classroom documentation.

___ Assisted in writing a ____ grant that received $____ in funding.

___ Analyzed difficult group dynamics to recommend alternative teaching methods.

___ Authored skill and self-esteem enhancement units for high-risk students.

___ Created and provided in-service training for ____ staff from ____ districts.

___ Designed interactive learning activities for ____, ____, and ____ classes.

Skill Lists and Sample Sentences for

WRITER/REPORTER/COPYWRITER

These Skills May Also Be Used as Skill Headings

___ Account Management
___ Acquisition/Review
___ Ad Scheduling/Response Tracking
___ Advertising Copywriting
___ Advertising Design
___ Advertising Research/Placement
___ Annual Reports
___ Book Proposals
___ Broadcast News Writing
___ Brochures
___ Business/Corporate Writing
___ Business Plans
___ Catalog Copywriting
___ Collateral Materials
___ Columnist/Commentator
___ Community Awareness Campaigns
___ Contract Writing

___ Copywriting
___ Corporate Campaign Writing
___ Corporate Communications
___ Corporate Presentations
___ Curriculum Development
___ Direct Response Copywriting
___ Editorial Management
___ Feature Articles
___ Fund-Raising Campaigns
___ Governmental Bulletins
___ Grant Writing
___ Graphic Design
___ Jingle/Songwriting
___ Job Descriptions
___ Key Account Management
___ Magazine/Article Writing
___ Manual Development

___ Manuscript Evaluation
___ Marketing Literature
___ Media Buying
___ News and Event Reporting
___ Newsletter Writing
___ Newspaper Reporting
___ Newswriting
___ Online User Documentation
___ Operations Manuals
___ Policy/Procedures Manuals
___ Position Papers
___ Press Releases
___ PR Literature/Campaigns
___ Product Packaging Copywriting
___ Project Conceptualizing
___ Project Management/Scheduling
___ Query Letters

___ Radio/TV Advertising
___ Reports/Briefs/Journal Articles
___ Research/Fact Verification
___ Sales Catalogues
___ Scientific Writing
___ Scriptwriting
___ Senior Editing Member
___ Software Documentation
___ Speech/Presentation Writing
___ Store Signage/Design
___ Story Research/Development
___ Technical Writing
___ Textbook Editing/Writing
___ Training Materials
___ User Manuals
___ Video Scripting
___ Web Content Development

Sample Sentences Using Some of the Skills Listed Above

___ Wrote training manuals as management team member.
___ Developed video scripts for ___, ___, and ___ videos.
___ Wrote technical documents including ___ and ___.
___ Wrote and issued press releases for ___ events.
___ Developed copy for parts catalogs with ___ circulation.
___ Authored position papers on sensitive issues such as ___.
___ Wrote governmental bulletins for ___ and ___.
___ Wrote copy for ___ direct mail campaigns.
___ Provided editorial management to staff of ___ writers.
___ Researched and verified facts for staff of ___ writers.
___ Performed media buys for major corporations such as ___.
___ Worked with instructors to develop ___ curriculum.
___ Developed Web content for site generating ___ daily hits.
___ Authored online user documentation for ___ and ___.
___ Researched and wrote job descriptions for ___ positions.
___ Developed copy for ___ product packaging.
___ Designed ads, wrote copy, and presented to clients.
___ Conceptualized and presented ad campaigns/story lines.
___ Trained and mentored ___ editing and writing staff.
___ Wrote jingles for key accounts such as ___ and ___.

___ Managed ___ advertising accounts with responsibility for ___, ___, and ___.
___ Provided acquisitions editing for division publishing ___ titles annually.
___ Scheduled $___ in annual advertising and tracked response rates.
___ Wrote advertising copy for key accounts such as ___, ___, and ___.
___ Designed advertising campaigns and storyboards for a $___ account.
___ Conducted market and buyer research to place ads with ___ radio stations.
___ Gathered financial and corporate mission information to create annual reports.
___ Wrote broadcast news segments on ___, ___, and ___ topics.
___ Developed brochures and marketing literature for key accounts such as ___.
___ Authored full range of business documents including ___, ___, and ___.
___ Worked with ___ to write business plan that resulted in $___ of funding.
___ Developed collateral materials for corporations with revenues in excess of $___.
___ Served as monthly columnist and commentator for the ___.
___ Designed and implemented community awareness campaigns for ___ and ___.
___ Wrote magazine articles featured in ___, ___, and ___.
___ Coauthored over ___ grants, which resulted in over $___ in funding.
___ Developed extensive expertise in graphic design and newsletter layout.
___ Created a variety of manuals for ___, ___, and ___.
___ Evaluated over ___ manuscripts for ___, ___, and ___ projects.
___ Edited over ___ textbooks for the ___ and ___ markets.

When and How to Use Transferable Skill Statements

When you use transferable skill statements, make sure they are specific, not general. For example, read the Before statement below. It could have been written about any job or any person, so it has little meaning or impact on employers. Don't put general statements like this at the top of your resume or in your summary of qualifications statements. Many people put statements like the Before statement in their resumes, yet they never provide documentation that proves they have such skills. If you state you have a particular skill, then provide enough specifics to convince employers that you do indeed have that skill. Which of these statements is more convincing?

BEFORE   Background demonstrates proven organizational and communication skills.

AFTER   Working directly with the President and staff of 35 sales representatives in 3 states to service 200 key accounts required strong organizational and communication skills.

If you use the statements listed below, beef them up with numbers and specific descriptions so that employers are convinced you have the skills described.

Transferable Skill Statements

___ Able to motivate staff to meet project deadlines.

___ Strong problem-solving skills proven by increased sales.

___ Work independently, successfully meeting quotas.

___ Strong technical and written communication skills.

___ Easily understand and solve technical problems.

___ Eager to perform work to maximum satisfaction of clients.

___ Strong managerial and organizational skills.

___ Team player interested in achieving all departmental goals.

___ Team player who consistently supports management.

___ Proven ability to develop strong customer and team rapport.

___ Customer service oriented, with goal of repeat business.

___ Enjoy working as a team member as well as independently.

___ Commended for reliability and trustworthiness.

___ Proven ability to work in fast-paced, difficult environments.

___ Able to lead others in high-demand situations.

___ Proven skills resolving problems and tense situations.

___ Enjoy working with public and diverse populations.

___ Able to coordinate many tasks simultaneously.

___ Self-motivated, hardworking individual.

___ Willing to do whatever is necessary to get the job done.

___ Background demonstrates proven organizational and communication skills.

___ Proven history as a team player, motivating others to meet objectives.

___ Excellent interpersonal, verbal, and written skills.

___ Success-driven team player who continually meets and exceeds goals.

___ Proven history of improving operations and increasing profitability.

___ Strong mathematical, spelling, and grammatical skills.

___ Learn technical information quickly.

___ Able to teach myself by reading manuals and performing "hands-on" work.

___ Serve as liaison between management, customers, and staff.

___ Able to handle challenges—proven history of increased productivity.

___ Coordinated a variety of tasks in stressful and fast-paced environments.

___ History of flexibility—able to handle constant change and interruptions.

___ Able to prioritize and operate proactively.

___ Self-starter who applies individual initiative to get the job done.

___ Very detail-oriented with excellent analytical and project-tracking skills.

___ Recognized for ability to juggle multiple tasks and meet deadlines.

___ Strong problem-solver who is resourceful and able to work independently.

___ Deal effectively with a diverse clientele while solving problems.

___ Able to promote public relations while dealing with irate/difficult customers.

___ Dynamic, outgoing individual able to develop strong rapport with customers.

---

6 Twelve Questions to Shape and Control Your Image

You've learned that the content of your resume determines how effective it is. If your resume has strong content that matches employers' needs, it will generate more interviews. If it has weak content, it will generate fewer interviews. The content, or descriptions, of each of your job titles and skill headings can also have a significant impact on the salary that potential employers think you are worth.

Writing powerful content is probably the hardest part of resume writing. Most job seekers feel overwhelmed tackling this task. They know they have great skills but can't seem to describe them in an impressive way. To help, I've created the Twelve Questions that guide job seekers at every level in projecting a strong image. These questions will help you identify and describe the best of your skills.

In hundreds of job search workshops I've taught, many people will go through the questions and then say things like "Oh, these questions really don't apply to my situation," or "There's no way I can use numbers to describe my work history. It just won't work." But after I walk through the same questions with them in detail, they say, "Oh, yeah, I do see how this applies to me. I guess I *can* use numbers." I encourage you to put maximum effort into understanding how these questions apply to your situation. I've used this system with thousands of job seekers and it can help you—no matter what level you're at or industry you're in—to create content that elevates and expands your image. And this translates into more interviews and higher salary offers. So challenge yourself to use and apply these questions. It is well worth your investment of time and effort.

To illustrate that the questions can apply to all positions and industries, we'll look at how the first question can be used to describe four very different jobs. Question 1 is "Whom did you work for or with? Will mentioning them strengthen your image?" Reviewing the examples below, you can see the salary spread for these positions would be from about $18,000 to $90,000 per year. Yet answering the same question created powerful content for each position. Take a moment and notice that each statement begins with a job function followed by whom the job seeker worked with. This sentence structure works well because it emphasizes one of your primary job duties, then strengthens it by stating whom you worked or coordinated with, supported, or supervised.

Data Entry Clerk
- Keyed in financial data for up to 200 key accounts per day, coordinating with 10 field agents and branch manager.

Road Crew Lead
- Led a crew of up to 15, working with site inspectors, permit officials, and architects to ensure building code compliance.

Project Manager
- Managed individual projects valued to $ $1/4$ million, delegating workflow to a staff of 10 design engineers, drafters, and administrative staff.

Vice President of Operations
- Directed this *Fortune* 500 corporation through a major turnaround, successfully increasing sales over $1.3 million in a 2-year period, as senior management consultant to the Board of Directors.

The 7-Up Marketing Strategy

When 7-Up was introduced to the market, a lot of planning and strategizing went into launching it as a leading soft drink. One strategy was to link its image to Coca-Cola and Pepsi by naming it the "Uncola." The makers of 7-Up linked its image to Coke and Pepsi by displaying these products in the backgrounds of its commercials. This strategy put 7-Up on the same playing field as the big guys. (Off-brand sodas have not employed such strategies and aren't viewed as being in the same league as Coke and Pepsi, and their sales reflect this.)

As a job seeker you'll want to apply a very similar strategy. You want to link your image to the important titles of supervisors, companies, organizations, key accounts, products, and staff that you have experience dealing with that are similar to those that you will deal with in your next job. This elevates your image and establishes that you already have experience at the level needed in the job you want. The four examples you just read are powerful because each person's image was linked to someone at a higher or impressive level that relates to the job they want. Each of the Twelve Questions provides examples that guide you in shaping and linking your image.

Answer *All* Questions for Each Title or Skill Heading

Whether you're creating a skill-based or a chronological resume, you may have a combination of job titles and skill headings to describe. It's important that you answer all of the Twelve Questions for each individual title or skill heading. Let's use Sandra, a law library manager, as an example. Below are her title and three skill heading sections from her resume. Review each one to see how she answered the first question, "Whom did you work for or with?" You'll notice that each answer is slightly different.

University of Washington Law Library Manager

- Managed a 600,000-volume law library, coordinating academic reference requirements with 78 teaching departments.

Law Firm Library Management

- Supervised law library department, supporting one of the nation's top law firms employing a staff of 340 attorneys and 30 partners.

Library Budget and Fiscal Control

- Controlled budgets ranging up to $350,000 annually, allocating funds for procurement of reference material upon advisement of law department deans and attorneys specializing in over 30 fields of law.

Supervision and Training of Library Staff

- Supervised and trained over 35 law library staff including computer systems manager, research assistants, document clerks, and administrative staff.

To create the statements above, Sandra asked herself, "As a law library manager for the University of Washington, whom did I work for or with? As a library department supervisor, whom did I work for or with? When I controlled the budget, whom did I work for or with? As a staff supervisor, whom did I work for or with?"

If one of the questions doesn't apply to your situation, then go on to the next one. Relax! Remember that your resume doesn't have to be perfect. It merely needs to show employers how your experience relates to the job you want. You'll beat out the majority of your competitors for this reason alone.

QUESTION 1: Whom did you work for or with? Will mentioning them strengthen your image?

Reading the examples below, whom would you pick to interview—the people described in the Before examples or the After examples? As you can see, naming whom each person worked for, or with, expanded and elevated each person's image. For emphasis, I've underlined appropriate phrases that answer this question.

BEFORE   **Secretary**
- Maintained correspondence, reports, and contracts for this national supplier of electrical equipment.

AFTER   **Administrative / Executive Support**
- Provided executive support to <u>President and Vice President</u>, which included preparation of contracts, reports, and correspondence for this national supply company.

BEFORE   **Retail Sales Clerk**
- Traveled throughout 12 stores, cashiering, dealing with customers, and solving problems.

AFTER   **Customer Service / Regional Support**
- Worked directly with <u>Regional Manager</u>, traveling to 12 stores to audit store procedures.
- Dealt with up to <u>200 customers</u>, accounting for up to $20,000 daily.

BEFORE   **Branch Manager**
- Managed branch operations and staff preparing loans.

AFTER   **Branch Manager—Escrow / Loan Operations**
- Managed branch generating over $22.3 million in loans annually, coordinating with <u>Corporate Vice President</u> and <u>12 leading financial institutions</u> to process commercial escrow and loan operations.

As you write your resume, think of the type of job you want. Have you already worked for, or with, staff or organizations at a similar level? If so, mention their job titles or the names of such organizations. This will create an image that you are qualified and experienced in the type of job you want. When answering this question you may want to include

- Titles of supervisors or staff you have supported
- Names of departments you coordinated with
- Names of key accounts
- Names of similar organizations you have worked with
- Names of well-known product lines you have serviced

- Types of industries or businesses you have dealt with
- Regional, national, or international references
- Status of company such as *Fortune* 500 ranking

QUESTION 2: Will describing the size of the department you worked for strengthen your image?

From the examples below, whom would you pick to interview—the people described in the Before examples or the After examples? Whom do you think you would be willing to pay more money? You can see that describing the size of the company or department for which each person worked creates a more qualified image, and will result in more interviews and higher salary offers. For emphasis, I've underlined appropriate phrases that answer this question.

BEFORE **Accounting Assistant**
- Assisted with all accounting duties from general ledger to financial statements.

AFTER **A/R and A/P Management**
- Maintained over 2,000 A/R and A/P accounts including preparation of financial statements for firm with annual revenues in excess of $140 million.

BEFORE **Warehouse Worker**
- Oversaw warehouse operations including supervising employees, parts kit prep, shipping/receiving, and quality control.

AFTER **Warehouse Management**
- Managed a 50,000-square-foot warehouse, supervising a staff of 10 in all areas including parts kit preparation, shipping, receiving, and quality control.

BEFORE **Nurse**
- As Charge Nurse, managed a cardiac unit with 5 registered nurses.

AFTER **Cardiac Unit—Charge Nurse**
- Managed a Cardiac Unit with 35 beds, supervising 5 Registered Nurses supporting a staff of 75 physicians including cardiologists, internists, gerontologists, and oncologists.

As you write your resume, determine if the size or function of the business or department you have worked for is impressive, relates to, or is similar to the size or function of the company or department you want to work for. If so, include this information. You may find it helpful to flip through the resume examples we've reviewed in earlier chapters and look at the various ways each resume addresses this question. Here are some ways you can describe the size of a company or department:

- Total sales revenues
- Number of employees
- Number of divisions or branch offices
- Physical size in square footage or other measurement
- Size of region, such as a three-state area

- Number of staff or departments you supported
- Number of accounts, organizations, customers, or units serviced
- Dollar value of assets, merchandise, equipment, or inventory

QUESTION 3: Will using numbers to describe your responsibilities strengthen your image?

Using numbers in your resume descriptions helps to show the depth of your experience. Review the examples below. Whom would you choose to interview for a position—the person in each Before description or the person in the corresponding After description? Again, whom would you be willing to pay more money? Since the majority of job seekers write weak resume content, you will stand out and look more qualified by using numbers and painting a "big picture" of your skills and experience. For emphasis, I've underlined appropriate phrases that answer this question.

BEFORE   **Outside Sales Representative**
- Market to established accounts and cold call prospective accounts to sell exterior building products.

AFTER   **Territory / Key Account Management**
- Manage a <u>5-state territory</u> composed of <u>125 key accounts</u> generating revenues of $2.5 million annually.

BEFORE   **Teacher**
- Taught English and grammar to high school classes.

AFTER   **Grade 9–12 English and Grammar Instructor**
- Developed lesson plans <u>implemented districtwide in 10 schools</u>.
- Taught English and grammar to <u>4 classes of 140 students</u> from diverse social and economic backgrounds.

BEFORE   **Gas Station Attendant**
- Cashiered, supervised night clerks, managed shift operations, and completed store accounting procedures.

AFTER   **Customer Service / Operations Management**
- Managed customer service, operations, and accounting for <u>branch generating $200,000 in monthly sales</u>.
- <u>Supervised 10 customer service staff</u> and <u>trained 50 additional staff in 10 branch locations</u>.

As you write your resume, brainstorm to discover ways you can use numbers to describe all the areas of your responsibility. Include any areas of responsibility that match or are similar to those in jobs you want. Here are some ways you can use numbers to describe job responsibilities:

- Volume of sales, cash, receipts, or transactions you have been responsible for
- Number of departments, divisions, staff, customers, or accounts you have been responsible for or coordinated with
- Number of projects, contracts, documents, units, or products you have been responsible for

- Dollar value of projects, contracts, assets, merchandise, equipment, or inventory you have been responsible for
- Highest dollar value of individual projects or contracts you have negotiated or managed
- Total value of all projects or contracts you have been responsible for

QUESTION 4: Did you create, reorganize, conceive, or establish any procedures or systems?

On an ongoing basis we all strive to find ways to increase productivity and company profitability but often discount our accomplishments in these areas. Many people are surprised when they make lists of all of the systems and procedures they have created or implemented throughout their careers. As you can see below, describing what each person developed, implemented, and designed adds depth to their resume and better highlights the skills they have to offer employers. For emphasis, I've underlined appropriate phrases that answer this question.

BEFORE **Assembler**
- Assembled electronics products, managed and set up production assembly.

AFTER **Production Setup and Control**
- <u>Developed, set up, and managed production assembly line,</u> which <u>increased production by 15%</u> and shipments over $ $^1/_4$ million annually.

BEFORE **Program Manager**
- Developed call-back and discount system, which increased add-on sales and account penetration.

AFTER **National Program Manager**
- <u>Developed and managed sales program implemented corporate-wide</u> in 5 national regions, which <u>increased customer base from 950 accounts to over 1,500 accounts in 6 months.</u>

BEFORE **Floor Supervisor**
- Oversaw retailing space, displays, and use of schematics. Supervised, scheduled, and trained staff.

AFTER **Operations Design / Departmental Management**
- Managed operations for 100,000-square-foot facility with sales of $24 million annually.
- <u>Increased annual sales by 15% by designing schematic systems</u> that were implemented in 15 departments.

Such achievements are important because they present an image of these individuals as being hard-working, self-motivated team players who care about increasing company profits and revenues—all of which are traits that employers want. Here's a short list of questions to help you remember some of the procedures you may have developed in your jobs:

- Have you set up systems for filing, accounting, customer service, sales, budgeting, purchasing, or other areas?

- Have you created new forms, production methods, or workstation layouts? If so, describe them.

- Have you developed employee or customer service procedures, guidelines, policies, manuals, or other documentation?

- How widely was the system implemented? How many departments or staff used the system?

- What was the result or success of the system that was implemented?

QUESTION 5: Have you increased productivity, saved money, or reduced labor?

Employers want and need employees who can solve problems. Of the examples below, which ones present an image of each person as being innovative and able to help employers save money, cut costs, and increase productivity and profitability? Which examples will be more likely to motivate an employer to call the applicant for an interview? For emphasis, I've underlined appropriate phrases that answer this question.

BEFORE **Mail Specialist III**
- Developed new bulk-mail processing forms that reduced number of forms to be completed by public.

AFTER **District Forms Design / Cost Savings**
- Developed new bulk-mail permit forms that <u>reduced number of forms required from 3 to 1</u>.
- System was implemented in 1,500 offices with <u>estimated paper and labor savings of $ 1/4 million annually</u>.

BEFORE **Receptionist**
- Reorganized engineering file system and created template document files for use by 25 engineers.

AFTER **Creation of Engineering Template Documents / Cost Savings**
- Created over 100 template documents utilized by 25 engineers billing work at $35 an hour.
- Templates <u>cut engineers' document processing time by 15%</u> with <u>a cost savings of over $76,000 annually</u>.

BEFORE **Clinic Manager**
- Managed clinic, supervising staff, bookkeeping, and annual billing.

AFTER **Neurology Clinic Manager / Increased Billings**
- Managed clinic to support a staff of 8 neurologists, generating over $3.4 million in annual billings.
- <u>Increased billings by 15%</u> by documenting and charging for all procedures performed.

As you can see, a person's achievements can far exceed their job titles. For example, the receptionist saved her company over $76,000 per year by implementing a computerized template system. Doesn't this present an entirely different picture of her "than just being a receptionist"? This type of information helps employers select you as a top candidate. The following questions may also help you answer Question 5:

- Have the systems you designed cut paper costs, labor costs, or manufacturing times?

- Have the systems you implemented increased new accounts, repeat business, sales, profitability, or productivity?

- How widely used is the system you created? How many departments or staff use your system?

- Have you trained staff in the use of these systems? If so, how many?

- Will listing the job titles of people you have trained, their duties, or the departments they worked in show the depth of your knowledge in a particular field, department, or job function?

QUESTION 6: Did you have responsibility for special projects? If so, how large were they?

At some point, most people are given responsibility for special projects, but most of us forget about each individual project. Yet if we think back and remember projects that relate to and support our job objectives, we can greatly improve our resumes. Here are three examples where job seekers had either not included the special projects they were responsible for or had included very little about their special projects. As you can see, one even held the title of special projects manager but had only listed "Drafter" as his title. Again, whom would you be more likely to interview or give a higher starting salary?

BEFORE **Drafter**
- Considerable experience using AutoCAD as a drafter with a residential development firm.

AFTER **Special Projects Manager / AutoCAD R12 Operator**
- <u>Manage special projects</u> including plan notices and changes, for 3 branch locations, working directly with 2 architects and up to 20 engineering, internal marketing, and outside sales staff.

BEFORE **Driver**
- Worked with dock managers to set up new receiving systems.

AFTER **Streamlining Dock Operations / Project Management**
- <u>Developed dock acceptance systems</u> utilized by 50 key accounts such as Safeway, QFC, and Albertsons.
- New system cut dock processing time 15 minutes per delivery, enabling 25 more deliveries per day.

BEFORE **Administrative Assistant**
- Working with company President, researched, purchased, and implemented new computer system.

AFTER **Computer System Implementation**
- Purchased and <u>managed implementation of a $200,000 computer system</u> installed in 10 divisions.
- Consulted vendors in system setup, negotiated pricing, and coordinated installation in all sites.

All three of these people used the skills they gained from special projects to make career changes and land full-time positions, even though the special projects only lasted three to six months. Don't worry about how long you've performed a particular task. Instead, focus on what you've learned and accomplished. Here are some additional questions that may help you describe special projects:

- Have you been responsible for coordinating seasonal projects such as conferences or trade shows?

- Have you been responsible for implementing the use of new equipment, computers, or production methods?

- Have you been responsible for analyzing and improving any type of existing system or program?

- If so, how many people use your system? Has it resulted in cost savings, increased productivity, profits, or sales?

- In developing or managing special projects, whom did you coordinate with or deal with? Will mentioning their job titles, job functions, or the departments they worked for help to show the depth of your knowledge and skills?

QUESTION 7: Have you been complimented for special talents?

Most of us get complimented for those tasks we do well and enjoy. Few put this information in their resumes, and this omission is a mistake. It makes sense that if we get complimented it's for the very things that we're best at and enjoy—which, of course, can help provide strong material for a resume. Many people have told me that they don't include things they've been complimented for because it falls outside of their job descriptions. However, if it relates to their new job objective it should be included, as the examples below illustrate.

BEFORE   **Cook**
- Commended by restaurant manager for enabling kitchen to serve an additional 50 customers per day.

AFTER   **Departmental Coordination / Streamlining**
- Commended by Manager for <u>analyzing and implementing new workflow system</u> for department with 15 employees, which increased number of customers served per day from 200 to over 250.

BEFORE   **Janitorial Supervisor**
- Awarded for crew achieving highest quality service and maintenance of commercial buildings.

AFTER   **Crew Management / Top Productivity Award**
- Managed 4 work crews providing services for 5 commercial buildings totaling 200,000 square feet.
- Awarded for my crew achieving <u>highest quality service, productivity, and expense savings of 25 crews.</u>

BEFORE   **Newspaper Circulation Department Manager**
- Managed night shift, staff, and work schedules for the *Seattle Times* newspaper production department.

AFTER   **Operations Management / Increased Profitability**
- Managed departmental operations, supervising 68 staff producing over $2 million in product per month.
- <u>Recognized by management</u> for increasing profitability by 9% within a one-year period of being hired.

Don't be shy about telling employers what you have achieved and been recognized for. Here are a few more questions to help you uncover your special talents:

- Have you been complimented for solving problems that other staff find frustrating and don't want to do? If so, what were the problems? How many staff, customers, or departments were involved? What steps did you take to resolve the problem?

- Have you been selected to handle difficult projects? Difficult clients? Or difficult employee situations? If so, how large were the projects, and how many clients or employees were involved?

- What made the situation difficult? How did you resolve it?

- Are you really good at a particular task? Are you faster and better at it than other employees? If so, why?

- Do others rely on you for certain tasks even though such tasks fall outside of your job description? If so, what kinds of tasks have you been responsible for? How large or complex were the tasks?

QUESTION 8: Do you have technical or special skills relevant to your objective?

Many people have completed specialized training or developed technical skills on their own. However, many job seekers think that their job skills are not special. For example, the mechanic below felt that just stating he was an auto mechanic was enough and that everyone would certainly understand the depth of his skills. However, do you form a different impression of him when reading the After example? Provide enough detail about the technical or special skills you've gained so that you look like the best candidate.

BEFORE **Auto Mechanic**
- Completed AAA Certificate Program enabling me to service vehicles produced by top 5 manufacturers.

AFTER **AAA Certified Automotive Technician**
- <u>Awarded 5 AAA Certificates</u>, achieving a test score of 96.5 to service vehicles by top 5 manufacturers.
- Of 200 applicants completing program was commended as 1 of 5 for nationwide achievement.

BEFORE **Customer Service Representative**
- Answered customer questions regarding telecommunications systems and software.

AFTER **Technical Support / Customer Service Representative**
- Provided <u>technical support for telecommunication systems</u> valued up to $ 1/4 million per system.
- Served as key account representative to 50 accounts including Microsoft, Hewlett-Packard, and UPS.

BEFORE **Word Processor**
- Used word processing and spreadsheet programs to produce correspondence, spreadsheets, and newsletters.

AFTER **Executive Support / Computerized Office Applications**
- Provided <u>executive word processing and contract support</u> to 8 Department Managers.
- <u>Utilized MS Word and Excel to produce multimillion-dollar contracts</u>, correspondence, and spreadsheets.

As mentioned above, most people make the mistake of being too general when they describe their technical skills. Give enough description so that employers fully understand the depth of your technical expertise. These questions can help you describe technical skills:

- Do you use computer programs? If so, name the program and what you produce with the program.
- Do you provide technical support or training to other staff, departments, or customers? If so, how many?
- Will listing the job titles of people you have supported or trained, their duties, or the departments where they worked show the depth of your experience and knowledge in a particular field, department, or job function?

- What areas of technical or special knowledge did you have to learn to do your job? Describe such knowledge if it relates to and supports your job objective.
- Do you use technical tools, equipment, processes, or procedures to do your job? If so, list them.

QUESTION 9: Do you have experience training or supervising staff? If so, how many?

This is a very straightforward question. However, most of us think too narrowly when answering it. The first example below is a case in point. Originally this person wrote that he supervised two clerks per shift. However, cumulatively he had trained over 200 people. Which is more impressive? Ask yourself how many people you have hired, trained, or supervised during the entire time with a department, company, or over your career. Giving cumulative answers can really beef up your image.

BEFORE   **Assistant Manager**
- Trained employees, completed accounting records, and supervised store in absence of manager.

AFTER   **Branch Management**
- <u>Trained and supervised over 200 sales and customer service staff</u> working 3 shifts in 2 locations.
- Supervised staff completing accounting records, bank deposits, sales and expense reports.

BEFORE   **Sergeant, U.S. Army**
- Trained platoon, overseeing infantry, equipment servicing, and personnel schedules.

AFTER   **Departmental Manager**
- Managed staff of 45, overseeing equipment and preparing all departmental reports and documentation.
- <u>Trained a total of 750 executive, management, and administrative staff</u> over a 5-year period.

BEFORE   **Secretary**
- Provided administrative support to executive staff and trained new clerical employees as needed.

AFTER   **Training of Administrative Staff / Departmental Support**
- Provided administrative support to 5 departments including the Vice President and Department Managers.
- <u>Trained 45 administrative staff in customer service, word processing, and accounting functions.</u>

Be sure to think broadly about your staff training or supervisory skills and use numbers to show the depth of your responsibilities. These questions can also help you describe your training and supervisory skills:

- How many people have you trained at any one time? Or in total, throughout your entire career?
- What types of duties, skills, or systems did you train staff to perform or to use?
- How many people have you supervised at any one time? Or in total, throughout your entire career?
- Will mentioning their titles, job functions, or the departments they worked for further demonstrate the depth of your knowledge or experience?
- Was there any type of documentation, paperwork, or reports that you had to complete regarding your training or supervision of staff?

QUESTION 10: Have you received promotions that demonstrate achievement?

Many people are promoted several times throughout their careers, yet their resumes don't include this information. As a result, employers never learn about career progress and aren't able to consider it when evaluating applicant resumes. As you can see below, knowing that these individuals were promoted, why they were promoted, how quickly they were promoted, and the results of their promotions is very powerful. Use these examples to describe your promotion(s), and slant the information you provide to be supportive of your job objective.

BEFORE **Dry-Cleaner Manager**
- Promoted from Assistant Manager to Manager by recommending replacement of obsolete equipment.

AFTER **Operations Manager / Customer Service Administration**
- Managed customer service and daily operations for 2,000 customer accounts with sales of $ $1/4$ million.
- <u>Promoted to Manager, within two weeks of hire for implementing system that increased productivity by 25%.</u>

BEFORE **Head Bookkeeper's Assistant**
- Was consistently promoted since being hired as a posting clerk.

AFTER **Customer & Vendor Account Processing**
- Provided customer service for 1,200 A/R and A/P accounts with annual transactions of $1.5 million.
- <u>Within 6 months of hire was given full responsibility for customer and vendor account processing.</u>

BEFORE **Editor**
- Managed editing functions for computer division; receiving two bonuses for exceeding unit goals.

AFTER **Microsoft Press—Senior Editor**
- Managed all editing functions for Microsoft Press's computer division with sales of $20 million annually.
- Within last 6 months have received two salary advances for division achieving top sales of 7 divisions.

As the last example shows, be sure to include the times when you might not have been given a new title but in effect received a promotion because you were given new job duties or a higher salary. These additional questions can help you describe promotions or job advancement:

- Have you received a promotion, a new title, or additional job duties? If so, why? What did you accomplish?

- How long had you been employed with your company or department before being promoted or advanced?

- Will mentioning the range of your new job duties expand your image and improve your chances of getting the job you want?

- Were you in competition with other employees or departments in order to receive the promotion or award? If so, how many people, departments, or divisions did you compete with?

- Are personal traits like being success-driven, goal-oriented, or self-motivated a big reason you were promoted? If so, integrate such descriptions into the statements you write for your resume.

QUESTION 11: Have you received any awards or certificates that relate to your job objective?

Many people receive awards and certificates throughout their careers, yet they never put this information in their resumes. Or if they do, they don't provide enough information to show employers how it relates to the job they're applying for. Since most people don't put enough detailed information in their resumes to show the depth of their experience, those that do stand out and look the most qualified.

BEFORE **Horse Trainer**
- Received numerous awards for showmanship of quarter horses.

AFTER **International Award Winner / Master Equestrian Trainer**
- <u>Won International Championship and 35 First Place Awards</u> for showmanship of quarter horses.
- Trained over 2,000 quarter horses for clients throughout the U.S., Canada, and Hawaii.

BEFORE **Corporate Training**
- Completed corporate training program and acceptance to attend AT&T's National Management Program.

AFTER **AT&T National Management Certificate**
- <u>Completed AT&T's Management Program</u>; selected as 1 of 3 candidates from 3 divisions of 400 staff.
- Currently in line for fast track promotion to Regional Management position.

BEFORE **Boeing Assembly—Production Award**
- Analyzed and streamlined paper flow utilized by production personnel in 5 departments.

AFTER **Increased Productivity / Cost Savings Award**
- Analyzed and streamlined documentation systems utilized by 200 employees in 5 departments.
- <u>Received award</u> for increasing productivity and cost savings by over $34,000.

Be sure to include any awards, certificates, commendations, or letters of recommendation you received for meeting goals or improving performance or profitability that relate to and support your job objective. Be sure to show how the award or what you learned relates to your current job objective. These questions may also help:

- Why did you receive the award, commendation, or recommendation? What did you accomplish?

- If you completed an area of study to win an award or certificate, what did you study?

- How comprehensive was the area of study? How many hours or units did you complete?

- Will listing the courses, subject areas, units, equipment, or procedures you learned to use show the depth of your knowledge or experience in an area that is needed in the job you want?

- Did you compete with other employees or departments to win the award? If so, how many did you compete with?

QUESTION 12: Have you identified the top five skill requirements for the position you want?

Did you identify the top five skills required for the last job you applied for? Did you build your resume around those skills? When I ask a large group of people this question, only one in ten say they designed their resumes around the top skills required for the job. This means that most resumes are extremely ineffective and explains why statistics show such dismal results from using them. Most people never create resumes that match the job they're looking for. They merely list job after job, without slanting it to sound like what each industry or employer needs. By identifying the top five skills required for the job you want and building a resume around them, you'll automatically put yourself in the top five to ten percent of people applying for the job. In the left-hand column you'll see a list of skills required for an accounting position. In the right-hand column you'll see how skills gained at McDonald's can be slanted to match an accounting position.

Five Top Skills Required for Accounting Position	How McDonald's Experience Matches Top Five Accounting Skills
Light Accounting Experience	**Cash Accountability / Recordkeeping** • Accounted for up to $300,000 monthly, completing sales reports and maintaining cash in 3 tills.
10-Key	**Computerized Cashiering / 10-Key** • Utilized computerized cashiering system to balance hourly cash between $1,000 to $2,000.
Deposits, Reconciliations	**Safe Deposits / Balancing of Tills** • Balanced tills and prepared safe deposit records for each shift with deposits of up to $10,000.
Customer Service	**Customer Service / Problem Solving** • Dealt with up to 200 customers daily, resolving problems and promoting public relations.
Team Player	**Team Coordination** • Served as Team Leader, coordinating workflow of 10 staff in 3 departments.

Using this example as a guide, review the list of skills and skill headings you've developed. Have you done as good a job as this example does in showing how your skill headings and titles match the position you want? If not, strengthen them.

Many of the top skills employers list are the ones you will be required to perform on a daily basis. Be sure to include a full list of the primary job duties you have been responsible for that are the same or similar to the primary job duties you'll perform in the position you want.

In addition, employers want to hire well-rounded employees. Employers need employees with core skills such as typing, programming, or supervisory ability. But they also need employees who get along with other staff members, work well with customers, can solve problems, are self-motivated, and care about the job they do. The example above presents a well-rounded picture of this employee. He has core accounting and computer skills but can also deal with customers, solve problems, and coordinate with other team members. Make sure the skill headings and job titles you include in your resume present the full range of your skills and market you as a well-rounded employee.

Now that you've gotten the bulk of your skills onto paper, the next chapter will show you how to refine and prioritize the statements you put in your resume.

7 Strengthening Your Resume Content

Now that you've prepared a rough draft of your resume by completing the Six Steps Worksheets, you're ready to fine-tune it. To begin, we'll discuss the importance of using powerful skill headings and job titles in order to grab an employer's attention and sell your top qualifications in seconds. Then we'll discuss how to create resume statements that convey the depth of your skills and achievements and motivate employers to call you for an interview.

Use Advertising Secrets to Create Powerful Resume Headings

Advertisers use headlines to grab our attention and convey a message that is meaningful to us. Ad agencies spend millions of dollars studying and testing such headlines. Even slight changes in headlines can make a dramatic difference in the number of responses an ad generates. Which of the headlines shown below do you think would draw in a substantially higher rate of responses?

CUT YOUR ELECTRICITY BILL BY $600

HOME OWNERS! CUT YOUR ELECTRICITY BILL BY $600

Ads with headings like "Home Owners!" have been shown to yield up to twenty-four percent more responses. Take a moment and try to figure out why a heading like this is so much more effective. The secret, of course, is that it targets a group of people and speaks directly to them. Job seekers also see dramatic differences when they use titles and headings that speak to employers and are targeted. The same phenomenon is at work in the resume examples throughout this book and helps explain why they have generated such high interview rates. By using job titles or skill headings that are targeted to match each employer's needs and integrating them into the design of your resume, you too will see a dramatic rise in the number of interviews you generate.

The Power of Targeted Resume Headings

On page 104 you'll see Grant's Before resume. Initially, Grant had reacted quite negatively to several of the resumes I use in my presentation. He felt they looked like direct mail pieces. To turn Grant's thinking around, I asked him, "So you're saying that you don't want to use strategies that have been proven to increase salaries up to $20,000 to $30,000 or more per year?" Hearing this question, I saw understanding begin to dawn on Grant's face. He replied, "No, I'm not saying that. I just think these resumes look too fancy for a driver like me." I replied, "Then use the concepts you're learning but create a resume with design and headings that feel comfortable to you. Your resume doesn't have to look exactly like mine. Just be sure that it directs and controls the eye path and that your main skills or job titles stand out."

Two weeks later I ran into Grant in the parking lot. He was thrilled because his resume had landed him a $49,000 position that took his salary from $18 per hour to $24 per hour. Obviously, Grant had done a good job of identifying skills that the employer wanted to hear about. Even though Grant's resume design is not how I would have laid it out, it was definitely effective.

Grant D. Smith
(555) 555-5555

1515 Michigan Avenue
Chicago, IL 00099

Objective

Seeking a position as a Driver Sales Representative, utilizing the following route sales and account management experience:

Summary of Qualifications

- Over 10 years successful experience in driving/route sales.
- 5 years key account sales experience calling on chain stores such as 7-11.
- Strong Sales Achiever awarded for increasing sales $ 1/2 million annually.
- Proven ability to penetrate and develop competitive accounts.
- Class A, Commercial Drivers License operating a 2-ton delivery truck.
- Awarded for achieving lowest driving insurance premiums of 23 statewide routes.

Route Management / Sales Experience

- Increased average in-store inventories by 55%.
- Managed 250 key accounts in greater Chicago area, including draft, bottled, and packaged products.
- Promoted and supported seasonal promotions and increased sales during special events for Coliseum and Dome events.
- Awarded for Outstanding Sales Achievement for achieving top sales while competing with 20 route drivers during national play-off events and games.
- Consistently met seasonal promotion quotas and sales deadlines during all local and national football, basketball, and baseball season games.
- Managed cash of up to $ 1/4 million with many key accounts commending me to headquarters for eliminating charge backs and errors in invoicing to their accounts.

Problem Solving and Customer Service

- Instrumental in increasing route sales from $1.6 million to $2.1 million annually.
- Maximized sales by introducing new product lines and setting up seasonal promotions that increased stock turnover rate from 2 turns up to 7 turns in some stores.
- Due to outstanding relationships developed with store managers was given premium shelf space, which increased sales by more than 10% annually.
- Consulted clients regarding unique account needs and developed effective solutions.
- Created customized displays to promote special events and in-store specials.
- Made an average of 20 deliveries per day, calling on a minimum of 20 new accounts per month.

Employment History

Sales/Route Driver, Major Beverage Distributor 1990–1999
Sales/Route Driver, NW Beverage Chain Sales 1986–1990

Grant D. Smith   1515 Michigan Avenue
(555) 555-5555   Chicago, IL 00099

Objective

Seeking a position as an Account Executive utilizing over 10 years experience
in Beverage / Key Account Development and Territory Management.

History of Top Beverage Sales

- Over 10 years successful experience marketing beverage products to key
  accounts.
- Strong Sales Achiever awarded for increasing sales by $ $1/2$ million annually.
- Proven ability to penetrate and develop major competitive accounts.

BEVERAGE SALES / MAJOR ACCOUNT MANAGEMENT

- Increased average in-store beverage sales by 55% while managing a territory of 250
  key accounts in greater Chicago area, including draft, bottled, and packaged products.
- Promoted and supported seasonal promotions and achieved a consistent history of
  increased sales during major national sports events.
- Awarded for Outstanding Sales Achievement for achieving top sales while competing
  with 20 territory managers.
- Consistently met seasonal promotion quotas and sales deadlines.
- Gained extensive beverage sales experience working as a route driver.

Management of Territory, Key Accounts, and Customer Relationships

- Instrumental in increasing territory sales from $1.6 million to $2.1 million annually.
- Maximized sales by introducing new product lines and setting up seasonal promotions,
  which increased stock turnover rate from 2 turns up to 7 turns in many locations.
- Due to outstanding relationships developed with store managers was given premium
  shelf space, which increased sales by more than 10% annually.
- Consulted clients regarding unique account needs and developed effective solutions.
- Created customized displays to promote special events and in-store specials.
- Called on a minimum of 20 new accounts per month in addition to maintaining a
  consistent program to increase sales to all 250 key accounts.

Employment History

Territory Management (Route Driver), Major Beverage Distributor 1990–1999

Key Account Sales (Route Driver), NW Beverage Chain Sales 1986–1990

When you look at Grant's resume, where does your eye go very quickly? For most people, it's the "Route Management/Sales Experience" heading. Then where does your eye go? Probably to "Problem Solving and Customer Service." These skill headings present Grant as much more than just a driver. I'm sure that's why he got the interview. Then he landed the job because he was able to articulate the best of his skills.

But if a resume doesn't use powerful headings or titles, it's likely to fail no matter how nice it looks. Take time to study the sample resumes in Chapter 11 and use design elements such as bolding, centering, or graphic lines to get attention. But be sure that the headings and titles you use in your resume are what really pack the punch!

Create Customized Headings for Specific Positions

It's very likely that you will find jobs that require some skills or experience you possess but haven't listed in your resume. Let's use Grant as an example. Even though he landed a great position as a route sales manager, let's say instead he had wanted to apply for a position as an account executive marketing beverage products to major grocery chain accounts. This position would require that he call on regional chain managers in corporate headquarters for firms such as Safeway or Acme. With this in mind, go back to Grant's resume and read the headings. Do those headings make Grant sound qualified for an account executive position, or do they make him sound underqualified? On the surface it looks like Grant isn't qualified for such a job. However, like many job seekers, Grant has all of the skills needed for an array of different jobs. He merely needs to relabel his experience to match that expected of an account executive.

Take a moment and see how we made slight changes in the headings of Grant's After resume on page 105 that dramatically changed his image. Does this resume now create an image of Grant as being qualified for an account executive position? You'll also notice that we adapted several statements in this resume to better match this position.

As you find positions that request skills not already included in your resume, tweak the headings and modify or expand your job titles until they are a better match and create the image you want. Adapt the statements in your resume to stress particular areas of experience each employer may need. You can do this by utilizing keywords stressed in help-wanted ads or job descriptions. This process often takes only minutes yet yields big results in the form of more interviews and increased salary offers.

How Many Skill Headings or Job Titles Should You Use?

I like to use three or four skill headings or job titles in a one-page resume. Sometimes I use two or three main headings or job titles with a few subheadings underneath.

The goal is to keep your resume looking streamlined so that the reader's eye moves to and concentrates on your top skills or titles within that first critical five- to ten-second glance. Too many headings or job titles defeat this purpose. By reviewing the resume examples in Chapter 11 you can get a good feel for how many headings or titles to use.

How to Edit Your Resume Statements for Maximum Impact

Now let's walk through five steps designed to polish the statements you'll use in your resume. To illustrate, I've shown how Roger went through these steps below. In Step 1, write out your original statements. In Step 2, rewrite them by using past tense, action verbs. In Step 3, write out each edited statement. In Step 4, add numbers to quantify each element or area of experience you describe. Then in Step 5, write out your new, more powerful statement. Follow this five-step process to strengthen each statement you'll include in your resume.

Compare the original statements in Roger's Step 1 to the final statements in Step 5. In the last step, you'll notice that Roger's image and perceived experience level have been elevated dramatically.

HOW TO CREATE STRONG RESUME STATEMENTS

STEP 1: BEFORE STATEMENTS

- Under direction of site supervisor completed construction projects independently.
- Worked with subcontractors and tradespeople telling them what to do.

STEP 2: REVISE USING ACTION VERBS

- ~~Under direction of site supervisor~~ _{Managed and} completed ∧ _{various phases of} construction projects ~~independently.~~
- ~~Worked with~~ _{Supervised and delegated work to} subcontractors and tradespeople ~~telling them what to do.~~

STEP 3: AFTER SENTENCES WITH ACTION VERBS

- Managed and completed various phases of construction projects.
- Supervised and delegated work to subcontractors and tradespeople.

STEP 4: NOW QUANTIFY AND ADD NUMBERS

- Managed and completed various phases of construction projects <u>valued to $2 million.</u>
- Supervised and delegated work to ∧ _{crews of up to 12} subcontractors and tradespeople.

STEP 5: CREATE FINAL STATEMENTS

- Managed and completed various phases of construction projects valued to $2 million.
- Supervised and delegated work to crews of up to 12 subcontractors and tradespeople.

Use Action Verbs

Start each of your statements with an action verb. This will give them more impact. Action verbs can also help you express yourself more directly and eliminate unnecessary words. In Step 2 above, Doug eliminated three words by using "Managed" to replace "Was responsible for." By eliminating unnecessary words, you will save space for important achievements and make your resume easier to read.

You'll find a list of more than 500 action verbs in the Appendix on pages 314 to 315. Use it to vary the verbs used in your resume. Words like "managed" and "supervised" are good, but you can also use words such as "directed," "controlled," and "oversaw" as substitutes that add variety. Select verbs that add power to your resume. Match them to the level of responsibility you want and the salary you want. For example, let's consider a secretary who wants to move into management. She should use action verbs such as "managed," "directed," "controlled," "delegated," and "supervised" to promote her management skills. An executive's resume will be more powerful if it uses verbs such as "spearheaded," "launched," "reengineered," "restructured," and "strategized." Avoid using words that weaken your image (skills, abilities, entry level, clerk, worker, assistant, person, graduate, trainee, clerical, part-time, volunteer, help, laborer) unless these words are a direct match to the job you want.

Prioritize the Statements for Maximum Impact

Once you've edited and strengthened all of your statements, the next step is to prioritize them by importance. Put the most powerful statements first, where they will have the most impact. Compare the set of statements below. Can you see what a difference the order makes?

BEFORE
- Selected and delegated responsibility to 5 lead personnel.
- Coordinated with 20 subcontractors and directed project completion.
- Managed commercial projects valued to $1.5 million.

AFTER
- Managed commercial projects valued to $1.5 million.
- Coordinated with 20 subcontractors and directed project completion.
- Selected and delegated responsibility to 5 lead personnel.

Prioritizing all the statements you'll use in your resume gives you a good overview of your top skills and abilities. Next you'll use this information to craft an objective statement that markets those skills effectively.

8 Creating Powerful Objective Statements

Now that you've learned to how write dynamic statements for the body of your resume, you're ready to carry that knowledge into the process of crafting a powerful objective statement. In this chapter we'll review objective statements from real resumes. One increased its author's salary by $4,800 per year, and another helped an applicant gain an incredible $42,000 more per year!

To begin, we'll discuss whether or not you should use an objective statement. Then you'll be taken through the process of completing three different types of objective statements and selecting which one is the best for you. At the end of this chapter you'll complete a worksheet that will guide you step-by-step in creating a powerful objective statement.

Should You Use an Objective Statement?

An objective statement tells an employer why he or she has received your resume, what position or field you desire, and your qualifications. Pretend you're an employer. You can imagine what it would be like to sort through 200 resumes without objective statements on them. If job titles, areas of experience, or skill headings didn't jump out and get your attention, you'd have no idea what each person was qualified to do. And you certainly wouldn't have the time to read each and every resume to figure it out. Even if you thought you knew where each person fit—chances are you'd be wrong!

If You Don't Include an Objective Statement

Even though it's usually best to include an objective statement, you can create an effective resume without one. However, you need to make certain that it is very clear to employers what kind of position you are qualified for as soon as they glance at your resume. For example, look at Sheila's resume on page 143. It's clear that she wants a bookkeeping or office management position in which she can use her experience supervising staff and overseeing customer service administration. Even though Sheila didn't use an objective statement, her carefully designed resume more than doubled her interview rate and increased her annual salary by ten percent. If you choose not to use an objective statement, make sure that your job titles and skill headings stand out, just as Sheila did, and that they specify the type of job you want. Otherwise, you may lose interviews.

If you omit the objective statement from your resume, then it's wise to also specify the type of job you want in your cover letters. It's also important to know that many employers who process resumes by scanning them into computer databases don't scan cover letters. It's therefore wise to include an objective statement in your resume if you know that it will be scanned. This is also true with employers who accept resumes via e-mail. They may read your cover letter but probably won't enter it into their databases. So if you're submitting your resume and cover letter via e-mail, then it's also wise to include an objective statement in your resume.

If You Know the Position You Want to Apply For

If you want a specific position, it's good to state this in your objective so employers will clearly understand what you want and if they can provide it. For example, Beth wanted a better position as an executive secretary. This was the only type of position she would consider. Therefore, our goal was to write an objective statement that projected a strong image of her executive secretarial skills. Here's what we came up with:

DO

OBJECTIVE:

Position as an Executive Secretary utilizing my
Executive Support, Project Management, and Computer Expertise.

The description shown above projects a very competent image. It pulls together three key areas of Beth's experience as strong reasons to hire her as an executive secretary. Compare it to Beth's original statement below. Which statement will be more likely to get Beth the type of position she wants? As you can see, naming a specific position and then backing it up with your skills make a strong objective statement.

DON'T

OBJECTIVE:

Seek a secretarial position offering challenge and growth.

Drawbacks to Stating a Specific Objective

There can be drawbacks to naming a specific position. You may find that openings for the position you want are not as available as you thought. Or you may decide you want to consider several positions. Or you may find a position that you qualify for but has a different title than the one you named in your objective statement. In these instances you may lose interviews if you don't adapt or broaden your objective statement. The best way to handle this situation is to make several versions of your resume. Create different objective statements for each type of position you want. If this is not practical, then create a version with a broader objective statement—one that focuses on the skills you want to use rather than specific job titles.

Emphasize Skills Rather than Competing Titles

In your objective statement, avoid listing job titles that conflict with one another. Tara has been a restaurant manager, a production manager, and a retail sales manager. If she were to create an objective statement that included all three of these titles, employers would question the type of job she really wants and what she's really qualified for. It's better for Tara to create one resume for each type of position she wants. If this isn't possible, then she should create an objective statement that markets a range of skills common to all positions. Compare the first two objective statements on the next page. The second clearly markets Tara more effectively. The third statement has been modified slightly for use when applying for a restaurant manager position.

DON'T

OBJECTIVE:

Seek a Restaurant Manager, Production Manager, or Retail Sales Manager position.

DO

Seek a position utilizing over 10 years experience in Operations Management, Staff
Supervision, and Workflow Scheduling with history of increased sales, production, and profits.

DO

Seek a position utilizing over 10 years experience in Restaurant Operations Management,
Staff Supervision, and Workflow Scheduling with history of increased sales, production, and profits.

Avoid General Statements

Avoid naming general skills in your objective statement. For example, Ed's resume had this
statement at the top of it, which is similar to the objective statements used in many resumes:

DON'T

OBJECTIVE:

Seek a position utilizing my people skills.

What exactly does "people skills" mean? It could mean customer service, sales, nursing, or
counseling skills. This statement doesn't tell an employer anything important because it's too
general. When employers read statements like this, they tune out. They want to be convinced of
a person's *specific* skills and abilities. Read Ed's revised objective statement below. It gets right to
the point.

DO

OBJECTIVE:

Seek a position utilizing over 5 years Customer Service Experience managing 300 customer
accounts with proven ability to interface with a diverse customer base and resolve problems.

Don't Describe What You Want

Every employer wants an employee who is willing to give one hundred percent and do his or her
best. Objective statements that mention the desire for challenge, adequate compensation,
respect, or growth opportunities come off sounding self-oriented rather than company-oriented.
Employers don't want to hire people who are only interested in what they're going to get from
a company. Take a look at these examples:

DON'T

OBJECTIVE:

• Position that will compensate me for my work and provide continuing growth opportunities.
• Seek a challenging position with opportunity for advancement.
• Seek a position with a major firm that will result in increased responsibility.

Do these statements tell an employer what the applicant is willing or able to do for the company? Do they present a strong image, or do they project a weak image that wastes resume space? By stating your specific skills and abilities, you will tell employers what you can give, rather than what you can take. Your motto should be "What can I do for this company?" instead of "What can this company do for me?"

Powerful Objective Statements

Following are examples of three different variations or ways to create an objective statement. Which one do you think is the strongest? Next you'll learn to write each kind—and learn why the third is especially powerful.

Seek a Financial Management position utilizing my background as a C.P.A., Portfolio Manager, and Accounting Supervisor.

OR

Seek a position utilizing my Certified Public Accounting, Financial Administration, and General Accounting Management experience.

OR

Seek a Financial Management position utilizing 10 years C.P.A. experience:

- Directing financial and accounting functions for 5 divisions with revenues in excess of $120 million annually.
- Overseeing portfolio and financial planning for fixed assets and investments totaling $12 million.
- Supervising staff of up to 45 accounting and administrative personnel.
- M.B.A., University of Colorado 1984.

Objective Statements and Significant Salary Increases

Next we'll review two sets of objective statements that significantly increased Marilyn's and Frank's salaries, respectively. Let's start with Marilyn's story. Marilyn had just taken nine months off to care for her new baby and wanted to reenter the work force. I still remember how unsure and tense Marilyn was when she asked, "I was in the $32,000 range. Now I'm not even sure I can start back to work at that salary—but I really need that to pay for daycare. What do you think?" I told her that I thought she could make up to $40,000.

While completing the Twelve Questions in Chapter 6, Marilyn let me know that she had supervised up to 142 full-time and seasonal staff. Of course, this needed to be in her resume. But Marilyn got very concerned and said, "But I didn't manage these people all the time. It was only for a few months each year." Since Marilyn hadn't had this duty full-time, it scared her to put it right at the top of her resume. I told her it takes a lot of skill to integrate and supervise an additional one hundred people in peak seasons. These are valuable skills that she could market for a new management job. After we discussed it, Marilyn included this information in her objective statement.

She called me about a month later. She had just turned down a position paying $57,000 because the commute was too long. Then about a year later, I saw Marilyn while I was giving a presentation. She shared this story with the participants: "The last time I talked with Regina, I had just turned down a $57,000 offer. Then I accepted a $74,000 position. Now I'm looking at a minimum salary of $80,000—but only a year ago I was asking Regina if I could get back in the work force at $32,000."

Frank's story is also memorable because his new resume took him from a lower-level clerical position to an office management position. He bounded into my office, beaming that he had landed a job that gave him an office with a door and a $4,800 annual increase! Both Marilyn's and Frank's resumes used an objective statement like the last one shown above. Comparing the three statements above, the last one is the most powerful—it's also the one that I've seen generate the greatest number of interviews and salary increases. The worksheets on the next four pages show how we created dynamic objective statements for Marilyn and Frank.

Objective Statement That Landed a $42,000 Salary Increase

Strong skill headings and job titles are an important part of creating powerful objective statements. Below you'll notice that Marilyn had been an assistant store manager, an account supervisor, and an outside sales representative. She wanted an operations or departmental management position, but her titles weakened her image, so we replaced them with stronger skill headings. We then used these skill headings to create three different objective statements.

OBJECTIVE: Operations or Departmental Manager

Job Titles	New Skill Headings
Assistant Store Manager	Operations / Departmental Management or Staff Supervision
Account Supervisor	Customer Service Management
Outside Sales Representative	Key Account Management

In box one on the following page, Marilyn created two different objective statements by naming the position she wanted, the three skill areas that matched her objective, and the years of experience she had.

In box two, Marilyn created another objective statement by naming the skills she wanted to use in case she found a position that wasn't titled "Operations or Departmental Manager."

The objective statement that landed Marilyn the $42,000 salary increase is in box three. To create this objective statement, Marilyn reviewed the main sections of her resume and put check marks next to the strongest statements that showed experience in each of her skill areas. Marilyn then used these statements to create her objective statement.

The worksheet on page 117 will help you create all three types of objective statements. Do so, then select the one you feel is the strongest. I urge you to create the third type of objective statement, one that takes an objective and combines it with a supporting list of experience.

1) Name a Specific Position

Seek an *Operations Management* position utilizing my *Staff Supervision, Departmental and Customer Service Management* experience.

OR

Seek an *Operations Management* position utilizing over 10 years *Staff Supervision, Departmental and Customer Service Management* experience.

2) Name Your Skills

Seek a position utilizing my *Operations, Departmental and Customer Service Management* experience.

BEST STATEMENTS FROM SECTIONS OF MARILYN'S RESUME

Job Title: *Assistant Store Manager* Skill Heading: *Operations/Departmental Management*

√ • Directed operations for facility generating sales in excess of $6 million annually.
√ • Supervised staff of up to 142 sales and customer service employees.
 • Generated sales of $1 million per month, three years in a row for December sales.
 • Set up mail order department, increasing sales by 23% in first year of operation.

Job Title: *Account Supervisor* Skill Heading: *Customer Service Management*

√ • Managed customer service department processing $120,000 in monthly orders.
 • Trained and supervised a staff of 12 Customer Service Representatives.
 • Managed computerized customer database and reporting for 2,000 key accounts.
 • Resolved all account returns to ensure satisfaction, repeat and referral sales.

Job Title: *Outside Sales* Skill Heading: *Key Account Management*

√ • Oversaw 200 commercial accounts, negotiating individual sales up to $125,000.
 • Achieved fastest start-up performance in Seattle branch.
 • Consistently ranked in top 5% competing with 60 Regional Sales Representatives.
 • Negotiated contracts and coordinated equipment requirements.

3) Combine Your Objective with Your Qualifications

OBJECTIVE & QUALIFICATIONS

Seek an _Operations or Departmental Management_ position

utilizing over 10 years experience:

- Directing operations for facility generating sales in excess of $6 million annually.
- Supervising staff of up to 142 sales and customer service employees.
- Managing customer service department processing $120,000 in monthly orders.
- Overseeing 200 commercial accounts, negotiating individual sales up to $125,000.

Objective Statement That Landed a $4,800 Annual Increase

Frank also needed to revamp his image. Below you'll notice that he had been a receptionist, a CRT specialist, and an accounts receivable clerk. His goal was to become an office manager. While these job titles show diverse office experience, they don't convey that he is qualified to become an office manager. Notice that in the box below Frank listed his job titles and then replaced them with skill headings. He then used these skill headings to create strong objective statements.

OBJECTIVE: Office Manager

Job Titles	New Skill Headings
Receptionist	Front Office Administration / Executive Support
CRT Specialist	Account Management or Customer Service
A / R Clerk	Bookkeeping or Accounts Receivable

In box one on the following page, Frank created two different objective statements by naming the position he wanted, the three skill areas that matched his objective, and the years of experience he had.

In box two, Frank created another objective statement by naming the skills he wanted to use in case he found an interesting position that wasn't titled "Office Manager."

The objective statement that landed Frank the salary increase is in box three. To create this objective statement, Frank reviewed the main sections of his resume and put check marks next to the strongest sentences that showed experience in each of his skill areas. Frank then used these statements to create his objective statement section.

The worksheet on page 117 will help you create all three types of objective statements. Complete them, then select the one you feel is the strongest. I urge you to create an objective statement like the third type, which combines your objective with your qualifications.

1) Name a Specific Position

Seek an _Office Management_ position utilizing my _Executive Support, Customer Service, and Bookkeeping_ experience.

OR:

Seek an _Office Management_ position utilizing over 7 years _Office Administration, Executive Support, and Bookkeeping_ experience.

2) Name Your Skills

Seek a position utilizing my _Office Administration, Executive Support, and Bookkeeping_ experience.

BEST STATEMENTS FROM SECTIONS OF FRANK'S RESUME

Job Title: _Receptionist_ Skill Heading: _Front Office Administration / Executive Support_

✓ • Managed front office administration to support staff of 15.
✓ • Provided secretarial support to President and sales staff.
 • Prepared all contract documents for individual projects valued to $1 million.
 • Set up tracking system that decreased processing time 10%.

Job Title: _CRT Specialist_ Skill Heading: _Account Management or Customer Service_

✓ • Managed 1,500 computerized customer accounts.
 • Coordinated with 20 field agents to process up to 200 claims daily.
 • Served as liaison between 5 departments and sales agents.
 • Prepared correspondence and claim verifications.

Job Title: _A / R Clerk_ Skill Heading: _Bookkeeping or Accounts Receivable_

✓ • Maintained bookkeeping for 1,200 A / R accounts.
 • Negotiated payment schedules and authorized credit to $2,500.
 • Set up new accounts and verified credit references.
 • Prepared weekly, monthly, and quarterly receivables reports.

3) *Combine Your Objective with Your Qualifications*

OBJECTIVE & QUALIFICATIONS

Seek an *Office Management* position utilizing the following background:

- Managing front office administration to support staff of 15.
- Providing secretarial support to President and sales staff.
- Managing 1,500 computerized customer accounts.
- Maintaining bookkeeping for 1,200 A / R accounts.

OBJECTIVE WORKSHEET

1) NAME A SPECIFIC POSITION

Seek a _____ position utilizing my _____,

_____, and _____ experience.

OR

Seek a _____ position utilizing over _____ years of

_____, _____, and _____ experience.

2) NAME YOUR SKILLS

Seek a position utilizing my _____,

_____, and _____ experience.

3) COMBINE YOUR OBJECTIVE WITH YOUR QUALIFICATIONS

OBJECTIVE & QUALIFICATIONS

Seek a _____ position utilizing the following background:

- _____
- _____
- _____
- _____

9 What You Should and Shouldn't Tell Employers

Many clients come to me because they've sent out resumes but haven't gotten interviews. Not surprisingly, many of their resumes included irrelevant or even damaging information. This chapter will help ensure that you don't end up in a similar predicament. You'll learn how to eliminate any information that will keep you from getting interviews. And on the flip side, you'll learn more about what to include and how to word it in order to generate more interviews.

Let's go back to a fundamental question: "What do employers want to see on resumes?" They want to see and read information that is relevant to the position you are applying for. Employers want to be reassured and feel confident that they are making the right choice in interviewing and ultimately hiring you. Therefore it's imperative that your resume project an image that meets their needs. Because your resume is first and foremost a marketing tool, it should include any experience, skills, or knowledge that will get you in for an interview. The flip side of that is making sure that nothing in your resume creates any doubts about you, or your skills, in the mind of an employer reading it.

Analyze all the information that you consider putting into your resume. Supplying the wrong data, or presenting it inadequately, can damage your chance for an interview. If it supports your objective, include it. If it doesn't, then leave it out. Word all information to maximize the image you want to project. Remember, employers must eliminate dozens of applicants as they sort resumes. If employers read anything about you that makes you appear undesirable, your resume will be tossed out. We'll consider the pros and cons of including or excluding certain data and where it should be placed on the following pages. There are no strict rules about selecting or omitting data. You will need to judge the relevancy of information you provide based on your objective and the image you want to project.

One-Page versus Two-Page Resumes

How long should a resume be? Many employers prefer a one-page resume because of the volume of resumes they receive and the time it takes to sort them. However, a two-page resume can be effective if you highlight your most important data on the front page. If you put important information on the second page without highlighting it on the front page, employers may not be motivated to turn to the second page and it may never be seen. This can cause you to lose interviews and possibly a job.

To maximize the success of a two-page resume, ask yourself, "What are my top selling points? Have I drawn attention to them on the front page of my resume? If appropriate, have I included them in my objective?" Be sure you can answer "yes" to each of these questions before you send out a two-page resume.

I generally recommend preparing a one-page resume for several reasons. Getting your background onto one page makes you narrow your focus to your strongest skills. This also helps you to be more directed and articulate when presenting those skills in an interview. Some people include too much detail in their resumes and create three- and four-page resumes that ramble. These resumes are so long and boring that no one reads them. I always wonder if the people I'm reading about are this long-winded and talkative at work, which is not a good impression to give prospective employers. If you do go onto a second page, then make it concise and use plenty of white space.

Extensive Experience Warrants a Two-Page Resume

Consider creating a two-page resume if you have extensive experience that matches your objective. Job seekers in the salary range above $30,000 often require two-page resumes. Executives and managers with more than a five-year work history normally require a two-page resume. Professionals such as computer programmers, scientists, nurses, and professors often require a two-page resume due to the technical nature of their work. Many professionals are also heavily involved in associations, have published articles, or have special training that is important to list. Many job seekers have several areas of responsibility at work, which makes each of their job descriptions longer. Using subheadings beneath main job titles and skill headings is a good way to break down this experience so that it is easy for an employer to see main areas of expertise at a glance.

How Far Back to Go in Your Work History

Normally you only need to cover your last ten years of experience in a resume, but there are exceptions to this rule. If you have older experience that strongly supports your objective, you may want to include it. However, you'll need to de-emphasize that it is older experience.

Many clients come to me because they are screened out on paper due to their age. They have listed dates of employment or education, which made it easy for employers to calculate their current age. This is especially a problem when a job seeker is forty-five or older. As employers imagine the traits of an ideal candidate, they may develop a preconceived image of the candidate's age, education level, and experience. They then screen resumes accordingly. Here's how to deal with employment dates.

When to Include Dates

Include dates of education and employment when they portray you at an age that fits the image and position you want. If your age may make an employer feel you are a risky candidate because you are either "too young" or "too old," then omit dates completely, de-emphasize them, or cut back your work history. It's easy for employers to guess your age if you have dated information in your resume.

For example, Sue graduated from college in 1965 and got her first job in 1966. If you subtract 1965 from the current date of 1999, you know it's been thirty-four years since she graduated. You can assume she graduated from college at the age of twenty-two, and now is at least fifty-six years old. Be sure to calculate your age using this method if you use dates in your employment and education sections. This will help you determine whether to include or exclude dates.

Gaps in Employment

If you need to conceal gaps in employment use "year-to-year" versus "month-to-month" dates.

Month to Month:	6/1990–Present	**Year to Year:**	1990–Present
	12/1987–1/1990		1987–1990
	3/1984–12/1986		1984–1986

As you can see in the month-to-month example, it's easy to spot gaps in employment. Starting from the bottom, there was a full year of unemployment from December 1986 to December 1987. There was also a five-month gap from January 1990 to June 1990. The year-to-year format concealed these employment gaps. This technique alone has helped many of my clients get more interviews. If you feel that this is misleading, don't worry, because this technique is widely used in resume writing. In addition, you will have to provide your full work history when you complete detailed applications. Remember, the name of the game is to get as many interviews as possible and to use whatever marketing techniques that help you get them!

Streamline Several Positions with One Employer

If you have held several positions with one employer you can save space by using this design technique:

ORIAN STORES INC.   1987–Present

Full-Charge Bookkeeper

- Managed a full set of books for this outlet with sales in excess of $4 million annually.
- Implemented computerized accounting system and trained management staff in new systems (1988–Present).

Payroll Accounting

- Managed payroll department in absence of Bookkeeper.
- Processed time cards, calculated tax and benefit deductions for 200 employees.
- Cross-trained in all bookkeeping and clerical functions (1984–1987).

ALLIED MANUFACTURING   1982–1984

Accounts Receivable

- Maintained over 150 A / R accounts, posting $30,000 in monthly transactions.
- Negotiated payment schedules with clients.

If You've Worked for Only One Employer

If you have worked for only one employer, use a design like the one on the next page to demonstrate the diversity and depth of your skills. Don't lump your experience into one big paragraph. Break it into job titles or skill categories, as this example illustrates. Notice how much better this directs and controls the eye path rather than one job title or one big paragraph would.

SMITH & THOMAS PUBLISHING COMPANY 1991–Present

Human Resource Management

- Managed human resource functions for staff of 200 in 3 divisions, with annual payroll and benefits in excess of $6 million.
- Launched company expansion programs that doubled staff within a 2-year period.
- Implemented risk management, production safety, and sexual harassment programs.

HRIS Computer Conversions

- Directed conversion of manual payroll and HR reporting systems to a computerized HRIS department employing 20 staff.
- Researched and purchased $120,000 network system.
- Trained executive, management, and administrative staff in system operations.

Program Development

- Developed training program and manuals that increased productivity by 15%.
- Created and implemented a cross-training program that increased effectiveness in vacation and sick-leave coverage.
- Awarded for "Outstanding Innovation and Increased Productivity."

If You've Worked for Temporary Agencies

The format below works well if you've worked for several contract or temporary placement agencies. Instead of listing each agency, label the type of work you performed and list the agency you did the most work with. Then give the length of years that you worked as a temp. This helps your work history look stable and creates space for other job descriptions. Read the examples below for ideas:

DESIGN ENGINEER, Contract Employment—Volt Technical 1996–1997

- Designed HVAC projects with professional fees ranging from $150,000 to $2 million.
- Served as project leader to team of 12 drafters working on 8 projects.

OFFICE ADMINISTRATION, Manpower Inc. 1996–1997

- Managed front office administration and reception to support a staff of up to 45.
- Provided secretarial support to executives and administrative employees.
- Demonstrated the ability to step in, learn new tasks quickly and efficiently.
- Due to these abilities my temporary assignments were lengthened and my duties expanded while completing contract and temporary assignments.

How to Describe Volunteer Experience

If your volunteer experience supports your objective then you may want to include it. When you describe volunteer experience, don't label it as such. After all, just because it's not paid experience doesn't mean that it's not as valid as paid experience! List it just as you would any job. State your title or skill heading, the organization, and your dates of volunteer work. Remember, during an interview you can always let an employer know your experience was as a volunteer. It's to your advantage to describe volunteer experience exactly as you do paid employment in order to generate more interviews. I've found that many people downplay their volunteer experience, yet many have had more responsibility as a volunteer than in paid employment. If this is your case, don't downplay your skills. Use your volunteer experience as a stepping stone to a better job with more responsibility. If you feel you must tell employers that your experience was volunteer, then add a statement like the last one in the example below:

PROJECT COORDINATOR, Youth Mission 1996–Present
- Coordinated fund-raising projects that raised over $75,000.
- Supervised and delegated work assignments to groups of up to 40 volunteers.
- Managed events and coordinated with city officials to accommodate up to 5,000 attendees per event.
- Worked extensively with the Executive Director as a volunteer coordinator managing diverse projects.

How to Describe Your Education

If your education is one of your strongest selling points, consider placing it at the top of your resume. If your education is not a major selling point then put it at the end of your resume.

If you have completed high school but have not gone to college, it is usually better to omit education from your resume. Many employers prefer at least two years of college. Listing high school alone draws attention to the fact that you don't have a college education, and this can sometimes prevent you from getting an interview. In our degree-conscious society you don't want to focus attention on what could be viewed negatively. Omit the education section entirely if you feel your education is extremely weak when compared to others applying for the position you want.

If you are a recent high school or college graduate with a short or erratic work history, the strategy is different. In this case, it is to your advantage to include your education. If you worked while completing high school or college, then list the dates you attended school. Employers will see that your employment dates overlap the dates you were in school. Most employers will understand an erratic work history if it's because you worked while completing your education.

Special Areas of Study

If you specialized in a specific area of study, graduated with honors, or participated in extracurricular activities that support your objective, then you may want to describe these activities. Ask yourself if it is beneficial to include this information. When describing educational activities, first draw attention to the activity and then list what college or high school you attended. Here's an example:

DO
- Business & Office Administration Concentration, Bellevue High School—GPA 3.5
- Manager—Supply & Equipment Store, Redmond High School

DON'T   Bellevue High School
Business & Office Administration Concentration
GPA 3.5

Redmond High School
Supply & Equipment Store Manager

College with a Degree

If you have a college degree then it's not necessary to list the high school you attended because this can weaken your image. Generally, it's better to save space by streamlining your education section. The exception would be if you specialized in an area that supports your objective or if you received high honors in high school. Weigh whether or not to include high school information based on the image it creates. List your degree or area of study, the college or high school you attended, the date you graduated (unless the date gives away your age in a negative way), and your GPA. You can often get this information onto one line.

DO   • B.A.—Business Administration, University of Iowa 1986—GPA 3.7

OR

• B.A.—English, University of Washington 1982

DON'T   University of Wisconsin
Saratoga, Wisconsin
B.A. in English
1982–1985

College without a Degree

If you have taken numerous college courses but have not graduated, group areas of study together that support your objective but omit irrelevant coursework. For example, a bookkeeper may have completed the following courses:

DO   • Accounting & Financial Analysis, Bellevue Community College 1981–1983

DON'T   • Bellevue Community College 1981–1983:

Accounting I & II	Assertiveness Training
Financial Statistics	Supervisory Skills for Female Managers
Business Communications	Pottery

If the years you attended college are recent and span two or three years, then list them. This is a substantial amount of study. Listing them is a good strategy, particularly if you are competing against other applicants with degrees. In this case, your work experience combined with your college education will often be considered equivalent to someone with a degree and no experience. If the dates are older and reveal your age in a negative manner, then drop them and specify the number of years you studied instead.

DO	• Accounting/Financial Analysis, Bellevue Community College, 3 Years

OR

	• Accounting/Financial Analysis, Bellevue Community College 1990–1993
DON'T	• Accounting/Financial Analysis, Bellevue Community College 1960–1962

If You Attended Several Colleges

Unless the colleges or universities you attended are prestigious, list only the most recent college you attended. The last college you attended will have a complete transcript of the courses you have taken and where you completed them. If an employer wants to verify your education, you can request that a transcript be forwarded to her or him from your last college.

Describing College Coursework, Projects, and Internships

If your college coursework is your strongest qualification then devoting a major portion of your resume to it can often strengthen your resume. This is especially true if you have little experience or are making a career change. The following format has been proven to be very effective at landing higher-paying positions for recent graduates.

The example below describes coursework gained from an A.A.S. Degree in CAD Technology. This format can be used to list and describe any college or university coursework. To make a list of the skills or knowledge you've gained from your coursework, review the academic competency and program literature you received from your instructional department. Then list areas of study or skills that you gained that can make you look qualified and knowledgeable of the types of jobs you want. Stating the number of hours studied as well as hands-on training or experience you've gained also works extremely well.

A.A.S. Degree in CAD Technology
AutoCAD R13—1,000+ Hours

Completed 1,440 hours of CAD and manual drafting in a program recognized for hands-on training—ITT Technical Institute. Maintained 3.72 GPA while working full-time.

AutoCAD Programming	Architectural Drafting	Load, Stress, and Heat
Menu Programming	Civil/Topographical Maps	Loss Calculations
Symbols, Library Development	Mechanical Fasteners, Gears, Casts	Project Management
3-D Drafting Techniques	Industrial Piping & Flow Diagrams	Cost Estimating
Electronic Logic Diagrams	Structural Steel & Concrete Assemblies	Project Status Reports
Applied Physics	Printed Circuit Layout	Planning & Scheduling

If You Gained Hands-on Experience

Many college or university programs require that you perform the work you are being trained to do, either in a class setting or with an employer. The example on the next page is from a student who completed a computer science degree. As you'll see, his class set up and managed computer systems for classrooms throughout the college campus. The class provided technical support and troubleshooting services to instructors and staff in four departments. We've marketed his experience just like real, paid employment because the students were performing work functions just like they would for an employer. Again, this format can be used to market skills gained from any college program in which you've obtained hands-on experience.

Networking / Technical Support

<u>Network Administration</u>

- Assigned trustee rights; created users and login scripts; installed operating systems, work-stations, and print service; and administered security rights.
- Supervised installation of Novel Netware, Microsoft NT, network cards, and cabling.
- Installed Wide Area Network high speed phone line, serial and parallel communications.

<u>System Troubleshooting</u>

- Consulted with Program Managers to troubleshoot systems in 4 departments.
- Installed hard drives, floppy drives, monitor cards, and CD-ROMs.
- Upgraded 486 PC lab to Pentium PC lab. Managed computer teams.

<u>User Training—Computer Applications</u>

- Designed Access software package for Computer Department to track 100 clients.
- Led teams of 8 developers in design of front- and back-end Access programming.
- Taught operating systems and Microsoft applications to 15 computer users.

<u>User Training—Computer Applications</u>

- Created accounting information system using Visual Basic; retail accounting system using Access; information systems and presentations using PowerPoint, Access, Excel, and Word; and developed optimization techniques in SQL Server Database Programming.

Describing Short-Term Projects

While completing a major in business administration, Sue served as a marketing consultant to an electronics outlet. She wanted to capitalize on this experience, and move from being a secretary to a management trainee. Because she wasn't paid for this experience, she wasn't sure if she should include it. But she did, and Sue's new resume landed her a trainee position with a major telecommunications company.

MARKETING CONSULTANT, Pacific Video & TV

- Increased annual sales by 30% by creating and implementing an innovative advertising program.
- Identified a specific market that no other competitors were marketing to.
- Implemented a marketing plan utilizing products and advertising targeted to this market.
- Designed window and in-store displays as well as radio and newspaper copy.

Including or Not Including Your Grade Point Average

Include your cumulative GPA if it is 3.5 or higher. If it is lower than 3.5, but the GPA for your major is 3.5 or higher, include the GPA for your major and don't mention your cumulative GPA.

DO
- B.A.—Business Administration, University of Kansas—Major GPA 3.5

DON'T
- B.A.—Business Administration, University of Kansas—Cumulative GPA 2.2

Corporate Training

If you have completed several corporate training seminars, streamline and summarize them. If there is a particular program or long-term course you've taken that strongly relates to your job objective, describe it fully.

DO
- Corporate Training: Credit Management & Personnel Administration

DON'T
- Sylvester Institute, Credit Management, 1 Day 1965. Motivational Center, Personnel Techniques, 2 Days 1978. XYZ Training Center, Sales & Customer Service, 3 Days 1980.

DO
- Advanced MS Word and PowerPoint Training for Executive Presentation Materials
- Corporate Newsletter Development, Slide Presentations, and Marketing Literature Design

DON'T
- MS Word and PowerPoint

As you write descriptions for your training, ask yourself, "What was the primary focus of this training? How can I label this training so that it sounds supportive of my objective? What areas of my training will help sell me for the position I want?"

Professional Memberships

Include professional memberships if they are relevant to your objective. Decide if this information is more or less important than other data, and include or exclude it accordingly. For example, Susan wants a position as a bookkeeper. She has a great deal of secretarial experience, but very little paid bookkeeping experience. As a member of an accounting association, she set up its bookkeeping records and maximized this experience by placing it at the top of her resume:

Bookkeeping / Budget Control
- Set up bookkeeping system for the Northwest Accounting Association.
- Maintained records for 1,000 members.
- Tracked expenses to control a $20,000 budget.

You may not wish to give details regarding your professional memberships, as Susan did, yet you may want to list them. In this case your resume might read like this:

Professional Memberships:

- **Board Member,** Northwest Accounting Association
- **Events Management,** Greater Seattle Women's Business Association

Leave Off Addresses of Employment

Don't list address, city, and state for each employer you've worked for. It takes up space and does not reveal anything important to an employer. Listing the address, city, and state for each employer also makes the eye jump around a lot. Compare the two samples below. Which one do you think is more appealing and has better design?

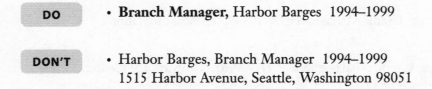

DO
- **Branch Manager,** Harbor Barges 1994–1999

DON'T
- Harbor Barges, Branch Manager 1994–1999
  1515 Harbor Avenue, Seattle, Washington 98051

Personal Information

Personal information is not normally required on a resume. However, some of your personal information may support your objective. My personnel agency placed electronic assemblers at ATL, a manufacturer of ultrasound equipment. The department supervisor was always interested in applicants with jewelry making or needlepoint skills. She found that employees with these hobbies had the manual dexterity needed for assembly work. They also had the ability to focus on small, detailed work for long periods. She consistently hired applicants with no relevant work experience but who enjoyed these hobbies. In this instance, it was a plus to describe my applicants' hobbies in their resumes.

Most of the time, however, you shouldn't list hobbies on your resume. It's more important to use resume space for job and skill descriptions. Below are several bits of information that you *shouldn't* put on your resume:

• Height and weight	• Social Security Number	• Marital status
• Date of birth	• Citizenship	• Race or sex

Airlines are one of the few employers who can legally request your height and weight information. A flight attendant needs to be physically fit and able to handle emergency situations, such as lifting sick or wounded passengers. Listing your height and weight would not be appropriate for most office or business positions.

On the other hand, if you meet the physical requirements for a position and you know that employers are interested in this data, then by all means tell them. For instance, a laborer who has had a perfect attendance record, is in excellent health, and can lift significant weight would benefit from listing this information on his or her resume. This is clearly personal information, yet these are also strong selling points. Want ads for construction workers often request personal information such as what tools the applicants own and whether or not they have reliable transportation. If you're applying for such a position and own these tools and have reliable transportation, then include this information because it is a selling point. This information could cause you to be the one called for an interview. If you are willing to travel, have a security clearance, are bondable, or possess any other traits that make you look more qualified for a particular position, be sure to include them. If they don't make you look more qualified, then exclude them.

Salary History

Do not list your salary history on your resume. If it is requested in an advertisement, and you feel you need to include it, put it in your cover letter. Give a range of your past salaries or a range for your current salary requirement. For example:

> My salary history has ranged from $15,000 to $20,000 annually.
>
> My current salary requirement is in the $18,000 to $22,000 range.

Be careful when stating salary requirements so that you don't oversell or undersell yourself. Giving a range minimizes the risk that you will be screened out of an interview. Don't include your salary if doing so might be a negative.

Reason for Leaving Employment

Don't include reasons for leaving employment on your resume. When you repeatedly explain why you've left each job it sounds like you are making up excuses and apologizing for your work history. When completing applications, consider using one of these replies to explain why you left a particular position:

- Career advancement
- To continue education
- To seek full-time employment
- Workforce reduction

Maintaining Your Confidentiality

If you are worried about listing the name of your current employer on your resume then consider leaving off the company's name. Instead, give a description of the type of firm you work for:

- **Copyright Attorney,** employed with a major law firm 1987–Present

To further ensure the confidentiality of employers contacting you, type CONFIDENTIAL RESUME above your name. In your cover letter, include a sentence like the one below if employers will need to contact you at work.

You may contact me CONFIDENTIALLY at work (555) 555-555 between 7:00 A.M. and 3:00 P.M.

If You Have Relocated

Several of my clients have had problems getting interviews because they had recently moved to our state. In writing their resumes, they had included the city and state for each job they had held. Since these positions were out-of-state, it was obvious to employers that they were not long-term residents of the area. Many employers have told me they have had problems with out-of-state employees and tend to avoid hiring them. Tony, a construction manager, encountered this problem with his old resume. When he came to me he had been getting about one interview for every twenty resumes he sent out. He hadn't considered his out-of-state employment as a possible cause. We certainly beefed up his resume and made it better, but the real key was eliminating references to his out-of-state employment. In only four weeks he received seven interviews from the ten resumes he sent out, and he accepted a position he really wanted.

If you have recently moved from one state to another, it is wise to leave out all references to the cities and states where you were employed. It's also wise to provide a current address within the city or area you seek employment in. If you don't have a permanent address, ask a friend if you can use his or her address on your resume. You might also consider getting a P.O. box in the area where you seek employment. If you live more than forty-five minutes away from the company you are applying to, employers may be concerned that you'll have a hard time getting to work. This can be another good reason to get a P.O. box in the area you want to work in. Be sure to cover your bases so that you appear to be an applicant who can easily get to work. Otherwise you may lose out on interviews and possibly a job.

Military Employment

I recently met with Fred, the vice president of a technical college. He is a retired military officer. Talking about military resumes, Fred shared a story about how his human resources staff skipped over military personnel and didn't consider them as qualified applicants. His college had an open budget and fiscal control position, and a Desert Storm logistics commander had applied for the position. After this applicant had been turned down for the position, Fred took a look at his resume. Since Fred was familiar with what the applicant's duties had been in the military, he knew the applicant was qualified. But the HR manager had rejected the resume because it was written with military language that she didn't understand.

As a logistics commander, the applicant had been responsible for tracking expenses and determining when and where to allocate funds for multimillion-dollar projects. They were exactly the skills required for the college position. However, the HR manager never got past the image of someone in the desert, wearing fatigues and army boots. As a result, this person's resume shot him in the foot—so to speak. When you read the first description below, it's easy to see why the HR manager didn't think this person would fit into the budgeting position. In contrast, the second example sounds like someone with skills needed for the college position.

USING MILITARY LANGUAGE

Desert Storm Logistics Commander

- Oversaw Desert Storm projects with responsibility for military field equipment, logistics, tracking of budgets, and allocation of project funds.

Project Budgeting and Funds Allocation

- Managed multimillion-dollar projects tracking expenses, allocating funds, and overseeing up to $20 million in equipment and supplies.

If you have a military background, be sure to describe it so that it sounds like the type of job you are applying for. For example, Betty, a Specialist 5, was a command clerk. Before interviewing Betty, I didn't have the slightest idea of what a Specialist 5 was or what a command clerk does. Many personnel managers or hiring officials won't know what military terms or classifications mean either. Here's what Betty's resume looked like:

U.S. Army, Specialist 5 / Command Clerk 1994–1998

- Oversaw command post and managed all administrative functions.
- Communicated with 45 officers and enlisted soldiers.
- Gave orders to clerical staff.

Instead of using the army's titles and descriptions for Betty's experience, we used transferable skills. Here's how we described her army background:

BRANCH / ADMINISTRATIVE MANAGEMENT, U.S. Army 1994–1998

- Managed all administrative functions for branch employing 45 executive staff.
- Prepared confidential reports and correspondence.
- Directed clerical projects and delegated duties to administrative staff.
- Maintained database, tracking over 1,500 employee accounts.

Associations and Religious Affiliations

If your involvement with an association or church group supports your objective then consider including it, but ask yourself if an employer could have a negative reaction when reading it. If so, leave it off. Some of my clients have strong religious beliefs and feel they only want to work in appropriate environments. So they feel it's important to list their church involvement. This, of course, could work for or against them depending on the job market and the religious beliefs of the employers they apply to. It's a gamble and gives control to employers. It can allow employers to screen the applicant out on paper. A better way to approach this situation is to leave religious information off the resume and generate as many interviews as possible. This allows the applicant to examine each work environment and see if it meets his or her needs. This puts applicants in control of the screening process. They are then screening employers out instead of employers screening them out.

Personal and Professional References

Provide three business and three personal references on a separate sheet of paper. For business references list the person's name, title, company, address, and phone number. For personal references, list each person's name, address, and phone number. I've included a sample reference sheet on the facing page.

You may assume that when a person says, "Sure, I'll be a reference for you," that this person will present you favorably. However, that's not always the case. Employers will ask your references to describe your reliability, temperament, work habits, strengths, and weaknesses. Such questions may cause your references to hesitate or give answers about you that are not always positive. Therefore, it's important to ask each of your references how they will describe you when answering these questions. If their answers are not positive, then take them off your reference list.

AMY HAMSTEDDER
1515 16th N.E.
Normandy, Wisconsin 57803
(555) 555-5555

PROFESSIONAL REFERENCES

Mr. David Smith, President
Safeco Transmissions
2435 98th Avenue
Tacoma, Washington 98379
(555) 555-5555

Ms. Susan Berry, Billing Manager
Newfound Company
34567 116th N.E.
Fort Worth, Texas 79873
(555) 555-5555

Dr. Richard Petroskie
Newborn Clinic
3457 78th Street
Detroit, Michigan 38767
(555) 555-5555

PERSONAL REFERENCES

Christine Nims
23456 277th S.E.
Bothell, Washington 98765
(555) 555-5555

Roger Daltry
38790 30th Avenue
North Bend, Washington 98037
(555) 555-5555

Sheila Watson
1245 Fiscus Avenue
Bellevue, Washington 98006
(555) 555-5555

10 Designing and Printing Your Final Resume

Now that you've polished the rough draft of your resume, you're ready to critique and test the effectiveness of its design. In this chapter, you'll also learn how to use typefaces, appropriate paper, and printing methods to create a professional image that commands an employer's attention.

Direct the Reader's Eye to Your Strengths

Take a moment to glance at the resume on the next page. What section of this resume do you tend to focus on? Most people say the middle section. What design elements do you think I purposely used to direct and control the path your eyes take as you glance at the resume? As you can see, the horizontal lines help to pull your attention into the middle of the resume. Its centered headings also make this section stand out, whereas the headings in the top and bottom sections are flush left. Staggering or offsetting headings in this way frames the middle section. Using bulleted statements also pulls your eye into the middle section. All of these design techniques make the middle section grab the reader's attention almost immediately.

You've already learned that employers spend as little as five to ten seconds glancing at a resume before discarding it. Therefore, your design must direct an employer's attention to your top skills or job titles in that critical time frame. The resume on the next page does this very effectively. If you review the sample resumes presented in earlier chapters, you'll see that they all look different but are equally effective in directing the eye path. Each resume also uses skill headings or job titles that match the jobs being applied for. If the skill headings or job titles didn't match, then the resumes wouldn't be effective and would likely fail. Therefore, it's important to consider skill headings and job titles as elements in an effective resume design.

Use Design to Maximize or De-emphasize

The resume on the next page uses design elements to emphasize Linda's skills. In contrast, it uses placement and spacing to de-emphasize Linda's work history. Review the skill headings in Linda's resume. Then read the "Work History" section to see where Linda gained these skills. Would it have weakened Linda's image if Howard's Malt Shop was listed at the top of her resume? Yes. This is a good example of design that de-emphasizes sections that are weak—or less relevant—than the body of the resume.

Linda began work for Howard's Malt Shop in her junior year of high school. The owners were gone most of the time and found that Linda was extremely reliable. When they opened new ice cream parlors, they chose her to train and supervise new employees. Within a year of graduating high school, Linda had trained five store managers and helped to set up each store. Yet most people—including employers—would think experience at an ice cream parlor was insignificant. This resume took Linda from an ice cream parlor to a management position with a food wholesaler and increased her salary from $7.50 per hour to $12.00 per hour.

LINDA PHILLIPS
1234 Passyunk Avenue
Philadelphia, PA 19155
(555) 555-5555

OBJECTIVE

To obtain a Management Trainee position utilizing my experience managing operations, overseeing customer service, training staff, and preparing computerized reports.

OPERATIONS MANAGEMENT / CUSTOMER SERVICE

- Managed opening and closing of facility, overseeing operations with sales of $20,000 monthly.
- Coordinated with 10 stores to process $125,000 in annual orders.
- Supervised disbursement of orders with store managers.
- Assisted owner in design of media and print advertisements.
- Knowledge of payroll taxes and processing (10-Key by touch).
- Took orders from key accounts and ensured orders were completed on a timely basis.

STAFF SUPERVISION / TRAINING

- Supervised and trained 9 employees in hostessing and cashiering.
- Trained 5 store managers in bookkeeping, payroll, purchasing, inventory maintenance, product pricing, and cashiering.
- Scheduled 2 shifts and work hours for weekends, holidays, and special events.
- Advised owner of employee performance.

COMPUTERIZED OFFICE APPLICATIONS

- Processed projects utilizing MS Word and Lotus 1-2-3.
- Prepared purchase orders, invoices, sales receipts, and correspondence.
- Developed databases for client accounts and accounts receivable processing.
- Utilized Quick Books to prepare checks and run accounts receivable reports.
- Handled multiline phones with multiple extensions.
- Typing at 60+ wpm with 10-Key at 345 spm.

EDUCATION

A.A.S. Degree in Marketing, Smith's Business College

WORK HISTORY

Operations / Customer Service Management, Howard's Malt Shop 1996–Present

Test the Effectiveness of Your Design

Once you've completed your resume, hold it up and ask several people where their eyes go first, second, third, and then fourth. If they're not drawn immediately to the top information you want employers to see first, then you need to redesign your resume. Another great test is to give people who are experienced in your field a copy of the ads for the positions you want to apply for, and tell them the salary you want. Ask them to review the ads and then ask them to review your resume. Once they've done so, ask them if they think the headings and job titles in your resume are strong enough to grab an employer's attention. Then ask if the statements you've used throughout your resume present an image of you that is well qualified and matches the salary you want. This process can provide you with valuable feedback. For example, if you're told that a particular heading or title makes your image drop significantly, then consider modifying or presenting your skills in a different manner. You may feel a little hesitant about getting such feedback, as we can all feel a little defensive about our writing and resumes. But by opening yourself to others' impressions, you can learn how employers will respond to your resume. This feedback can help you create a top-notch resume. Now that you've learned how to create a resume with strong design and test its effectiveness, we'll discuss how to produce and print a polished, professional resume.

Formatting and Printing Tips for Producing a Professional, Polished Appearance

You've learned how important it is to control the image you present in your resume. The printing and paper that you use to produce your resume also project a certain image. In today's job market, virtually all resumes are printed with laser or ink-jet printers, which look sharp, crisp, and professional. Typewritten resumes look much less professional and can't compete effectively with laser-printed ones. If you don't have access to a laser printer, then take your resume to a service bureau and have it word processed and printed. This will cost anywhere from ten to twenty-five dollars a page, but is an insignificant expense to ensure that employers find your resume attractive to look at.

Use Narrow Margins to Save Space

Most of the resumes in this book have top, bottom, left, and right margins of half of an inch. It's OK to use narrow margins as long as you allow plenty of white space between sections. Just be sure that your resume doesn't look crowded and that the reader's eye is directed quickly and easily to your top sales points.

Typefaces and Point Sizes

It's best to use familiar typefaces like Times Roman or Helvetica that are easy to read. These typefaces also scan well. Set the text of your resume in 12 point, titles and primary skill headings in 14 point, and subheadings in 12 or 13 point. Then review your resume. Are the type sizes and styles easy to look at? Do they create a professional image? Some typefaces, such as Helvetica, are larger than Times Roman so they must be sized down. Ten-point Helvetica is often equivalent to twelve-point Times Roman.

Use Bulleted Statements

To make your resume easy for employers to read, use short, bulleted sentences rather than block paragraphs. When you look at a resume with bulleted statements, you feel like you can start and stop reading anywhere. But when you look at a large block paragraph, it feels like you have to commit to reading the entire paragraph. Since employers respond in the same way, they may choose not to stop and read paragraphs.

Use Quality Printing and Paper

Have your resume printed or photocopied onto a high-quality twenty-four-pound bond paper. A light cream or off-white paper with a laid or textured finish will stand out in a stack of white photocopied resumes. Avoid anything that is too flashy—such as lime green paper or stiff card stock—that will make you look unprofessional. Also, avoid speckled or parchment papers. Both have light and dark spots that don't fax or scan well. Print your resumes and cover letters on matching paper. Send them in a matching envelope. It's usually best to type the addresses on your envelopes, unless you have excellent penmanship. Most quick-print shops carry a variety of stationery from which to choose.

Executive Resumes

Executives will do well to print their resumes on stark white twenty-four-pound bond paper with a high cotton content. This paper looks (and is) more expensive, and creates the preferred image for executives in the $100,000 to $200,000 range.

Include All Contact Information

Be sure to include your mailing address, area code and phone number, voice mail number, e-mail address, and link to your homepage resume or URL if you have a website. However, always keep in mind that this information will be available to anyone and everyone if you post your resume on the Internet. If there is any information that you want kept confidential then do not include it. If you post your resume online, consider using a blind e-mail box for employers to contact you through. This service is offered by most resume posting sites to maintain your anonymity.

11 Sample Resumes That Will Blow Away Your Competition

This chapter contains a wide range of resume examples from job seekers with annual incomes from $20,000 up to $120,000. All of the examples employ strategies that produce dramatically more interviews and salary increases. As you browse through this chapter, you'll notice that each resume example uses skill headings or modified job titles targeted to each person's job objective. This is substantially different from the average resume, which includes skills or job titles that may be totally unrelated to the job seeker's career objective. Whether you choose to use a chronological or a skill-based resume, be sure that all of the skill headings and titles in your resume match and support your job objective.

Tips on Using the Resumes in This Chapter

Use the resume examples in this chapter to help you shape the content of your resume, rather than just copying information that seems to fit your background. A copied resume is a weak resume compared to one that describes your unique skills, abilities, and achievements. Next to each resume you'll find tips for describing skills and experience that will grab an employer's attention. Use these suggestions along with the Twelve Questions in Chapter 6 to create your own powerful resume.

On the next pages is an index of the resume examples in this chapter and throughout the book; they are grouped by career field. At the beginning of each section you'll see a list of the resumes contained in that section. This makes it easy to find resumes for specific fields. Below each list of resumes are skill section lists. These alphabetized lists make it easy to find descriptions of specific skills. First look for resumes that match the types of positions you've held and that you want. Then make a list of the skills you have developed or that are needed in the jobs you want.

It's important to look at a broad range of career categories. For example, Melissa had been an office manager and a retail sales associate. First, she turned to the Administrative/Clerical and Customer Service/Retail sections and found six resumes with information that matched her background. Next, Melissa made a list of additional skills she possessed, such as purchasing, computer implementation, inventory control, staff supervision, and budget control. She then read the alphabetical skill sections and found that the Accounting/Bookkeeping, Sales/Marketing, and Management categories also listed resumes with skill sections that matched her background. In this way, Melissa saw how others described many of the skills she has and used their resumes as a guide to create her own.

A Word about Layouts and Formats

My favorite resume formats appear on pages 143, 146, 153–54, 159, and 166. Styles like these have consistently generated the highest number of interviews and substantial salary offers, so my strongest recommendation is that you use one of these formats. However, I've also provided a wide range of layouts that have all been extremely successful. (If you're in a class with other students who may be applying for jobs with the same employers, the layouts in this chapter will help you create a resume that is unique in appearance. When employers receive dozens of resumes that look alike, it can make them suspicious that they are copied and don't reflect each applicant's unique skills.)

Good luck! By following the examples in this chapter you'll be pleased with the response your new resume generates!

ACCOUNTING/BOOKKEEPING

Assistant to Controller, 53
Bookkeeper/Office Manager, 143
C.P.A./Chief Financial Officer, 174
Full-Charge Bookkeeper, 144
Laborer to Bookkeeper, 145
Senior Staff Accountant, 146
  A/R and A/P Management, 92
  A/R Clerk, 116
  Accounting Supervisor, 53
  Acquisitions Management, 174
  Asset Management, 53
  Audit Division Management, 174
  Banking/Finance Administration, 174
  Bookkeeping, 143, 144, 145, 146, 149
  Budget Control, 146
  Cash Flow Management, 174
  Computer Conversion, 144
  Computer Experience, 145
  Computerized Bookkeeping, 145
  Contract Administration, 53
  Contract Negotiation, 156
  Cost Accounting, 53
  Cost Containment/Savings, 181
  Financial Administration, 112, 174
  Financial Modeling, 152
  Full-Charge Bookkeeper, 144
  General Accounting, 53
  Inventory Control, 149, 166
  Job Costing, 146
  Outsourcing, 174
  Payroll/Benefits Administration, 121, 146
  Procurement Budgets, 181
  Project Accountant, 53
  Project Management, 53
  Purchasing/Inventory Control, 145
  Regional Management, 53
  Revenue Expansion, 174
  Vendor Account Processing, 100
  Vendor Coordination/Savings, 166

ADMINISTRATIVE/CLERICAL

Legal Administrative Assistant, 147
Office Assistant/Receptionist, 148
Office Manager, 149
Senior-Level Executive Assistant, 150
  Account Management, 116
  Accounts Specialist, 148
  Administrative Assistant, 148
  Administrative Management, 150
  Computer Implementation, 150
  CRT Specialist, 116
  Data Entry Clerk, 89
  Delivery of Training Programs, 150
  Departmental Administration, 151
  Departmental Support, 147, 148
  Division Administration, 150
  Executive Support, 98, 116, 150
  Forms Design, 95
  Front Office Administration, 116, 148
  Inventory Control, 149
  Legal Document Preparation, 147
  Management of Office Staff, 122, 143
  New Office Setup, 149
  Office Administration, 122
  Operational Analysis, 150
  Receptionist, 116

COLLEGE AND UNIVERSITY STUDENTS

B.A. Degree, Liberal Arts, 151
M.B.A. Degree, 152

CURRICULUM VITAE

College Vice President, 153–154

CUSTOMER SERVICE/RETAIL

Customer Service Manager, 155
Customer Service Representative, 13, 236
Management Trainee, 136
Retail Manager, 156
  Account Management, 166
  Assistant Department Manager, 165
  Branch Management, 20, 99, 144
  Buying and Vendor Sourcing, 156
  Cash Accountability, 164
  Cashier, 36–37
  Computerized Applications, 136, 236
  Credit Representative, 17
  Customer Service, 13, 37, 143, 145, 147, 151, 155, 162, 167
  Delivery of Training Programs, 155
  Department Manager, 166, 167, 168
  Departmental Coordination, 37
  Departmental Documentation, 147
  Directory Operator, 12–13
  Human Resources Management, 156
  Inside Sales Support, 235
  Launch of Retail Operations, 155, 156
  Marketing Management, 13
  Marketing Skills, 187
  National Account Administration, 236
  New Store Opening, 156
  Opening/Closing Operations, 164
  Operations Management, 37, 93, 136, 155
  Order Administration, 37
  P&L Responsibility, 156
  Produce Manager, 165
  Public Relations, 143, 151
  Report Development, 236
  Retail Management, 34
  Retail Sales, 164
  Retail Sales Rep, 187
  Sales Order Processing, 236
  Shipment Verification, 236
  Staff Supervision/Training, 37, 136
  Store Layout and Design, 156
  Store Manager, 156
  Technical Sales, 187
  Training of Field Service Teams, 155
  Video Store Management, 162
  Waitress, 36–37
  Warranty Administration, 188
  Workflow Coordination, 37

EDUCATION

College Vice President, 153
Computer/Electronics Instructor, 157
K–8 Teacher, 158
  Business Instructor, 153
  Campus Director, 153
  College Instructor, 157
  Electronics Instructor, 157
  Grade 9–12 English Instructor, 93
  Primary Teacher, 2
  Special Education, 158
  Student-Parent Liaison, 158

HEALTHCARE/MEDICAL

Clinic Manager, 159
Medical Assistant, 160
Registered Nurse, 161
Surgical Technologist, 162
  Billing Management, 159
  Case Management/Documentation, 193
  Counselor, 193

Family Counseling, 193
Medical Office Administration, 159
Multidisciplinary Team Member, 194
Neurology Clinic Manager, 95
New Medical Office Setup, 159
OB/GYN OR Rotation, 162
Patient Assessment, 161
Patient Education, 161
Program Management, 193
Purchasing—Medical Products, 159
Staff Scheduling, 160
Standards of Care/Research, 161

HIGH SCHOOL

Clerical Experience, 163
Fast Food Experience, 164
Business Computer Training, 163, 164
Cash Accountability, 164
Computerized Applications, 163
Customer Service Skills, 163, 164
Fast Food to Accounting, 102
Opening/Closing Operations, 164
Retail Sales/Customer Service, 164

HIGH-TECH

AutoCAD/Manual Drafter, 165
Electronics Engineering Tech, 166
Network Administrator, 167
Webmaster/Site Developer, 168
Account Management, 166
AutoCAD R12 Operator, 92
Budget Control, 168
Computer Troubleshooting, 166
Design Applications, 167
Electronic Production/Repair, 166
Help Desk Supervision, 167
Inventory Administration, 166
Networking/Technical Support, 167
PCB Repair/Rework, 166
Product Development, 191
Project Management, 165, 168
Setup Bench Testing System, 166
Special Projects Manager, 165
Supervision of Technical Staff, 168
System Troubleshooting, 167
Technical Support, 98
Testing and Certification, 191
User Training, 167

HOSPITALITY AND FOOD SERVICE

Executive Chef, 169
Restaurant Manager, 170
Chain Management, 170
Cook/Department Coordination, 97
Cost Control Measures, 169
Culinary Accreditation, 169
Front and Back House Operations, 170
Operations Director, 170
P&L Responsibility, 169, 170
Profit and Revenue Expansion, 169, 170
Purchasing/Budget Management, 170
Reengineering of Operations, 169
Sales Rep—Hotel Catering, 187
Staff Management, 170

HUMAN RESOURCES

Human Resources Generalist, 171
Human Resources Manager, 172
Applicant Screening, 171
Benefits Coordination, 171
Delivery of In-house Training, 171
Division-Wide Human Resources Management, 172
Employee Orientation, 171
HRIS Computer Conversions, 122
Human Resource Management, 122
Human Resources Administration, 172
Human Resources Law and Hiring Guidelines, 171
Maintenance of HRIS Systems, 171
Management of Human Resources Budget, 172
Management of Human Resources Staff, 172
Organizational Restructuring, 172
Placement of Temporary Staff, 16–17
Recruitment Management, 171
Reengineering of Operations, 172
Salary Analysis/Job Classification, 171
Senior Management Consulting, 172
Training of Management Staff, 171
Union Labor Relations, 172

LICENSED PROFESSIONALS

Architect, 173
Certified Public Accountant, 174
City Attorney, 175
Civil Engineer, 176

Acquisitions Management, 174
Cash Flow Management, 174
Construction Supervision, 173
Consulting/Municipal Departments, 175
Design Engineer, 122
Financial Administrator, 174
General Manager, 174
Human Resource Management, 174
Institutional/Commercial Design, 173
Land Development, 176
Production Planning and Control, 174
Project Management, 173, 176
Revenue and Profit Expansion, 174
Risk Management, 175
Utility Engineering, 176

MILITARY

To Management Consultant, 177
To Marketing/Management, 178
Branch Management, 131
Budgeting and Funds Allocation, 131
Company Sergeant, 99, 152
Computer System Management, 177
Cost Reduction/Labor Control, 177
Division HR Management, 177
Financial Administration, 177
IS Planning and Procurement, 177
Logistics Planning, 177
Marketing Management, 178
Operations Management, 177, 178
Process Reengineering, 177
Program Management, 177
Project Budgeting, 177
Reprogramming and Testing, 177
Senior Management, 177
Total Quality Management, 177

PARTS, PRODUCTION, WAREHOUSE

Parts and Service Manager, 179
Production/Materials Manager, 180
Purchasing Agent, 181
Warehouse Manager, 182
Assembler, 94
Computerized Systems, 182
Contract Negotiation, 181
Cost Savings, 181
Freight Forecasting/Cost Savings, 181
Inventory Management, 180
Management Reporting, 180

Manufacturing Reengineering, 180
MRP, Production Planning, 180
Operations Design, 94
Procurement Budgets, 181
Production Lead, 36–37
Production Management, 180, 182
Production Setup and Control, 94
Project Management, 181
QC/Inspection, 197
Receiving/Shipping, 182
Senior Management Reporting, 180
Staff Supervision, 181
Strategic Planning, 180
Subcontractor Relationships, 180
Systems Reengineering, 180
Vendor Sourcing, 180, 181
Warehouse Management, 92

REAL ESTATE/PROPERTY MANAGEMENT

Commercial Property Manager, 183
Real Estate Broker and Agent, 184
Acquisitions and Market Analysis, 183
Administrative Management, 183
Apartment Complex Manager, 183
Management of Facilities, 183
Manager—Builder Services, 184
Multi-State Management, 183
Portfolio Management, 183

SALES AND MARKETING

Account Representative, 17
Driver Sales Representative, 104
National Marketing Manager, 185
Regional Sales Division Manager, 186
Retail Sales Representative, 187
Senior Account Executive, 188
Business Development, 186
Distribution Management, 191
International Product Launch, 191
Major Accounts Management, 17, 188
Manufacturing Rep/Liaison, 188
Market Expansion, 191
Marketing Consultant, 126
Marketing General Management, 186
National Program Manager, 94
National Sales Management, 188
Outside Sales Representative, 17, 188
Product Development, 186, 191
Project Management, 186

Regional Sales Management, 188
Route Management, 104
Sales/Contract Administration, 186
Strategic Planning, 177
Supervision of Contract Servicing, 188
Territory Management, 105, 188
Training of Sales Force, 189
Warranty Administration, 186

SENIOR MANAGEMENT/EXECUTIVE

CFO/General Manager, 174
COO—National Manager, 189–190
International Marketing Executive,
      191–192
Acquisitions Management, 174
Analysis/Process Reengineering, 177
Branch Operations Manager, 190
Business Management, 150
Cash Flow Management, 174
Computer Administration, 96, 177
Cost Reduction/Labor Control, 177
Country General Manager, 191
Country Product Launch, 191
Delivery of Training Programs, 150
Departmental Administration, 166
Departmental Manager, 99, 176
Distribution Management, 191
Division Launch/Management, 174
Equipment Specifications/Testing, 191
European Market Manager, 191
Financial Administrator, 174
Human Resources Management,
      174, 177
International Management, 173, 191
IS Planning and Procurement, 177
Logistics Planning, 177
Manufacturing Team Management, 152
Market Positioning, 189
National Marketing Manager, 185
Operations Group Manager, 190
Operations Management, 114, 177
Production Planning and Control, 174
Regional Management, 189
Reprogramming and Testing, 177
Revenue and Profit Expansion, 174
Sales Force Development, 186, 189
Senior Management Consultant, 178
Senior Manager/C.P.A., 174
Service Manager, 179
Strategic Planning, 189

Staff Supervision/Training, 155, 156
Total Quality Management, 177
V.P. of Operations, 89

SOCIAL SERVICES

Counselor/Case Manager, 193
Social Worker, 194
Case Management, 194
Chemically Dependent Clients, 194
Crisis Line Counselor, 193
Family Counseling and Support, 194
Multidisciplinary Team Member, 194
Outreach Facilitator, 193
Program Development, 122
Project Coordinator, 123
Psychiatric Counseling, 193

TRADES

Automotive Technician, 195
Carpenter, 196
CNC Machinist, 197
Commercial Truck Driver, 198
Construction Manager, 199
Master Tradesperson, 200
Auto Systems/Service, 98, 179, 195
Construction Jobs, 196, 199, 200
Driver Positions, 96, 198
Electrician, 200
Fleet Maintenance, 195, 198
Heavy Equipment Operator, 198
Janitor, Crew Management, 97
Licensed Plumber, 200
Machine Shop, 197
Road Crew Lead, 89
Trades Management, 199, 200
Welder, 200

WRITING/JOURNALISM

On-Air News Reporter/Writer, 201
Science Reporter/Writer, 202
Award-Winning Writing, 201, 202
Editor, 100
Environmental Impact Writing, 202
Hard News and Features, 201
Health/Medical/Science Writing, 202
Interviews and Research, 201, 202
News Producer and Staff Manager, 201
Technical Writing, 202
Writing to Meet AMA Guidelines, 202

BOOKKEEPER/OFFICE MANAGER

SHEILA SMITH

BOOKKEEPER / OFFICE MANAGER

5050 S.E. 30th
Scranton, NJ 12345
(555) 555-5555

BOOKKEEPING

Established complete accounting system for new plant generating annual sales of $12 million annually, working directly with company President and CFO.

- Processed payroll for 65 employees and 1,250 A/R and A/P accounts.
- Handled complete set of books, cash disbursements, cash receipts, sales journal, general ledger postings, and bank reconciliations.
- Prepared financial statements and summarizations for 5 internal departments.
- Completed and submitted all payroll and excise tax reports.
- Processed billing for approximately 200 daily invoices and collected on bad debts.
- Maintained personnel and insurance files, updated employee status, calculated and submitted yearly pension and W-2 forms.

OFFICE MANAGEMENT

Managed office administration to support President and staff of 35.

- Converted all operations to computerized system and directed the implementation of a $200,000 computer system including analysis and selection of software.
- Trained management and sales staff in computer usage, sales, and inventory tracking.
- Consulted with exporters to compile export forms and packing slips for national and international shipments.
- Coordinated with insurance administrators to process claims.
- Attended executive staff meetings, composed senior correspondence, and prepared a variety of confidential reports and proposals.

SUPERVISION OF ADMINISTRATIVE STAFF

Supervised and trained 40 accounting, administrative, and customer service staff.

- Coordinated and assigned daily workflow for up to 5 departments, including hiring of temporary employees to meet seasonal work demands.
- Cut administrative turnover by 40% by instituting effective training programs.

CUSTOMER SERVICE ADMINISTRATION / PUBLIC RELATIONS

Developed strong rapport with 450 key accounts and vendors, as well as employees.

- Elicited customer concerns and resolved problems to maintain excellent public relations.
- Provided speedy and accurate follow-up on orders ranging up to $250,000 per order.
- Coordinated a variety of tasks in this fast-paced customer service environment.

EDUCATION

Bookkeeping & Office Administration, Lynnwood Academy

EMPLOYMENT HISTORY

Full-Charge Bookkeeper, Amsterdam Constructors 1990–Present
Full-Charge Bookkeeper, Smith & Sons Manufacturing 1985–Present

---

Accounting Resume Tips

WHEN PREPARING A RESUME FOR ACCOUNTING POSITIONS, DESCRIBE . . .

- Full range of your accounting or bookkeeping experience as well as additional duties you are responsible for, such as office or branch administration, staff supervision, or information systems management, if they match your job objective.

- Size of the company or department you worked for in terms of monthly or annual revenue, number of employees, number of divisions or locations, and standing of company, such as whether it is in the *Fortune* 500.

- References to the firm as an international, national, or regional organization.

- Number and titles of staff you worked with or consulted in each of your jobs, such as the president, CFO, or department managers.

- Number of A/P, A/R, and G/L accounts you were responsible for and the dollar amount of cash receipts, payables, and receivables you managed.

- Number of bank accounts you managed or reconciled.

- Dollar amount of payroll and number of employees you prepared payroll for or maintained benefits for.

ABBY KINNICK
13278 290th N.E., Louisville, WI 98008 (555) 555-5555

FULL-CHARGE BOOKKEEPER

Seek a challenging position as a Full-Charge Bookkeeper utilizing

- Over 9 years experience in office management, bookkeeping, and customer service.
- Proven history of self-motivation with ability to manage projects and meet deadlines.
- Ability to improve accounting and departmental operations for increased profitability.

AREAS OF EXPERIENCE

BOOKKEEPING	OFFICE MANAGEMENT	COMPUTER
A/R, A/P, G/L, Payroll	Supervision & Training	Conversions/Testing
Sales Journals, Billing	of Clerical Personnel	Work with Programmers
Bank Reconciliations	Workflow Scheduling	
Financial Statements		**PROGRAMMING**
Credit Verification	**CUSTOMER SERVICE**	BASIC, COBOL, RPG,
	Problem Solving	Fortran, Assembler

SUMMARY OF ACHIEVEMENTS

BOOKKEEPING Maintained A/R, A/P, and billing for over 1,500 accounts and payroll for up to 55 employees.

- Developed a variety of summary reports—A/R, payroll, staff utilization, sales, and cost reports.
- Researched and verified customer credit applications.
- Prepared quarterly reports and excise tax returns.
- Posted entries to sales journals and general ledger.
- Handled banking transactions and reconciled statements.
- Assisted with preparation of financial statements.
- Processed employee credit applications.

BRANCH OFFICE MANAGEMENT Managed branch office administration, overseeing general office, reception, and bookkeeping functions to support staff of 55.

- Supervised and trained clerical staff and delegated workflow.
- Maintained personnel files and insurance claims.
- Dealt with insurance administrators resolving claims problems.
- Developed OSHA & WSHA reports. Prepared union contracts.
- Purchased and inventoried office supplies.

COMPUTER CONVERSION Oversaw and implemented conversion of manual system to a Digital Mainframe Computer with PIC operating system.

- Worked with programmers in design/testing of software.
- Developed a variety of computerized spreadsheet reports.
- Completed a Computer Programming/Accounting Program at ITT, which included programming in BASIC, COBOL, RPG, Fortran, and Assembler Languages.

Arnold Helms
(555) 555-5555

210 30th Street
Crabtree, AL 56789

OBJECTIVE

A position utilizing my bookkeeping, office administration, and customer service skills.

COMPUTER EXPERIENCE		OFFICE ADMINISTRATION
FoxPro	Excel	Accounts Receivable & Payable
Quicken	MS Word	Computerized Billing
Peachtree	WordPerfect	Payroll / Recordkeeping
Database Administration	Data Entry	Multiline Phones

COMPUTERIZED BOOKKEEPING

- Maintained over 800 A/R accounts and approximately 100 A/P accounts.
- Prepared biweekly payroll for up to 8 employees.
- Prepared all deposits and reconciliations for 3 checking accounts.
- Converted manual payroll, A/R, A/P, and checking to computerized system.
- Set up computerized accounts and developed client database.

PURCHASING / INVENTORY CONTROL

- Purchased and maintained $10,000 worth of inventory for 55-unit condominium.
- Purchased all supplies for building, office, pools, and grounds from 15 vendors.
- Prioritized weekly and monthly responsibilities, consistently meeting all deadlines.
- Kept detailed records, documented purchases, and tracked inventory.

CUSTOMER SERVICE

- Coordinated with state, county, and city officials in completion of purchase orders.
- Provided cost estimates, project options, and company policy guidelines to customers.
- Dealt effectively with irate customers, resolving conflicts and negotiating payments.
- Provided quality service by assessing and fulfilling customer needs.

EMPLOYMENT HISTORY

Computerized Bookkeeping	A-1 Mechanics, Inc.	1994–1999
Purchasing/Inventory Control	Hotel Procurers	1991–1994
Inventory Control/Customer Service	Balboa Distributors	1990–1991
Customer Service/Purchasing	General Vehicle	1988–1990

EDUCATION

Computer Applications—Certificate	B.C.T.I.	1999
Pre-Law Studies	Bellevue Community College	1997
Legal Clerk Training	U.S. Army	1985

More Accounting Tips

- Types of tax reports you prepared and filed, and if you filed them monthly, quarterly, or annually.
- Number and titles of staff you supervised or trained, as well as the range of duties they performed.
- Responsibility for preparing financial statements or balance sheets.
- Dollar amount of budgets you managed and what the budgets were allocated for.
- Dollar amount of billing you managed or prepared, and the number of accounts you supervised.
- Dollar amount of assets you controlled and capital equipment you purchased.
- Types of accounting reports you prepared, who they were forwarded to, and what they were used for.
- Types of special projects you may have been responsible for, such as implementing new computer systems or relocating and setting up your office.
- Types of computerized accounting systems and software you used, implemented, or supervised. The dollar value of such systems, how many departments or facilities they were located in, and if you helped to improve the system in any way.

More Accounting Tips

- How many departments, and the names of departments, you coordinated with to complete accounting reports or to do your job, and the titles of key staff you served as a liaison to.

- Categories of accounting duties that you were responsible for, such as invoicing, inventory control, billing, job costing, payroll, banking, leasing, or purchasing using numbers as much as possible to describe each duty.

- Level of profit and loss responsibility you held demonstrated by what your firm's or department's monthly, quarterly, or annual sales or revenues were and by what percentage you cut losses or stayed within budgets.

- Systems or ideas you implemented that you received awards, promotions, or commendations for, with examples of how successful they were.

- Names of key accounts or organizations you dealt with that have high name recognition.

- Education and training you've completed, as well as certifications or licenses you hold, with greater detail provided about skills or knowledge that relates to the field of accounting or bookkeeping.

Charles Delay
P.O. Box 2920
Dallas, TX 78933
(555) 555-5555

**Seeking a position utilizing over 10 years
Accounting & Job Costing experience, which includes**

- Managing senior-level accounting functions for firm with 6 corporations, 12 divisions, and revenues of $31 million annually, working directly with President and Board of Directors.
- Overseeing job costing, payroll, and benefits administration for staff of up to 90.
- Managing multimillion-dollar budgets, job costing, internal audits, depreciation, sale of assets, division mergers, corporate portfolio, and worldwide investments.

Senior Staff Accountant, Cable Management Services 1995–Present

- Managed accounting functions for this worldwide cable management firm composed of 6 corporations with 12 divisions and total sales of $31 million annually.
- Directed corporate accounting for 4 subsidiary divisions with revenues of $12 million annually.
- Established initial accounting system for primary corporation and oversaw the integration of corporate acquisitions and sales.
- Developed and managed auditing team; annual budgets and depreciation/sale of assets.
- Provided senior accounting consulting to CFO and Corporate Managers to implement strategic growth plans.
- Prepared journal entries and financial statements using computerized system.
- Analyzed and reconciled all general ledger accounts using Lotus 1-2-3. Created and enhanced Lotus 1-2-3 worksheets for general ledger accruals.
- Prepared monthly and quarterly payroll tax reports and various state business reports.

Management of Job Costing / Payroll & Benefits, Abrams Publishing 1994–1995

- Managed job costing for 3 departments generating revenues in excess of $9 million annually.
- Supervised ADP payroll administration for staff of 90, directed preparation of payroll tax reports, 401K reports, and 125B Cafeteria Plan.
- Oversaw processing of 2,500+ computerized A/P accounts.

Full-Charge Bookkeeper, Construction Assets, Inc. 1992–1993

- Managed full-charge bookkeeping for this multimillion-dollar corporation, working extensively with VP, CFO, and Regional Manager.
- Prepared journal entries, computerized payroll, payroll taxes, accounts receivable and payable, account reconciliations, budgets, and financial statements.

Education

Business Technology Degree in Accounting and Computer Programming
North Seattle Community College
Recipient of Distinguished Scholar Award—GPA 4.0

LEGAL ADMINISTRATIVE ASSISTANT

STEPHEN CARTER   3489 284th Street, Brownsville, OR 98203   555-555-555

Seeking a Legal Administrative Position

LEGAL ADMINISTRATIVE ASSISTANT PROGRAM ———————

Legal Document Preparation

- Prepared pleadings, briefs, case and statutory citations, jury instructions, transmittal letters, and legal correspondence for family, civil, and criminal litigation.
- Researched and interpreted Washington Court Rules, Revised Code of Washington, and Uniform System of Citation for case documentation and Court Calendaring.

Legal Transcription / Records Management

- Transcribed and prepared legal correspondence and documents from written notes and verbal dictation—typing at 60 wpm.
- Followed ARMA rules to set up alpha and numeric client files, client billing, and fee arrangements.

Computerized Legal Office Applications

- Utilized WordPerfect, Windows NT, PowerPoint, and Excel to prepare legal documents, presentation materials, billing, and database files.

DEPARTMENTAL SUPPORT ————————————————

Customer Service

- Dealt with up to 200 customers per day, coordinating with up to 4 departments to meet customer needs.

Departmental Documentation

- Utilized computerized system to access and verify customer accounts and track up to $70,000 in returns per month.
- Prepared till balance documents, inventory reports, and credit card transactions.
- Awarded "Employee of the Month" for achieving highest accuracy rating in processing more than 1,000 monthly customer transactions.

Staff Training & Supervision

- Trained and supervised up to 20 staff in customer service, account documentation, inventory control, merchandising, and opening and closing procedures.

EDUCATION / EMPLOYMENT HISTORY———————————

Legal Administrative Assistant Program, Renton Technical College 1999.
Customer Service Specialist, Wal-Mart Department Store 1997–1998.
Sales Associate, JC Penney 1996–1997.
Medical Transcriptionist Program, Seattle Vocational Institute 1994–1995.
Customer Interviewer, Marc Marketing Research 1993–1994.

Administrative/ Clerical Resume Tips

WHEN PREPARING A RESUME FOR ADMINISTRATIVE, SECRETARIAL, OR CLERICAL POSITIONS, DESCRIBE . . .

- Size of the company you worked for in terms of annual sales, number of employees, or offices if this is impressive and sounds like the type of company you want to work at.

- Number and titles of staff or departments you provided administrative or clerical support to.

- Type of work you performed and range of duties you completed, being sure to prioritize and list your most important job functions first and eliminating those that might weaken your image.

- Size of projects you were responsible for, such as preparing contracts with fees ranging from $20,000 up to $500,000 or purchasing up to $50,000 in office supplies each year.

- Number and titles of staff you trained or supervised, either in each job or cumulatively throughout your career.

- Range of job functions you trained staff in, as this often demonstrates the breadth of your office skills and knowledge. To train someone, you must also know that skill or job function.

More Administrative Tips

THIS RESUME CONTAINS IDEAS ABOUT . . .

- Titles and number of departments and staff you coordinated with to do your job, obtain information from, or resolve problems with.

- Number of customers and names of key accounts that you communicated with on a daily or monthly basis as well as the range of revenues generated from large accounts you dealt with.

- Types of problems you were responsible for resolving and how successful you were.

- Number of phone lines you answered, the number of extensions you transferred calls to, and the type of phone systems you are familiar with, such as PBX or Rolm.

- Type and dollar value of any kind of equipment you researched, purchased, or advised management to purchase.

- Kinds of office systems you implemented or improved and if your improvements resulted in increased productivity, labor or cost savings.

- Special projects you managed such as office relocations, international travel arrangements, greeting VIPs, organizing trade shows or special events, etc. Provide details of how many people you did this for or how many attended the events.

Samantha Naples
2389 S.W. 80th
Los Angeles, CA 98202
(555) 555-5555

OBJECTIVE & QUALIFICATIONS

Position as an Administrative Office Assistant utilizing the following experience:

- Managing front office administration while providing support to the firm's President and 20 management and field representative staff.
- Preparing correspondence, quotes, and proposals using WordPerfect, MS Word, and Lotus 1-2-3.
- Overseeing the mail department and coordinating delivery of critical documents to support 8 departments.
- Completing a Certificate in Office Automation and Executive Secretarial Procedures, Griffin Business College.

ADMINISTRATIVE EXPERIENCE

ACCOUNTS SPECIALIST / ADMINISTRATIVE ASSISTANT, Safeco Consulting Division
- Served as Administrative Assistant to Branch Manager, being responsible for screening, prioritizing, and forwarding internal requests from 12 departments to the Branch Manager or to appropriate departments.
- Processed and verified up to 1,000 legal documents for claims ranging in value from $500 up to $100,000.
- Coordinated customer service and claims processing with bank officials, bank customers, insurance agents, and interoffice employees. Composed and edited client correspondence using dictaphone.
- Maintained general ledger postings with Ten-Key at 327 spm and Typing at 100 wpm.
- Achieved a 98% accuracy rating in processing of documents and correspondence while maintaining a high production volume in a fast-paced, demanding work environment.

FRONT OFFICE ADMINISTRATION, Abrams & Williamson, Inc.
- Managed front office, providing secretarial support to the President and 8 management staff.
- Prepared correspondence, certificates, quotes, proposals, and summaries utilizing WordPerfect 5.0.
- Managed mail department, being responsible for successful delivery of confidential and critical documents to support staff in 6 departments.
- Controlled a purchasing budget to maintain office and engineering supplies; purchased office equipment, computer system, and related maintenance services.
- Handled an 8-line phone system with 20 extensions.

DEPARTMENTAL SUPPORT / SECRETARIAL LEAD, Systems Control
- Provided secretarial support for 3 departments, which included composing and editing correspondence.
- Served as Word Processing Lead to secretarial staff in all departments, being responsible for initial orientation after hire, word processing training, and problem resolution.
- Set up new filing system to accommodate over 25,000 files, purge and store out-of-date documents.
- Managed mail operations for 8 departments and coordinated with department managers including

Marketing	Accounting	Medical
Administration	Claims	Eligibility
Data Processing	Customer Service	

ALICE COOPER
200 N.E. Northup Way
Dupont, RI 08004
(555) 555-5555

OBJECTIVE

Challenging Office Manager / Administrative Assistant position using my ability to manage projects, streamline procedures, and deal extensively with customers.

AREAS OF EXPERIENCE

Dictaphone	Collections	Computers
Correspondence	Bookkeeping	IBM & Macintosh
Typing 65 wpm	Inventory Control	Order Entry, Word Processing
10-Key by Touch	Shipping/Receiving	Payroll, A/R, A/P, Inventory
PBX & Multiline Phones	Travel Arrangements	Excel Spreadsheets
Purchasing Office Supplies	Appointment Scheduling	Database Design/Maintenance

OFFICE MANAGEMENT

NEW OFFICE SETUP

Managed and reorganized distribution office including credit management/collections operations.
- Corresponded with corporate headquarters daily.
- Developed and maintained job logs, customer accounts, inventory, invoicing, accounts payables and receivables.

WORKFLOW SCHEDULING

Directed administrative functions to support staff of 25 as Assistant Office Manager.
- Managed workflow of clerical and shipping personnel.
- Responsible for inside sales, expediting, and order entry.
- Trained sales and accounts payable staff.

INVENTORY CONTROL

Controlled inventory for 3 warehouses in 2 states.
Compiled year-end spreadsheet reports.
- Ordered stock and maintained vendor relationships.
- Processed parts requisitions, coordinating with production, Q.C., and shipping departments.

BOOKKEEPING

Managed general ledger, payroll, A/R, A/P, sales journals, personnel records, and bank reconciliations. Managed petty cash, controlled budgets, and purchased office supplies and equipment.

EDUCATION

Accounting and Office Procedures Certificate, Edison Technical School

EMPLOYMENT

Assistant Office Manager, Dupont Awning 1996–Present
Office Administrator, Northwest Symmetrical Products 1990–1995
Inventory Control, Packaging Services, Inc. 1988–1990

More Administrative Tips

HERE ARE MORE TIPS TO DESCRIBE . . .

- Volume and type of work you or the administrative staff you supervised or trained were responsible for.

- Your typing, ten-key, and shorthand speed as well as your level of accuracy.

- Types of computer systems and peripheral equipment you have experience with.

- The names of leading software packages you have experience with, as well as what you used the software for, such as producing spreadsheets to track and control budgets ranging up to $ 1/2 million, create customer databases, or prepare executive correspondence.

- Advanced operation of software you've used such MS Word mail merge, newsletter, or math calculation functions.

- Number of documents, files, or shipments you were responsible for processing or maintaining on a daily or monthly basis.

- Number and types of vendors or outside organizations you communicated with or negotiated with and how this related to your job.

More Administrative Tips

◆ If you are an executive secretary, use job titles and skill headings that sell your experience supporting senior staff as the resume on this page illustrates.

◆ If you are a receptionist wanting to move to a higher-level position, label your reception experience "Front Office Administration" or "Branch or Corporate Reception." These headings create a higher-level image. Consider using additional skill headings to elevate your image and describe your general office skills, such as "Departmental Support," "Computerized Office Applications," or "Assistant to Executive Staff."

◆ If you are a general office clerk, then be sure to quantify your duties such as how many staff you work with, how many files you maintain, how many phone lines you answer. You'll also want to use skill headings like those above to elevate your image.

◆ If you are working in, or applying for a job in a specific field such as a legal or medical secretary, be sure to describe the range of your specialized knowledge and use terms that are targeted to your field. For example, "Legal Transcription" is stronger than "Transcription." "Medical Office Administration" is stronger than "Office Administration."

Carl Roland
(555) 555-5555   applicant@abcd.net

2109 Seventh Avenue
Baltimore, MD 38573

SENIOR-LEVEL EXECUTIVE ASSISTANT

offers expertise in Management of Office and Division Administration;
Supervision of Administrative Staff; Streamlining of Business and Office Procedures;
Management of Accounting and Customer Service Departments proven by

- Serving as Senior Executive Assistant to top-level executives, which required seasoned business acumen and ability to manage highly sensitive matters and reduce staff workloads.

- Supervising administrative staff and managing division operations including accounting, finance acquisition, contract negotiation, vendor services, marketing, and customer service administration.

- Achieving high production through typing and shorthand at 100 wpm, having excellent accuracy, and proven ability to complete time-sensitive, critical projects with a Top Security Clearance.

EXECUTIVE ASSISTANT TO NATIONAL DIRECTOR
World Health Organization 1985–Present

Executive Support to Division Heads
- Managed administrative operations to support 5 Division Chiefs with responsibility for hiring, scheduling, supervision, and training of 22 administrative staff.

Division Administration—Office of National Director
- Managed division administration for Office of the National Director, with responsibility for controlling complicated calendar and scheduling with U.S. Health Departments.
- Interfaced with all levels of staff, including high-government officials with responsibility for coordinating confidential meetings, preparing and transmitting sensitive documents.

Administrative Management of International Projects
- Managed all administrative functions for international projects as Assistant to Directors of European and Asian Divisions and 24 Mission Chiefs on worldwide health missions, prior to position as Executive Assistant to National Director.

Divisional Operational Analysis & Improvement
- Analyzed and streamlined work practices by implementing computerized systems, which eliminated redundant work by 32% and resulted in total annual savings of $100,000.

Implementation of IT Systems / Database Design
- Analyzed existing IT and database systems for three divisions. Successfully streamlined and developed two major databases to track work output of 50 administrative staff; assess division project performance; create and consolidate monthly reports for all divisions.

Delivery of National Training Programs
- Served as Trainer/Facilitator for WHO's national orientation and training program. Determined key staffing needs and updated curriculum used in all divisions.

Business Management
- Owned and operated a service business, increasing revenues by 300% within three years of opening, prior to employment with WHO. Developed business plan, policies, and procedures; secured financing; managed staff; negotiated contracts; and controlled operational budgets.

B.A. DEGREE, LIBERAL ARTS

Frances Delaney
200 N.E. Poplar Drive
Indianapolis, IN 92304
(555) 555-5555

OBJECTIVE
*Seek an internship position utilizing my
Events Promotion, Marketing, Public Relations, and Administrative experience.*

EVENTS DEVELOPMENT & PROMOTION

University of Saskatoon—Promoted and led a variety of events to support the University's body of 600 students in four-year and master's degree programs, which included

- Assisting the Student Services Director and coordinating New Student activities.
- Creating over 200 brochures and flyers for events and seminars for Welcoming of Incoming Students, On-Campus Safety Issues, and Student Government Elections.
- Drafting the Student Constitution as an elected member of the student body. Coordinating student membership meetings, Student Fees Committee, and documenting related projects.

DISTRICT EVENTS MANAGEMENT

Vice President of Administration for DECA Program—Managed events and meeting schedules for students from 4 school districts participating in setup and management of a student business sponsored by ARCO.

- Coordinated production and marketing of 20 consumer items, took meeting minutes, organized annual report, and attended business management program.
- Hosted Seafair activities and events registration at a major shopping mall.

DEPARTMENTAL ADMINISTRATION

Office of Vice President, WFM Corp.—Interfaced with 6 branches coordinating local and national meetings, including scheduling of airline, hotel, and transportation for Office of Vice President.

- Coordinated support and facility requirements for corporate meetings.
- Trained 5 general office clerks in use of MS Word, Excel, and data entry programs.
- Oversaw front office reception, processed mail for 3 departments, reorganized existing filing system, and maintained documentation for staff of 10 Sales Representatives.

PUBLIC RELATIONS / CUSTOMER SERVICE

Dealt with hundreds of customers daily, processing sales of up to $65,000 per month.

- Assisted customers in making product selections, solved problems, utilized computerized cash registers, and controlled and maintained $225,000 in inventory.

EDUCATION
Bachelor of Arts Degree in Liberal Studies, University of Saskatoon
Associate of Applied Science Degree, Singleton Community College

EMPLOYMENT WHILE COMPLETING EDUCATION
Departmental Administration, N.W. Marine Supply 1997–Present
Public Relations / Customer Service, The Keg Restaurants 1995–1996
Office of Vice President, WFM Corp. 1991–1994

Tips for College & University Students

AS A STUDENT OR RECENT GRADUATE, DESCRIBE . . .

- Internships or practicums you've completed, emphasizing skills you've gained that match the jobs you want. For example, Frances was a student activities coordinator but emphasized the experience she had developed in events promotion rather than her title.

- Skills you've developed in paid employment or volunteer positions that match and support your job objective. Again, it may be important to use skill headings rather than job titles.

- Number and titles of staff you worked for or with, in each internship, volunteer, or paid position. Emphasize titles of staff that are like the staff you will work with in the job you want.

- Number and titles of staff you may have trained and the range of job functions you trained them in. Show how the training you provided relates to skills needed in the job you want.

- Size of organizations you interned or worked for, such as total number of employees, *Fortune* 500 ranking, or total revenues.

More College Student Tips

DESCRIBE . . .

◆ Key terms used in your career field to describe the primary job duties you were responsible for, or areas of knowledge you developed, that in some way relate to the jobs you want.

◆ Systems or procedures you implemented or improved.

◆ Length of each internship or number of hours completed, if impressive.

◆ Grades, commendations, or recommendations you received as a result of internships completed.

◆ Major papers you wrote and research conducted, primarily if they relate to your career goal.

◆ Presentations you gave on topics related to your career goal.

◆ Awards you were given if they in some way relate to the jobs you want. Why you received them and how many people you competed against to win each award.

◆ Scholarships for education or learning activities. For example: "Four-Year Full-Tuition Scholarship Awarded Based on High SAT Scores and Instructor Recommendations."

◆ Use these suggestions along with the advice in Chapters 4, 5, and 6 to build a strong resume that effectively markets your education.

Ralph Randall
(555) 555-5555   ralph@abcd.net

34 Post Road Hill
Wishing, MT 89012

BUSINESS OPERATIONS ANALYST

Offers expertise with Fortune 500 corporations with responsibility for Financial Modeling, Gross Margin Improvement, Revenue Forecasting, Strategic Pricing & Production Analysis coupled with Software Programming, Operations Management, and Training Program Development experience, which includes

Creating financial models to forecast revenue and volume impact on manufacturing expansion, which cut project costs by $75,000 as a Cross-Functional Analyst.

Achieving savings of $275,000 and improving gross margin by 26% as an Operations Manufacturing Analyst.

Developing applications using C, C++, SQL, and FORTRAN with comprehensive knowledge of hardware and software including Windows, DOS, Word, Excel, and Access.

Completing the M.B.A. Program at Montana University with published Master's Thesis entitled "Business Analysis and Maximization of Production and Profits."

FINANCIAL ANALYST, GENERAL MOTORS 1998–Present

Development of Financial Tracking System
- Created financial models to forecast annual revenue of $600 million with projected 7.2% revenue increase. Developed financial tracking system to calculate costs, which eliminated reentry of data and omitted high percentage of data errors, resulting in estimated savings of $75,000.
- Worked directly with CFO to develop regional financial forecasting reports.

OPERATIONS ANALYST, WESTINGHOUSE 1996–1997

Management of Manufacturing Team
- Managed manufacturing team in charge of electronics production, which took output from $1.3 million to over $2.1 million by fiscal year-end.

Production Design / Cost Savings
- Analyzed production activities for two of Westinghouse's high-value products, which included designing jigs that cut labor costs by over 38%. Designed parallel processor algorithms to create an integrated parts pulling and project scheduling system that cut work-in-progress by 31.5%.
- Achieved annual savings of $275,000 and received Westinghouse On-Time Delivery Award.

DIVISION MANAGEMENT, U.S. ARMY 1992–1996

Operations & Staff Management
- Promoted to Company Sergeant with responsibility for division of five sergeants managing a total staff of 135 personnel. Implemented division-wide training program. Controlled $12 million of equipment and managed personnel and accounting administration.

EDUCATION

M.B.A. Degree, University of Montana 1998
Thesis published by Montana University Press, July 1999

CURRICULUM VITAE

Frank Dumont
(555) 555-5555   applicant@abcd.net

35 Adams Road
Carston City, NY 00123

VP / REGIONAL DIRECTOR—ACADEMIC MANAGEMENT

Offers over 10 years experience in Education Management, Supervision of Academic Departments, Compliance with Federal Funding Programs, Fiscal Control, Facility Development and Management, and College Marketing Programs proven by

- Managing up to 5 college campuses with total revenues in excess of $45 million annually, successfully increasing enrollment by over 35%.
- Supervising staff of 150 including Directors of Student Services and Academics, Financial Aid Officer, Instructional Staff, and Administrative personnel.
- Managing curriculum development and accreditation functions for 40 courses. Controlling budgets of $6.1 million and supervising financial aid and accounting departments.
- Serving as a Board Member for the New York State Education Commission; authoring books and articles on educational topics; and serving as a speaker for national education conferences.

SENIOR-LEVEL MANAGEMENT—CAMPUS OPERATIONS

Vice President of Academics, Business & Medical Training Institute 1995–Present
- Directed operations for 5 campuses, generating sales in excess of $45 million annually.
- Supervised Academic, Financial Aid, Placement, Instructional, and Records Departments.
- Ensured academic operations adhered to federal and accrediting agency regulations.
- Supervised Financial Aid and Accounting Departments as Controller prior to this position.
- Managed accounting functions and prepared financial statements, controlled $6.1 million annual budget and conducted internal audits.
- Coordinated program reviews with accrediting auditors.
- Reorganized, updated, and computerized accounting department taking department from noncompliance to compliance with ongoing maintenance of accreditation.

Regional Director, Northeast College of Business 1990–1994
- Directed 6 campuses serving over 2,100 students and generating revenues of $12 million.
- Increased student enrollments and resulting revenues by 37.5% while improving profitability.
- Supervised staff of 150 including Academic Deans for 12 programs, Financial Aid, Instructional, and Administrative personnel.
- Controlled annual budget in excess of $5 million with responsibility for procurement of books, supplies, and capital equipment.

Academic & Operations Director, Northeast College of Business 1984–1990
- Directed campus operations generating annual revenues of $6.1 million serving 750 students.
- Doubled student enrollment by implementing a comprehensive marketing program.
- Trained, supervised, and evaluated staff of 31 including financial aid and instructional staff.
- Taught multiple programs including Business Operations, Supervision and Leadership, and Business Law in the Workplace prior to promotion as Campus Director.

Curriculum Vitae Tips

- A curriculum vitae is somewhat different than a resume because it puts a heavy emphasis upon academics. CVs also tend to be longer than the average resume and can run from two to five pages. Resumes written for international positions where extensive details are requested all the way back to high school or elementary education may be even longer.

- CVs emphasize academic achievement such as degrees, honors, and awards received; grade point average; academic research completed; papers written, published, or presented; scholarships and sponsorships; inventions or patents; honorable mention in trade magazines or other sources; a curriculum taught or developed; and professional affiliations.

- Many curricula vitae follow traditional formats but are ineffective because of this. As illustrated in Chapter 4, traditional chronological formats are often not an effective marketing tool for job seekers who need to market skills rather than their most recent positions.

- When developing your curriculum vitae, decide what area of your background is most related to the job you want.

More CV Tips

- If your skills are most important, then create a skill-based resume that uses skill headings to match your career goal. Then follow your skills section with detailed academic information such as education, publications, presentations, and affiliations.

- If your work experience is most important, then put your work history first.

- If education is your strongest qualification, then begin the resume with a heavy emphasis on academics followed by either a skills section or an employment section.

- You may be wondering if it's safe to deviate from a traditional CV format that starts with academics. While working as a job placement specialist for the University of Washington, Bothell, I helped students create CVs for application to highly competitive graduate programs. Using a format like the one here, the student affairs office saw a significant increase in acceptance of students into such programs.

- This proves that it is most important to sell your best marketing points first rather than sticking with a format that markets weak points first.

EDUCATION

Master's in Education, University of New York 1991
Master's in Business Administration, University of New York 1988
Bachelor of Arts Degree in Accounting, University of New York 1986

EDUCATIONAL PUBLICATIONS

Motivational Strategies for Increased Learning, McGraw-Hill, 1998
"Use of Universal Symbols in Teaching At-Risk Students," *Education* Magazine, Summer, 1997
"Personal Rewards of Teaching," *Educators Quarterly,* 1997
Identifying Self-Esteem Problems as Basis of Learning Dysfunction, McGraw-Hill, 1995
"Peer Involvement in the Classroom," *Education* Magazine, Spring, 1994

PRESENTATIONS, NATIONAL EDUCATION CONFERENCES

Motivating Instructional Staff, National Private College Conference 1999
Methods to Increase Student Enrollment & Retention, NE Educators Conference 1998
Increasing Private College Profitability, Administrators Career Development Conference 1997
Curriculum Design That Exceeds Accreditation Requirements, NE Educators Conference 1996

PROFESSIONAL AFFILIATIONS

Board Member, New York State Education Commission 1995–Present
President, East Coast Chapter of Education Administrators 1995–Present
Vice President, Baltimore Instructor's Learning Institute 1993–1994

SCHOLARSHIPS

Full-Tuition Scholarship for Master's in Education Program, University of New York
Two-Year Scholarship for Completion of B.A. Program, University of New York

AWARDS & HONORS

Top Educator Award, New York State Educators Association 1998
Dean's List, All Quarters of 1990–1991

REFERENCES & FURTHER DETAILS UPON REQUEST

CUSTOMER SERVICE MANAGER

Dorothy Killigan

15 Freemont Avenue

Plainview, KS 53486

(555) 555-5555

CUSTOMER SERVICE MANAGER

**offers expertise in Management of Customer Service Operations;
Administration of Major Accounts & Contract Negotiation;
Development & Delivery of Customer & Staff Training Programs;
and Management of Regional Service Teams proven by**

- Directing Customer Service Operations generating up to $1.8 million in revenues and supervising teams servicing $6.5 million of CAD computer equipment and software.

- Managing service of 450 key accounts including Microsoft, IBM, Hewlett-Packard, and AT&T.

- Exceeding sales and service quotas by 14%, representing $150,000 in annual revenue expansion, exceeding production by 9% and cutting account response time by 18%.

- Holding a B.S. in Business Administration from Kansas University.

CUSTOMER SERVICE / OPERATIONS MANAGEMENT

CAD Software Systems 1995–Present and Excel Distributors 1990–1995

Management of Customer Service & Call Center Operations
- Supervised Customer Service and Call Center Departments employing 15 staff who serviced 450 key accounts generating $1.8 million annually.
- Took division from a 85% customer satisfaction rating to a 99% rating by auditing on-site service and conducting customer surveys to identify needs.
- Negotiated major contracts with General Managers and Procurement Directors generating up to $100,000 in annual revenue per contract.

Delivery of Division-Wide Customer Service Training Programs
- Developed and installed infrastructure for division-wide customer service training program, which included authoring customer service manual, policies, and procedures.
- Established quarterly training modules for all staff to ensure top performance.

Training of Field Service Teams
- Authored individual training manuals for 32 products and directed delivery of training to 10 field service teams.
- Established performance criteria and evaluation system for each field service team.

Launch of New Business Operations / Niche Market Development
- Launched wholesale distribution business, achieving revenue growth of 38% by opening 3 new locations and taking sales to $1.5 million in 4 years.
- Outsold leading competitor by researching competitive products and needs of competitor's client base, which resulted in winning over 65% of competitor's business.
- Researched and set up overseas production facility, which cut costs by $250,000.
- Sold the business at a 350% profit over original investment within 3 years of operational management and expansion.

Tips for Customer Service and Retail Resumes

WHEN WRITING A RESUME FOR CUSTOMER SERVICE OR RETAIL POSITIONS, DESCRIBE . . .

- Number and type of customers you deal with on a daily or monthly basis. For example, are your customers corporate clients or residential homeowners? Use descriptions that match the types of jobs you want.

- Geographic locale your customers are from, or that you service, such as a national or regional customer base.

- Dollar amount of revenues generated by the store or department you work in, or manage, or from customers or accounts that you service.

- Types and number of products or product lines you market.

- Kind of feedback or positive comments you receive from customers or your superiors regarding the level of service you provide.

- Size of organization you work for, such as the firm's total annual revenues, number of employees, or customers it services.

- Number of customers or staff you have trained, the range of their titles or job functions, and type of training provided.

More Retail Tips

◆ Number of staff you supervised in each position, or throughout your entire career, as well as the range of their job titles or job functions.

◆ Size of the store or department that you work in or manage in terms of square feet or dollar value of inventory.

◆ Type and number of products or product lines that you market or manage, total sales generated from them, and the number and type of vendors you deal with.

◆ Names of key accounts you service, especially if they are well recognized in your field.

◆ Increases in sales, profitability, or inventory turnover you've achieved.

◆ Reductions in cost, vendor pricing, unpaid accounts receivable, or employee turnover you've achieved.

◆ Dollar amount of operating, marketing, advertising, procurement, or payroll budgets you manage.

◆ Wide range of duties you perform, such as management of customer and vendor relationships, store design, inventory control, purchasing, seasonal planning, staff scheduling, theft prevention, or facility maintenance.

Mike Chaney
(555) 555-5555   mike@abcd.com

P.O. Box 528
Smithe, CO 88383

RETAIL OPERATIONS MANAGER

**offers expertise in Revenue and Market Base Expansion;
Strategic Planning; New Business Launch; Store Design; Product Line Development;
Customer Relationship Management and Supervision of Management Staff proven by**

Analyzing market trends, developing new product lines, and creating a mixed media advertising program that increased sales up to 41.7% per product, achieving gross sales of $11.1 million.

Overseeing all areas of retail operations including human resource management, financial administration, purchasing, and budget control to maintain a 34% profit margin.

Management of Retail Operations	Product Management
Revenue Expansion / Strategic Planning	Product Design & Planning
Sales & Inventory Planning	International Vendor Sourcing
Staff Supervision & Management	Package / Pricing Strategies
Profit & Loss Management	Emerging Market Analysis
Stringent Cost Control Measures	Annual Sales Forecasting

MULTISITE RETAIL MANAGEMENT
Bagworth Sporting Apparel 1985–Present

Retail Operations—Launch & Management
Launched and managed 4 retailing establishments marketing high-end sporting apparel to an affluent market, successfully building revenues to $11.1 million annually. Developed clothing and footwear line consisting of 210 products marketed in 1,000 square feet of retail space.

Revenue & Cost Control with Full P&L Responsibility
Managed all aspects of financial control for all locations with responsibility for sell-through rates and product profitability with margins of 34% over gross costs. Developed and controlled payroll and related budgets. Installed a computerized inventory system that cut labor requirements by 26%. Saved $35,000 by negotiating long-term lease.

Annual Contract Negotiations—International Vendor Sourcing
Negotiated annual contracts with 32 international vendors. Purchased up to $2.5 million annually and worked closely with vendors designing new product lines.

Retail Design & Merchandise Planning
Designed store layout including signage, interior merchandising/floor plans, exterior fixturing, and window and showcase design, consistently meeting projected expense budgets.

HR Management—Retail Operations
Hired, trained, and supervised 45 retail staff including Store Managers, Purchasing Agents, Accountant, Sales, Stocking, and Customer Service personnel. Developed HR training manuals, corporate policies, and procedures. Managed payroll and benefits administration. Complied with state and federal hiring guidelines.

COMPUTER/ELECTRONICS INSTRUCTOR

Terry Smite
(555) 555-5555

Roosevelt Ave #310
Vancouver, AK 32385

Community College / Voch-Tech Instructor with over 10 years experience teaching Beginning to Advanced Computer classes.

SUMMARY OF COMPUTER LESSON PLANS DEVELOPED AND TAUGHT

Intro to Microcomputers	**Program Applications**	**Software—Beginner to Advanced**
Beginning Computers	Spreadsheets	MS Word, WordPerfect, Wordstar
Computer System Overview	Databases	Excel, Access, FoxPro
Multifunction Applications	Word Processing	PowerPoint, Publish It
Intro to DOS	Custom Software	**Internet / WWW Applications**
Intro to Windows	CADD Overview	Internet Explorer, Netscape
Intro to Database Applications	Accounting	FrontPage, PageMill, Photoshop
Intro to Programming	Utility Applications	Navigating the Web

COMPUTER INSTRUCTOR, Columbia College 1995–Present

- Taught over 700 students attending Introduction to Microcomputer and Advanced Computer Classes, during tenure with Columbia College for classes of up to 25 students.
- Introduced innovative teaching techniques that increased class attendance by 15% over average attendance rates.
- Managed up to 3 classrooms with over $150,000 of computer equipment, software, and training materials.
- Supervised Computer Lab serving up to 50 students with responsibility for hiring and training staff of Instructional Assistants.
- Introduced final exams in the computer lab in place of handwritten exams.
- Advised Department in selection, purchase, and installation of new computer systems.
- Wrote a grant request that resulted in obtaining $ $1/4$ million in funding with end result of new computer lab being built, and being given position as Grants Administrator.

ELECTRONICS INSTRUCTOR / SUPPLEMENTARY COMPUTER MODULES, Rex College 1994–1995

- Taught Basic Electronics, AC-DC, Introduction to Semiconductors, and Overview of General Avionics and introduced use of computers via 10 modules into the electronics curriculum.
- Set up and supervised Electronics Lab serving up to 75 students.
- Created and taught basic computer usage for 50 students who were new users.

RELATED INDUSTRIAL EXPERIENCE

Manager—Manufacturing Engineering / Electronics Testing, Sundstrand 1990–1995.
Manager—Microprocessor Controlled Systems, CX 1986–1990.
Quality Engineer—Undersea Electronics Systems, Honeywell 1980–1986.

Education Resume Tips

WHEN PREPARING A RESUME FOR EDUCATION POSITIONS, DESCRIBE . . .

- Range or categories of subjects you taught, particularly those that match your goal, as illustrated in the columns of these resumes.

- Number of students you've taught in each individual class or throughout your entire career.

- Diversity of students you've dealt with such as multicultural, at-risk, ESL, gifted, or remedial.

- Size of classes you taught or managed in terms of number of students in attendance.

- Level of student success your classes achieved such high grade point averages, high attendance levels, or high number of awards or scholarships received by your students.

- Learning labs, curriculum, or modules you developed; and the technologies or special tools you integrated into such labs or curriculum.

- Number of teachers or other staff you trained, their titles, what you trained them in, and how extensive the training was. If the training was in-school, district-wide, regional, or national training

More Education Tips

DESCRIBE . . .

◆ Size of the school or district that you taught in and titles of key staff or outside agencies you coordinated with to do your job.

◆ Extracurricular activities you developed, directed, or participated in that relate to your job objective.

◆ Professional training you've completed and certifications you hold that relate to the teaching position you want.

◆ Administrative duties such as completing attendance or district records.

◆ Grants you've written, funds you've managed, or special equipment you've obtained for your school, and what the dollar value of funds or equipment was.

◆ Meetings you may have headed or other types of consultation you may have provided, as well as what the meetings or consultation accomplished, and the titles of staff you dealt with.

◆ Level of parent conferencing or volunteer involvement you achieved and how it impacted your classrooms and students.

◆ Skills you developed in nonteaching positions that contribute to your skill as an educator, such as staff supervision, administrative management, counseling, community leadership, or organizational management..

Charles Tygen

12012 Franklin Ave. SE
Macon Springs, MT 53442
(555) 555-555

K-8 Certified Teacher

Seeking an Elementary Teaching position utilizing experience:

Developing curriculum and teaching classes of up to 32, including gifted and special needs students; achieving high levels of parent involvement in student tutoring.

Integrating Macintosh, MECC, and Jostens computer learning systems into existing and newly created lesson plans.

Holding a Master of Education Degree, Dean's List, University of Montana with K-8 Teaching Certificate with Science and Chemistry Endorsements.

K–8 including Special Education, At-Risk, and ESL Students

Areas of Instruction
Reading, Science, Mathematics, Geography, Music, Art, and Physical Education

Chapter 1 Reading Programs
Comprehension and Word Attack Skills
Dolch Sight Program
Spelling/Grammar
Testing/Botel

Student and Parent Liaison
Parent/Teacher Conferencing
Remedial Instruction
Self-Esteem Building

Special Education
Behavior Disabilities
Developmentally Handicapped
Mainstreaming of ESL and
At-Risk Students

5th Grade Teacher, Smithe Elementary, Stoque School District 1996–Present
• Taught math and reading for up to 100 students per day.
• Consulted with educational supply firm to develop reading curriculum that was adopted district-wide and served as a teacher trainer for new programs.
• Developed and managed math remedial program to support 20 teachers district-wide.
• Served on the Stoque School District math and reading curriculum team.

1st & 2nd Grade Teacher, Reed Elementary, Reed School District 1994–1995
• Integrated two grade levels into one classroom using multiage learning techniques.
• Set up class computer program utilizing Jostens/MECC systems. Taught basic Windows and word processing concepts to students.
• Implemented a computer tutoring program using 10 volunteer tutors.

1st Grade Teacher, Franklin Elementary, Redmond School District 1993
• Developed and taught a literature-based, whole language reading program using Dolch Sight Program, comprehension, and word attack skills.
• Created math enrichment and reading support plans as well as classroom planning systems that were utilized by 15 elementary teachers.

2nd Grade Teacher, Pride Elementary, Stoque School District 1992
• Set up student writing and storybook reading programs coupled with computerized system that allowed students to create art for each writing or reading project.
• Integrated science kit program that increased student research, analysis, and reasoning skills, which were adapted for all learning styles from mainstream to learning disabled to gifted students.

CLINIC MANAGER

Donna Evon
(555) 555-5555

42346 323rd St.
Paluma, HI 98108

> *Clinic Manager offers expertise in Group Practice Management with proven history of Expanding Revenues, which includes*
>
> - Managing group practice composed of 5 surgical clinics generating annual revenues of $16 million.
> - Hiring, training, and supervising a staff of over 47 back and front office personnel including Medical Assistants, X-ray Technicians, Laboratory Techs, Bookkeeping, and Reception staff.
> - Implementing professional marketing plans that increased revenue base by 18.3%.

MANAGEMENT OF MULTIPLE SURGICAL CLINICS
Paluma Physician Group 1987–Present

Surgical Clinic—Business & Revenue Expansion
- Managed 5 clinics staffed by 20 General, Vascular, and Thoracic Surgeons.
- Grew practice from 2 to 5 clinics during rapid expansion accomplished within 2 years.
- Worked closely with physicians to develop mission statement and corporate procedures.

Clinic Administration—P&L Reporting
- Managed all phases of clinic administration with responsibility for P&L Reporting.
- Supervised accounting, billing, patient appointments, and surgical scheduling.
- Controlled operating, payroll, and miscellaneous project budgets totaling $2.5 million.

Procurement of Medical Equipment & Supplies
- Researched and purchased capital equipment including X-ray and ultrasound systems.
- Managed relationships with 12 primary vendors for medical and paper supplies.
- Set up inventory control and equipment depreciation schedules utilizing QuickBooks.

Setup of New Clinic Operations
- Managed setup of 3 clinics with responsibility for site location and lease negotiation.
- Maintained close supervision of each project, keeping principals advised of progress.
- Purchased and facilitated installation of phone, medical imaging, and computer systems.

Medical Insurance Billing & Administration
- Met with Insurance Providers to set up billing procedures and ensure billing compliance.
- Supervised monthly billing with responsibility for reconciling any billing discrepancies.
- Complied with Radiology, OSHA, and Board of Health guidelines.

Implementation of Computerized Systems
- Converted manual billing to computerized system in first two clinics managed.
- Implemented new billing systems in all clinics as software became obsolete.
- Streamlined patient tracking and billing, which decreased repetitive data entry by 24%.

Clinical Administration—Computerized Applications
- MS Word, DR Software Medical Package, MacroKey, Quicken, and QuickBooks

Professional Licenses and Education
- Registered Nurse, University of Hawaii 1988

Healthcare Resume Tips

WHEN PREPARING A RESUME FOR HEALTHCARE POSITIONS, DESCRIBE . . .

- Type of clinic, hospital, or medical units that you worked for that are related to the type of job you want.

- Number of medical staff you coordinated with or supported, including their job titles and medical specialties.

- Number of internal departments, medical specialty units, or outside organizations you coordinated with to do your job or to facilitate patient care such as orthopedics, X ray, or respiratory care.

- Number of medical staff you trained or supervised, the range of their job duties or titles, and the total volume of patients or workload they were responsible for and that you oversaw. Type of in-service training you delivered.

- Number of beds in your ward or unit. Number of patients you cared for or provided services to on a daily or annual basis.

- Number of medical charts or other documentation you maintained or reviewed.

- Types of patients you cared for such as pediatric or geriatric, the disease processes, and medical procedures you performed or became familiar with.

MEDICAL ASSISTANT

Elizabeth Dornan
2387 33rd Avenue
San Francisco, CA 94000
(555) 555-5555

Seek position as a Medical Assistant in Cardiology utilizing experience: —————

- Setting up and managing stress testing labs and treadmill tests for 200 patients per day.
- Offering broad background as a Float serving in Cardiology, Neurology, Primary Care, Nephrology, Oncology, and Pulmonary Care Units.
- Setting up EKG laboratories and managing phone triage, patient/hospital scheduling, records maintenance, and billing.
- Hiring, training, evaluating, scheduling, and supervising medical assistant staff.

Cardiology Medical Assistant / Supervisory Experience —————

- Researched and set up several treadmill testing laboratories developing expertise in Administration of treadmill testing, EKGs, Holter monitor hookups, pacemaker checks, trans-telephonic checks, and venipuncture.
- Set up a neurology laboratory at Virginia Mason Clinic to support 10 physicians.
- Gained multi-specialty experience in hospital scheduling, patient referral to other specialists, phone triage, computerized scheduling, billing, and posting.
- Managed patient crises and prioritized critical activities in addition to lab management.

Clinical Trial Supervision—Cardiology

- Conducted in-depth trials for cardiac care patients with responsibility for administering treadmill tests, EKGs, venipuncture, and blood pressure checks.
- Provided follow-up, which included dose titration, use of concomitant medicines, and physician intervention following FDA-approved protocol and drug regimes.

Medical Assistant Certification and Cardiology Training

- Certified Medical Assistant, Virginia Mason Clinic In-House Training.
- Training to Conduct Clinical Trials—7,000+ hours Diagnostic Ultrasound, Pulmonary Function Testing, Transderm-Nitro Protocol 15.
- Complete list of 20 training programs attended can be provided.

Staff Scheduling / Management

- Owned firm that provided services to commercial properties valued to $12 million.
- Hired, trained, scheduled, and supervised employees; developed bids for projects valued to $30,000; held full responsibility for project management, site evaluation, and final project approval.

Employment History —————

Owner, Great Stokes Commercial Painting Service 1995–Present.
Clinic Administration / Medical Assistant, Internal Medicine Specialists 1994–1995.
Clinical Trial Supervision, California Cardiology Clinic 1992–1994.

More Healthcare Tips

DESCRIBE . . .

- Range of patient populations you've dealt with, such as multicultural, ethnic, underprivileged, or at-risk groups.

- Types of patient education or counseling you provided, and to whom you provided such services.

- Types of medical equipment you used or were responsible for, if you calibrated or ensured proper functioning of such equipment, and the dollar value of such equipment.

- Names or floors of departments you worked on, which shows specific or diverse experience you wish to market.

- Administrative duties you performed, such as taking of medical histories, controlling medical records, managing drug supplies, ordering inventory, dealing with vendors or suppliers, resolving billing disputes, or preparing reports.

- Supplies you ordered, how many units you controlled drugs for, or what the dollar volume of monthly or annual billing was that you managed or processed.

- Type of computerized systems you used to document patient care, schedule surgeries or staff, transmit records, or communicate with outside clinics or hospitals.

REGISTERED NURSE

BOB STOCKER, R.N.

1523 Simon, Sax TX 71234   555.555.5555

SUMMARY OF QUALIFICATIONS

Seeking acceptance into the Family Nurse Practitioner Program utilizing

18 years RN experience providing full range of care to patients and families of all ages from economically and culturally diverse populations. Managing a medical unit serving over 30,000 patients annually. Training and supervising over 40 RNs with direct responsibility for total patient care, narcotics control, assessment, and risk management.

FAMILY NURSING EXPERIENCE

General Practice	Preventive Care	Quality Control/Case Management
Adult & Pediatric ENT	Annual Physicals	CQI of Unit Operations
Minor Trauma	Women's Health	Family Systems Assessment
Orthopedic Injury	(Prenatal to 5th Month)	Physician and Agency Referrals
GYN Treatment	Well-Child Checks	PEDS/Adult Psychiatric Intervention
Adult Medicine	School/Sports Physicals	Medication Management

PATIENT ASSESSMENT / CASE MANAGEMENT

- Practiced independently, performing health histories, physical examinations, and triage including initiation of acute emergent care.
- Ordered and interpreted diagnostic studies including lab work, X rays, and EKGs.
- Performed diverse medical procedures including suturing, casting, splinting, nasal packing, debridement, respiratory care, and pelvic exams.
- Provided comprehensive primary care to first-, second-, and third-generation families.
- Delivered holistic care focusing on the patient and family as an integral system and facilitated home health, long-term, disability, rehabilitation, and acute care services.

STANDARDS OF CARE / ACADEMIC RESEARCH

- Established standards of care for hospital-wide implementation.
- Researched and instituted FastTrack Program, providing expedient cost-effective care.
- Developed timeline studies to track treatment modalities, length of stay, and patient loads to determine staffing and scheduling requirements for 66 physicians and nurses.
- Authored and copyrighted Emergency Department guidelines for Native American care to deal with barriers to delivery and acceptance of "Western" medicine.
- Conducted a comprehensive community assessment of Pierce County on teen pregnancy currently under review by the Health District for policy and community change.

PATIENT EDUCATION

- Provided patient education in health promotion and disease prevention including stress management, nutrition, life-style changes, pregnancy, family planning, and counseling.

PROFESSIONAL LICENSE & EDUCATION

- Registered Nurse, Certified Emergency Nurse, Neonatal Resuscitation Certificate
- Advanced Cardiac Life Support, Trauma Nurse Core Certification, BLS Instructor
- BSN Degree, Texas A&M University; Practical Nurse Certificate, Tampa College

---

More Healthcare Tips

WHEN PREPARING HEALTHCARE RESUMES, ALSO DESCRIBE . . .

- Academic or work-related research you've performed and if your employer or an outside agency used it. If used, how widely was it used and by whom.

- Papers or findings you've presented. How many staff you presented the information to, and their titles, and if the information was presented as in-service training or at regional, national, or international conferences.

- Your attendance or heading of staff and administrative meetings, or strategic planning sessions, and what such meetings entailed. Titles of staff who attended such meetings.

- Attendance in professional organizations including how large the membership was and what you did for the organization.

- Type of leadership roles you may have assumed, such as being the lead in crisis or emergency situations on a particular ward or unit, and the number and type of staff you led in such a role.

- New systems or procedures you implemented, how widely they were used, and if they were successful in cutting costs, improving productivity or quality of care.

SURGICAL TECHNOLOGIST

Samuel Frankel
(555) 555-5555

42346 323rd
Seattle, WA 98000

Seek a Surgical Technologist position utilizing the following background:

- Scrubbing to support staff of 60 physicians, RNs, and technicians for 19 operating rooms.
- Completing 1,440 hours surgical training with 550 hours surgical technology experience.
- Managing staff, processing computerized accounts, and opening and closing procedures.
- Holding a Surgical Technologist Certificate from Renton Technical College.

SURGICAL TECHNOLOGY—CLINICAL ROTATIONS

Transplants / General Surgical OR Rotation, Harborview Medical Center
- Scrubbed for this major referral hospital, supporting 19 operating rooms.
- Set up cases for Neurology, Orthopedics, Plastic/Reconstructive, Genitourinary, Gynecology, ENT, Gastrointestinal, General, and Cardiovascular surgeries.
- Set up for Kidney Transplants, AAA, Craniotomy, and Total Joints required preplanning with Circulator to prep inpatients for donor transplants.

General Surgical OR Rotation, Health South
- Supported 10 operating rooms, selecting cases, arranging OR, and setting up equipment for Endoscopic procedures, Bilateral Mastectomies, Breast Biopsies, ACL Repair, Septoplasty, Tonsillectomy, Tympanoplasty, Herniorrhaphy, and Turp.
- Washed and sterilized equipment needed for next surgical case.

OB/GYN OR Rotation, Evergreen Medical Center
- Set up for C-section, cleaned rooms after procedure, and stocked unused supplies.
- Set up for vaginal births in patient birthing rooms. Set up for circumcisions in the nursery. Transported patients as needed.

Endoscopy Rotation, Overlake Medical Center
- Set up rooms for cases such as Colonoscopy, EGD, ERCP, and PEG Placements.
- Assisted physicians in retrieving specimens; cleaned scopes and operated sterilizer.
- Prepared patient for procedure, reviewed completeness of medical file, restocked supplies after procedures, and cleaned up post-procedure.

Central Supply, Riverside Hospital
- Gained experience in 4 Divisions—Decontamination; Assembly; Sterilization–Gas; and Steam, Wrapping, and Labeling. Packed cases for surgeries.
- Utilized ultrasonic cleaner and autoclaves.

MANAGEMENT & CUSTOMER SERVICE EXPERIENCE

Operations Manager, Blockbuster Video
- Supervised staff of 4 servicing 1,000 accounts with revenues of $4,500 per month.
- Managed inventory, computerized account processing, opening/closing procedures.

Customer Service, Franklins Fine Furniture
- Served up to 200 customers per day, marketing products and cashiering.
- Stocked and inventoried products and maintained merchandising floor.

More Healthcare Tips

DESCRIBE . . .

- Development of policy or procedural manuals or training materials detailing the delivery of patient care or of administrative documentation; how many different departments, units, clinics, hospitals, or total staff used the materials.

- Range of services you provided or supervised, such as front office or back office management.

- Type of lab work you performed, collected, or coordinated; the types of patients you provided this service for; and the disease processes that were involved.

- Type of phone triage or support you provided patients, such as nurse counseling or pre-assessment of traumas.

- Type of community agency referrals you made or coordinated to deliver a wide range of patient care and services.

- Type of family counseling or education you provided, how many families you've counseled, and the diverse issues or problems involved.

- Total years of experience you have if this is a strong qualification.

- Key terms and phrases hiring officials emphasize in job openings, such as being a "multidisciplinary team player."

Suzanne Rawlings
(555) 555-5555

880 Summercourt Pl.
Tampa, FL 29844

Seeking a position utilizing my Office and Customer Service experience coupled with training in Computerized Applications.

MARKETING COORDINATOR / EXECUTIVE SUPPORT

- Assisted office manager and 6 sales agents with financing for a citywide restaurant chain with 15 locations.
- Provided marketing and general office support to executive staff for this multimillion-dollar corporation.
- Assisted sales agents with project organization and file maintenance.

COMPUTERIZED OFFICE APPLICATIONS

- Utilized Excel, MS Word, and MS Works on IBM and Mac systems.
- Prepared correspondence, spreadsheets, newsletters, brochures, and input data entry to support sales staff.
- Utilized mail merge to prepare bulk mailings of 200 form letters.
- Type 50+ wpm with 10-Key at 230 spm.

CUSTOMER SERVICE

- Trained 5 employees in cashiering, sales, and customer service.
- Provided sales and service to 200 customers daily, resolving problems.
- Coordinated customer service with 15 employees and 5 managers.
- Accounted for up to $2,000 per day, making all deposits and safe drops.
- Utilized manual and computerized cashiering systems for 3 years.
- Bilingual in English and Spanish.

TRAINING—COMPUTER / OFFICE APPLICATIONS

- Completed over 500 hours training in Business Math, Accounting, Marketing, Word Processing, and Computerized Keyboarding.
- Tampa High School, Graduated January, 1999.

Employment While Completing Education

Marketing Coordinator, JoBaker Real Estate, 1997–1998
Customer Service/Hostess, Interlake Pancake House, 1996–1997
Customer Service/Cashier, Doug's Video, 1995–1996

High School Resumes

WHEN PREPARING A RESUME FOR A HIGH SCHOOL STUDENT, DESCRIBE . . .

- Range of skills developed on the job and in classroom settings as the accompanying resumes illustrate.

- Number of customers dealt with in retail, sales, or food service positions.

- Dollar volume of cash that you handled, and the frequency and number of tills that you balanced.

- Number and titles of supervisors and other staff that you worked with or supported.

- Volume of work that you prepared or processed, such as the number of products you packaged, number of letters typed, or number of files you maintained.

- Number of phone lines you answered, volume of calls you took, and the number of staff or departments you transferred calls to.

- Dollar amount of inventory that you helped to stock or order, and the square footage of stores or space that you stocked or displayed merchandise in.

- Daily duties you performed, such as verifying checks, processing credit card charges, cleaning facilities, stocking shelves, or taking customer orders by phone.

Terry Shaw
Springdale Road #12
Reeseville, SC 48333
(555) 555-5555

**Seek a Retail Sales position utilizing my
Customer Service and Opening / Closing experience.**

**Customer Service
Retail Sales**

- Dealt with up to 400 customers, processing sales of $2,000 daily.
- Handled over 200 customer complaints and returns monthly.
- Prepared daily pickup orders for up to 100 customers.
- Accounted for over $10,000 of inventory.
- Resolved problems by coordinating with customers and staff.
- Set up innovative window displays, stocked and priced merchandise for distribution to 5 branch locations.

**Opening/Closing
Operations**

- Trained 4 staff members in sales and production procedures.
- Assisted branch manager in employee scheduling.
- Opened and closed daily operations including
  - Setup of 10 workstations and equipment.
  - Cash drawers for 4 tills.
  - Electronic equipment for drive-through station.
  - Preparation of 200 stock items utilized by 16 employees.

**Cash
Accountability**

- Approved checks for up to 20 accounts daily.
- Utilized computerized cashiering systems for over 12 months.
- Processed bulk orders for up to 15 staff, with sales and receipts totaling over $40,000 monthly.

**Business
Computer Training**

- Completed over 440 hours of Business and Computer Training at Reeseville High School:

MS Word	PowerPoint	Excel
Form Letters	Brochures	Spreadsheets
Mail Merge	Business Cards	Calculations

Work History
Customer Service and Opening / Closing, Taco Time
Customer Service and Closing, Old Time Buffet
Customer Service / Bagger, Albertsons

AUTO CAD/MANUAL DRAFTER

Don Conrad
(555) 555-5555 e-mail jobhunter@abcd.idt.net

23458 Werth Avenue
Salt Lake City, UT 93334

Seek an AutoCAD Operator position utilizing 5 years experience:

AutoCAD R14 Operator........_providing drafting support for 3 branch locations._
Special Projects Manager......_overseeing special plan notices and changes._
Construction Manager....._supervising new construction projects._

AutoCAD R14—2,400 Hours Hands-On Experience
CAD Technology / A.A.S. Degree—3.95 GPA, ITT Technical Institute

AutoCAD Programming	Project Management	Structural Steel & Concrete Assemblies
Creation of Script Files	Cost Estimating	Civil/Topographical Maps
Menu Programming	Applied Physics	Industrial Piping
Paper Space, Model Space, X Refs	3-D Drafting Techniques	Layering Standards

AutoCAD R14 Operator / Special Projects Manager (Architectural) Burnstead Homes

- Provide drafting support for 3 branch locations, working directly with 2 architects and up to 20 engineering, internal marketing, and outside sales staff (for new residential development firm).
- Manage special projects including special plan notices and plan changes upon approval.
- Draft details for mechanical, electrical, engineering, and structural systems.
- Oversee up to a dozen projects routinely, as well as accommodating additional priority projects.
- Review, update, and correct plans submitted by outside architects.
- Revise up to 5 plans daily with a dozen or more sheets during peak periods.
- Operate AutoCAD running under DOS, Windows 3.11, Windows 95, and Windows NT.
- Considerable experience customizing AutoCAD environment and programming with autoLISP, layering systems, model space, beam calculations, printing/plotting, and troubleshooting.
- Extensive knowledge of Excel 7.0, Word 7.0, and WordPerfect 6.1.

Construction Manager, Conrad Construction

- Managed construction of 4 chalet-style cabins including rough framing, roofing, exterior finish, interior details, windows, plumbing, electrical, and decking.
- Reviewed plans and coordinated with inspectors, architects, and buyers to complete projects.

Project Management—Installation, CRE (Courtney Remodeling)

- Managed and completed an average of 4 remodel projects monthly, working directly with clients.
- Followed hand drawings and layouts to install refacing products.

Assistant Department Manager, B & P Food Chain

- Managed staff of 12 for department generating sales in excess of $1.5 million annually.
- Oversaw opening and closing operations, budget and inventory control, sales projections, scheduling, quality control, and merchandising for department of 25,000 square feet.

Drafting Resume Tips

WHEN PREPARING RESUMES FOR POSITIONS LIKE CAD/DRAFTING, DESCRIBE . . .

- Number of engineering staff you provide drafting for as well as their titles.

- Type of drafting you do, such as architectural or mechanical. Use keywords that match the jobs you want.

- Types of computer programs and software you are familiar with that in any way relate to skills needed in drafting positions.

- Types of projects you do drafting for, such as commercial, institutional, or residential.

- Range of fees for projects you perform drafting of, such as projects generating design fees of $10,000 to $250,000 per project.

- Dollar value of the buildings, equipment, or items you provide drafting of, such as commercial buildings ranging in value up to $12 million.

- Types of individuals or organizations you communicate with outside of your office, such as building officials and architects.

- Number of drafting projects you complete monthly or coordinate simultaneously.

Dan Parkins

(555) 555-5555   e-mail EETguy@abcd.idt.net

2534 15th Avenue
Vermont, AZ 83334

> **_Seek an Electronics Engineering Tech position_**
> _utilizing the following experience:_

Electronics Troubleshooting.....testing mother boards, memories, processors, and monitors.
PCB Repair.....diagnostics, rework, and repair to component level.
Electronics Engineering Technician/A.A.S. Degree.....1,900 hours, ITT Technical Institute 1998.
Electronics Inventory/Savings.....managing a $4.5 million inventory and reducing stock 70%.
Subcontractor Management.....cutting contract costs by $385,000.

TEST TECHNICIAN, Sony Electronics ———————————— February 1997—Present
Computer Troubleshooting / Setup of Bench Testing System
- Provide testing/troubleshooting of monitors, mother boards, hard drives, video cards, CPUs, memory boards, floppy drives, CD-ROMs, network cards, and modems.
- Support 7 field techs and 8 production crew for firm with sales of $12 million annually.
- Serve as sole notebook PC test repair tech for the company.
- Set up and implemented testing/troubleshooting system, servicing 30 accounts with $8 million in sales.

Inventory Administration / Cost Savings
- Manage production/repair inventory in excess of $4.5 million to manufacture 2,000 systems monthly.
- Reduced inventory 70% and shortened production lead time by testing items before return to vendors.
- Prepare P.O.s, match invoices, verify warranties, and maintain database for 25,000 units sold.

Vendor Coordination / Cost Savings
- Negotiated contract that saved the company $385,000 in a 5-month period.
- Cut vendor turnaround by 84% by reducing return time from 6 months to 4 weeks.

Customer Liaison / Account Management
- Deal with approximately 30 key accounts on a daily basis including Metro/King County Municipal Departments, King County Courthouses, and First National Bank branch locations.

PCB REPAIR / REWORK, Volt Temporary Service ——————— November 1996—January 1997
Electronic Production / Repair
- Repaired and assembled approximately 6,000 PCBs. Corrected flow solder errors including single resistors, 200-pin network connectors, capacitors, integrated chips, voltage regulators, and inductors.
- Built monitors from ground up with casings, CRTs, main boards, connecting power, and video cables.
- Followed schematics to properly assemble boards including through-hole soldering.

SUPERVISION / OPERATIONS MANAGEMENT, Wonder Bakery — February 1992—October 1996
Staff Supervision and Departmental Administration
- Supervised and trained up to 15 staff in production/shipping functions, processing 59,000 units weekly.
- Coordinated work schedule for 3 shifts and delegated duties.
- Maintained bookkeeping for 10 key accounts and coordinated with main plant to input orders.

NETWORK ADMINISTRATOR

Valerie Ashworth
(555) 555-5555

34 St. View Drive
New Orleans, LA 98108

Seek a Network Administration position utilizing the following background:

- Managing 4 networking systems serving 200 clients in 4 departments.
- Maintaining Microsoft NT and Novell Network for systems in 3 facilities.
- Serving as Access Team Leader, training users and creating applications.
- Managing operations and staff for branch with sales of $1.2 million.
- A.A.S. Degree in Computer Science, New Orleans Technical College 1999.

Networking / Technical Support

Network Administration

- Assigned trustee rights, created user and login scripts, installed operating systems, workstations and print server, and administered security rights to serve 200 clients.
- Supervised installation of Novell Netware, Microsoft NT, network cards, and cabling.
- Installed Wide Area Network high-speed phone line, serial, and parallel communications.

System Troubleshooting

- Consulted with Program Managers to troubleshoot systems in 4 departments.
- Installed hard drives, floppy drives, monitor cards, and CD-ROMs.
- Upgraded 486 PC lab to Pentium PC lab. Managed computer teams.
- Solved difficult user problems such as operating system and software errors.

Creation / Supervision of Help Desk

- Created and supervised a help desk that centralized system work requests.
- Selected and trained staff of interns providing network troubleshooting.

User Training / Computer Applications

- Designed Access software package for Computer Department tracking 100 clients annually.
- Led teams of 8 developers in design of front and back end Access programming.
- Taught operating systems and Microsoft applications to 150 computer users.

Design Applications / Operating Systems / Software

DOS 6.22	Assembler	Lotus Organizer	RBase
Windows 98	InfoModeler	Microsoft Schedule Plus	QuickBASIC
Windows NT	Lotus 1-2-3	Visual Basic	Turbo C

- Created accounting information system using Visual Basic; retail accounting system using Access; information systems and presentations using PowerPoint, Access, Excel, and Word; and developed optimization techniques in SQL Server Database Programming.

Employment, Holmes Manufacturing 1990—Present

Departmental Management

- Managed departmental operations and staff of 15 for branch with sales of $1.2 million.
- Trained staff in all areas of customer service, sales, closing and opening operations.
- Completed departmental reports and managed 10 vendor accounts.

Customer Service Administration

- Oversaw customer service and administration to serve up to 200 customers per shift.
- Set up and maintained base of 7,500 computerized customer accounts.
- Coordinated with 5 departmental managers and staff to meet customer needs.

Network Administration Resume Tips

WHEN PREPARING RESUMES FOR THIS FIELD, DESCRIBE . . .

- Complexity of the network you managed, such as how many terminals or PCs it included, how many locations or buildings it was distributed in, how many users accessed the system.

- Operating systems, platforms, and network software used.

- Dollar value of the total computer system you managed.

- Various functions you performed to manage the network such as creating user and login scripts.

- Number and titles of staff you coordinated with to maintain the network.

- Number of technical staff you trained or supervised, as well as their titles or descriptions of their job duties.

- Type of programming languages or software you've used and the range of applications you created.

- Number of users you've trained, including their job titles or job functions.

- Supportive skills such as project management or system acquisition.

Web Development Resume Tips

WHEN WRITING WEBMASTER OR WEB DESIGN AND DEVELOPMENT RESUMES, DESCRIBE . . .

- Operating systems and platforms you designed sites to run on.

- Software products used to create, launch, and maintain each site.

- Size of each site in pages or number of hits generated.

- Type of applications integrated into each site that you developed, such as customer response forms, databases, or online ordering systems.

- Success of your site in terms of awards, number of visitors, important reviews, or dollar amount of e-commerce transacted.

- Names of key accounts, customers, or employers you've designed sites for.

- Number of technical staff or users you've trained.

- Supportive skills you possess such as project management and scheduling, mock-up design, proposal development, vendor selection, and negotiation.

Reese Jones, Webmaster & Designer

Online Portfolio: http://www.abcddesign.com
1313 7th Avenue, Trenton, OH 87323
555-555-5555   rjones@abcddesign.com

Webmaster seeks position utilizing professional experience including

Development & Launch of Small- to Large-Scale Award-Winning Websites
Retaining Key Clients such as Microsoft, Amazon.com, and Netscape
Employing Internet PR Strategies Resulting in Sites Generating up to 1 Million Monthly Hits
Development & Integration of Site Features that Increased Visitor Base by 35%
Designing High-End, Professional Graphics, and Website Video Segments
Supervision of Technical Teams

Website Development & Management

Independent Designer 1990–Present   Sun Micro Web Designer 1996–Present

Development of Corporate Websites Designed and launched corporate websites ranging from 100 to 400 pages, generating up to 5 million hits per month per site.

Mock-Up of Commercial Sites Created layout and mock-up sketches for complex commercial sites selling up to 100 products per site.

Site Design / HTML / JAVA / CGI Conceived artistic look and authored 300 pages of informational literature. Utilized HTML, Java, Perl, and CGI scripts to create custom applications to run on UNIX systems. Created visitor forms to submit ordering or information requests.

Website Awards & Reviews Received Best of the Web, PC World Award, Cool Site, Top 100 Site, and Gold Mine Awards for all sites.

Launch & Web Ranking Maintenance Achieved high search rankings in HotBot, Yahoo!, Alta Vista, Webcrawler, Northern Lights, Infoseek, MetaCrawler, and Excite. Increased annual hit rate by a minimum of 35% per site.

Website Design Tools Utilized Homesite, PageMill, FrontPage, Photoshop, Gif Animator, NetObjects Fusion, DeBabilizer, Illustrator, Premiere, Soundforge, NetShow, Java, Shockwave, AlienSkin, Macromedia Fireworks, CGI, Perl, Sequel Server, HTML, VRML, and DHTML to design sites and create E-Commerce Applications and Active Server Pages.

Web Applications Gained extensive experience in HTML, naming protocols, file extension, gif transparency, ALT and HTML tag generation, effective use of bandwidths, animated gifs, and use of sound, video, and chat within websites.

Project Management & Budget Control Managed project budgets ranging from $10,000 to $200,000 with responsibility for initial conception, artist rendering to illustrate mock-up pages, and project scheduling to final launch.

Supervision of Technical Staff Hired, trained, and supervised teams of Web Designers and Programmers with responsibility for delegating project workflow and final product review.

View Samples of My Web Design Projects at http://www.abcddesign.com

EXECUTIVE CHEF

PO Box 10, Tulsa, OK 72123   555-555-5555   milner@abcd.com

Executive Chef with Operations Management Experience Offers

- Background in Restaurant Development & Positioning and Profit & Loss Management.
- F&B Purchasing, Vendor Management, Cost & Quality Control, Menu Reengineering.
- Commercial Kitchen Setup, Capital Equipment Acquisition, and Staff Management.

Summary of Achievements as an Executive Chef

- Directing restaurant, banquet, and resort operations for up to 6 Supreme Restaurants.
- Overseeing operations generating annual sales of up to $12.4 million per restaurant.
- Analyzing operations and implementing outsourcing programs that increased profitability.
- Implemented corporate catering programs that increased revenues by 32%.
- Awarded for achieving "Top Sales Expansion" in the Midwest Region.

Multiunit Restaurant Management, Supreme Restaurants, Inc. 1992–Present

History of Increased Profits

- Developed, planned, and managed opening of 12 new restaurants in addition to 6 managed on an ongoing basis for this national chain generating revenues in excess of $125 million annually.
- Controlled F&B revenues of $30 million and succeeded in maintaining a 21% profit margin.
- Supervised and trained 125 chefs, cooks, stewards, bar, and service personnel.

P&L Responsibility—Cost Control Measures

- Held full P&L responsibility for all restaurant operations including capital equipment acquisition ranging up to $2 million per site.
- Cultivated and developed vendor relationships, which proved effective in negotiating low pricing, expediting orders, and receiving highest quality products.
- Kept abreast of changing market conditions and healthy eating attitudes in order to successfully incorporate new menu ideas and retain existing clientele as well as attract new markets. Saved over $1.1 million by negotiating major contract with leading vendor.

Reengineering of Commercial Kitchen Operations

- Redesigned kitchen operations and expanded cooking facilities, which resulted in a 33% increase in output that allowed each unit to meet targeted meal capacities serving up to 300 patrons per hour.

3-Time Winner of Annual Operations Award

- Received 3 Annual Operations Awards for Innovation in Restaurant Management, Team Building, and Revenue Expansion.

Culinary Accreditation & Educational Background

- A.A.S. Culinary Arts with Accreditation by Culinary Institute of America
- University of Houston, Conrad Hilton School of Hotel & Restaurant Management Program

---

Hospitality Resume Tips

WHEN PREPARING RESUMES FOR HOSPITALITY OR FOOD SERVICE POSITIONS, DESCRIBE . . .

- Volume of sales you generated, or the restaurant or hotel generated, on a monthly or annual basis.

- The number of customers that you, the restaurant, or hotel serviced on a monthly or annual basis.

- Type of restaurant or hotel you worked for, such as a five-star hotel, French cuisine restaurant, or deluxe resort.

- Number of beds, size of seating or accommodations, or square footage of the hotel or restaurant.

- Number of buildings you managed or were in some way responsible for.

- Types of services or departments you managed or worked in, such as front desk reception, reservations, hosting, seating, banquet facilities, commercial kitchen, food and beverage operations.

- Number and titles of hotel or restaurant staff you managed or served as a lead to.

- Workstation layout, interior or exterior design, menu development, or advertising that you developed and its impact on sales.

Sample Resumes That Will Blow Away Your Competition   169

Robert Allman   P.O. Box 324, Vermont, MI 12334   555-555-5555

RESTAURANT OPERATIONS DIRECTOR

seeks a position utilizing experience:

Developing, Launching, and Managing New Restaurant Operations
Analyzing Markets & Positioning Restaurant to Maximize Revenues
Managing Reservations, Service, Banquet, & Commercial Kitchen Operations
Controlling F&B Purchasing, Payroll, & Operational Budgets
Management of Banking & Vendor Relationships

MULTIUNIT RESTAURANT MANAGER & PROPRIETOR

Magnifique Roasting & French Bakery 1995–1999
The Shore's Restaurant 1990–1994

Launch of Premiere Restaurant Chain

• Conceived, launched, and managed Magnifique Roasting & French Bakery, driving revenues to over $1.2 million per unit within 6 months of launch.

• Built chain to 3 units within 3 years with total responsibility for profit and loss, strategic market and menu planning, cultivation of banking relationships, unit accounting, tax compliance, vendor sourcing, and contract negotiation.

Management of Hosting, Food Service, Kitchen & Bar Operations

• Managed front and back house operations for The Shore's, taking revenues from $5.2 million to $6.1 million within 2 years of management, for national chain with total revenues of $36 million.

• Directed reservations and service to approximately 12,000 clients per month for this 8,000 sq. ft. facility, which catered to an affluent market.

Supervision of Restaurant Staff

• Supervised crew of 75 employees including Restaurant Managers, Head Chefs, Cooks, Bar Managers, Food Service Directors, and Hospitality and Wait Staff for Magnifique.

• Managed all phases of Human Resource Administration including hiring, training, performance evaluations, benefits administration, and compliance with hiring laws.

Control of F&B, Labor & Operating Budgets

• Controlled an annual F&B purchasing budget of $1/2 million; payroll budget of $350,000 and capital equipment investment and leasehold improvement budget of $633,000.

Profit & Revenue Expansion

• Launched promotional campaigns and delivery programs that increased new business by 36% and expanded sales by $323,000.

• Redesigned menu plans, cooking stations, and workflow patterns, which increased productivity by 12.9% and resulted in significant impact on meal delivery times.

Restaurant Market Analysis & Niche Positioning

• Generated consistent revenue increases by analyzing regional restaurant markets and customer demographics to create niche products, promotional campaigns, and delivery programs that have proven highly effective in all restaurants managed.

• Advised V.P. of Operations for The Shore's in niche market development with many strategies being applied nationwide.

HUMAN RESOURCES GENERALIST

Stanton Benchman

35 Franklin Road, Wasaw, MI 34267
(555) 555-5555 bench@abcd.net

MANAGER OF HR GENERALIST FUNCTIONS

Offers background overseeing HR Generalist & Recruitment Staff
for Administrative Offices & Manufacturing Facilities employing 750 Personnel

- Workflow Management
- Recruitment Campaigns
- Applicant Screening
- Employee Orientation
- Delivery of In-House Training Programs
- Salary Surveys & Work-ups
- Benefits Coordination
- Compliance with HR Law and Hiring Guidelines

MANAGER—HR GENERALIST DEPARTMENT
Bidwell Manufacturing 1995–Present

Supervision of HR Generalist & Recruitment Staff
Supervised 12 HR Generalist and Recruitment staff for this international firm with 5 administrative offices and 31 manufacturing facilities.
Trained HR Generalist staff in recruitment of 125 job classifications with salary levels to $75,000.

Management of Administrative & Manufacturing Recruitment Campaigns
Managed recruitment of staff for Accounting, Customer Service, Administration, Engineering, Production, Marketing and Sales, and Contract Compliance Departments.
Recruited and hired over 230 key personnel through High-Tech and Tradeshow Fairs; and by implementing an aggressive recruitment/ad campaign targeted to university graduation programs.

Training of Management Staff in Hiring Guidelines
Delivered annual training to 95+ Department Managers on current HR Law and Hiring Guidelines. Instructed managers in conducting interviews, performance evaluations, disciplinary actions, and exit interviews in compliance with regulatory guidelines. Developed Affirmative Action Reports and Workers' Compensation Logs for submittal to and verification by management staff; recorded and reported staffing and personnel issues.

Management of In-House Training Program
Managed training programs for all job classifications including worker safety in production environments, sexual harassment awareness and reporting for supervisors, and documentation of workers' compensation claims.

HRIS System Management
Managed complex HRIS computer system to track over 10,000 applicants entered into HR database. Utilized system for applicant screening and evaluation, maintenance of HR, and employee performance records.

Salary Analysis & Job Classification Development
Conducted market salary analysis for engineering and production design classifications. Wrote job descriptions, salary advancement schedules, and manuals detailing benefit packages.

Benefits Administration
Coordinated with health insurance and 401K plan administrators to ensure that all new employees were enrolled properly. Served as liaison to resolve employee insurance claim disputes and to control benefit costs.

EDUCATION
Bachelor of Arts Degree, University of Wasaw 1990

More HR Tips

DESCRIBE . . .

- Departmental or operational budgets you manage.

- Special projects you implement, such as employee relocation, training, or workforce reduction plans.

- Types of curricula, equipment, or processes you train employees or executive staff to use.

- Knowledge you have of state and federal hiring guidelines to ensure regulatory compliance and to minimize exposure to litigation.

- Experience in, or knowledge you have of, benefits administration and labor contract negotiation.

- Accomplishments in reducing turnover, and improving productivity and profitability.

- Special events you attend, coordinate, or manage, such as national recruitment conferences or career fairs.

- Types of computer systems you use to maintain recruitment data, document personnel records or on-the-job incidents, and how large or extensive such systems are.

- Training you have completed or certifications you hold related to HR management.

Ralph Cannon
15 South Center
Plainview, KS 53486
(555) 555-5555

**Seeking a position utilizing over 10 years experience in
HR Management, Staffing, and Recruitment for Major Corporations**

with success in National Staffing; Risk & Litigation Control; Implementation of Labor Relations Programs; Administrative & Operational Analysis; Employee Training Programs; and Senior Management Reporting demonstrated by

- Directing HR Administration including hiring and training of 750 full-time and 300 seasonal staff employed in customer service, production, and administrative departments.

- Managing staff of HR professionals providing support to 20 international locations.

- Supervising all areas of FLSA, NLRB, Title VII, Workers' Compensation, OSHA, WSHA, EEO, and ADA guideline and regulatory compliance.

- Conducting analysis of workflow procedures in all departments and consulting V.P. of National Operations regarding strategic planning to reengineer inadequate systems.

HUMAN RESOURCE MANAGEMENT
U.S. and Overseas Manufacturing & Distribution, Inc. 1991–Present

HR Administration—National Operations
Directed HR Operations for 20 distribution centers and 2 administrative branch offices employing a total workforce of up to 1,050 employees.

Supervision of HR Generalist Staff
Managed staff of 10 HR Generalists who carry out recruitment, staffing, training, and employee relation programs for over 200 work classifications.

Management of Facility HR Budgets
Controlled HR budgets allocated to each facility with responsibility for expense control that resulted in a 15% reduction in the combined national budget of $4.3 million.

Employee & Union Labor Relations Counseling
Provided labor relations counseling to 45 management staff to promote positive employee relations and ensure compliance with labor union contracts including disciplinary action, promotion, or relocation of employees.

Senior Management Consulting / Organizational Restructuring
Guided senior management staff including V.P. of National Operations, CEO, and CFO in change management, organizational restructuring, and workforce reduction or expansion.

Reengineering of Operational Systems / Increased Production
Traveled to and analyzed operating procedures in all 20 distribution centers to upgrade work methods and implement a nationwide management training program, which resulted in a 19.5% increase in production and a 8.9% increase in profitability.

EDUCATION
Bachelor of Science in Psychology, Maryland University
Over 2,000 hours Professional Training in HR Management, HRIS Administration, ADA, SHRM, and Sexual Harassment

ARCHITECT

Troy Newton
(555) 555-5555   newton@abcd.net

Central Avenue, #10
St. Louis, MO 38293

LICENSED ARCHITECT
DESIGN OF INSTITUTIONAL & COMMERCIAL PROJECTS

Offers 10 years of experience in all phases of Architectural Design, Site Development, Project Management, and Construction Administration proven by

- Managing architectural design of new construction for institutional and commercial projects ranging in value up to $40 million per project; and supervising staff of up to 30 architects, designers, and drafters.
- Designing projects for *Fortune* 100 corporations, national franchise organizations, and financial institutions including Albertsons Stores, Olson's Supermarkets, Jay Jacobs, and U.S. Bank.
- Overseeing Construction Management for a wide range of projects including concrete, steel, and wood structures; and directing all phases of site planning, site development, design documents, and detailing.
- Holding an Architectural License in the State of Missouri with a B.S. Degree in Architecture.

Institutional & Commercial Design
- Designed new construction for institutional and municipal projects, such as University of Missouri Research Facility, City of St. Louis Police Department, and elementary schools for St. Louis School District.
- Designed roofing membrane for remodel of 75 QFC and Albertsons Stores in 6 states.
- Coordinated project requirements with civil, electrical, and mechanical engineers, developing extensive knowledge of UBC, CDLU, and BOCA code revisions. Coordinated permits with building officials and resolved building and zoning disputes.

Civil Engineering & Site Development
- Designed street improvements, sanitary and storm drainage control systems for municipal projects including government-owned multi-housing complexes, which required extensive coordination with contractors and city inspectors.

Construction Supervision & Project Management
- Managed commercial construction projects with responsibility for supervising a staff of up to 100 subcontractors and tradespeople.
- Conducted on-site inspections, approved work orders, coordinated with vendors, planned and requisitioned materials, establishing a solid reputation for bringing projects in on time and at budget with high quality control standards.
- Served as Client Representative interfacing with contractors to resolve contractual issues; consulted clients regarding builder selection, bid and proposal review, and final bid evaluation.

Employment History
Architect, Design Associates 1995–Present
Construction Manager / Proprietor, Newton Commercial Construction 1987–1994

Partial List of Design & Construction Projects

Commercial	Institutional	Municipal
Albertsons Stores, Inc.	Bainbridge High School	St. Louis Public Works Facility
Nordstrom Store Renovation	UW Research Facility	Redville Fire Station
Microsoft Complex Design	Farmview Hospital	Redfern Hatchery Building
Windemere Business Park	Schick Counseling Center	Forestry Center Building

Tips for Licensed Professionals

- When preparing a resume for professional positions, describe the range and categories of skills you've developed that are required or important within your career field.

  If you are a professional involved in engineering, architecture, construction, or related positions describe the following:

- Number and range of types of projects you've developed or managed, as well as the dollar value of such projects or range of fees for such projects.

- List of projects you've been responsible for, including the name and type of facility as well as unique attributes of each project.

- Number of staff you've supervised or trained as well as their titles.

- Project management, scheduling, budget control, and administrative duties you've been responsible for.

- Range and types of internal and external organizations or departments you've coordinated with, such as city building departments.

- Key terms and buzzwords used in your industry integrated into headings for your resume.

CELIA WARD, CPA
555-555-5555 cward22@abcd.com

#312 City Towers
Seattle, WA 98108

CFO / GENERAL MANAGER

offers expertise in Management of Corporate Accounting for a Fortune 500 Corporation; Strategic Planning as a Board Member; National & Global Market Planning; Revenue & Profit Expansion; and Supervision of Division Management staff proven by

- Managing accounting for manufacturing operations generating $25 million annually with history of increasing output by 250% and profitability by 19% while cutting finance charges by 27%.
- Directing Division Managers in 35 facilities responsible for total workforce of 325 employees.
- Opening and managing the Alaska Division of Ernst & Young with responsibility for branch audit staff servicing major accounts with revenues of up to $400 million.
- Providing seasoned experience as a Certified Public Accountant with a Master's Degree in Business Administration from the University of Washington.

CHIEF FINANCIAL OFFICER
Sundstrand Manufacturing, North American Division 1995–Present

NATIONAL OPERATIONS MANAGEMENT

Oversee financial administration and general management for corporation manufacturing $25 million in products with responsibility for directing staff of 35 Division Managers with indirect responsibility for 300+ engineering, manufacturing, shipping, and administrative employees.

Division-Wide Revenue & Profit Expansion Increased gross profit margin by 19% through implementation of division-wide measures that reduced reject rates and labor costs; and redesign of production workflow systems and scheduling, which increased output by 250%.

Outsourcing, Materials Planning & Control Reengineered MRP system and established needed controls to provide current reports on in-house inventory levels, production capacity, and labor and equipment availability, which allowed divisions to plan and accept large-scale projects.

Manufacturing Division—Acquisitions Management Directed purchase and merger of new manufacturing division. In 6 months new division generated a 15% profit margin. Established corporate structure and implemented accounting, internal control, and computer systems.

BANKING & FINANCIAL ADMINISTRATION

Cultivated banking arrangements resulting in letters of credit and other financing instruments in excess of $½ million and negotiated reduction in financing charges by 27%.

Cash Flow Management Managed cash flow and negotiated foreign exchange transactions. Prepared monthly and annual audited financial statements. Set pricing for all manufactured products successfully reversing trend of 27.3% annual loss to profit in only 6 months.

HUMAN RESOURCE MANAGEMENT

Implemented an employee relations program and bonus plan that reduced union membership by 83% and reduced turnover by more than 32.5%.

SENIOR MANAGER—CERTIFIED PUBLIC ACCOUNTANT
Ernst & Young 1985–1995

LAUNCH & MANAGEMENT OF CORPORATE AUDIT DIVISION

Opened and managed the Alaska Division of Ernst & Young, managing branch audit staff servicing key accounts such as Alaska Airlines, Rainier Brewing, Kodiak Lumber Mills, and Unigard Insurance.

CITY ATTORNEY

Sandra Jones
33 Florida Way
Salisville, FL 99234
(555) 555-5555

**Seeking the Municipal Attorney position for the City of Salisville
utilizing the following experience:**

- Serving as Interim Municipal Attorney for the last 2 years with 8 years prior experience as an Assistant Municipal Attorney for the City of Salisville.
- Being a Member of the Florida State Bar and California State Bar.
- Holding a Juris Doctor Degree from New York College of Law coupled with a Bachelor of Science in Business Administration from Florida State University.

INTERIM MUNICIPAL ATTORNEY

City of Salisville 1997–Present
Assistant Municipal Attorney, City of Salisville 1989–1997

Legal Representation of City of Salisville

Currently serve as Interim Municipal Attorney with responsibility for legal representation of the City employing 250 staff and serving a population of 1,500,000.

Consulting to Municipal Departments

Consult all municipal departments regarding full range of legal issues and serve as part of senior management team with emphasis on

- **Human Resources:** Oversee all legal issues for staffing of 250 employees including court representation, labor union contracts, and internal communications.
- Advise all departments regarding correct disciplinary procedures and employment agreements and contracts for represented and unrepresented employees.
- **Law Enforcement:** Serve as General Council to the City Police Department with responsibility for civil forfeiture and criminal violations proceedings.
- **Building, Utility, & Land Use:** Consult with Building, Utility, and Finance Boards to ensure regulatory compliance of City expansion and growth plans.
- Write city ordinance and regulations, which are reviewed and passed by City Boards and City Council.
- Provide emergency and day-to-day legal counsel to department heads.

Legislative Advisor to City Council

Research legislative and legal issues and advise city council members of pending litigation, emerging and community concerns including potential outcomes of issues. Develop options and actions for review, voting, and adoption by city council.

Senior Management Advisor

Act as part of the Senior Management Team advising Municipal Manager and Mayor in all legal issues.

Risk Management—Civil & Criminal Court Proceedings

Consult with municipal insurance providers to negotiate settlement or recommend denial of claims made against the City of Salisville. Analyze risk in any proposed action by the City and advise departments accordingly. Oversee civil litigation and represent the City in criminal court proceedings and before hearing boards.

More Tips for Licensed Professionals

FOR POSITIONS IN LEGAL OR MEDICAL FIELDS, DESCRIBE . . .

- Areas of specialties you've developed skills in, such as family law or assessment of cardiac disorders, if such specialties relate to your career goals.

- Number and type of legal cases you manage or the number of patients your practice provides medical services for.

- Titles of senior staff and names of organizations or departments you consult with or report to.

- Legal or medical board certifications, as well as license numbers and states licensed in.

- Size of the organization you work for in terms of dollar revenue generated, budget amounts you manage, or total staff employed.

- Names of organizations you work for or deal with—particularly those that have high name recognition in your field.

- Number of legal or medical staff you manage or train.

- Range of administrative functions you perform, such as preparation of trial documents or medical reports, legal or medical office management, marketing of professional services, or delivery of staff training programs.

More Tips for Licensed Professionals

DESCRIBE . . .

◆ Success you've achieved in bringing projects in on time, maintaining high quality standards, or winning large contracts.

◆ Value and types of contracts or sales agreements you manage or negotiate.

◆ New plans, products, or services you have developed or launched; how comprehensive and successful they were.

◆ Research you've conducted that has been utilized by your firm, how such research has impacted the firm's success, and how widely the research has been implemented.

◆ Any patents, new procedures, or techniques you've developed and their success.

◆ Trade or industry papers or presentations you've given; the number and range of titles of professional staff you presented to at in-house, regional, national, or international conferences.

◆ Awards or professional designations given to you by professionals or organizations in your field.

◆ Types of professional associations you participate in, the sizes of such organizations, and your involvement with them.

Randall Ferguson, PE
99 Ambaum Blvd. South
Brighton, NJ 53491
(555) 555-5555

Seeking a Civil Engineering position utilizing over 10 years experience:

Providing design and consultation as a Civil Engineer for projects valued to $120 million with a proven reputation for bringing projects in on time, at budget, and to client satisfaction.

Managing staff of up to 20 civil engineers and drafters with responsibility for all phases of project design and construction management.

Holding a Master's in Science Degree in Civil Engineering from the University of New Jersey.

Manager—Civil Engineering Department, HR Consulting 1995–Present
- Managed design of municipal, institutional, and commercial projects conforming to county, city, and Department of Transportation guidelines.
- Drafted proposals and bids, researched and planned preliminary phase, and conducted on-site inspections.
- Supervised civil engineering staff designing utilities, street, and parking lot; surface water management, fire and sewer mains, land development, and diverse municipal projects.
- Interfaced with clients, architects, contractors, surveyors, building officials, permit, and utility departments to ensure timely completion of all projects.

Land Development—Civil Engineer, Wood & Associates 1993–1994
- Managed land development projects utilizing computerized design to contain costs for surface water management, utility, and transportation projects.
- Submitted in-depth permit applications with consistent history of receiving expedient approval due to accuracy of all details provided.
- Coordinated construction activities, inspected work in progress, and certified completion.
- Supervised staff of 12 drafters, managed project schedules, delegated workflow, prepared proposals, and verified billing statements.
- Received 5 bonuses for successfully bringing in major projects on time and at budget.

Civil Engineer—Utilities Division, City of Brighton 1985–1993
- Designed public-sector sewer improvements, storm water pollution systems, road drainage projects, bridge and road improvement projects, and wastewater and hydraulics systems.
- Coordinated with Department of Environmental Regulation to resolve all DER concerns to reach final inspection approval.
- Solicited, reviewed, and made recommendations for selection of outside contracting services, which sometimes required scheduling and directing multiple vendors for each project.
- Developed applications for exception to county, city, and Department of Transportation requirements, which required thorough analysis of existing codes and effective presentation of reasons for needed exception.

Civil Projects Engineer, Wall Engineering 1984–1985
- Designed civil projects such as filtration beds and discharge control facilities for surface water management systems. Designed structural engineering projects for commercial clients.

Detailed Project List Provided upon Request

MILITARY TO MANAGEMENT CONSULTANT

Doug Ottinger
(555) 555-5555

Route #2000
Sylvester, KS 85930

Results-Oriented Senior Management & Organizational Consultant

*with proven success in Regional / Division Management,
Strategic Planning and Organizational Reengineering proven by*

- Managing regional operations for 16 divisions employing 4,500 staff with proven success in process reengineering which cut operating and programming costs by over $1/2 million.

Regional Manager & Organizational Consultant, USAF 1989–Present

OPERATIONS MANAGEMENT

- **Systems Analysis & Process Reengineering**—Reengineered documentation systems for personnel departing a central location; reduced unfilled personnel requirements by 41%.
- **Cost Reduction & Labor Control**—Developed and analyzed survey data as part of management consultant team chartered to improve shift production, end solution reduced operating costs by $120K annually, directly contributing to division being selected "Best Management Consulting Division" from 12 divisions.
- **Operational Risk Management**—Conducted risk assessment of personnel operations for every job function performed within 10 sections and successfully identified multiple risk factors.
- **Logistics / Supply Planning & Allocation**—Led multifaceted logistics reception team to accommodate 14,000 personnel, which required coordinating with airport and customs to ensure round-the-clock service.
- **Total Quality Management**—Facilitated four strategic planning sessions consulting CEO and Division Vice Presidents in defining division-wide goals, action plans, and performance measures. Strategic planning followed the Malcolm Baldridge criteria for TQM organizational restructuring.
- **Performance Measurement**—Overhauled training and self-inspection programs for 5 departments, successfully taking customer satisfaction rates from 75% to 87% with section being rated "Excellent."

NATIONAL COMPUTER SYSTEM IMPLEMENTATION

- **IS Planning, Procurement & Installation**—Managed software development, hardware acquisition, and implementation of new distributed database system to over 98 federal agencies throughout the nation.
- **Software Development / Reprogramming**—Directed flawless reprogramming and testing efforts of two divisions for nationwide personnel system database; change affected over 1.2 million personnel records.
- **Functional Analysis & Program Management**—Implemented first document management/ imaging system valued at over $200K for personnel records, which significantly reduced backlog of data inquiries.
- **Project Manager / Team Leader**—Led joint team of field operations staff and technical programmers that resolved a complex data system interface problem and avoided 4,000 work-hours in programming charges.

Master's Degree in Administration from Kansas University

Military to Civilian Resume Tips

WHEN PREPARING RESUMES FOR POSITIONS OUTSIDE OF THE MILITARY, DESCRIBE . . .

- Number of staff you trained or supervised. If you were a sergeant, replace your military title with a skill heading like "Operations" or "Unit Management," using terms that sound like the jobs you want.

- Range of job functions performed by staff you supervised or trained.

- Dollar value of inventory or equipment you were responsible for, but avoid using terms like weapons or armaments.

- Titles of superiors you reported to, but convert the titles into civilian language. For example, a division commander could be called a "Division Manager" (adjust title to size of division managed).

- Administrative tasks you completed such as inventory control, maintenance of personnel records or payroll, use of computerized systems, purchasing, budget management, maintenance of activity logs, management reports, preparation of confidential or judicial documents.

- Number of departments or units you coordinated with to do your job, along with names and functions of the departments, such as purchasing or logistics.

More Military to Civilian Tips

- Dollar value of military facilities you managed or building systems you were responsible for.

- Dollar value of military contracts you administered or negotiated, titles of staff or types of vendors you negotiated with, and what you negotiated for.

- New systems or procedures you developed, streamlined or implemented; and the success of such systems in cutting costs or improving productivity.

- Leadership responsibilities such as directing teams, managing projects, and meeting organizational goals or deadlines.

- Types of awards you received. Translate them into civilian terms, i.e., U.S. Defense Medal becomes "Top Service Award."

- Number of hours of training you received, and the function of the training translated into civilian terms that match the jobs you want. "Weapons Operation & Maintenance" can be converted to "Equipment Operation & Maintenance."

- Soft skills you developed, such as the ability to work successfully in adverse, high-stress situations, manage heavy workloads with high quality output, or lead teams to achieve top performance.

Scott Handleton
273 420th Avenue, Burgis MA 08492
555-555-5555
handleton@abcd.net

SEEKING A MARKETING or MANAGEMENT POSITION

utilizing my experience in Divisional Staff Supervision, Marketing Analysis & Business Management Consulting, which includes

- Supervising up to 325 staff on an annual basis, coordinating internal customer support for 10 departments, and managing $3.1 million of inventory.

- Serving as a Senior Management Consultant providing strategic marketing plans to local and national businesses.

- Holding a Business Administration Degree in Marketing from Maine University.

Department & Operations Management
Managed and trained 325 staff on an annual basis rotating in from 3 divisions with responsibility for tracking, control, and disbursement of equipment and supply inventories exceeding $3.1 million.

- Interfaced with 10 external departments to ensure timely release and return of materials and to document usage requirements or returned damaged goods.
- Redesigned inventory accounting and scheduling systems that increased availability by more than 37% and resulted in significant productivity improvement in all divisions.

Senior Management Consultant
Consulted senior management clients in manufacturing, retail, wholesale, insurance, and financial industries regarding plans to expand product lines and increase profitability and sales.

- Worked closely with principals analyzing existing business operations and future plans to determine feasibility or suggest options for maximum growth.
- Commended by all clients for substantially improving productivity and market position.

Business Administration Instructor
Instructed Business Administration graduates for an international business school specializing in training of foreign students for entry into the American marketplace.

- Developed curricula encompassing advanced marketing and management.
- Led classes of up to 30, which included presentations to corporate sponsors.

Work Performance & Achievement Awards
- Led Department in Receiving "Top Performance" and "Top Service" Awards.
- Received 4 U.S. Army Achievement Awards with an Honorable Discharge.

EMPLOYMENT HISTORY
Department & Operations Management (Supply Specialist), U.S. Army 1996–Present
Senior Management Consultant, AG Consultant 1993–1996
Business Administration Instructor, Westhill International 1991–1992

NORMAN SMITH
(555) 555-5555

32345 Tacoma
Tacoma, PA 43236

AUTOMOTIVE SERVICE MANAGER

offers background Managing Multiple Service Operations, Supervising Automotive Technician and Service Staff, Overseeing Warranty & Customer Service Departments, and Managing Vendor Sourcing & Related Contracts with proven history of Increased Revenues and Profitability:

• Directing staff of 125 sales, parts, auto technician, machinist, inventory, purchasing, installation, accounting, and clerical personnel for operations with sales of $6.5 million.

• Managing major fleet accounts, controlling operating budgets of up to $1.5 million, and overseeing outsourcing of $600,000 in rotating stock.

• Launching new operations, developing training and performance guidelines, customer service policies, and production quotas for all units.

MANAGER OF
SERVICE, WARRANTY & CUSTOMER SERVICE OPERATIONS
1990–Present Detailed employment history follows

Service Manager, Smith's Auto Supply
• Managed parts store generating sales of $6.5 million annually specializing in servicing of truck fleet accounts as well as marketing to the general public.
• Controlled operational, payroll, inventory, and expense budgets of up to $1.5 million.
• Supervised up to 125 full-time and seasonal staff on an annual basis.
• Analyzed market trends to select top selling parts and to ensure in-store availability as well as maintaining merchandising strategies that significantly increased stock turns.

Automotive Service Manager, D&G Sales & Service, Inc.
• Managed Warranty Sales, Parts, and Repair Service for luxury car repair shop servicing Lexus, Mercedes Benz, and Rolls Royce vehicles generating annual sales of $4 million.
• Grew account base from 2,500 clients to well over 4,000 within a 2-year period by implementing service callback and referral request programs.
• Controlled in-house inventory valued in excess of $1.2 million.
• Supervised staff of 30 technician, sales, and parts control personnel.

Automotive Servicing Technician Supervisor, Walt's Ford Dealership
• Supervised crew of 12 automotive technicians, for this busy dealership servicing commercial fleets and private accounts, with sales totaling $3.1 million annually.
• Analyzed and reengineered service operations achieving a 35% increase in profits.

EMPLOYMENT HISTORY
Automotive Servicing Technician Supervisor, Walt's Ford Dealership 1998–Present
Automotive Service Manager, D&G Sales & Service, Inc. 1993–1997
Service Manager, Smith's Auto Supply 1990–1993

Parts, Production, and Warehouse Resume Tips

WHEN PREPARING RESUMES FOR THESE POSITIONS, WHICH HAVE MANY RELATED FUNCTIONS, DESCRIBE . . .

◆ Size of the company, department, or facility you work for or manage in terms of annual revenues or production levels or square feet of inventory, manufacturing, or warehousing space.

◆ Number and titles of staff you supervise or train and the range of job functions they perform.

◆ Range in dollar value, number, and types of products or parts produced, procured, or warehoused each month or on an annual basis.

◆ Number of different products or product lines manufactured.

◆ Type of manufacturing processes used to produce parts, such as high-tolerance machining or vacuum forming.

◆ Types of inventory control systems used to manage inventories, such as JIT.

◆ Number of vendors that materials or services are procured from, and if the vendors are local, regional, national, or international suppliers.

More Parts, Production, and Warehouse Tips

DESCRIBE . . .

- Number of customers or accounts that purchase produced parts or products.

- Names of major accounts serviced and range of revenues generated by such accounts.

- Range of contracts you oversee or ensure fulfillment of in terms of revenues generated by such contracts or types of companies purchasing products.

- Number and types of different shifts of employees you manage, lead, or train.

- Types of equipment used in production, parts, or warehousing operations and value of such equipment if you are responsible for servicing, managing, or purchasing it.

- Range of job functions you are responsible for, such as materials planning and requisition, staff management, development of training programs, strategic planning, or human resource management.

- Administrative responsibilities such as preparation of production, inventory, or warehousing reports; profit and loss; review of time cards or payroll approval; expense allocation or budget control.

- Management and cost control of shipping or freight services.

Bruce Jesse
555-555-5555

34 Fitzgerald Street
Walter, NJ 33421

Production / Materials Manager with 10+ Years Experience offers expertise in

- Manufacturing Management with Responsibility for Supervision of Plant Operations with 72 Staff
- Materials Requisition for up to 7 Divisions with Full MRP & Cost Tracking Responsibility
- Inventory & Parts Control, Purchasing & Subcontractor Management for Division with $13.5 Million in Sales
- Implementation of Computerized Production Programs for Manufacturing of 2.1 Million Parts Annually
- Costing, Production Planning & Control of a $3/4 Million Operating Budget

Production Manager, eXtreme athletic equipment, inc. 1996–Present

Management of Multiple Production Departments
Managed production of 4 departments manufacturing athletic equipment for division with sales of $7.2 million annually. Supervised vacuum forming, die cutting, assembly, and electronics department.

Systems Reengineering—Implementation of JIT Program
Reengineered systems in all departments and instituted consistent inventory control measures. Developed JIT system that increased warehouse capacity by 23% and streamlined production procedures. Redesigned workflow and purchased automated assembly equipment that doubled output and increased profits by 12%.

MRP, Production Planning & Quality Control
Planned production for all departments with responsibility for individual contracts ranging to $1.2 million per order, with senior-level decision making responsibility for MRP, production scheduling, final assembly, and quality control. Requisitioned up to $300,000 in parts and equipment for individual, major contracts.

Cultivation & Management of Subcontractor Relationships
Cultivated and managed relationships with over 200 national and international vendors. Negotiated substantial savings by maintaining positive, enduring relationships with leading subcontractors.

Materials Manager, Hendricks Manufacturing 1990–1996

Materials Management & Vendor Sourcing for 2 Divisions
Managed materials sourcing and in-house inventory for 2 divisions generating sales of $13.5 million annually. Instituted pricing models that increased profits by 8%. Centralized inventory control system, which resulted in up-to-the-minute inventory reporting that was critical in quoting high-volume fast turnaround orders.

Support of R&D and Prototype Development
Worked closely with R&D, engineering, and prototype departments to source and price materials for new or customized products. Researched material production requirements such as tensile strength, aging, and wear for manufacturing of critical, close tolerance parts.

Development of Complex Production Schedules
Created complex production schedules built upon material availability from over 200 sources. Developed receiving inspection standards and triggers to verify material availability, which increased output by 19%.

Senior Management Reporting
Reported to the Vice President of Manufacturing, advising of division production, profitability, and seasonal and industry planning to maximize market.

PURCHASING AGENT

Sandra White
(555) 555-5555

P.O. Box 10
Tulsa, OK 72345

Purchasing Agent

offers expertise as Engineering & Manufacturing Liaison to Fulfill Parts Requirements; Management of Procurement Budgets; Bid Solicitation; Contract Negotiation & Vendor Management; Capital Equipment Acquisition; Quality Control & Cost Containment

Over 10 Years of Purchasing & Acquisitions Experience includes

Managing procurement of up to $12 million per project.
Directing acquisition of capital equipment acquisition for 10 national facilities.
Controlling multiple concurrent projects with total procurement of up to $20 million.
Overseeing a staff of Junior Purchasing Agents and Contract Administration Specialists.

National & International Purchasing Agent
AeroDynamics, Inc. 1990–Present

Cross-Industry Procurement

- Procured up to $20 million annually in electronics, computer, construction, and professional services contracts, for this *Fortune* 500 firm with global sales of $1.2 billion.
- Served as Engineering & Manufacturing Liaison and Buyer for 7 overseas manufacturing facilities.
- Received highest rating from Regional Managers among national purchasing team.
- Researched and implemented a prepaid purchasing program that cut ordering time by 25% and increased manufacturing turnaround by 33%.

International Sourcing / Cost Savings

- Saved $1.7 million on 2 major international purchasing contracts by having developed long-standing relationships with the world's largest vendor of electronic components.
- Negotiated $350,000 savings on shipping container purchase and bundled package of overseas freight rates.
- Saved $89,000 on purchase of large quantity of computerized process controls for newly instituted manufacturing processes by negotiating an option-to-renew clause.

Project Management—Supervision of Purchasing Staff

- Managed a staff of 12 Junior Purchasing Agents and Contract Administration Specialists with responsibility for managing parts requisition programs and division performance.
- Delegated purchasing and project assignments to requisition parts to service 9 National and International facilities.

Education & Professional Training
NAPM Certified Purchasing Agent and NIGP Certified Purchasing Officer
B.A. in Business Administration

More Parts, Production, and Warehouse Resume Tips

WHEN PREPARING RESUMES FOR THESE POSITIONS, ALSO DESCRIBE . . .

- Systems or procedures you've analyzed or reengineered and the success of such systems or procedures.

- Computer systems you've implemented and what the systems are used for, and the success of such systems in cutting production times or reducing manual labor requirements.

- Development of written policies or procedures manuals for parts control, manufacturing processes, or warehousing standards.

- Safety issues you've dealt with or have responsibility for. Implementation of safety programs in production or warehouse facilities, including handling of hazardous materials or dangerous equipment.

- Coordination with state or federal officials or agencies, such as OSHA and WSHA representatives, to ensure environmental, worker, and facility safety.

- Types of reports or documentation you've completed to document on-the-job incidents or worker injuries, or to comply with regulatory reporting guidelines.

DENNIS LUCAS

32 Vicker Road
Scranton, OH 43236
555-555-5555

SEEKING A WAREHOUSE MANAGEMENT POSITION

utilizing background Managing Inventory in Multiple Warehousing Facilities and Supervising Staff in 7 Departments with strong history of Increased Warehouse Efficiency, Production Output, and Operating and Inventory Savings.

WAREHOUSE MANAGEMENT, Automotive Distributors 1995–Present

Management of Warehousing Operations & Staff

- Directed all warehousing operations including receiving, inspection, invoice approval, light assembly, quality control, shipping, delivery, and dispatch for 4 locations with combined inventory in excess of $12 million.
- Hired and supervised staff in all areas described above, which included scheduling for 3 shifts, performance evaluations, and implementation of safety systems.

Control of Inventory in Multiple Warehousing Locations

- Managed inventory in all locations, which totaled over 400,000 sq. ft. of facility space to house 2,500 products with wholesale values up to $2,700 per part.
- Directed off-site Warehouse Managers in implementation of inventory systems.

Management of Operating Budgets

- Controlled master budget for all warehousing facilities totaling $350,000. Worked closely with CFO and Controller to develop effective inventory accounting systems.
- Cut annual operating costs by 12% by centralizing inventory stores in each location, creating a logical, systematic receiving, assembly, and shipping system.

JIT Inventory Systems—Decreased Discrepancies

- Worked closely with Director of Manufacturing to implement JIT system that integrated with existing inventory control systems in all warehousing locations.
- New system resulted in decreasing inventory discrepancies by over 27.6% and saved more than $220,000 annually.

Production Planning—Increased Output

- Planned production of up to 60 staff performing light assembly and producing up to 3,100 units per day that were allocated to all locations for final assembly.
- Commended by Director of Manufacturing for increasing light assembly output by 350 units per day, which provided a substantial positive impact on final production.

WAREHOUSE SUPERVISOR, Shearson Distributors 1990–1995

Management of Receiving, Warehousing & Shipping Operations

- Managed a $1.5 million inventory, which rotated bimonthly, with responsibility for supervising up to 23 staff working three shifts.
- Converted many manual tracking systems to an integrated computerized system.

EDUCATION

A.A. Degree with Core Studies in Logistics Management, Scranton College 1994

COMMERCIAL PROPERTY MANAGER

Norm Dicson
555-555-5555

34 Tillis Ave
Memphis, TN 21230

Commercial & Residential Property Manager

*offers expertise Managing Commercial, Mixed-Use, and Premiere Residential Complexes;
Holding P&L Responsibility with Proven History of Increased Profits & Cost Containment;
Supervising Major Remodel Projects Valued to $2.5 Million per Project;
Overseeing Subcontractor Management & Contract Negotiation for All Trades;
and Developing Business Plans Resulting in Full Financial Funding for New Acquisitions.*

Multi-State Property Management

- Directed a field management team of 6 District Managers overseeing 85 site locations, 125 partnerships, and 7,000 units located in 6 states generating $120 million annually.
- Analyzed profit and loss for each region and implemented cost containment programs that increased profitability by 32%, being awarded "Regional Manager 1997 and 1998."

Management of Multiuse High Rise Facilities

- Directed and controlled financial and operational functions of a 220,000-square-foot, multiuse, high rise facility comprising residential housing, commercial offices, a 150-room hotel, 3 restaurants, and 2 lounges, generating revenues of $56 million annually.

Residential Portfolio Management

- Managed a residential portfolio consisting of 967 garden-style deluxe apartments and 18 developments in rural and metropolitan markets. Increased tenancy to 97.5% by implementing effective marketing and customer service programs.

Apartment Complex Manager

- Managed a 1,200-unit premiere apartment complex catering to individuals in the $200,000+ income range, generating over $12.5 million in annual revenues.

Commercial & Residential Property—Administrative Management

- Hired and managed subcontracting crews for all major remodels, including trades coordination for electrical, plumbing, structural, landscaping, HVAC, and elevator remodels, overseeing capital improvement budgets of up to $2.5 million per project.

Acquisitions & Market Analysis

- Conducted extensive market and property analysis for acquisition of commercial and residential properties to ensure the maintenance of 40% operating ratios.

Employment History

Regional Manager, National Property Management 1995–Present
Commercial Property Manager, SeaWest Ventures 1990–1995
Apartment Complex Manager, Premiere Apartments 1985–1990

Real Estate Resume Tips

WHEN PREPARING RESUMES FOR POSITIONS IN REAL ESTATE OR RELATED FIELDS, DESCRIBE . . .

- Types of real estate that you marketed or managed the sale or maintenance of, such as residential, commercial, or mixed-use properties.

- The range in dollar value of the properties you marketed.

- The total annual sales you generated, or the value of properties or portfolios you managed.

- The size of the real estate firm or corporation you worked for in terms of its total annual revenues or number of offices nationally or internationally.

- Number of customers or accounts that you dealt with or serviced on a monthly or annual basis, including names of key customers or accounts that are well known in your field.

- Range of contracts in terms of dollar value that you negotiated with clients or with vendors, and what types of contracts were involved.

- Marketing plans or strategies you implemented, such as lead development programs, direct advertising campaigns, referral bonus programs, or specialized staff training, which in some way improved sales.

More Real Estate Tips

DESCRIBE . . .

◆ Computer systems you may have implemented and if they improved sales or agent efficiency.

◆ Range and titles of outside organizations you coordinated with to do your job, such as title or escrow companies, real estate attorneys, city or county building departments.

◆ Reports or administrative paperwork that you were required to complete such as real estate contracts, broker reports, sales/expense reports, or payroll records.

◆ Number and range of titles of staff that you supervised and trained, and what the total volume of sales were that they generated or the total value of properties that they managed.

◆ Geographic region that you, your sales office, or brokerage serviced.

◆ Awards you or your staff received and why.

◆ Titles of senior staff or partners that you consulted or advised and what you advised them of.

◆ How much you increased sales or profits, either for your own personal sales, your team's sales, or your brokerage, and how you did this.

Noreen Fee

45 Ashton Road
Big Bend, TX 85726
555-555-5555

TOP PRODUCING REAL ESTATE BROKER

offers proven expertise Managing the Highest Producing Franchise for Prudential; Directing Commercial & Residential Sales; Expanding Regional Revenues; Maximizing Division Profitability; Developing & Supervising a Top Sales Force.

BROKER / BRANCH MANAGER, Prudential Real Estate 1996–Present

- Took sales from $50.8 million to over $80 million annually by expanding agent sales force and by providing extensive training in lead development and closing strategies.
- Conducted daily, weekly, and monthly sales goals meetings to monitor all active transactions and assist agents with any sales or lead development problems.
- Recruited top sales agents from competing agencies and negotiated salary compensation schedules, which resulted in high motivation while increasing sales and division profits.
- Managed a force of up to 12 agents soliciting and marketing both commercial and residential properties.
- Implemented division-wide use of laptop computers, which increased listings by over 38% due to ability to capture impulse listings by agents while in sellers' homes.

MANAGER—BUILDER CONTRACTS DIVISION, Century 21 1990–1995

- Developed and launched the Builder Contracts Division, taking revenues to over $35 million within a 3-year period.
- Demonstrated viability of program and spearheaded adoption regionwide in 32 brokerages resulting in each branch managing its own Builder Contracts Division.
- Worked closely with VP of Marketing to institute profitability standards, quality control measures, inventory turnover requirements, and sales expectations for each division.
- Expanded base of branch offices offering Builder Contracts from 4 locations to 8 locations and expanded base of builders from 3 to 10.
- Trained over 60 agents from all divisions in effective marketing and management of Builder Services.

REAL ESTATE AGENT, John L. Scott 1987–1990

- Generated annual sales of $21 million marketing residential properties ranging in value from $150,000 up to $1.2 million and receiving 8 Top Sales Awards.
- Gained exposure to commercial property sales, which led to subsequent position with Century 21 as the Manager of the Builder Contracts Division.

EDUCATION
Bachelor of Arts Degree—Business & Marketing Concentration
University of Texas 1987

NATIONAL MARKETING MANAGER

Cynthia Moyers
4312 55th Street
Huntsville, AR 21411
(555) 555-5555

OBJECTIVE

Sales Management position utilizing my national marketing, direct sales, and supervisory experience, with opportunity for high income potential.

MARKETING & MANAGEMENT ACHIEVEMENTS

Developed and managed national marketing program, generating sales in excess of $15 million from 12 major U.S. operations.

- On-line to meet current sales projections—establishing 2,000 new accounts in 1999.

- Extensive experience developing and implementing outside sales, telemarketing, and direct mail campaigns.

- Business and operational development has included recruitment, hiring, and training of sales and support staff.

- Developed and managed annual budgets, controlled expenses, purchased capital equipment, and oversaw accounting systems.

NATIONAL MARKETING MANAGER 1992–Present
National Transfer, a Division of Home Management, Inc.

- Created national marketing program and established 12 U.S. sales operations. Within 2 months generated a client base of over 300 accounts. On-line to meet 1999 projection of opening 2,000 accounts.

- Traveled nationally marketing services to *Fortune* 500 corporations, national property management firms, and the general public. Conceived and developed telemarketing program, direct mail campaigns, promotional advertising, sales presentations, and customer service operations. Negotiated program approval with Board of Directors. Hired and supervised subcontractors for promotional designs, office systems, and installations.

- Monitored communication and marketing efforts in 7 subsidiary divisions to ensure quality control and compliance with company policies/procedures. Established new offices in hub cities. Recruited, supervised, and trained sales, telemarketing, and support personnel.

- Devised and implemented computerized spreadsheet program to maintain national client base, sales, and account data from corporate headquarters. Managed budgets, projected sales, controlled costs, oversaw purchasing, accounts payable, and receivables.

More Sales Tips

DESCRIBE ...

◆ Type of contracts you negotiated, including the range in dollar value of such contracts from the smallest to the largest contract you negotiated.

◆ Number of wholesale or retail distributors you dealt with or managed that distribute products you were responsible for marketing, as well as the annual sales generated by such distributors, and if the distributors were local, regional, national, or international distributors.

◆ Systems or strategies that you have implemented which increased sales, repeat business, or referrals, and the percentage increase achieved.

◆ Number and titles of sales staff you recruited, managed, trained, or served as a lead to along with the sales volume they generated.

◆ Names of departments or divisions you managed and the sales volume they generated.

◆ Analysis of competitive products, current, or emerging markets, or new technology that you have conducted that has been instrumental in increasing sales, improving market penetration, or effectively positioning products for top sales.

Rebecca Weldon   1310 Franklin
555-555-5555 weldon@abcd.com   Wooten, VA 11223

REGIONAL SALES MANAGER

seeks a position utilizing the following experience:

- Managing sales division servicing 1,200 governmental, corporate, and institutional accounts that generated $37.8 million in annual revenues.

- Launching Regional Marketing Program with responsibility for development of Service and Warranty Program and Customer Service Administration.

- Negotiating individual contracts ranging from $1/4 million to $1.9 million per project.
- Receiving "Top Division Manager Award" competing with 14 managers nationwide.

WEST COAST SALES DIVISION MANAGER
Reynolds Office Equipment & Leasing, Inc. 1995–Present

Management of West Coast Sales Division Managed division generating sales of $37.8 million being responsible for servicing of over 1,200 governmental, corporate, and institutional accounts. Awarded as "Top Division Manager" competing with 14 Division Managers nationwide.

Implementation of Regional Marketing Program Launched new regional marketing program for 17 primary product lines with 46 secondary product lines. Negotiated contracts ranging up to $1.9 million per contract.

Development of Service & Warranty Program Developed and instituted infrastructure for service and warranty program, which increased revenues by 13%. Warranty program offered trade-in discounts on major product lines, which resulted in retaining 97% of existing business.

Niche Market Development Analyzed market trends, emerging technology, and needs of major clients to recommend appropriate product line development to Senior V.P. which resulted in the development of 5 new products that increased sales by 11.7%.

Supervision of Division Sales Force Hired, trained, and supervised staff of 10 Sales Account Executives who covered a 9-state territory. Commended for ability to lead each salesperson in meeting or exceeding annual sales quotas.

GENERAL MANAGER—PROPRIETOR
Sarnal Paper Products 1990–1995

New Business Launch Developed and launched this paper products supply firm building sales to $2.7 million within 5 years. Specialized in servicing of city, county, state, and federal accounts making large volume purchases.

P&L / Financial Administration Managed all aspects of financial administration from bidding, procurement, and vendor management to control of operating and expense budgets.

EDUCATION
B.A. Degree, University of Virginia
M.B.A. Program, Texas A&M University
Certified Management Planner

RETAIL SALES REPRESENTATIVE

SANDRA WASHINGTON
4336 600th S.E.
Valla Harta, NM 55027
(555) 555-5555

OBJECTIVE

Outside Sales Representative position utilizing my ability to generate and close sales, and promote public relations.

SUMMARY OF MARKETING SKILLS:

Sales	Supervision
Customer Service	Personnel Training
Public Relations	Vendor Contact
Product Promotions	Inventory Control
Merchandising	Cash Accountability
Market Analysis & Trends	Displays

SALES EXPERIENCE:

Technical Sales

- Generated sales in excess of $\$^1/_2$ million annually in high-tech and electronic merchandise.
- Managed an in-house inventory of up to $100,000.
- Dealt with vendors selecting products.
- Utilized catalogs and manufacturer's literature in sales presentations.
- Trained staff in sales, customer service, merchandising, and cash control.

- Achieved high closing ratio by gauging customer response and adjusting presentations to resolve customer concerns.
- Dealt with a diverse range of clientele in fast-paced and demanding situations.

Sales Representative

- Dealt with high volume of customers promoting the sale of catering services at a major hotel.
- Consistently met sales projections.
- Received an award for achieving highest sales.
- Ordered up to $375,000 in annual catering products.
- Monitored market and sales trends to maximize sales.
- Served on "Excellence in Customer Service Committee."
- Trained new employees in sales and customer service procedures.

EDUCATION

Marketing Program, Honor Roll, Valla Harta Community College
Medical Administration Coursework, MedLine Technical College
Medical Assistant Program, Health Careers Center

WORK HISTORY

Inside Sales, U.S. Army Exchange 1995–1999
Sales Representative, Airlines Hotel 1992–1994
Administrative Assistant, Medical Services 1990–1992

More Sales Tips

- Types of administrative paperwork you are responsible for, such as sales contracts, revenue reports, submittal of product specifications, expense reports, or sales forecasts.

- Strategic planning you conducted, what it involved, if it was implemented, and its success in increasing sales or profits.

- Level and titles of key staff you gave presentations to, including the size of audience and what the presentations included.

- Trade show hosting or coordination, including the volume of customers you contacted, level of new leads developed, or sales generated from such events.

- Type of sales you were responsible for, such as inside, outside, commercial, governmental, institutional, aerospace, engineering, medical, major, or key account sales that relate to the positions you want.

- Consultation you provide to senior executives, internal departments, or customers regarding the development or reengineering of products, what the products or new processes involved, and what the long-term success of such products was along with the titles or job functions of the staff you consulted.

Scott Ridell
234 Northridge Hwy.
Corpus Christi, TX 82347
(555) 555-555

More Sales Tips

DESCRIBE . . .

- Number and types of internal departments you coordinate with to do your job, such as R&D, engineering, production, or order fulfillment.

- Number and type of outside organizations you coordinate with to do your job, such as manufacturers, vendors, or freight forwarding firms.

- Knowledge you have developed of manufacturing, distribution, or warehousing operations that relate to the job you want.

- Types of marketing activities you are responsible for, have developed, or implemented, such as local, regional, or national marketing programs; telemarketing; direct mail; lead development; or mixed media campaigns.

- Training you provided customers, including their titles or job functions and what the training involved.

- Sales or achievement awards you've received, why you received them, and how many sales representatives or divisions you competed against.

- Type of travel you undertook, why you traveled, how often you traveled, and the territories or regions you covered.

SENIOR ACCOUNT EXECUTIVE OVERSEEING NATIONAL ACCOUNTS OFFERS THE FOLLOWING BACKGROUND:

Managing base of 300 regional and national accounts generating up to $1.3 million per account with combined revenues exceeding $12.5 million.

Negotiating long-term contracts with residual revenues up to $2.7 million over life of contract with key decision makers such as Corporate Presidents, CEOs, COOs, and CFOs.

Expanding client base by 37% by launching a service program for all regions managed, which increased profitability for all product lines by 8.7% and represented $1.8 million in new profits.

National Accounts Management, Industrial Supply Corporation 1996–1998

Major Account Development Managed Southwest Region composed of 6-state territory in addition to 50 national accounts with responsibility for marketing a line of 35 industrial supply products. Achieved 3rd year sales goals within 12 months by analyzing past sales history of each account, competitor services, and market position to develop customized incentive programs for all accounts. Called on senior decision maker at each account to negotiate long-term 2–3 year contracts that locked in product pricing and incentive structures and secured corporate profits.

Vendor Consultant—Product Design Consulted with 12 manufacturing vendors to create products customized for common manufacturing needs, resulting in distinctive edge over leading competitors.

Regional Manufacturing Representative, Vacuum-Formed Parts 1990–1995

Tri-State Territory Management Managed 125 accounts in a 3-state region, becoming the top sales producer within 18 months and securing 78% of business previously contracted to two competitors. Worked with engineers to develop vacuum-formed parts and prototypes when this was not being done as an industry standard.

Supervision of Contract Service Staff Supervised contract service staff with responsibility for monitoring contracts, manufacturing scheduling, and purchasing to ensure on-time order fulfillment.

Outside Sales Representative, Automotive Warranty Inc. 1990–1995

Launch of Warranty Program Launched fleet warranty agreement program for this national warranty corporation, which increased sales by 29% and contributed to annual revenue of $12 million. Expanded sales of warranty program from 2 to 5 states, which resulted in taking service department from 35 staff to over 70 in 2 years of growth. Recognized by National Marketing Director as "The Top Sales Performer" competing with 30 outside sales representatives.

EDUCATION
M.B.A.—Emphasis in Marketing
Graduated with Highest Honors from University of Hawaii

Kent Drummond
555-555-5555 kdrummond@abcd.com

23 Sylvester Road
Rochester, NY 11123

COO—National Management

offers expertise in Management of U.S. Sales Force, Strategic Planning, and Development of National Distribution Channels with History of Increased Revenues and Profitability in all Regions and Divisions Managed, proven by

- Launching national, regional, and divisional marketing programs with responsibility for national operations generating revenues of $93 million.
- Directing staff of 12 Regional Managers and 112 Sales Representatives.
- Reporting to Board of Directors with full P&L responsibility for all divisions.

FINANCIAL ADMINISTRATION
National and Regional Sales and Profit Forecasting
Control of Multimillion-Dollar Operating Budgets
Merger & Acquisition Management
Market, Pricing & Product Positioning

REGIONAL MANAGEMENT
Launch of National Marketing Programs
National Sales Force Development
Company-Wide Systems Reengineering
Major Contract Negotiation

CHIEF OPERATING OFFICER

Provita Beauty Products, Inc. 1987–Present

COO / General Manager—National Operations 1995–Present

Responsibility for National Performance
Managed national operations, guiding revenue growth from $67 million to $93 million within the last 2 years with responsibility for national financial performance.

Director of National Sales Force
Hired, trained, and supervised 12 Regional Sales Managers with indirect responsibility for staff of 112 Sales Representatives calling on wholesalers throughout 50 states.

Channel Development & Management
Increased distribution channel by 32% by cultivating partnerships with distributors catering to upscale department stores. Updated merchandise to maximize turns and profits.

Regional Marketing Manager, Midwest Division 1993–1994

Launch of Divisional Marketing Program
Conceived and launched marketing program for the Midwest division, taking revenues from $22 million to over $29 million.

Leading Sales Force to Exceed Revenue Goals
Guided Director of Sales and team of 17 Sales Representatives in successfully exceeding sales growth, margin, volume incentive, and productivity targets set on an annual basis.

Delivery of Division-Wide Training Programs
Developed and delivered training programs to management staff in all divisions. Programs resulted in a documented 12% productivity increase division-wide.

Executive Resume Tips

WHEN PREPARING RESUMES FOR EXECUTIVE POSITIONS, DESCRIBE . . .

- Size of the corporation or divisions you manage in terms of total annual revenues, number of employees, number of offices or locations, or ranking as a *Fortune* 500 corporation.

- Growth in revenues or profits you have achieved, with a description of what level you have grown sales to in contrast to original levels of sales or profits.

- Reach of your responsibility, such as global business operations, international marketing, or regional management.

- Type of industry and categories of industry knowledge you possess or specialize in, if such information matches the executive positions you want.

- Type and number of products, product lines, or services your company markets, manufactures, or distributes.

- Responsibility for fiscal administration that you hold, including profit and loss management, acquisitions management, reporting to board of directors, and strategic planning, with descriptions of how far-reaching and comprehensive these duties are.

More Executive Tips

DESCRIBE THE FOLLOWING:

- Dollar range of budgets you manage and what they are used for.

- Amount of capital equipment or assets you manage or procure annually.

- Dollar value of facilities you manage, including annual operating expenses and total square footage.

- Number of management staff you are directly responsible for, including their titles or job functions.

- Number and titles, or job functions, of staff you are indirectly responsible for; how many locations or divisions they are employed in; and if the divisions are local, national, or international facilities.

- Computer or information systems that you have purchased or implemented; how large the system was in terms of number of locations, users, or terminals; cost of the system; and impact the system has had upon productivity or cost savings.

- Range of human resource management functions you perform, such as labor contract negotiation, supervision of HR management staff, regional or national workforce planning, or division-wide benefits administration.

PROVITA BEAUTY PRODUCTS, INC.—continued

Operations Group Manager, West Coast Region 1992–1993

Reengineering of Distribution Infrastructure
Managed the West Coast Region, taking revenues from $10 million to $14 million within 18 months. Developed regional sales force, reengineered infrastructure for distribution and operating systems, and developed long-term contracts with base of 32 distributors. Consulted with V.P. of Marketing on a daily basis to apprise of goal attainment.

Branch Operations Manager, Portland Headquarters 1990–1991

Financial / Branch Administration
Gained extensive financial management experience being responsible for administration of headquarters office that distributed a 67-item product line. Worked with West Coast Operations Group Manager to develop strategic market plans, forecast sales, and control expense and labor budgets of up to $3 million. Assisted with acquisition and merger of competitive beauty product line.

Sales Manager, Portland Headquarters 1988–1990

Territory Management—Revenue Expansion
Managed a staff of 5 Sales Representatives successfully increasing sales by 13% within 1 year of management. Coached sales staff in negotiation of distribution agreements and marketing to major department stores such as Nordstrom and The Bon Marche. Developed sales training manuals and worked closely with Branch Operations Manager in redesigning distribution methods.

Sales Representative, Greater Portland Area 1987

Launch of Fast-Track Career Growth
Within 6 months of hire attained first-year goals, and at year-end received promotion to Sales Manager, which started fast-track career growth with Provita Beauty Products. Since leaving this position, grew responsibility from sales of $5.7 million to $93 million.

EDUCATION
Master's in Business Administration, University of New York
Bachelor of Arts Degree, Puget Sound University

PROFESSIONAL TRAINING
Over 3,000 hours of Corporate Training includes completion of certified coursework in Fiscal Administration, Merchandise & Market Analysis, HR Administration, Implementation of Computerized Systems, Community Relations Building

Rebecca Healey
555-555-5555   healey@abcd.net

234 Cottman Blvd.
Brooklyn, NY 32512

INTERNATIONAL MARKETING EXECUTIVE

offers extensive expertise in Country-Wide and Regional Marketing Launches
within European and U.S. Markets; Emerging Market Development;
Niche Product Marketing; Major Contract Negotiation;
and Management of Sales and Product Development Workforce proven by

- Launching European marketing plan that captured 16.3% of emerging market and increased revenue stream by 59%, resulting in $15 million of new sales annually.

- Supervising staff of Regional Sales Directors with proven ability to build solid teams that consistently exceed annual revenue goals.

- Holding a Master's in Business Administration from Boston University.

COUNTRY MARKETING MANAGER
Customized Computing Systems 1997–Present

Country-Wide Product Launch / Distribution Management
- Managed launch of commercial product line throughout Europe, establishing effective distribution channels through base of wholesalers and retailers.
- Supervised staff of 12 Regional Sales Directors and guided them in the identification and exploitation of target markets, regional marketing plans, cooperative advertising programs, channel management, branch administration, and staff development.

Capture of Emerging Markets—Increased Revenue Stream
- Increased CCS emerging market share by 16.3%, which increased revenue stream by more than 59% and represented $15 million in new revenues over a 3-year period.
- Guided international distributor network in the identification of major market segments, such as engineering and architectural firms for large format printing line and key corporate/governmental clients, working closely to negotiate and close multimillion-dollar sales contracts.

Development & Delivery of Country Product Lines
- Developed customized networked product line to meet requirements for major governmental accounts ranging up to $1.5 million per contract.
- Created European marketing plan for networked product line and consulted U.S. product development teams in the delivery of products suiting the specific needs of assigned geographic regions.

Equipment & Software Specification, Testing & Certification
- Consulted with IT and MIS Directors of major accounts to develop equipment and software architecture for networked systems composed of 100 to 200 terminals.
- Worked extensively with system engineers and software designers to create and test customized applications and ensure total product Q&A and certification.

More Executive Tips

WHEN PREPARING RESUMES FOR EXECUTIVE POSITIONS, DESCRIBE . . .

- Range and dollar value of major contracts you manage or negotiate, and titles of key staff you negotiate with.

- Key industry experience or buzzwords that will interest employers hiring for executive positions, such as P&L Management, Channel Management, Product Development and Launch, Global Market Expansion, International Operations Management, or Revenue Expansion.

- Systems or procedures you have implemented or redesigned; new marketing or product development programs you have initiated.

- Impact your efforts have had upon increasing sales, improving profit margins, reducing or eliminating turnover, expanding product lines, or developing new markets. Describe what you did and how successful it was by using numbers and percentages to show increases in sales or reductions of expenses.

- Training programs you have developed and delivered for management, marketing, manufacturing, accounting, administrative, or other staff, including the creation of policy and procedures manuals, company hiring guidelines, or technical documentation.

More Executive Tips

DESCRIBE . . .

- Types of accounts you manage the servicing of, such as those involved in aerospace, manufacturing, engineering, or high-tech industries, or that are categorized as commercial, governmental, institutional, or major accounts.

- Market, competitor, or product analyses you have conducted to better position your firm's products or services and what the positive outcome has been in terms of gaining increased market share or new accounts.

- Level of your firm's marketing or distribution reach to a regional, national, or international level.

- Technical expertise you have developed in consulting, engineering, or research and development, as well as regarding new products or the improvement of existing manufacturing methods.

- Number of distributors you manage and the total revenues they generate, as well as total number of products or product lines they provide or distribute.

- Professional licenses, certifications, degrees, or patents you hold that are related to the executive positions you want. Papers written or presentations you have given, including the number and titles of staff presented to.

CUSTOMIZED COMPUTING SYSTEMS—continued

MARKETING DIRECTOR—AFRICAN OPERATIONS 1994–1996

Marketing Launch—Development of Channel Distribution Network
- Launched networked product line throughout Africa, building revenues to $37 million within 3 years by developing and managing a channel of 35 distributors.
- Hired, trained, and supervised a staff of 20 Account Executives, System Designers, and Software Engineers.
- Developed country marketing plan and led marketing team in exceeding first-year goals by 8%, second-year goals by 12.5%, and third-year goals by 14%.
- Coached Account Executives in closing major contracts ranging up to $750,000.
- Consulted with V.P. of Marketing and V.P. of Networked Systems Division to advise of major contract awards and forecast manufacturing requirements.
- Commended for "Top Regional Sales" competing with 3 marketing managers.

MARKETING MANAGER—SOUTHWEST U.S. OPERATIONS 1989–1993

Niche Market Identification—Regional Marketing Launch
- Managed Southwest Region of 10 states, taking revenues from $18 million to $27 million within 2 years of management.
- Identified niche market in federal accounts and set up marketing division that captured 32% of market and represented over 53% of revenue expansion.
- Hired and supervised staff of 10 Key Account Representatives calling on governmental and institutional accounts.

EDUCATION
Master's in Business Administration, Boston University
Bachelor of Science Degree in Electronic Engineering, University of Washington
Bachelor of Arts Degree, Puget Sound University

PROFESSIONAL ASSOCIATIONS
Past President—International Marketing Association
Member of Board of Directors—European Software & Printing Association
Active Member Within Each Country's Chamber of Commerce

COUNSELOR/CASE MANAGER

Fred Banarby
555-555-5555 barnaby@abcd.net

3539 Vernon Road
Waco, TX 38572

Seeking a Counselor or Case Management position
within a Crisis Intervention or Mental Health Setting with experience:

- Providing crisis counseling and serving as an advocate in ER and police department settings for high-risk populations including responsibility for suicide intervention and referral.
- Counseling mentally ill patients in group and individual sessions within a psychiatric ward.
- Maintaining case management files to meet agency and federal reporting requirements.
- Holding a Bachelor of Arts in Psychology from North Dakota University, 1999.

COUNSELING / ADVOCACY

Crisis Line Counselor, Sexual Assault Center 1996–Present

- Counseled more than 250 victims of sexual assault via crisis line as well as being on call to meet with victims in emergency room and police department settings, advising them of legal and prosecutorial options and serving as an advocate before legal representation was obtained.
- Provided intervention counseling for assault victims contemplating suicide and facilitated referral to external support agencies.
- Advised clients and families of evidence collection and documentation procedures. Made appropriate referrals to police, legal, and support agencies.
- Counseled adult and high-risk adolescent victims from diverse socioeconomic backgrounds.

Psychiatric Counseling, Intern at North Dakota State Hospital 1995–1996

- Conducted initial assessment of more than 100 mentally ill individuals suffering from drug abuse and consulted with staff psychiatrist to develop appropriate treatment plans.
- Counseled individual patients as well as leading group counseling sessions.
- Maintained case files, medical charting, and history/effect of prescribed medications.

Outreach Facilitator, Community Service Organization 1993–1994

- Served as liaison to rural community of Native Americans with a population of 3,500 residents. Facilitated scheduling and delivery of services provided by the Visiting Nurse Service.
- Documented client medical histories including incidence of alcoholism and drug abuse.
- Provided emergency counseling and intervention until appropriate support could be accomplished by the Visiting Nurse Service.

ADDITIONAL EMPLOYMENT WHILE COMPLETING EDUCATION

Student Research Assistant—North Dakota University
Sales Associate—Central Post Exchange

More Human Services Tips

DESCRIBE . . .

◆ Titles of key staff, as well as their medical specialties, that you coordinate with to do your job. Names and types of outside agencies that you coordinate with to facilitate client or patient services.

◆ Types of training you developed or delivered to other staff, including how many staff you trained in total and the largest number of staff you trained at one time.

◆ Administrative duties you have been responsible for, such as budget management, expense control, payroll administration, regulatory compliance, and reporting.

◆ Key industry terms human services employers will be interested in, such as Caseload Management, Family Counseling, Crisis Intervention, Clinic Management, or Supervision of Human Services Staff.

◆ Grant or fundraising activities you have been involved in, such as grant writing, events promotion, or corporate solicitation.

◆ Coordination or management of volunteer programs you have been involved in, including the number of volunteers and their assigned duties.

◆ Training, degrees, licenses, or certifications completed or that you currently hold.

Morgan Farmer
234 Holmes Road, Winchester WY 99923
(555) 555-5555

SOCIAL WORKER—ACTING STAFF DIRECTOR

offers diverse experience in Inpatient and Outpatient Settings within Psychiatric, Mental Health & Rehabilitative Units; Individual Therapy & Psychiatric Evaluations; Coordination with Multidisciplinary Teams; and Program Administration proven by

- Offering Program Management experience as an Acting Staff Director with responsibility for facilitating client care with team of 60 physicians, psychiatrists, RNs, and case managers.
- Managing heavy client caseloads with responsibility for initial assessment, development of treatment plans, and monitoring and charting of patient progress.
- Holding a Master's in Social Work with MH Specialization, Summa Cum Laude, coupled with a B.S. in Psychology from the University of Pittsburgh 1991.

CASE MANAGEMENT
CHEMICALLY DEPENDENT, DISABLED & HIV-POSITIVE ADULTS

Ridgemont Group Homes and Mt. Vernon Psychiatric Hospital 1992–Present

Case Manager—Chemically Dependent Clientele Managed caseload for group home providing counseling and rehabilitation services for chemically dependent adults in accordance with SCA policies. Conducted psychological assessments and developed treatment plans for mood, depression, personality, and anxiety disorders combined with substance abuse protocols.

Case Manager—Developmentally Disabled Clientele Provided direct care for adults with developmental disabilities in residential settings. Established medical, counseling, behavioral, vocational, and recreational goals as part of a comprehensive program plan for each client.

Counselor—HIV-Positive Adults Counseled adults who were recently informed of positive HIV status. Psychological counseling included addressing depression and anxiety, and providing agency referrals to assist with obtaining healthcare and financial assistance.

Multidisciplinary Team Member Served as part of multidisciplinary team of physicians, psychiatrists, RNs, and physical therapists to develop whole-system treatment plans for individuals and family systems. Dispensed medications following physician orders.

Family Counseling Counseled immediate family regarding treatment plans and facilitated appropriate referrals to family members with related issues. Consulted with external service agencies to assist family members in obtaining treatment funding and authorizations.

Case Documentation & Compliance Maintained all case records in compliance with state and federal guidelines as well as each agency's reporting requirements. Documented patient treatment plans, progress, and/or alarming changes in behavior for referral to other units.

PROGRAM MANAGEMENT—ACTING STAFF DIRECTOR

Served as Acting Staff Director in Absence of Program Manager at
Ridgemont Group Homes and Mt. Vernon Psychiatric Hospital.

In this capacity, supervised up to 4 Case Managers overseeing a total client load of
approximately 120 patients in all areas described above.

AUTOMOTIVE TECHNICIAN

Paul Butterfield
(555) 555-5555 e-mail bfield@abcd.net

324 40th Street
Tippo, MS 22088

Seek an Automotive Technician position
utilizing the following experience:

Automotive Shop Repair .....2,340 hours experience in a N.A.T.E.F. and A.S.E. College Certified Shop.
Certified Technician .....holding current Brake, ABS Systems, and Emissions Control Tech Certifications.
6 Years Mechanic Experience ..... in automotive, truck, and small engine repair.
Crew Supervisor ..... supervising staff and delegating workflow to repair $1/2 million of equipment.
A.A.S. Degree in Automotive Technology ..... completed with 3.86 GPA in December, 1999.

AUTOMOTIVE SHOP REPAIR, N.A.T.E.F., and A.S.E. Certified Program _____ 1996–1999

Engine System Diagnostics & Repair
- Performed engine removal/replacement, cylinder head and cylinder block reconditioning, timing component replacement, and engine systems setup. Diagnostics and repair of lubrication, cooling exhaust, fuel and emissions systems. Engine diagnosis and compression tests.

Computerized Engine Control Systems
- Tested, diagnosed, and repaired computerized engine systems on autos and light trucks including speed controls, ride level sensors, anti-lock brake sensors, crankshaft and camshaft sensors, Hall effect sensors, Schmidt triggers, analog/digital converters/inverters, photocells, electronic voltage regulators, diodes, transistors, and resistors.

Manual & Automatic Transmission & Transaxle Repair
- Serviced, adjusted, and performed general maintenance on automatic and manual transmissions/transaxles including constant mesh gears, spur gears, bevel gears, synchronizers, shift mechanisms and interlocks, bearings and thrust washers, power flows, and ratios.

Steering & Suspension Systems / Driveability Technician
- Performed steering system repair including diagnosis of steering column noises, binding problems including tilt mechanisms, power and non-rack and pinion steering problems. Diagnosed MacPherson strut, short- and long-arm suspension systems, and performed needed repairs.

Automotive Electrical Systems
- Diagnosed and repaired autos and light trucks including basic wiring, Ohm's Law, lighting systems, switches, relays, microswitches, storage batteries, battery testing, charging systems, accessory circuits/systems, fuses, power distribution, and fusible links.

AUTO MECHANIC & RELATED EXPERIENCE _____ 1988–1996

Truck Fleet Mechanic, Fleet Management Services
- Maintained and repaired fleet of trucks and jeeps including engine systems diagnostics and repair.

Automotive Tune-ups—Mechanic Assistant, Excel Automotive
- Performed tune-ups, parts repair and replacement, diagnostics, emissions, and body repair.

Truck A/C Line & Fitting Assembly, Mac Truck Division
- Torqued A/C lines and fittings to tolerance specifications per build paper.

Small Engine Mechanic / Crew Supervisor, Hunts G.C.
- Trained and supervised 20 staff in diagnosis and repair of $1/2 million of small engine equipment.

Trades Resume Tips

WHEN PREPARING RESUMES FOR TRADE POSITIONS SUCH AS AUTO TECHNICIAN, DESCRIBE . . .

- Type of vehicles and automotive systems you repaired, such as autos, trucks, and heavy equipment, including specifics such as engine, steering, and suspension, transaxle, and electrical systems. Include details that illustrate your knowledge of each system.

- Total number of vehicles you've repaired and what your production level was on a daily or monthly basis.

- Type of tools and equipment you have experience using or that you own and are required for the jobs you want.

- Titles and duties of staff that you have trained, supervised, or served as a lead to in this type of work and the volume of work that they produced.

- Related skills you've gained from other positions that are needed as an automotive tech, such as customer service, inventory control, or workflow scheduling.

- Number of years or hours of hands-on experience you have in this line of work. Professional training you've completed or certifications you hold related to this field.

CARPENTER

CARPENTER

More Trades Tips

WHEN PREPARING RESUMES FOR POSITIONS IN THE CONSTRUCTION TRADES, DESCRIBE . . .

- Dollar value and type of projects you've worked on, such as commercial, mixed-use, high-rise, residential, or renovation projects.

- Categorize the type of work you do, such as remodeling, finish work, or journey-level carpentry if this matches the type of jobs you want.

- Specialized skills you've developed, such as being a master carpenter, and the equipment you've used.

- Number of staff or subcontractors you hired, trained, or supervised, along with their job titles or job functions.

- Hands-on experience or knowledge you have of trades and building systems, such as electrical, plumbing, or foundations.

- Type of construction you've worked on, such as concrete tilt-up construction, steel high-rise, or wood frame construction.

- Dollar range of projects you've bid or estimated, and responsibility for materials specification or take-offs.

- Skills you have in reading blueprints or schematics, or in making hand drawings.

CRAIG YOUNG
JOURNEYMAN FINISH CARPENTER
4337 89th Street, San Francisco, CA 94111

(555) 555-5555

OBJECTIVE

Journeyman-level position with emphasis in finish work for remodeling/alteration projects.

AWARD-WINNING CARPENTRY DESIGN

- Developed a regional reputation for project design and finish carpentry with projects receiving the Regional Project Design Award from *Sunset Magazine*, with full articles detailing before and after examples of two projects.

REMODELING

- Generated 75% of new remodels from strong customer referrals, specializing in the remodeling of homes valued at or above $ $1/2$ million.
- Remodeled diverse projects with fees ranging up to $200,000 per project that include additions, kitchen and bath remodels, saunas, skylights, decks, and commercial tenant improvements.
- Gained experience in all phases of construction remodeling including roofing, drywall, alteration of electrical and plumbing systems, pour and finish of concrete work.
- Sought out by new clients based on having a solid reputation for giving special care in project management including the protection and cleanup of affluent homes and accessories.

CABINETRY—FINISH WORK

- Managed final phase of finish work on 99% of all jobs, throughout my 10-year career as a Journeyman Finish Carpenter.
- Designed, built, and installed cabinets; fitted and installed finish trim in all applications including Formica; hung and fit doors.
- Developed an excellent callback rate by contractors who consistently receive extremely positive feedback regarding my ability to follow through and please demanding, high-end customers.

CARPENTRY

- Established a consistent, full-time 6-year employment history being booked back to back in the completion of finish carpentry of homes in the $400,000+ range as well as light and heavy commercial jobs with fees of up to $1 million.
- Completed hands-on work in all phases of foundations, floors, walls, roofs, and stairs with ability to perform layout and design.

EDUCATION

A.A. Degree, San Pueblo College
Land Surveying Certificate, San Diego Junior College

WORK HISTORY—FULL PROJECT LIST PROVIDED UPON REQUEST

Remodeling	1994–Present
Carpentry—Commercial (Limited Residential)	1989–1993
Cabinet Maker	1985–1989

CNC MACHINIST

Charles Wilson
(555) 555-5555

34 State View Drive
Akron, IN 33135

Seek a CNC Machinist position utilizing the following background:

- 650 hours experience operating CNC Fadal and Haas mill machines and Takisava lathe machines.

- 10 years Machinist experience producing precision, close tolerance parts includes supervising machine shop operations with responsibility for QC, production, material, and labor planning.

- Combined study of 4,150 hours in Machine Technology with current certificate in Machine Shop Program and an A.A.S. Degree equivalent in Machine Technology.

Machine Technology
CNC Machine Programming, Setup & Operation

CNC Machine Certificate, total of 1,650 hours CNC and Machine Technology—Akron College
Machine Technology Degree, 2 years totaling 2,500 hours—Ukraine Technical College

Machinist and Shop Foreman Experience

Machinist—Conventional Mills & Lathes, Smith's Forge Corporation 1996–1999
- Operated lathes and vertical boring mills to cut drill collars up to 30 feet long and rings from 10" to 100" in diameter from aluminum and stainless steel.
- Machined various parts from nonmagnetic steel.
- Trained 5 employees in lathe and boring mill machine operations.
- Promoted from Advanced Specialist I to Advanced Specialist II within 6 months of hire.

Machine Shop Foreman—Quality Control / Parts Inspection, Anista Elevator 1993–1998
- Managed shop with 20 machinists operating conventional mills, lathes, grinders, drill presses, and stamps to produce machined parts for escalators and elevators.
- Conducted on-site inspections to determine damage or malfunctioning parts for hundreds of accounts.
- Analyzed drawings and parts specifications to repair or machine new parts.
- Managed machining of steel, brass, and aluminum precision parts ranging from .050" to 50".
- Maintained lifts, meeting an extremely fast turnaround requiring high-quality performance.

Machinist Foreman—Supervision of Junior Machinists, Tractor Factory 1980–1993
- Supervised 60 senior and junior machinists operating conventional mills, lathes, grinders, drill presses, stamps, and honing machines to produce hydraulic parts for tractors.
- Machined precision, close tolerance hydraulic parts made of steel, cast iron, and brass.
- Consistently led department in meeting production quotas and maintaining low rejection rates.
- Served as part of 4-person supervisory team overseeing total of 250 employees with responsibility for material and labor planning.

More Trades Tips

- All phases of shop work you were responsible for, such as bidding, production planning, materials requisition, machine setup, visual inspection, quality control, and final approval.

- Size of the shop or company that you worked for in terms of total annual sales, total staff, or total annual production.

- Responsibility you held for managing or delegating work assignments.

- Descriptions of the types of equipment you serviced, such as 2-ton boiler systems, or parts that you fabricated, such as precision parts ranging from .050" to 50".

- Success you've achieved in implementing new systems that have increased productivity or cut costs and what this involved.

- Success you've achieved in maintaining high quality control and low rejection or material waste rates.

- Management and administrative skills you've developed, such as shop management, crew supervision, workflow planning and scheduling, purchasing, vendor coordination, inventory control, shift setup, equipment maintenance, sales forecasting, development of production reports, or use of computerized systems.

More Trades Tips

WHEN PREPARING
RESUMES FOR TRADE
POSITIONS SUCH AS
A SEMI DRIVER OR
COMMERCIAL BUS DRI-
VER, DESCRIBE . . .

- Type and size of vehicles you drove, such as a 53-foot flatbed or a 100-seat interstate bus.

- Type and value of freight you transported and the number of states you traveled to.

- Number of customers or passengers you dealt with monthly or annually.

- Number of years experience you have driving and the total miles you have driven.

- Type of commercial driving licenses you hold and related endorsements.

- Number of drivers you've trained or supervised and what their job duties were.

- Knowledge of automotive systems and maintenance requirements.

- Administrative duties such as completing freight documentation, delivery records, maintenance logs, estimating delivery times, preparing incident or accident reports, dispatching inbound or outbound traffic, planning truck loads, or proper handling of hazardous materials in compliance with required regulations.

INTERSTATE SEMI DRIVER
Charles Wilson (555) 555-5555

Delaware Road 310
Franklin, TN 98108

Seek a Commercial, Over-the-Road Driving Position Utilizing

- Over 5 years OTR Semi Driving experience hauling freight to all 48 mainland states with loads ranging in value to $5 million per trip.

- Over 5 years experience as an Interstate Coach Driver covering a 5-state region and over 3 years experience serving as a Lead Driver/Heavy Equipment Operator.

- Responsibility for training and supervising drivers, overseeing fleet maintenance, completing freight documentation and field notes, and ensuring highest quality service to key accounts.

- Commercial Driver License Class A Tanker Endorsement and DOT Card with Driver Safety & Production Awards Received Every Year of Employment.

Semi Driver, National Freight 1993–Present

OTR Driver

- Logged over 1 million miles driving semi-tractor and 53-foot refers, dry box, and flatbeds to all 48 states with responsibility for loads ranging in value from $150,000 up to $5 million per trip.
- Hauled a wide range of freight, including meat and poultry products, agricultural supplies, high-value electronics, and automotive equipment.

Interstate Dispatch—Supervision & Training of Drivers

- Served as Interim Dispatcher, managing all inbound and outbound traffic for movement of 500 trailers and staff of 30 drivers. Utilized 10-code and 2-way radios to communicate with drivers on the road to solve equipment and shipment problems.
- Trained drivers in completion of bills of lading, field note taking, P.O.A., safety, and HAZMAT training.

Coach Driver, Greyhound Bus Lines 1987–1993

Interstate Driver

- Drove interstate buses through a 7-state region, traveling over 5,000 miles per round trip and logging more than 1 million miles, receiving consecutive annual "Safe Driver Awards."

Customer Service—Documentation

- Managed customer service for 100-seat interstate buses, which included collecting tickets and cash fares, verifying departure and arrival schedules, coordinating freight forwarding and delivery to arrival terminals, safe loading and unloading of passengers, and documenting any on-board incidents.

Driver—Heavy Equipment Operator, Medland Construction Services 1984–1986

Lead Driver / Operator

- Served as Lead Driver to staff of 12 with responsibility for operation of over $5 million of trucks and heavy equipment including tandem dump trucks, loaders, excavators, dozers, backhoe, overhead crane, and cat.

Fleet Maintenance

- Managed daily maintenance of fleet and served as liaison between all drivers and in-house service department to ensure safe operation of all vehicles and equipment. Scheduled outside servicing as needed.

CONSTRUCTION MANAGER

Rick Rouchester
P.O. Box 421, Bend, OR 32839
(555) 555-5555

Seeking a position utilizing over 10 years Construction Management, Supervisory, and Contract Administration experience:

- Serving as Construction Manager for a 300-unit complex valued at $37 million.
- Supervising crews of up to 67 laborers, carpenters, and plumbers.
- Developing bid requests and take-offs for projects ranging up to $12 million.
- Conducting site inspections to maintain quality control and keep projects on schedule with a proven history of bringing projects in on time and at budget.

CONSTRUCTION SUPERVISOR, Windemere Property Management Services 1997–Present

- Managed renovation of a 300-unit complex valued in excess of $37 million.
- Consulted principals in renovation and labor costs totaling $5.3 million.
- Supervised construction crews of up to 67 laborers, plumbers, and carpenters.
- Developed bid requests, selected and hired subcontractors for major renovation.
- Maintained master schedule to ensure on-time and at-budget project completion.
- Consulted with Complex Manager in renovations to meet tenant and market needs.
- Received substantial bonus for bringing project in on time and at budget with no accidents or workers' compensation claims processed during project.

PROJECT MANAGER—COMMERCIAL CONSTRUCTION, R.R. Inc. 1988–1996

- Managed commercial building projects for new construction ranging in value from $1.5 million up to $12 million per project.
- Negotiated commercial remodeling contracts with fees of up to $250,000 per project.
- Developed take-offs and worked closely with construction managers coordinating subcontractors and requisitioning construction materials.
- Supervised up to 3 crews concurrently working throughout the state of Oregon.

SITE MANAGER, BJ Construction 1985–1987

- Managed new residential construction projects valued up to $2.5 million.
- Supervised initial framing to final project completion and customer move-in.
- Customized residential floor plans to meet client needs and to control costs.
- Conducted site surveys and worked with architects and permit officials as needed.

EDUCATION

University of Nebraska
University of Alaska Anchorage
Community College of the Air Force

More Trades Tips

- Phases of each project that you managed, from initial design to site management to final approval.

- Titles of staff or superiors you reported to or worked with, as well as names of internal departments or divisions you coordinated projects with.

- Titles of external staff or organizations you communicated with regarding projects, such as city building officials, architects, engineers, and land surveyors.

- Success you've achieved in bringing projects in on time and at budget.

- Dollar range of project budgets you managed or controlled, such as materials requisition and payroll expenses.

- Type of customers or accounts you serviced and the total annual revenue generated from them.

- Design skills, such as developing layouts or using AutoCAD systems.

- Awards or bonuses you've received for project design or the on-time completion of projects.

- Professional training, licenses, or certifications related to this field.

CONSTRUCTION SUPERVISOR—MASTER TRADESPERSON
15 YEARS COMMERCIAL EXPERIENCE
Norton Newberry

315 Route S., Scranton, OH 83756   (555) 555-5555

CONSTRUCTION MANAGEMENT

CONSTRUCTION SUPERVISOR Specialized in management of commercial and institutional construction projects, overseeing up to 10 concurrent new construction projects ranging in value from $2 million up to $25 million.

TRADES MANAGEMENT Hired plumbing, electrical, carpentry, roofing, structural, foundation, site development, and surveying crews for all projects. Reviewed subcontractor work, issued change orders, and approved final work completion to high QC standards.

BID MANAGEMENT Reviewed and selected bids and proposals with proven history of bringing projects in on time and at budget. Developed construction schedules for all phases of work and delegated duties to site supervisors and leads.

MASTER TRADESMAN
OHIO STATE PLUMBER &
ELECTRICAL CONTRACTOR LICENSES

LICENSED PLUMBER Supervised installation of all phases of plumbing systems for commercial projects, including boilers, plumbing, heating, water mains, sewer, fire safety systems, and exterior drainage systems.

ELECTRICIAN—BOCA CERTIFIED Supervised installation of power and lighting circuits, electrical fixtures, wiring, motors, generators, UPS, controllers, switchboards, voltage and frequency regulators, HVAC systems, instrumentation, compressor control circuits, transformers, and automatic bus transfers. Read and interpret schematic diagrams. Compute voltage, resistance, current, and power.

CERTIFIED WELDER Performed or directed fabrication and installation of piping and structural systems including use of gas tungsten welder, oxyacetylene torches, sheet metal roller, carbon-arc welding, MIG, TIG, stick arc, flux core welding, hydraulic pipebender, and required safety and fire fighting equipment. Inspected all welds to ensure quality control. Read and interpret blueprints with thorough knowledge of all welding symbols.

BUILDING CODE COMPLIANCE Served as Construction Liaison to city and county building departments with responsibility for ensuring permit compliance to required codes and facilitating inspections by building/permit officials.

KEY PROJECTS

COMMERCIAL CONSTRUCTION New construction of TGIF Restaurant, Scranton Community Clinic, and Microsoft Manufacturing Facility. Remodel of Ohio Target Store and HVAC Renovation of Windermere Office Complex.

GOVERNMENTAL / INSTITUTIONAL PROJECTS New construction of Scranton Elementary, Scranton Fire Station, and Scranton Art Museum.

EMPLOYMENT HISTORY

INDEPENDENT CONTRACTOR Riley Commercial Construction 1985–Present.
CONTRACT EMPLOYEE National Construction Services 1990–1993.

Debbie French
555-555-5555 deb@abcd.net

Richmond Road #12
Smithsburg, NV 66573

ON-AIR NEWS REPORTER & WRITER

---

*offers expertise as a News Producer with Responsibility for
Development, Scheduling, and Coordination
of Hourly and Weekly On-Air News Programming proven by*

- Writing over 2,500 On-Air Reports for Hard News, Feature, and Entertainment Segments for major TV and Cable stations with responsibility for story idea development, research, interviews, and coordination with news directors and production staff to facilitate on-air delivery.

- Supervising hourly news production for a leading cable station, which included selecting and editing stories from live feeds for breaking stories and 5-minute segments.

- Holding an M.B.A. and a B.A. in Broadcast Journalism from Nevada State University.

ON-AIR REPORTING, WRITING & PRODUCTION
GSAU, CBS Affiliate, and CNN Freelance Writer 1990–Present

Freelance News Writer / Reporter
- Wrote and produced segments for live newscast including hard news, features, and entertainment as well as live updates to advance and promote news stories for later broadcast.

Short Hard News & Feature-Length Segments
- Researched, wrote, and produced news copy for 2- to 3-minute news slots and 3- to 6-minute features utilizing source material from station-originated stories and news feeds.

Production Planning
- Worked with Executive Producer planning news schedule and top stories. Coached Anchors regarding statistical details for technical stories in preparation for features.

Research & Interviews for On-Air News & Entertainment Reports
- Logged over 2,000 hours of interviewing and research time obtaining story details from public and government officials, celebrities, authors, foreign dignitaries, corporate officers, and other noteworthy individuals.

On-Air Award-Winning Segments
- Received numerous awards for short news pieces as well as features written as a Freelance Reporter for local cable television, politically oriented radio segments, children's television networks, and health-oriented programming.

NEWS PRODUCER & STAFF MANAGER
UXBT Cable Television 1993–1994

Hourly News Production
- Selected and edited news stories from satellite feed, covering daily stories from around the globe to supplement hourly 5-minute cable news broadcasts.

Coordination of Programming Requirements
- Managed news production staff preparing copy for on-air reporting. Coordinated all programming requirements with anchors, editors, camera crews, and graphics staff.

JOURNALISM AFFILIATIONS
Society of Professional Journalists—Secretary-Treasurer

Writing & Journalism Resume Tips

WHEN PREPARING RESUMES FOR WRITING AND JOURNALISM POSITIONS, DESCRIBE . . .

- Type of stories or news reports that you have researched and written that match the types of jobs you want.

- Titles of key staff or the names of internal departments that you coordinate with, such as news directors, producers, photographers, or copy editing or production departments.

- Size of the paper, magazine, radio, cable, or television station that you report or write for in terms of circulation, audience, or industry ranking, such as being a "#1 station in a #3 market."

- Length or frequency of publication (or broadcast) of your stories or reports, such as writing for a daily or weekly newspaper, or writing five-minute feature segments.

- Type of research you conducted, who you interviewed, such as celebrities or leaders in specific industries.

- Awards or commendations your writing has received, why you received them, and whom you competed against to win.

More Writing and Journalism Tips

DESCRIBE . . .

- Areas of writing or reporting that you specialize in that relate to the types of positions you want.

- Numbers and titles of staff supervised or trained, and the job duties that they perform that relate to the field of writing or journalism.

- Geographic reference as to the reach of the stories you have written or reported, such as for a national magazine, global network, or local cable station, if such references match the positions you want.

- Success you've achieved in consistently meeting production deadlines.

- Total number of articles or reports you've written or total number of hours of experience you've gained on the job or on the air.

- Experience you have gained in nonwriting or nonreporting fields but that has added to your knowledge of the types of stories or reports you write.

- Involvement in professional organizations that enhances your skill as a writer or reporter and what such involvement includes.

- Professional training or degrees that relate to the types of positions you want.

STACY KEANON
3538 Birch Road, Memphis TN 90900
555.555.5555

SCIENCE REPORTER / WRITER

with extensive experience Writing for National Newspapers and Magazines on diverse Science, Environmental, Medical, Health Care, and Community Issues with background:

- Spanning over 10 years as an Award-Winning Science Reporter and Writer commended for ability to convey scientific and technical jargon, making it highly readable with greater impact.

- Interviewing thousands of experts in science and related fields and writing over 300 published articles as well as hundreds of scientific and medical collateral pieces.

- Working with all levels of newspaper and magazine staff, including editors-in-chief, camera crews, photographers, illustrators, and reporters, to coordinate and complete writing assignments.

SCIENCE / MEDICAL / TECHNICAL WRITER 1991–PRESENT
Award-Winning Articles Published in *Sierra* magazine and *USA Today*
Broad Science Writing Experience Shown Below—Full Project/Employment History on Request

Science Writing for National Magazines & Newspapers Developed and managed all aspects of science writing projects including research, expert interviews, statistical verification, and translating of dense technical and science information into lay terms. Worked closely with editors-in-chief, staff photographers, and illustrators to create dynamic, eye-catching graphics to accompany articles.

Health & Medical Issues Writing Researched and wrote diverse range of articles covering health and medical issues, such as latest AIDS research and treatment, women's healthcare issues, community health concerns, emerging concerns regarding resistant bacteria, and pros and cons of social health care.

Environmental Impact Writing Researched and wrote articles on urban growth and related impact on wildlife population and migration, river and stream ecology and restoration, water quality control and health issues, and upgrading of wastewater management systems to accommodate expanding populations.

Technical / Medical Collateral Writing Researched and developed technical/medical collateral materials for pharmaceutical firms, healthcare providers, insurance administrators, medical equipment manufacturers, medical laboratories, and scientific research firms to market products and services.

Writing to Meet AMA Style Guidelines Developed medical collateral materials following American Medical Association style guidelines ensuring that content submitted by consultants and scientific experts was complete, accurate, and met regulatory compliance. Created appropriate scientific charts and tables. Consulted with photographers and illustrators to provide direction for publication design and look.

Award-Winning Science Writer Received Science Writing Award from Science Writers Guild and National Merit Award from The Science Writers Association. Commended for readability and distillation of highly technical subjects with an ability to involve the lay audience and touch community lives.

Research & Interviews with Leaders in Scientific & Related Fields Interviewed leaders in science, pharmaceutical, biology, medical manufacturing, community health services, world-renowned hospitals, and medical clinics as well as local, state, and federal officials involved in projects described above.

EDUCATION & HONORS
Master's Degree in Advanced Journalism Studies, University of Tennessee
B.A. Degree in English, University of Tennessee
4-Year, Full-Tuition Scholarship for B.A. Program
Technical Writing Award, Science Writers Conference

12 Cover Letters That Increase Salaries and Land More Interviews

Now that you've put together a great resume, you're ready to create an equally important part of your job search package—the cover letter. Cover letters are used to introduce yourself and explain to employers why you are contacting them. Many employers won't accept a resume if it is not submitted with a cover letter. In today's job market, proper business etiquette requires that you include a cover letter with your resume. If you don't include one, then employers may assume that you are not familiar with the business world and you may lose interviews. Throughout this chapter, you'll learn secrets to the creation of cover letters that position you as a top candidate and consistently generate more interviews.

Don't Let Your Cover Letter Miss the Mark

Let's start by considering what happens when employers screen cover letters. Christine's experience is typical. As an assistant sales director, Christine was asked to select a few people to interview for a sales position. She was excited about the project and thought she'd have about twenty or thirty cover letters and resumes to review. She was shocked when she received a box of 200 cover letters and resumes to sort that night. When she first began, Christine wanted to read each cover letter and resume, but soon realized she had spent thirty minutes reading only ten cover letters and resumes.

She knew she would be up all night if she didn't develop a faster method. So Christine asked herself what skills were most important for the job. Since it was a sales position, she decided she would look for the word "sales" in the cover letters and would look for job titles that reflected sales experience in the resumes. She then began glancing at each letter. If nothing stood out, she didn't take the time to read the letter. Instead, she immediately turned to the resume, running her finger down it and looking for sales experience. If either the letter or resume didn't describe sales experience, she set them aside to be filed.

All of the 200 applicants who applied for the position Christine screened knew that it required sales experience. But only twenty-eight of them had highlighted their sales background. That meant that more than eighty-five percent of the applicants did not market their skills effectively in their cover letters or in their resumes! This shows how important it is to highlight and draw an employer's eye to important skills in your cover letter.

Design Your Letter to Save an Employer Time

Christine's story also points out that the average cover letter takes too long to read. As a result, many cover letters are skipped over and never read. To increase the likelihood that employers will read your letter, you need to design it so that it saves them time. You can do this by using main headings or bolded statements that match the positions you are applying for. Such strategies will direct the employer's eye to your top qualifications and sell your skills in four to five seconds. Look at the cover letters on pages 208 and 210 and note that the paragraph headings are set in boldface type. This markets important information in seconds and cuts employers reading time—which dramatically increases the chance that your letter will be read.

Make Your Content Powerful

After you've gotten an employer's attention, the content of your cover letter must convince an employer to interview you. I think of cover letters as being much like the opening and closing statements that attorneys give when representing a client in court. Attorneys carefully analyze the facts that prove why their clients should win, then they structure and prioritize their arguments for maximum impact. You want to do the same thing with your cover letters. To build a convincing case of your qualifications, you need to analyze and address what each employer is looking for. Let's walk through an example to show how this process works.

Pretend that you want to apply for the driver/delivery position shown below. Read the ad and consider writing a cover letter for it. On a scrap piece of paper make a list of the personal traits, characteristics, and abilities you think would be important to put in your letter in response to this ad. Don't cheat by jumping ahead—you'll learn more if you do this before you read further.

> **DRIVER/DELIVERY PERSON** 2+ years experience driving and delivering high-value products in the Puget Sound area. Customer Service experience dealing with corporate accounts required. Salary $28,000. Resume to Ms. Perry, Personnel, XYZ Co., 1456 Harborview Avenue, Bremerton, WA 98121.

How many personal traits and skills did you list? When I share this exercise with job seekers, they often come up with a list like the one on the left shown below. But the ad asks for the five specific skills and areas of knowledge that are listed on the right. Which list do you think will be more likely to grab an employer's attention for this ad? This exercise shows why most people write such weak cover letters. Job seekers often get off on tangents that seem to relate to what the employer wants to hear, but such cover letters fall short because they don't address the specific skills employers are requesting.

What Most People List		5 Skills or Areas of Knowledge Requested
Bondable	Knows the Area	2+ Years Driving Experience
Trustworthy	Likes to Deal with People	Delivering High-Value Products
Dependable	Attention to Detail	Knowledge of the Puget Sound Area
Excellent Driving Record	Accounting Skills	Customer Service
Self-Motivated	Time Management	Corporate Accounts

Keeping the delivery driver ad in mind, look at the original letter on the facing page. Then compare it to the bulleted letter on page 206. Which one has the stronger design and content? Which one emphasizes the five skills or areas of knowledge requested in the ad? On the basis of these letters, whom would you call for an interview? Whom do you think you would be willing to pay more money?

Many job seekers perform this exercise but think these strategies don't apply to them because they are in higher-level positions or come from other industries. However, the process you just learned applies to positions at all income levels and to all career fields. In a moment we'll illustrate this by analyzing two more positions with higher salaries and more complex job descriptions.

Ronald Taft
457 Avalon Street
Bremerton, WA 98121
(555) 555-5555

September 20, 1999

Ms. Diane Perry
Personnel Manager
XYZ Delivery and Shipping
1456 Harborview Avenue
Bremerton, WA 98212

Dear Ms. Perry:

Enclosed is my resume for the Driving position you recently advertised in the *Seattle Times*.

I have several years driving and delivery experience. My work history is stable and I am looking for a position that offers challenge and adequate compensation. I have enjoyed working with customers in the right employment settings but prefer independent work as a driver/delivery person. My driving and customer service experience seems to qualify me for this job.

I look forward to an interview. You may contact me at (555) 555-5555. Thank you.

Sincerely,

Ronald Taft

Ronald Taft
457 Avalon Street
Bremerton, WA 98121
(555) 555-5555

September 20, 1999

Ms. Diane Perry
Personnel Manager
XYZ Delivery and Shipping
1456 Harborview Avenue
Bremerton, WA 98212

Dear Ms. Perry:

Enclosed please find my resume for the Driving position you recently advertised in the *Seattle Times*. As you will note, my experience includes

- **Over 5 years driving experience within the Puget Sound area**
- **Making deliveries of up to $250,000 in cash and high-value merchandise**
- **Providing customer service to corporate accounts such as IBM, Microsoft, and U.S. Bank**
- **Excellent driving and safety record with history of reliability and trustworthiness**

My experience delivering high-value merchandise within the Puget Sound area combined with my customer service experience makes me well qualified for this position. I look forward to an interview and may be contacted at (555) 555-5555. Thank you for your time and consideration.

Sincerely,

Ronald Taft

Who Is Your Audience and What Do They Want to Hear?

When job seekers analyze the delivery driver ad, they often miss at least two of the five skills requested in the ad. When job seekers respond to longer ads, it gets worse. They then overlook large numbers of skills or requirements that they should address in their letters. To help you identify what needs to be in your letters, you should learn three key strategies. These strategies will make you an expert in writing cover letters and are based on marketing methods proven to increase sales.

- First, identify your audience—those employers you will be contacting.
- Second, determine what their needs are.
- Third, figure out what you need to tell them in order to make a sale and land an interview.

To illustrate these strategies, we'll analyze two ads that are more complex. Reading the ad below, you'll notice that it's for a leading air express company and stresses experience in a corporate environment. Knowing this about our audience provides valuable information to help us present the correct image in a cover letter. By reading the ad and listing each keyword or area of experience it requests, we can identify what this employer's needs are. Using this information, we can then determine what we need to tell this employer in order to get his or her attention and land an interview.

In the first column below, I extracted keywords and skills from the ad and grouped them into related areas. In the second column, I labeled each group of skills with skill headings by using keywords from the ad.

Now review the letter on the next page to see how I used the skill headings in the right-hand column as paragraph headings. Also note that the image presented by each of the bolded headings matches the image required for this position and meets the needs of our audience.

ADMINISTRATIVE SECRETARY Can you keep pace with the leading air express company? We have an immediate opportunity for a multitalented Executive Secretary in our corporate office. Highly responsible position involves secretarial and administrative support for treasury supervisors and department heads, including coordinating corporate contributions, providing accounts payable entries, support for all SEC filings, mail/file maintenance and special projects. The ideal candidate will have 2 years secretarial or administrative experience, type 65 wpm, 10-key at 120 spm, and be highly proficient with MS Word and Excel. Also need the ability to create and maintain PC databases. Notary Public License, legal secretary experience, ability to proofread and use marking software, and basic understanding in accounting and financial terminology a plus. Salary $34,000+.

Keywords and Skill Requirements

- Multitalented Executive Secretary in Corporate Office $\longrightarrow$ Legal Secretary Experience
  Notary Public License
  2 years Secretarial or Administrative Experience
  Type 65 wpm, 10-key at 120 spm, MS Word and Excel
  Proofread, Use Marking Software
- Secretarial and Administrative Support for Supervisors and Dept. Heads $\longrightarrow$
  Coordinating Corporate Contributions
- Understanding of Accounting and Financial Terminology $\longrightarrow$
  Providing Accounts Payable Entries, SEC Filings,
  Mail/File Maintenance, Special Projects
- Create and Maintain PC Databases $\longrightarrow$

Skill Headings

- Executive Assistant/Legal Secretary

- Corporate/Departmental Support

- Accounting/Financial Administration

- PC/Database Management

Virginia Lutz
32583 83rd Avenue NE
Juneau, AK 98311
(555) 555-5555

November 15, 1999

Ms. Diane Perry
Personnel Manager
XYZ Delivery and Shipping
1456 Harborview Avenue
Anchorage, AK 98212

Dear Ms. Perry:

Enclosed please find my resume for the Administrative Secretary position recently advertised in the *Anchorage Times*. Briefly, I have outlined my top qualifications for this position.

Executive Assistant / Legal Secretary

While employed with XYZ Company, I provided legal secretarial support, which included preparation of contracts ranging from $250,000 to $2.5 million. In this capacity I was responsible for verifying contract data, financial calculations, proofreading, and the use of marking software.

Corporate / Departmental Support

As an Executive Assistant I provided departmental support to a staff of 10, including the President and Vice President of Finance. My duties included administrative project management and contact with department heads in 5 branch locations. Completing a diverse range of projects included benefit administration and research, acquisition of network computer systems, and employee relocation programs.

Accounting / Financial Administration

As an Assistant to the Vice President of Finance, I prepared and verified financial statements, annual budgets of up to $2 million and strategic business plans utilizing MS Word and Excel. My typing speed is in the range of 80 wpm with a high degree of accuracy.

PC / Database Management

Working with senior management staff has required setting up and maintaining a variety of computer tracking systems, such as databases for contract administration, customer account data, accounting, and reporting requirements.

Sincerely,

Virginia Lutz

Develop Strong Skill Headings and Job Titles

When analyzing the administrative ad, most job seekers come up with skill headings like "Secretarial and Administrative Skills," "Computer Skills," and "Basic Accounting." However, these headings do not match the image or salary level of this position. A stronger image is created by selecting keywords from the ad, such as "Executive Secretary," "corporate office," "support department heads," and "legal secretary" to create skill headings that do match the level of this position. Some words such as "skills," "basic understanding," and "terminology" shouldn't be used because they create an image of the applicant being less experienced than the ad requires.

Note, too, that I changed "Executive Secretary" to "Executive Assistant" because executive assistants are often given more responsibility for decision making and project coordination—which this position requires. I then combined "Executive Assistant" with "Legal Secretary" to create the heading of "Executive Assistant/Legal Secretary." I used the keyword "Corporate" combined with "Departmental Support" to create the heading of "Corporate/Departmental Support." I then combined "Accounting & Financial" with "Administration" because many executive assistants are responsible for compiling and completing accounting and financial reports, documents, and paperwork. You can use "administration" or "administrative" to mean paperwork that you've handled. This resulted in the skill heading of "Accounting/Financial Administration." To strengthen "PC and Database Skills," I merely replaced "Skills" with "Management" to create the skill heading of "PC/Database Management." Creating and maintaining databases will require managing them so this is also accurate and truthful.

When you analyze ads, don't get hung up on being perfect and don't let your comfort zone keep you from creating strong skill headings. Combine keywords and skills to create powerful headings or bolded statements that project an appropriate image. Now read another ad below. Then review the skill headings I created and see how I used them in the letter on the next page.

CEO/GENERAL MANAGER *Fortune* 500 firm expanding into the global market is looking for a General Manager to oversee facility and employee expansion programs, formulate budgets with P&L responsibility, develop strategic marketing plans, forecast sales and market trends. Requires ten years senior management/CEO experience managing firms generating revenues in excess of $2.5 million. Experience supervising up to 200 staff in multisite locations. Broad knowledge of human resources management, labor laws, and union contract negotiation. Experience in national and international marketing strategies preferred. Able to present business development plans to Board of Directors and win approval for major projects. Salary $130,000.

Keywords and Skill Requirements

- CEO/General Manager/Senior Management ————▶
  Manage firms with sales of $2.5 million plus
- Formulate budgets with P&L responsibility ————▶
- Human resources management, labor laws, and ————▶
  union contract negotiation
  Oversee facility and employee expansion programs
  Supervising up to 200 staff in multisite locations
- Global Market ————————————————▶
  National and international marketing strategies
  Develop strategic marketing plans, forecast sales and
  market trends
- Present business development plans to Board of Directors ————▶
- Win approval for major projects

Skill Headings

- Chief Executive Officer/General Manager

- P&L Responsibility
- Multi-Division HR Management/
  Corporate Expansion Programs

- Global Market Planning

- Reporting to Board of Directors

Ralph Sanders
256 Quentin Road
San Francisco, CA 93923
(555) 555-5555

January 17, 2000

Ms. Diane Perry
Personnel Manager
XYZ Delivery and Shipping
1456 Harborview Avenue
Bremerton, WA 98212

Dear Ms. Perry:

In response to your advertisement for a General Manager/CEO, I have enclosed my resume and briefly outlined my top qualifications:

Chief Executive Officer and General Manager
As the Chief Executive Officer for ABC Company, I have been responsible for managing four divisions and growing the firm from $1.8 million to $3.6 million annually. In this capacity, I implemented cost reduction plans that increased profitability by 12%. My background includes senior management within sales, service, and production industries.

P&L Responsibility and Reporting to Board of Directors
Responsibility for fiscal and budgetary control has included analyzing organizational objectives, instituting cost control measures, lease management, and staffing allocation. Profit and loss responsibility has included tracking division profits and expenses on a monthly basis and reporting my findings to the firm's President and Board of Directors. As division needs were identified, I formulated and presented business development plans to the Board, winning approval for a one-time budget increase in excess of $400,000.

Multi-Division HR Management and Corporate Expansion Programs
Launching corporate expansion programs has required overseeing an HR Department for an initial staff of 200, which grew by 25% within a one-year period. In this function, I delegated hiring, recruitment, and training functions to the HR Manager and monitored union contract negotiations for all divisions.

Global Market Planning
Spearheading an international marketing program involved analyzing market trends and forecasts, competitive products, pricing, manufacturing capability, and marketing delivery systems. After a preliminary assessment of ABC Company, I conceived a marketing plan that expanded our sales force from a ten-state region to national coverage including development of the European market. This expansion was the primary thrust that increased sales over $1.8 million within a two-year period.

The position of General Manager/CEO that you have advertised matches my proven ability to drive company expansion and revenues. I am very interested in pursuing a discussion with you and sharing my thoughts on your global expansion plans. You may contact me through voice mail at (555) 555-5555. Thank you for your time and consideration.

Sincerely,

Ralph Sanders

Match Your Top Skills to Employers' Needs

Imagine that an employer wants skills A, B, C, D, and E. In your cover letter you address only A, D, and E. But in fact, you have B and C skills. If you leave out B and C, and your competitors highlight all five of the skills in their cover letters, who looks more qualified? They do.

If you find an opening for a position that you really want, be sure that both your cover letter and resume address, as closely as possible, the top four or five skills the employer is requesting. If you don't have a direct match to one of the skills, highlight a skill that is related. For example, Sandy found an ad for an executive secretary that requested experience supporting CEOs and senior management staff. She hadn't worked with staff at that level but had worked with division managers in three states. She could label her experience "Executive Support to Division Management." This creates the image that Sandy can support key management staff and handle top-level responsibility, which is what the employer really wanted. If you feel you are weak in one skill area, find an area in your background that has some thread of experience that does relate. It's better to market that experience than to leave holes in your qualifications. By providing a full range of your skills, you'll elevate and control the image you present.

Don't Send Resumes That Are Weaker than Your Letter

Most resume books, this one included, recommend that you use your cover letter to customize your resume. In this way you can address unique requirements for each ad or job opening. However, this often causes job seekers to create cover letters that are stronger than their resumes and indirectly encourages the use of weak resumes. When an employer who doesn't read cover letters receives a weak resume, the applicant may not get an interview because the employer scans the resume, thinks the applicant isn't skilled enough, and never even reads the cover letter. This results in lost interviews.

The key here is to make sure that your resume is just as strong as your cover letter. So it's wise to put your resume next to your letter when you've finished it. Then compare the image presented by both. If your letter is substantially stronger than your resume, you should strengthen your resume. An example of this is shown below. Randy wants a department management position in the $36,000 to $40,000 annual salary range. Read the skill headings in the left column. Then read the job titles in the right column, which were used in Randy's resume. Do the titles in the right column cause your image of Randy to drop? In this case Randy is much better off strengthening the titles in his resume so that they are just as strong as the headings used in his cover letter.

RESUME—JOB TITLES	COVER LETTER—PARAGRAPH HEADINGS
Shift Manager	Departmental Management
Crew Lead	Staff Supervision and Training
Assembler	Budget and Expense Control
	Material Requisition and Production Planning

Graph How Employers Will Respond to Your Cover Letter

Graphing, a technique that we learned in Chapter 1, can be used to ensure that your cover letters create the image you want and get you interviews. You'll see the body of Sarah's Before cover letter below. This letter was written for a $42,000-a-year restaurant manager position that requires overseeing multiple locations with sales of $6 million. Take a moment and read Sarah's letter. Then read the ad that Sarah was responding to.

> I am answering your ad for the Restaurant Manager position advertised in the *New York Daily News*. I believe I am very qualified for this position.
>
> My restaurant management skills include over 20 years experience as a manager in high-volume affluent restaurants. As a public school teacher I have utilized my communication skills to train staff in food service, kitchen, hospitality, and bar operations. As the owner of a gift card shop I also controlled purchasing budgets and coordinated with vendors.
>
> My computer skills include experience with word processing and spreadsheet programs. Please review my resume. You may contact me for an interview at (555) 555-5555.

RESTAURANT MANAGER—MULTIUNIT OPERATIONS Requires a minimum of 10 years experience managing multiple restaurant units with full P&L responsibility and supervision of 50 staff. Proven ability to manage purchasing and labor budgets with history of implementing cost-cutting measures. Must be able to develop and manage vendor relationships and negotiate volume and discount pricing. Background in start-up operations a must with ability to take existing units from low profit to high sales volume. Base salary $42,000 with a liberal bonus package based upon unit performance.

Is the image presented in Sarah's letter hard-hitting enough for this ad? Does her letter match the level of skills required in the ad? Or does the letter create an image that seems below the level of skills required? By graphing our response to Sarah's cover letter, we can anticipate how employers will respond to her skills and how motivated they will be to call her for an interview. Now look at each of the job titles and statements listed below that Sarah used in her letter. As you read them, decide if each title or statement causes Sarah's image to improve, weaken, or stay even with her goal. Then look at the facing page and see if you agree with how I graphed Sarah's image.

TITLES AND STATEMENTS IN LETTER FOR $42,000+ POSITION

—Manager of High-Volume Affluent Restaurants

—Public School Teacher

—Owner of a Gift Card Shop

—Utilized teaching/communication skills to train food service, kitchen, hospitality, and bar staff

—Controlled purchasing budgets and coordinated with vendors

—Computer skills including experience with word processing and spreadsheet programs

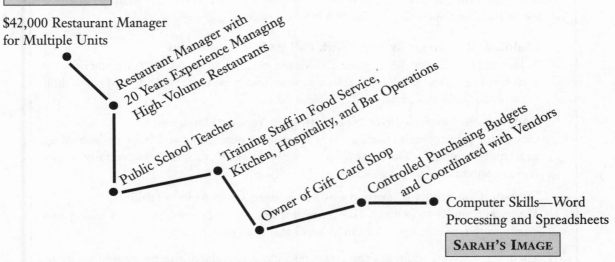

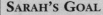

SARAH'S GOAL

$42,000 Restaurant Manager for Multiple Units

Restaurant Manager with 20 Years Experience Managing High-Volume Restaurants

Public School Teacher

Training Staff in Food Service, Kitchen, Hospitality, and Bar Operations

Owner of Gift Card Shop

Controlled Purchasing Budgets and Coordinated with Vendors

Computer Skills—Word Processing and Spreadsheets

SARAH'S IMAGE

What Happened to Sarah's Image in Her Cover Letter?

You probably think that the titles and statements in Sarah's letter present a weak image of her skills and don't market her strongly enough for the $42,000+ restaurant management position she wants. Sarah had landed a few interviews using her old resume but they were for entry-level management positions in the $20,000 to $28,000 range. So we can assume employers were also reacting to Sarah's letter as we have.

Now let's look at why we have a weak image of Sarah's skills. Sarah mentions that she has managed high-volume restaurants but doesn't tell us that she has managed multiple units. Therefore, most people assume she has only managed one restaurant at a time. They say this creates an image below her goal and graph her title of restaurant manager accordingly. They also feel that stating she has twenty years of experience may make her appear too experienced, and therefore too old, since the ad only requested ten years of experience.

The title of public school teacher makes Sarah's image drop dramatically as we imagine someone in an elementary school teaching children rather than managing adults in fast-paced restaurants. This title is then graphed much lower than her title of restaurant manager. However, knowing that Sarah has trained a wide array of restaurant staff makes her image come up but only slightly.

Then we read "Owner of Gift Card Shop," which makes Sarah's image take the worst dip. We envision her in a retail setting with rows of gift cards, which doesn't present an image of her as having the necessary skills to run multiple restaurants. Reading that Sarah was responsible for controlling purchasing budgets and coordinating with vendors makes her image come up slightly. Even though these skills relate, her image has been damaged too much and these skills aren't strong enough to get her image back on track. Last we read a statement about Sarah's experience with word processing and spreadsheet programs. While these skills may be useful, the employer hasn't requested them. Therefore, they neither raise nor lower her image.

Overall, the graph makes it very easy to understand why Sarah generated some interviews as well as understanding why the interviews were for jobs significantly beneath her salary range.

How Sarah Improved Her Image

Take a moment and read the body from Sarah's After cover letter on the next page. As you do, imagine how you would graph your response to each of the titles and statements in this letter. Then see if you agree with how I've graphed my response to Sarah's After letter.

Enclosed please find my resume in response to your ad for the Restaurant Manager position overseeing multiunit operations. Below is a brief overview of my skills:

Multiunit Restaurant Manager with Full P&L Responsibility
While employed with the Premier Restaurant chain, I managed up to six units during each fiscal period with full P&L responsibility. Total revenues ranged from $5.6 million to over $9.8 million in each region I managed.

Budget/Cost Control, Price Negotiation, & Vendor Management
One of my primary responsibilities was controlling purchasing and labor budgets of up to $2 million annually. During my tenure with Premier Restaurant, I successfully cut my region's purchasing costs by a total of $2.1 million.

Start-up Operations & Turnaround of Existing Units to Profitability
My background also includes launching five new start-up operations and taking two existing units from a loss position to profitability in only 6 months.

My experience directing multiunit restaurant operations combined with my proven ability to manage budgets, control costs, and bring units to profitability makes me well qualified for this position. I look forward to an interview and can be reached at (555) 555-5555. Thank you for your time and consideration.

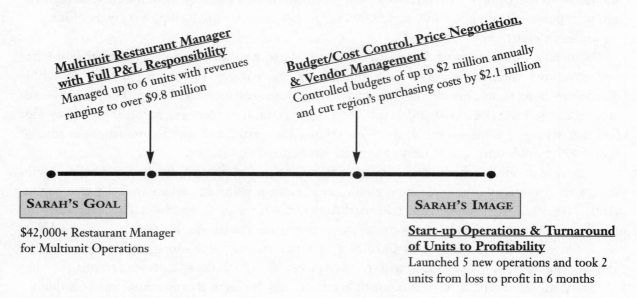

SARAH'S GOAL

$42,000+ Restaurant Manager for Multiunit Operations

SARAH'S IMAGE

Start-up Operations & Turnaround of Units to Profitability
Launched 5 new operations and took 2 units from loss to profit in 6 months

Use Graphing to Critique Your Cover Letter

As you saw, Sarah's new letter elevated her image to match the salary and responsibility level for the job she wanted. She achieved this by using much of the terminology from the ad to label and describe her skills. As you complete your cover letter, follow Sarah's example. Then graph your response to the main headings and statements in your letter. If any heading or statement makes your image drop significantly, create a stronger heading or statement. Your cover letter doesn't have to be perfectly on target. If some of your skills aren't an absolute match, that's fine. You can still generate a great response because most people's cover letters are so misdirected. Even if you have only a few of the important skills required, highlight them and get those cover letters out there!

Tips for Writing Letters That Get Results

Now we'll discuss some tips to ensure that your resume gets read and gets results. First let's talk about the importance of customizing your letters. You will generate a higher response rate with letters, resumes, and applications that are customized. In my last job search, I generated a one hundred percent response rate competing with 600 applicants for four very different positions. Job seekers in my classes have also reported a significant increase in interview rates—many reporting fifty to seventy-five percent response rates—after they began customizing their application packages. Because each employer and each industry may have differing skill requirements or concerns, it is imperative that you address how your skills match their unique needs. From my own experience and from what thousands of job seekers have told me, customizing often makes the difference between landing interviews and not landing them.

Employ Useful Redundancy

Many career and resume counselors advise that you avoid repeating anything in your cover letter that's in your resume. I disagree. Studies have shown that people must see or hear something up to seven times before it makes an impression on them! When employers spend so few seconds glancing at dozens, even hundreds, of cover letters and resumes, how can we expect them to remember much about any individual? By being redundant and reemphasizing our best skills in a cover letter, we can help an employer remember them. In this instance, redundancy is a useful strategy.

However, you'll want to avoid the *appearance* of repeating yourself by using different skill headings or titles in your letter than those you used in your resume. For example, if you use the title of "Executive Secretary" in your resume, you might use a skill heading of "Executive Support/Departmental Administration" in your letter. This reemphasizes the same set of skills but doesn't look redundant. You can apply the same strategy by lifting strong statements from your resume and then rewording them for your cover letter. Remember that both your letter and your resume should be stand-alone documents and each should sell your top four to five skills—which means that you'll have to repeat them. Job seekers often have concerns about repeating information from their resumes in their cover letters. In response to this, I tell them that I receive several calls from clients each week telling me about the success of their cover letters and resumes. These recommendations work—and will help you land more interviews.

Don't Use Gimmicks—They Don't Work

When a job seeker receives poor responses to his or her cover letters and resumes, they sometimes feel they have to go to extraordinary lengths to get an employer's attention. However, these strategies usually don't work. I've tested opening cover letter paragraphs like those on the next page and employers have consistently said they don't like them.

Employers often say such statements make the person seem desperate or too slick. They also say these statements seem much better suited for a direct mail flyer than in a professional cover letter. If you follow the cover letter strategies you're learning, you won't need to resort to gimmicks.

DON'T If you're looking for a top salesman who can double your sales, I'm the person to call.

People often tell me that I'm the best manager they've ever hired.

Give me a call and you'll be convinced I can turn your company's losses into profits—in no time flat.

Need a secretary who can handle pressure, solve problems, and manage details? If so, put my 10+ years of administrative skills to work in your office.

Control Information about Your Salary History

Many help-wanted ads request that you include your salary history in your cover letter. Including such information makes it easy for employers to screen out candidates whose salary requirements are too far above or too far below the salary being offered. For example, an employer wants to pay $1,800 a month for a customer service representative and receives a letter from someone whose salary has been $2,400 a month. The employer may decide the applicant will not be interested in the position at $1,800 and doesn't interview him. The job seeker may or may not have been happy with a salary of $1,800 but loses his chance to make that decision, as well as an opportunity to learn more about the position.

Just because salary information is requested doesn't mean that you have to supply it. If your cover letter and resume build a strong case for your qualifications, an employer will risk calling you even if you don't provide salary information. If it's a real sticking point, the employer will ask about your salary on the phone. When the employer calls, you've achieved your goal. You can then assess the position and decide whether or not you want an interview. To be on the safe side, I recommend not giving salary information in your cover letter. If you feel you must include salary information, then give a range. For example, if you will take $1,800 a month, but prefer a starting salary of $2,000, you might include a sentence that reads

My current salary requirement is in the range of $1,800 to $2,000 per month.

If you wish to increase your salary, for example, taking it from $55,000 to $65,000+, consider using a statement like this:

My current salary requirement is in the mid- to high-sixties range. If you would like further salary details, please contact me at (555) 555-5555.

Anatomy of a Cover Letter

Now we'll talk about what should be included in the body of your cover letter starting with your opening paragraph, then moving to those paragraphs that will sell your top qualifications, and closing with a paragraph that states your interest and requests an interview.

1. Address Your Letter to a Specific Person

Always address your letter to a specific person if at all possible. If you are responding to a help-wanted ad or a posted job opening and no name is listed, then do some research. Call the company that placed the ad or posted the opening and ask to whom you should submit your cover letter and resume. Be sure to get the correct spelling of the person's name along with his or her job title and phone number. Also ask if that person has a specific mailing address that should be included. In this way you can ensure that your cover letter is delivered to the correct person. Not having the name of a specific person to contact makes it difficult to follow up on your cover letter and application. It also makes it seem that you haven't done your homework, or that you are sending generic letters and resumes to many employers rather than writing individual letters to specific employers you want to work for.

2. Use the Introductory Paragraph to Tell Why You Are Writing

Generally, a cover letter comprises three to five short paragraphs. In the first paragraph, it's good to explain why you are writing the letter or if someone has referred you. Here are several good opening paragraphs that have been proven effective by thousands of job seekers:

DO Enclosed please find my resume for the _____ position you recently advertised.

OR

Sally Ingrams, manager of the _____, informed me that you have a _____ position open. She feels that my _____ and _____ experience matches this opening and encouraged me to contact you. Below, I have briefly outlined my top qualifications.

OR

Thank you for speaking with me today regarding my background in _____, _____, and _____. As you requested I have enclosed my resume for your review and have outlined the experience needed for your _____ department.

3. Use the Body of Your Letter to Present Your Case

In the second, third, and fourth paragraphs of your cover letter, you should build a case for your qualifications. Use bolded statements like those in the cover letter on page 206. Or use skill headings above main paragraphs like those shown in the cover letters on pages 208 and 210. Be sure that your cover letter addresses all of the main skills, areas of knowledge, and education requirements requested in ads that you answer.

Writing smooth sentences seems to be the most difficult and frustrating part of writing cover letters. To help, I've provided a few transitional statements that you can use to begin cover letter paragraphs. Review the cover letters on pages 208 and 210 to see how we've used statements like those below and at the top of the next page.

TRANSITIONAL PHRASES

- Overall, my _____ background includes . . .
- Having an in-depth knowledge of _____ allows me to . . .
- As a _____, I was responsible for . . .
- During my employment with _____, I . . .
- Over ten years of experience as a _____ has involved responsibility for . . .
- In addition, I have . . .

- I am very excited about this position as it will utilize the best of my abilities in . . .
- My background in _____, _____, and _____ combined with my ability to promote strong team relations has consistently resulted in . . .
- Implementing _____ and _____ systems has resulted in . . .
- As a _____, I have established a proven history of . . .
- My background demonstrates an ability to . . .

4. Make the Closing Paragraph Your Call to Action

Your final paragraph should be a call to action. State when you will contact the employer, or ask for an interview, and then thank the employer for his or her consideration. Say you will contact the employer the following week if you know the company name and phone number. This works better than saying you will call on a certain day. If something comes up and you forget to call that particular day, you won't end up looking like you have poor follow-through. In closing, your final paragraph might read

> I am very interested in this position and will contact you next week to schedule an interview. If you have any questions, please contact me at (555) 555-5555. Thank you for your time and consideration.

If you can't follow up because you don't have the company's name (when answering a blind ad), then state that you would like to schedule an interview. Your final paragraph might read

> I am very interested in this position and would like to schedule an interview with you. Please contact me at (555) 555-5555. Thank you for your time and consideration.

5. Use a Postscript (P.S.) to Grab Attention and Convince Employers to Interview You

After your signature, use a postscript to attract attention, get employers to read your letters, and call you for an interview. Direct mail marketers have tested and found that including a P.S. in a letter can substantially increase response rates. This happens since most of us will read a P.S. first, because we're curious about what it says.

When I applied to the University of Washington, Bothell, for a job placement specialist position, I used a P.S. in my cover letter. I was finishing up the first edition of *Proven Resumes and Confidence Builders* and knew that the book was my most convincing qualification since I only had a two-year degree. But I felt that sending a book would be too much to include with a cover letter. So I called and talked with Kathleen, the director of career counseling, who was the hiring manager for the position. I asked her if she would be interested in seeing several pages from my book and she said she would. In my cover letter I then included the following postscript:

> **P.S. As we discussed, I have enclosed several pages from my book, which further illustrate my skills in teaching resume, job search, and interviewing strategies.**

What would you do next if you read this P.S. in a letter that I had sent you? Most people say they would automatically turn to the pages of my book. That's exactly what Kathleen did. I had purposely included this P.S. so that I could direct Kathleen's attention to my book. In the face of heavy competition from people with bachelor's and master's degrees, I didn't want my book, my strongest qualification, to be overlooked. After Kathleen hired me, she told me that the hiring committee had decided they wanted to hire me even before they interviewed me. That's how impressed they were with the "paper package" I had submitted.

Many job seekers have reported that a strong P.S. landed them interviews. Morgan told me he had sent a letter to the human resource department of an electronics manufacturing firm. The letter was forwarded to department managers, and most weren't hooked by the P.S. But one of the managers was experiencing a problem Morgan had solved and described in his P.S. That manager called Morgan and then hired him. Here's what he put in his postscript:

> **P.S. Talking recently with Sam Reynolds, in your electronics production department, he let me know that you are experiencing problems with your wave flow solder machine. At ATP, I managed the same system and was responsible for calibrating it. By shutting the system down each evening for about 30 minutes and making close tolerance adjustments, I was able to cut daily rejection rates by over 15%. I'd be glad to share my experience with you.**

If you include a P.S., be sure that you use it to convey something that is important to the employer. Mention your experience and success rate using a particular piece of equipment or a computer program that you know the employer uses. You might include a detailed report (that's not confidential) or a newsletter that you've designed that is very impressive. Or you can include an article that you've written that shows your expertise in the field you are seeking. If you read an article about a company's product or services and you have relevant experience, use a P.S. to mention it.

Don't use a P.S. to tell employers how wonderful their company is and how much you'd like to work for them. They hear such comments all the time and they normally have little impact.

Only Use Generic Letters as a Last Resort

As mentioned before, you'll generate more interviews by writing customized letters. However, if you absolutely don't have the time to write individual letters, you can create generic letters that are effective. Even though I was hesitant, I created a generic letter for Stanley because he worked six days a week and many nights. He truly had no time to write letters. He was lucky to find two hours each Sunday to read help-wanted ads. Stanley wanted a better sales position, so we created a generic letter that emphasized the skills requested in several ads for sales openings. The generic cover letter saved Stanley a lot of time. All he had to do was copy it, slip it into an envelope, and mail it with his resume. Stanley's generic letter on the next page generated a little less than a fifty percent response rate.

If you wish to apply for positions that are very different, then it's important to write a generic letter for each type of position. For example, Gretta managed a headache clinic and was also a gemologist (she selected gems for a major jewelry firm). These positions are very different. Physicians aren't going to want to know about her gemology background and jewelry stores aren't going to want to know about clinic operations. Gretta needed two letters, one targeted for a clinic position and one targeted for a gemology position. In contrast, Stanley's single letter was effective for him because he only used it to apply for sales positions.

Stanley Schneider
1512 Second Avenue
Gary, IN 34567
(555) 555-5555

November 31, 1999

Attn: Recruitment

Please accept this letter as application for the Sales position you recently advertised. Briefly, I have outlined my sales background.

Record as Top Sales Producer
- Currently generate approximately $1 million in annual sales.
- Proven experience developing and managing major commercial accounts.

Willingness to Travel
- Past employment has required extensive travel in a marketing capacity.

Education
- B.A. Degree in Business Administration with experience setting up, managing, and marketing a high-profile business.

Sales Management and Account Administration
- Over 10 years experience marketing and managing a business has required extensive sales management, contract negotiation, and account administration skills.

Dedication to Quality and Customer Service
- My desire is to excel and achieve the best for myself, my customers, and the corporation for which I work. Excellent references can verify my dedication and loyalty to service.

The combination of my skills and experience match the qualifications you seek for this position. I am eager to meet with you to discuss employment opportunities. Please leave a message for me at (555) 555-5555 and I will return your call that day.

Sincerely,

Stanley Schneider

To create a strong generic letter, pull out five to ten ads for positions similar to the one you want. Make a list of all the skills required. Then group them together following the same process that is outlined on pages 207 and 209. Use skill headings or bolded statements that address the most important skills or those requirements that are repeatedly asked for. Since you'll be photocopying your generic letter and not typing it individually, you can use a salutation like "Attn: Recruitment" or "Attn: Human Resources Department." Never use gender-specific salutations, such as "Dear Sirs" because you may end up insulting the employer reading it. As you can see, you won't have a name so you probably won't be able to follow up. This is a pitfall of generic letters.

If you are like many job seekers you may be thinking that a generic letter is the way to go. However, you will not generate as strong a response with generic letters as you will with customized letters. I know that it is difficult to work, come home and take care of a family, and then find time to write resumes, cover letters, and applications. But your success rate is dependent upon the time and effort you put into marketing yourself for each individual job. Generic letters are better than getting nothing in the mail—but use them as a last resort only if you have no other alternative.

Use the Cover Letter Worksheet

The cover letter worksheet on the next page is an effective, fast, and simple tool for writing a cover letter. It's easy to fill in the blanks by writing bulleted statements for each skill listed in the ad or job posting you are responding to. Students and readers who have used this worksheet have told me hundreds of cover letter success stories.

Critique Your Letter

Once you've written your letter, take the time to review the list of questions below to critique it and see if there are any items you've missed.

- Is your letter addressed to a specific person rather than to "Human Resources" or "Personnel"?
- Does your letter use design elements like bolding, indenting, or underlining to grab attention?
- Does your opening paragraph explain why you are submitting your cover letter?
- Does your opening paragraph mention the title of the position or ad you are responding to?
- Does your opening paragraph mention a job number if one was referenced in the ad?
- Does your opening paragraph mention the name of someone if you were referred to the company?
- Do the skill headings or bolded statements in your letter match the top skills required for the job you want?
- Does the content of your letter make a strong argument for your qualifications?
- Does the body of your letter generate interest in you?
- Does the last paragraph call for action and ask for an interview?
- If applicable, does your last paragraph state a time when you will follow up?
- Does your letter use an effective postscript (P.S.)?
- Does the tone and content of your letter match the salary and responsibility level of jobs being sought?
- Have you graphed each title, skill heading, and statement in your letter and strengthened any that are weak?

Your Street Address
City, State Zip Code
(Area Code) Phone Number

Date

Name of Person You Are Contacting
Person's Title
Company Name
Address
City, State Zip Code

Dear Mr. or Ms. _____:

Enclosed please find my resume for the _____ position
you recently advertised. As you will note, my experience includes

- _____

- _____

- _____

- _____

- _____

The combination of my _____, _____,
and _____ experience makes me well qualified for this
position. I will contact you next week to discuss interviewing with you. If you
have any questions, please contact me at (your area code) your phone number.
Thank you for your time and consideration.

Sincerely,

Your Name

Follow Up on Your Letter

Once you've written your letter and mailed it, you'll increase your success rate by following up on it. If you don't, you'll be like the majority of job seekers who send hundreds of cover letters and resumes but never know what happened to them. By contacting employers to ensure that your letter and resume were received, you can put yourself ahead of your competition and stand out.

Already you may be thinking, "But I don't want to have to call and follow up. I just want employers to call me." I think there's nothing more frightening to most of us than following up on employment packages that we've submitted for job openings. It makes our hands get sweaty and our hearts palpitate. The fear of hearing "No, we're not interested in you" makes most of us procrastinate and never follow up.

It's natural to feel a little uncomfortable at the prospect of calling employers and asking if your letters have been received. Whenever I teach job search seminars I ask people to raise their hands if contacting employers seems a little scary. Usually more than half of the participants raise their hands, so these feelings are normal.

I know I was scared and breathless the first time I called to follow up on a cover letter I had sent in response to a help-wanted ad. Having closed my resume business, I had decided to go into the personnel field. I answered an ad for a personnel coordinator with a national placement agency. The ad listed the street address but didn't include the company name or phone number. When a week had passed and I hadn't received a call, I got out the yellow pages. Within a few minutes I found the agency's name and phone number.

The ad had stated, "No calls, please," which made me even more uncomfortable. But I really wanted that job so I called and spoke with Mr. Grant, the owner of the agency, who asked me why I thought I could do the job. Feeling shaky, I jumped in and told him I had owned a business writing resumes and had marketed over 1,500 job seekers. I explained that this, combined with my knowledge of hundreds of industries and job requirements, would allow me to quickly step in and market employees applying for positions through his personnel agency. He seemed quite interested and said, "Well, I do have someone in mind and I believe we'll hire her, but why don't you come in tomorrow?" Wow, was I happy when I got off the phone! To make the rest of this story short, I spent three hours at his office the next day, then had a second lunch interview that took two hours, and a final interview that took an hour and a half. I got the job because I took my fear by the horns, found the agency's phone number, and followed up on the cover letter I had mailed.

Job Seekers Report Landing Jobs after Following Up

Many participants in my workshops report similar success stories. One young man had been a weekend gas station manager and had completed an office automation course. He sent out more than 100 resumes and cover letters to ads for administrative positions along with letters to companies who hadn't advertised. After three weeks he was very depressed because he hadn't received even one interview. When I asked him if he had followed up on any of his letters, he said, "No, it's scary. Why would they want to talk to me anyway? I've only managed a gas station."

Boosting his confidence, I reminded him that he had supervised operations with sales of up to $50,000 per month overseeing six staff members, and that he had the highest grades in his computer class. After about thirty minutes he felt better. The next day he dropped in, and he was beaming. The very first job he had followed up on was at a brokerage firm. When he called the manager, she said she remembered his cover letter and resume but that they were already into their third round of interviews; however, she thought she could squeeze him in. He ended up interviewing with three of the brokerage partners the next day and was hired.

Another job seeker in a much higher salary range had been a senior sales manager making $70,000. He also reported he had sent off more than seventy-five resumes but hadn't landed any interviews. After hearing how important follow-up is, he contacted the national marketing director of a major medical instrument company and landed an interview. He was told they weren't interested in him for the $70,000 position but wanted to interview him for a $100,000 position. Boy, did that increase his confidence! Don't underestimate the power of follow-up!

If you submit your cover letter in response to a blind ad, one that only lists a P.O. box with no company name, you won't know what company you are applying to. Be careful—you could answer an ad for the company you currently work for. To learn what company placed the help-wanted ad, call the post office that handles the zip code listed in the ad's address. Ask the post office to give you the name of the company that holds the box number provided in the ad. Once you know which company has placed the ad you can decide whether to apply or not. You can also use this information to follow up, ensure that your cover letter has been received, and engage the employer in a conversation similar to the one I had with Mr. Grant. Few people take the time to find out what companies placed the blind ads they respond to. Therefore, very few job seekers call and follow up on their applications. The fewer the phone calls, the less competition you have. This puts you in a strategic position. By calling, you can put yourself way ahead of your competitors.

Answer Ads as Soon as Possible

Apply for each position as soon as possible. If you find an ad in a Sunday paper, answer it that night or the next day. If you wait too long, you may lose out. Large companies are more likely to keep and file all cover letters and resumes submitted to them, but many smaller companies do not. In several of the smaller firms I've worked for, a high volume of cover letters and resumes arrived during the first week after each ad was placed. If there were enough qualified candidates in that first batch, the rest of the letters and resumes received the following weeks were often not even opened. It was just too time consuming. So those candidates who sent their cover letters and resumes in too late never had a chance!

This has happened to many of the clients who have come to me because they aren't getting enough interviews and are struggling to find out why. When asked how soon they get their cover letters and resumes off in response to a Sunday ad, they frequently say something like "Well usually I get my letters in the mail by Thursday or Friday." When I explain this isn't soon enough they start getting their letters in the mail Sunday night or Monday. After this happens, many call me on Wednesday, Thursday, or Friday to say, "I can't believe I've already received an interview for the position I responded to this weekend." Time counts. Get your cover letters and resumes mailed as soon as possible!

I was shocked to read one consultant's advice to executives. He recommends waiting a few days after seeing an ad before responding to it. He even goes so far as to say it's good to wait a week or two before applying. He evidently thinks the executive hiring process is always long and drawn out. He seems unaware of the fact that a company may have already been looking for someone for weeks or months and could be on the verge of a hiring decision. My advice is to get those letters out there—and the sooner the better. Then be sure to follow up!

Use the Power of Fax and E-Mail

By faxing or e-mailing your cover letter and resume, you can also land more interviews. For example, Pamela found a help-wanted ad for a property manager position that included the company name, address, phone, and fax numbers. That night she faxed her cover letter and resume. When she called the next morning to follow up, she was set up for an interview two days later. During her interview, the employer took out a six-inch stack of cover letters and resumes. Holding them, she said, "I've received more than one hundred resumes and cover letters by mail. I don't have the time to read them all and have decided to interview only those people who fax their information to me. I've received seven faxed resumes and yours was one of them. I'm impressed that you followed up so quickly."

Fax or e-mail your cover letter and resume as soon as possible if a fax number or e-mail address is provided. Your last choice should be to mail your resume. Who knows, by the time your cover letter and resume are received by mail the position may be filled. Or enough faxed or e-mail resumes may have been received that the mailed ones may not be opened. Do whatever it takes to reach an employer as quickly as possible.

Contact Employers Who Haven't Advertised

In addition to applying for advertised positions, you'll also be wise to submit a cover letter and resume to employers who have not placed an ad but whom you would like to work for. To be effective, you need to avoid cold call letters that generate a poor response rate. A cold call letter is one that is written with little knowledge of each company or its needs. Many executive outplacement firms help their clients send out hundreds, sometimes a thousand, cold call letters. Yet cold call letters often have very low response rates. One leading outplacement firm's statistics show that cold call letters generate a three to four percent response rate for positions under $40,000, and that this drops to less than one percent for positions at or above $100,000. This means that job seekers submitting cold call letters can only expect to receive between one and four responses to every one hundred letters they submit. This is not much better than direct mail solicitations, which usually generate about a two percent response rate.

After spending the time and money to send out several hundred, or a thousand, cold call letters, many job seekers become extremely discouraged. The solution is to compile a dozen or so ads or job openings that are similar to those jobs you believe would be available with a company that hasn't advertised. By analyzing similar ads and job opening descriptions, you can then make an accurate assessment as to what an employer's needs are—even if that employer hasn't placed an ad. In this way you can create a cold call letter that is targeted or customized for your industry or the jobs you want.

In addition to what you'll learn from the ads and job opening descriptions, imagine that you work for each company. What level of position would you be employed in? What types of equipment, systems, products, or personnel would you be responsible for? What type of problems would you have to deal with? What are some of the biggest ongoing or seasonal problems faced by such a company?

Have you worked for a similar company or solved a similar problem in the past? What do you think is the biggest concern a decision maker has when hiring someone for the position you want? Address this information in your cold call letters. By doing such an analysis, you will increase the success of the cover letters you submit to employers who haven't advertised.

Target the Correct Decision Maker

When preparing your cover letters, whether for an advertised or an unadvertised position, be sure to target the correct decision maker and market yourself for positions at the correct salary and responsibility level. Sending your cover letter to the wrong person at the wrong level often results in failure. This had happened to Lance. He was a salesman making $75,000 in the freight forwarding industry. Over a five-month period he had not landed one interview even though he had contacted more than fifty employers. I asked what salary level he wanted and he said anywhere from $50,000 to $75,000. That's a big range in salary as well as level of responsibility. Many salespeople in the $50,000 range manage a two- to three-state territory with sales of $2 to $5 million. Lance told me he had been responsible for accounts in forty states with sales of $20 million.

When Lance called companies to get the name and address of the person he should send his cover letters to, he would ask to speak to senior sales managers. He would then inquire about sales positions in the $50,000 range and proudly state that he had managed forty states with sales of $20 million. He would get either a lukewarm response on the phone or submit his cover letter and never land an interview. The problem was that Lance was as qualified as many of the senior sales managers he spoke to or sent his cover letters to, so it was likely that many of them felt threatened by Lance's experience. To be more successful in both his phone conversations and in his cover letters, Lance needed to tone down his experience when going for a $50,000 job.

Better yet, he needed to target hiring officials such as a vice president of marketing, who is one or two levels above a senior sales manager, and wouldn't be threatened by his experience. To Lance's surprise, he found that senior staff at that level were interested to see how he could help their divisions or departments increase sales. By changing his strategy Lance substantially increased his interview rate and was ultimately hired for a job in the $75,000 range.

Similar problems occur when job seekers substantially elevate the image that they present in their resumes, but keep submitting cover letters for jobs at a lower level. Employers then believe such job seekers are overqualified and don't grant them interviews. It's not that the applicants aren't qualified for higher level jobs—it's that they're not even applying for them. To avoid such problems, be sure that your cover letters and resumes do not oversell or undersell you. Apply for positions at the appropriate salary and responsibility level that you want. Just like Lance, contact hiring officials that are at least one level above the position you want. These strategies are just common sense, yet many job seekers fail because they don't follow these simple guidelines when writing and submitting their cover letters.

You're Now Ready to Submit a Powerful Marketing Package

By applying the strategies provided throughout this chapter you will create a cover letter that is as commanding as your resume. Combining your letter and resume will allow you to submit a powerful marketing package that will put you in the top percentage of qualified applicants and will result in interviews and job offers for the positions you want.

13 Electronic Resumes and Internet Job Search Strategies

Many companies still select candidates to interview by visually reviewing resumes. But in today's electronic world more and more firms use automated resume tracking systems because they drastically reduce the time it takes to review, sort, and file large numbers of resumes. Using these systems, employers collect and store thousands of resumes in electronic databases. Such databases can then be sorted to find applicant resumes that contain skills, experience, or educational backgrounds that match specified job requirements.

This brave new electronic world means that you must have two versions of your resume. One is your nicely formatted version for human eyes, which we'll refer to as your "visual resume." And you'll need one designed for computers, which we'll call your "electronic resume." Later you'll learn how to create an electronic resume by converting your resume word processing file into plain text or ASCII (American Standard Code for Information Interchange) format.

To achieve job search success in today's electronic arena, use these two key points to guide you:

- First, you want to learn how to create a resume that will come to the top when an employer sorts for keywords or areas of experience that the company needs. You'll achieve this by knowing the type of job you want, the skills needed for such a position, and then effectively matching your skills to that position.

- Second, you want to use Internet job search strategies to find employer websites and job postings so that you can apply for them.

An Electronic Job Search Success Story

To begin, let's review how Doug used a skillfully constructed keyword resume to achieve job search success on the Internet. Doug was about to leave the military and had come to me to help him create an electronic resume. After only a month's time of using his new resume, he sent me this e-mail describing the success his e-resume had achieved:

> Remember me? Well I'm about to leave the military and go to just the job I wanted . . . thanks to the ProvenResumes program.

> If you remember, I shared with you a job ad for a position I wanted and then used it as the basis for building my resume. Well, I put my resume on the Internet at OCC.com (Online Career Center) and within days, that exact company called me and wanted to interview me. Needless to say, I went through the interviews and was hired!

> I'm recommending your system of creating keyword resumes to all my friends who are considering a civilian career! Thanks! Doug Ottinger

Although it's impressive to hear that Doug landed a position via the Internet, it's even more impressive to know that he had created his resume for one position with a particular company and that this firm selected Doug's resume from thousands of others that were posted.

So how did Doug do this? First, he determined the kind of job that would be a good match for the range of skills he had developed in the military. Then he searched the Internet for such positions and for companies he wanted to work for. Once he found such positions, he analyzed each job posting to identify the key skills, areas of experience, education, and technical requirements each employer was looking for. Doug then created a resume using keywords to describe specific skills that his target employer had used. It was Doug's effective use of keywords that caused his resume to be selected and resulted in his being interviewed and ultimately hired. Please keep in mind that the success you achieve will vary from Doug's experience and will be based on a variety of factors that will include, but may not be limited to, the quality and number of resumes you post online, how well qualified you are for the jobs you seek, and the prevailing market conditions in which you are seeking employment.

Keywords: Even More Important in the Electronic World

Before we look at Doug's Before and After resumes, let's talk about why keywords are such an important ingredient of scannable and electronic resumes. Scanners use software to read resume text and convert it into electronic data for storage, sorting, and retrieval in electronic databases. Many employers also provide resume building forms at company websites, pull posted resumes off of other resume posting sites, or accept resumes via e-mail. Resume data pulled from such sites can also be added to electronic databases.

All resumes stored electronically can then be sorted by key skills, experience, or education. Such items are referred to as *keywords*. For example, an employer looking for an accountant might enter the following keywords or phrases: *staff accountant, B.A. Degree in Accounting, full-cycle accounting, financial statements*, and *cost accounting*. A sort of all resumes in the database could be performed and those that contain all or some of these keywords would be identified. An employer could then read them on the computer screen, print entire resumes, or print abstracted data from some or all of the resumes.

Some automated resume tracking systems can read and retain the entire number of keywords contained in a resume. Other, usually older, systems may only be able to retain thirty-five or so keywords. Either way, you can see why keywords are the "magic door" for generating interviews with employers who use resume tracking systems. Keywords are, in short, how employers find you in their systems. If you don't supply the right keywords, then your resume won't be found, you won't be identified as a potential candidate, and you won't get interviews.

Now let's look at how Doug targeted his resume for a particular job, posted it to an online career center, and was hired. Doug had found an ad for a management consultant position, which appears at the top of the next page. Take a moment and read the ad. You'll see that it contains thirty-six keywords derived from thirteen keyword phrases. Like many employers do, it looks like this firm threw in the kitchen sink when writing the ad. Even though this is a typical strategy, most employers know it's unlikely that they will find an applicant with every skill they request. They basically search and settle for the one applicant who seems to have the best blend of soft skills, such as high achievement on the job or leadership, combined with hard skills such as those emphasized in this ad. With this in mind, Doug transformed his Before resume from one that emphasized military terms to one that emphasized keywords to describe skills and experience this employer wanted.

The Ad That Doug Analyzed and Responded To

Shown below is the ad for the "Management/Organizational Consultant" position that Doug analyzed and responded to.

Management/Organizational Consultant

Ideal candidate will have a <u>B.A. degree</u>, preferably in <u>engineering</u> with excellent <u>communication</u> and <u>team management</u> skills. Must have background in: <u>testing</u> and <u>evaluations systems</u>, <u>systems implementation</u>, <u>acquisition management</u>, <u>total quality management</u>, <u>government accounting</u> or <u>systems accounting</u>, <u>business process improvement/reengineering</u>, <u>change management</u>, <u>performance measurement</u> and <u>benchmarking</u>, <u>quality assurance</u>, <u>risk management</u>, <u>logistics/supply</u>, <u>software development/package implementation</u>, <u>federal contracting</u>, and costing estimating.

Take a moment and read the section from Doug's Before resume on the next page. If a computer sort were performed using eight keywords from the ad above such as *organizational/management consultant*, *testing systems*, *business reengineering*, and *risk management*, would Doug's Before resume be selected? You'll find that the only keyword contained in his Before resume is "Systems." Any resume that contains two or more of these keywords would be rated higher than Doug's resume. Those containing eight of the keywords would be rated highest.

Now take a look at the section from Doug's After resume. All eight keywords are included either in the skill headings or in the text of this resume. If a sort were performed for the eight keywords, Doug's After resume would be selected and would be rated as one of the best received. As a result, we can say it would grab the computer's attention.

Once that's accomplished, the next step is to ensure that Doug's resume will also grab an employer's attention when viewed by human eyes. As you've learned, employers analyze and select resumes based on the image they form of you. To see how an employer would react to Doug's Before and After resumes, read the bolded headings in Doug's Before resume and compare them to the bolded headings in his After resume. Which resume creates an image of Doug as being qualified as a management consultant? Which resume creates an image of Doug working around airplanes and bombs? Which one would come out on top when reviewed by an employer hiring a management consultant? Keywords must grab a computer's attention, but in the end the design, content, and image presented by your electronic resume must still grab an employer's attention and present an image of your skills that matches the position and salary you want.

How Many Keywords Should You Use?

The ad above includes thirty-six unique keywords and Doug's resume used twenty of them, which was well over fifty percent. Whenever possible, use a minimum of fifty percent of the keywords found in an assortment of ads for the type of positions you want. If possible, use all of them as long as you have the skills you're listing. You never want to lie or exaggerate by adding keywords to describe skills you don't possess. This strategy could land you an interview, or a call from an employer, but would backfire when employers see you don't have the skills you've marketed.

RELEVANT EXPERIENCE

October 1996-Present -- Chief, Planning & Innovations, 11th Bomb Wing

Assisted the Chief Operating Officer in all matters pertaining to planning, systems development, and competitive sourcing for the 11th Bomb Wing, consisting of 12 divisions and 4,800 employees.

October 1995-96 -- Military Personnel Flight Commander, 11th Bomb Wing

Served as senior advisor to COOs with responsibility for implementing all military personnel policies and programs for 3,500 personnel.

October 1990-1995 -- Requirements Analysis Chief, Air Wing Division

Served as technical advisor and personnel liaison between policy makers and information systems divisions. Led teams in planning, procurement, and training for implementation of $ 1/2 million computer system.

October 1989-1990 -- Personnel Utilization Chief, Missile Wing

Led, motivated, and trained crew of 20 individuals providing relocation, employment, and classification services for 3,700 military personnel.

REGIONAL MANAGER / ORGANIZATIONAL CONSULTANT, USAF 1989 - Present

OPERATIONS MANAGEMENT

- *Systems Analysis & Process Reengineering* -- Reengineered documentation systems for personnel departing a central location; reduced unfilled personnel requirements by 41%.

- *Cost Reduction & Labor Control* -- Developed and analyzed survey data as part of management consultant team chartered to improve shift production; end solution reduced operating costs by $120K annually; directly contributed to division being selected "Best Management Consulting Division" from 12 divisions.

- *Operational Risk Management* -- Conducted risk assessment of personnel operations for every job function performed within 10 sections and successfully identified multiple risk factors.

- *Logistics / Supply Planning & Allocation* -- Led multifaceted logistics reception team to accommodate 14,000 personnel, which required coordinating with airport and customs to ensure round-the-clock service.

- *Total Quality Management* -- Facilitated four strategic planning sessions consulting CEO and Division Vice Presidents in defining division-wide goals, action plans, and performance measures. Strategic planning followed the Malcolm Baldridge criteria for TQM organizational restructuring.

- *Performance Measurement* -- Overhauled training and self-inspection programs for 5 departments successfully taking customer satisfaction rates from 75 to 87% with section being rated "Excellent."

NATIONAL COMPUTER SYSTEM IMPLEMENTATION

- *IS Planning, Procurement, & Installation* -- Managed software development, hardware acquisition, and implementation of new distributed database system to over 98 federal agencies throughout the nation.

- *Software Development / Reprogramming* -- Directed flawless reprogramming and testing efforts of two divisions for nationwide personnel system database change affecting over 1.2 million personnel records.

- *Functional Analysis & Program Management* -- Implemented first document management/imaging system valued at over $200K for personnel records, which significantly reduced backlog of data inquiries.

- *Project Manager / Team Leader* -- Led joint team of field operations staff and technical programmers that resolved a complex data system interface problem and avoided 4,000 hours in programming charges.

Analyzing and Compiling Keywords from Ads

Analyzing help-wanted ads and job opening descriptions is essential in creating an effective resume—and it's even more important for electronic resumes. Now we'll walk through the process of analyzing ads, using Robin as an example. Since Robin wanted to create a resume to market her customer service skills, she began by collecting eight ads for a broad range of customer service positions that interested her. Next, she followed the steps below to compile keywords and keyword phrases for her resume:

Step 1: Underline all keywords and keyword phrases in each ad.

Step 2: Group keywords and keyword phrases into skill categories as shown on the next page.

Step 3: Create skill headings using keywords or keyword phrases for each group of skill categories.

Step 4: Prioritize and number the skill categories.

Step 5: Select the top thirty-five to forty-five keywords to create a keyword section for the top of the resume.

Step 6: Write statements using as many keywords as possible for use in the rest of the resume.

Many job seekers find only 25 to 35 keywords in the ads below, yet there are more than 160 keywords provided in 63 keyword phrases. Identifying all keywords and keyword phrases is important because you never know which keywords employers may use to sort resumes. The more keywords you include in your resume, the higher the chance is that your resume will be selected.

Step 1: Underline Keywords and Keyword Phrases

First, Robin underlined all keywords in the ads.

1. Customer Service/Order Entry
Great oral and written communication skills. MS Word and Excel. Strong data entry skills. 2- or 4-year degree. Knowledge of computer hardware a plus. Assist field representatives in the sales support center, process or change orders, provide product information.

2. Customer Service Rep
1+ years exp. in customer service or retail field. Will take inbound calls from customers nationwide, process warranty claims, log complaints, answer questions. Quote pricing, use database and customer inventory management systems to check stock.

3. Customer Shipment Representative
Excellent communication skills, computer literate with proficiency in MS Word and Excel. 1+ years experience with good job stability. Work at the customer service center for this international shipping company. Will track customer shipments and communicate shipment status to customers. Openings in documentation and customs departments.

4. Customer Service/Sales Support
Key account administration, customer service and administrative sales support to account executives by phone. MS Word and Excel. Detail-oriented team player with excellent follow-up, written and verbal communication skills. Duties: receiving, coordination and completion of shipments/documentation. Phones, general office, and data entry.

5. Client Services—New Accounts
Handle incoming customer calls to set up new accounts or change existing service; provide information about products and services; and maintain records of customer contacts. Strong customer service and problem resolution skills.

6. Customer Request Representative
Handle customer requests, inquiries, and complaints. Enter and access data using a computer terminal. High degree of accuracy required. Related work experience in similar environments such as commission, quota sales, billing, collections or key account servicing.

7. Inside Sales Support
Support inside sales staff, build customer relationships with key accounts, approve return authorizations, process orders, post AP/AR. Coordinate shipments, complete shipping documents. Must be team player able to work in fast-paced, high stress environments.

8. Order Processing/Customer Service
Process sales orders, commissions, reports for sales teams. Follow up with vendors and distributors, book appointments, process customer credit applications, complete sales paperwork for assigned sales team. MS Word, Excel, data entry, typing at 60+ wpm.

Step 2: Group Similar Skills Together

Robin grouped all of the underlined keywords and keyword phrases from the ads into skill categories as shown below.

Step 3: Label Skill Categories with Skill Headings

Next, Robin labeled each category with a skill heading.

Step 4: Prioritize and Number Skill Categories by Importance

In this step, Robin decided which groups of skills were most important and numbered them by importance.

6 Office and Administrative Experience
General Office
Answer Phone/Questions
Book Appointments
Post AP/AR
Typing 60+ wpm

3 Support of Inside Sales Team/Account Executives
Inside Sales Support
Administrative Sales Support
Support Account Executives
Assist Field Reps
Complete Sales Paperwork for Assigned Sales Team
Quote Pricing
Process Warranty Claims
Provide Product/Service Information
Process Reports for Sales Teams

1 Key Account Administration
Customer Service/Servicing of Key Accounts
Build Customer Relationships
Change Existing Service
Handle Customer Requests, Inquiries, and
    Complaints
Handle Incoming Customer Calls
Take Inbound Calls

Approve Return Authorizations
Log Complaints
Maintain Records of Customer Contacts
Set Up New Account

4 Shipment Verification and Documentation
Check Stock
Communicate Shipment Status to Customers
Communicate with Vendors by Phone
Coordinate Shipments
Follow-Up with Vendors and Distributors
Complete Shipping Documents
Receiving, Coordination, Completion of Shipments
Track Customer Shipments

5 Computerized Applications
Computer Literate
Excel, MS Word
Data Entry, Use Database Systems
Enter and Access Data Using a Computer Terminal
Use Customer Inventory Management Systems
Knowledge of Computer Hardware

2 Sales Order Processing
Order Entry/Process Change Orders
Process Customer Credit Applications
Process Sales Orders/Commissions

Step 5: Select the Top Thirty-five to Forty-five Keywords and Keyword Phrases

Next, Robin selected several top skills from each category and used them to compile the following keyword summary for her resume as shown on page 233. It's important to include a keyword summary at the top of your resume, as some resume tracking systems can only retain twenty-five to thirty-five keywords when searching resumes. A keyword summary at the top of the resume ensures that your most important keywords will be picked up before less important keywords.

> **KEYWORD SUMMARY -- CUSTOMER SERVICE REPRESENTATIVE**
> -- Key Account Servicing -- Build Customer Relationships
> -- Handle Incoming Calls, Requests, Inquiries, Complaints
> -- Process Sales Orders, Credit Applications, Return Authorizations, Warranty Claims, Sales Reports, Commissions
> -- Support Inside Sales Teams, Account Executives, Field Representatives -- Set Up New Accounts
> -- Excel, MS Word -- Data, Order Entry -- Database, Customer Inventory Management Systems
> -- Typing 60 wpm

Step 6: Write Resume Statements Using Keywords and Keyword Phrases

Robin created statements using seventy-three keywords or phrases from the ads that matched her experience. Below is a statement that uses these keyword phrases: "Inside Sales Support," "Support Account Executives," "Assist Field Reps," and "Complete Sales Paperwork for Assigned Sales Team."

> -- Provided <u>inside sales support</u> to a staff of 10 <u>Account Executives</u> and assisted 5 <u>Field Representatives</u> being responsible for <u>completing sales paperwork for assigned sales team</u> generating revenues of $12 million annually.

The statement above is used in the main section of Robin's resume under the subheading of Support of Inside Sales Team/Account Executives. If you read Robin's resume and compare it to the underlined keywords in the ads on page 231, you'll find that every statement in it is packed with keywords from the ads. This is an excellent example of how to extract keywords from ads to build a powerful electronic resume.

Anatomy of a Keyword Resume

As you'll see on page 236, the first section of Robin's resume is her Keyword Summary. In a computer sort for customer service representatives, this section would help to ensure that Robin's resume is selected. In the second section of the resume, two qualifications statements detail the depth and breadth of Robin's customer service representative experience. This section takes only a few seconds to read but would grab an employer's attention and start building a strong image of Robin's skills. The third section, or the body of Robin's resume, includes skill headings followed by keyword statements. In the last section of her resume, you'll see that Robin listed her education.

More Tips for Strengthening Keyword Resumes

In addition to hard skills, most want ads and job descriptions ask for soft skills and also provide a gold mine of miscellaneous terms unrelated to either hard or soft skills. While these miscellaneous terms often seem unimportant, they can dramatically strengthen your resume.

The Secrets of Describing Your Soft Skills

The eight ads Robin selected had included these soft skills: "Detail-Oriented Team Player," "Good Job Stability," "Oral, Verbal, and Written Communication Skills." So using these terms will grab a computer's attention. But when it gets to the human review of the resume, these terms are not as strong or as specific as they should be. For example, read the first statement in the "Overview of Qualifications" section in Robin's resume. You'll notice that it ends with the keywords "detail-oriented team player." Yet, it's the preceding descriptions in that statement which really convince you that Robin is a detail-oriented team player. The phrase good job stability could be described this way: "Maintained a 100% attendance record during 5 years of employment, which demonstrates dedication and good job stability." Notice how the keywords are included but are attached to specific details that back up the description. When describing soft skills, be sure to provide examples that prove you have such skills.

Secrets for Using Miscellaneous Phrases

Ads frequently provide industry, regional, or job references that aren't related to hard or soft skills, education, or training requirements. However, these terms can be a significant key in elevating your image and making you look extremely well qualified. For example, the ads Robin had found included these references: "Customer Service and Sales Support Center," "Documentation and Customs Departments," and "International Shipping Company." Read through the headings in Robin's resume on the facing page to see how she added these keywords to it. Do they strengthen her resume and make her seem even better qualified for the range of positions she wants?

Converting Your Keyword Resume to an Electronic Format

As we've already discussed, many employers use automated resume tracking systems that store resume data in plain text or ASCII file format. You want to convert your file into this format so that it can be accepted error-free by electronic resume tracking and e-mail systems. You will then use this file to print a hard copy of your resume for scanning, to copy and paste your plain text resume into online resume building forms, or to copy and paste your plain text resume into an e-mail message for transmission to employers or recruiters.

What Happens When Resumes Are Scanned

While newer and more sophisticated scanning systems can read, sort, and retain all text contained in a printed resume, older or less sophisticated systems are more limited. Newer systems can take a snapshot of an entire resume and reprint it just as it was submitted to an employer, keeping all formatting such as bolding, underlining, or italicizing intact. Older systems may only be able to display or reprint the resume data in very plain typefaces with all formatting removed; such systems also tend to insert errors as they remove formatting commands. Since you never know which type of system an employer is using, it's wise to create a plain text or ASCII version of your resume so that it will work well on both new and older systems.

On the facing page is a section from Robin's nicely formatted resume on page 236, which has been scanned and then reprinted from an older scanning system. This shows what can happen when older systems convert resume text into electronic data, removing all formatting commands in the process. The bolding, underlining, and graphic lines that Robin used to make her resume visually attractive have been removed and resulted in several errors or typos. Therefore, it's important that you learn how to create a resume file that lets you print a hard copy of your resume so that it can be scanned and then converted into plain text or ASCII format by an employer's scanning system without creating errors.

On page 237, Robin's nicely formatted resume with bolding and graphic lines seen on page 236 has been converted to plain text or ASCII format. While this resume is very plain and unattractive to human eyes, it will scan and can be inserted into e-mail messages error free. To convert Robin's resume, we followed the guidelines provided on pages 238 to 239.

^ROBIN HILDEBRAND 1515 S.E. 30th Street
0000(555)0000555-55550000000Seattle, WA 98105000000000000000000000000000000000000000000000000000000000000

^^KEYWORD SUMMARY - CUSTOMER SERVICE REPRESENTATIVE
-- Key Account Servicing -- Build Customer Relationships -- Handle Incoming Calls, Requests, Inquiries, Complaints
-- Process Sales Orders, Credit Applications, Return Authorizations, Warranty Claims, Sales Reports, Commissions
-- Support Inside Sales Teams, Account Executives, Field Representatives
-- Setup New Accounts
-- Excel, MS Word -- Data, Order Entry -- Database, Customer Inventory Management Systems
-- Typing 60 wpm

^OVERVIEW OF QUALIFICATIONS

-- Provided customer service for up to 400 key accounts and supported a staff of 15 marketing and field service representatives generating annual sales of $12 million which required strong skills as a detail-oriented team player.

-- Demonstrated proven skill in maintaining excellent customer relationships with Regional Managers and District Purchasing Agents, being responsible for all phases of customer order processing and administration.
0000000000000000000000000000000000000000000000000000000000000000000000000000000000000000000000000000000

ROBIN HILDEBRAND
(555) 555-5555

1515 S.E. 30th Street
Seattle, WA 98105

KEYWORD SUMMARY -- CUSTOMER SERVICE REPRESENTATIVE
-- Key Account Servicing -- Build Customer Relationships
-- Handle Incoming Calls, Requests, Inquiries, Complaints
-- Process Sales Orders, Credit Applications, Return Authorizations, Warranty Claims, Sales Reports, Commissions
-- Support Inside Sales Teams, Account Executives, Field Representatives -- Set Up New Accounts
-- Excel, MS Word -- Data, Order Entry -- Database, Customer Inventory Management Systems
-- Typing 60 wpm

OVERVIEW OF QUALIFICATIONS
-- Provided customer service for up to 400 key accounts and supported a staff of 15 marketing and field service representatives generating annual sales of $12 million, which required strong skills as a detail-oriented team player.
-- Demonstrated proven skill in maintaining excellent customer relationships with Regional Managers and District Purchasing Agents, being responsible for all phases of customer order processing and administration.

CUSTOMER SERVICE REPRESENTATIVE, Smith's Retail & Wholesale Distribution 1991-Present

Nationwide Key Account Administration / Sales Order Processing
-- Provided customer service to 400 key accounts generating annual revenues ranging from $10,000 to $ 3/4 million per account each year, working closely with clients such as Regional Managers and District Purchasing Agents.
-- Took incoming calls, handled customer requests, inquiries, and complaints; approved return authorizations or changed existing service, being recognized for building excellent customer relationships.
-- Managed sales order processing including data entry for up to 80 orders per day with responsibility for processing change orders, customer credit applications, and calculating sales team commissions.

Support of Inside Sales Team / Account Executives
-- Provided inside sales support to staff of 10 Account Executives and assisted 5 Field Representatives, being responsible for completing sales paperwork for assigned sales team generating revenues of $12 million annually.
-- Quoted pricing, processed warranty claims, provided product and service information, and prepared various reports for sales team as part of administrative sales support duties.

International Shipment Verification & Documentation
-- Coordinated, followed up, and communicated shipment status with customers, vendors, and distributors by phone.
-- Checked stock, tracked shipments, and managed receiving, coordination, and completion of required shipping documents for department processing over 10,000 shipments per month.

Computerized Applications / Documentation & Report Development
-- Utilized advanced functions of MS Word, Excel, and Internet for data entry, maintenance of database systems, and access of customer inventory management systems.
-- Developed broad knowledge of computer hardware and inventory tracking software, being computer literate in use of leading word processing and spreadsheet programs.

Office & Administrative Experience in Customer Service & Sales Support Centers
-- Supporting teams of up to 15 marketing and field service personnel has required broad general office skills including front office administration, reception and answering of phones and customer questions, booking appointments, posting AP/AR for hundreds of national accounts, and typing speed of 60+ wpm.

EDUCATION
-- A.A.S. Degree in Business Administration, Lucerne College 1992

ROBIN HILDEBRAND
1515 S.E. 30th Street
Seattle, WA 98105
(555) 555-5555

KEYWORD SUMMARY -- CUSTOMER SERVICE REPRESENTATIVE

-- Key Account Servicing -- Build Customer Relationships -- Handle Incoming Calls, Requests, Inquiries, Complaints
-- Process Sales Orders, Credit Applications, Return Authorizations, Warranty Claims, Sales Reports, Commissions
-- Support Inside Sales Teams, Account Executives, Field Representatives -- Set Up New Accounts
-- Excel, MS Word -- Data, Order Entry -- Database, Customer Inventory Management Systems -- Typing 60 wpm

OVERVIEW OF QUALIFICATIONS

-- Provided customer service for up to 400 key accounts and supported a staff of 15 marketing and field service representatives generating annual sales of $12 million, which required strong skills as a detail-oriented team player.

-- Demonstrated proven skill in maintaining excellent customer relationships with Regional Managers and District Purchasing Agents, being responsible for all phases of customer order processing and administration.

CUSTOMER SERVICE REPRESENTATIVE, Smith's Retail & Wholesale Distribution 1991 - Present

Nationwide Key Account Administration / Sales Order Processing

-- Provided customer service to 400 key accounts generating annual revenues ranging from $10,000 to $3/4 million per account each year, working closely with clients such as Regional Managers and District Purchasing Agents. Took incoming calls, handled customer requests, inquiries, and complaints; approved return authorizations or changed existing service, being recognized for building excellent customer relationships. Managed sales order processing including data entry for up to 80 orders per day with responsibility for processing change orders, customer credit applications, and calculating sales team commissions.

Support of Inside Sales Team / Account Executives

-- Provided inside sales support to staff of 10 Account Executives and assisted 5 Field Representatives, being responsible for completing sales paperwork for assigned sales team generating revenues of $12 million annually. Quoted pricing, processed warranty claims, provided product and service information, and prepared various reports for sales team as part of administrative sales support duties.

International Shipment Verification & Documentation

-- Coordinated, followed up, and communicated shipment status with customers, vendors, and distributors by phone. Checked stock, tracked shipments, and managed receiving, coordination, and completion of required shipping documents for department processing over 10,000 shipments per month.

Computerized Applications / Documentation & Report Development

-- Utilized advanced functions of MS Word, Excel, and Internet for data entry, maintenance of database systems, and access of customer inventory management systems. Developed broad knowledge of computer hardware and inventory tracking software, being computer literate in use of leading word processing and spreadsheet programs.

Office & Administrative Experience in Customer Service & Sales Support Centers

-- Supporting teams of up to 15 marketing and field service personnel has required broad general office skills including front office administration, reception and answering of phones and customer questions, booking appointments, posting AP/AR for hundreds of national accounts, and typing speed of 60+ wpm.

EDUCATION

-- A.A.S. Degree in Business Administration, Lucerne College 1992

Guidelines for Creating Plain Text and ASCII File Formats

The following instructions will show you how to create a new file in plain text or ASCII format, as well as show you how to convert an existing file to this format. Once you've created a resume file in this format, you can print it for scanning or use the file to post your resume to online resume banks or to paste it into e-mail messages.

To Create a New Plain Text or ASCII File: Open your word processing program and type in your resume. Then, from the File menu, use the Save As command and select "plain text or ASCII" as the file type. This creates a plain text file for you. Then follow the rest of the instructions below.

To Convert an Existing File to Plain Text or ASCII Format: Open your original file. Then select the Save As command from the File menu, enter a new file name, and select "text only, plain text or ASCII" as the file type (with some older computer systems you may need to save the file in DOS format). This will leave your original resume file intact and create a second plain text file for you. Converting your word processing file into plain text or ASCII file format can introduce errors into the file since it removes formatting commands such as centering, bolding, or underlining. So once you've created your plain text or ASCII file, re-open it and scroll through it to correct any errors that have occurred.

Formatting Your Plain Text File: Now format all of the text of your resume flush left. Stack your name and address as illustrated at the top of the resume on page 237. Put your name, skill headings, and job titles in capitals with blank lines above and below information you want to stand out. Don't use bold, italics, underlining, lines, boxes, tabs, bullets, columns, or centering. Use flush left, block paragraphs for job title and skill heading descriptions. If you use double hyphens, be sure that you include a space between them and adjacent words so that the words are scanned and sorted properly. Highlight all text and set it in Courier 10 with left and right margins of 1.25 inches and resave your file in the plain text or ASCII format. Generally, your lines should contain no more than sixty-five letters per line, so you may need to adjust your margins accordingly.

Saving the File with Line Breaks: Some employers may request that you save the file in "plain text format with line breaks." Saving with line breaks will put what is known as a hard return at the end of each line at whatever margins you've set.

Adjusting Line Length: You may find that the text lines of your resume are either too long or too short when you send your resume in an e-mail message or submit it online. If your lines are too long, then reopen your file and make your margins bigger so your lines are shorter. If your lines are too short, then make your margins smaller so your lines are longer. Once you've done this, then resave the file as a "plain text file with line breaks" or "text only with line breaks."

Use a Text Editor to Remove Any Remaining Formatting: Next open your plain text or ASCII file using the text editor that comes with your computer system. Windows computers, for example, come with Notepad. Opening the file in a text editor sometimes reveals additional garbage letters that occur when files are converted to plain text or ASCII format that you cannot see when using your word processing program. If there are errors, delete them, and then save your file with the text editor. Your text editor will then put your resume into a final format using raw ASCII language, which is accepted universally by database and e-mail systems. Print the file and check your hard copy to correct any other formatting errors, then save the file using your text editor. Use this file to print your scannable resume, and to copy and paste your resume into e-mail messages or into online resume building forms.

Printing Your Resume for Scanning and Faxing: Print original resumes for scanning and faxing on white or very light-toned paper. Gray, dark-toned, or speckled paper can cause errors when scanned or faxed. Don't fold or staple your resume, as creases and staple marks can also create errors when your resume is scanned or faxed.

Resume Length and Website Guidelines: Scannable and electronic resumes can generally be longer, with two to three pages being average. Always follow instructions regarding length or submission requirements provided at resume posting sites or employer websites as they may differ from these guidelines.

Use the Preview Option and Test Your Resume Before Submitting It: When using online resume building systems, be sure to take advantage of the preview option before you submit the final version of your resume. This will allow you to check your margins and make sure that your resume is easy to read. Also test your resume by printing it as well as copying it into several e-mail messages and sending it to yourself and friends before sending it to employers. Clean up any problems that you find. Even in the plain text format, employers will discount resumes that are sloppy, full of errors, or seem to be carelessly prepared.

Submit Two Versions of Your Resume: When you mail your resume to employers, submit both a nicely formatted resume and a plain text keyword resume for scanning. Put a Post-it note that says "Visual Resume" on the nicely formatted resume, and a note that says "Scannable Resume" on the scannable one. This way employers can select whichever format best suits their needs.

Get the Most Out of the Subject Line of Your E-Mail Messages

When you send your resume or cover letter via e-mail, use the subject line in your e-mail message to maximum advantage. For example, Ralph is an accountant and has found an ad requiring five years cost accounting experience. The ad also includes a job number. To create an effective subject line that will help to grab an employer's attention, Ralph's subject line could read

> **Subject:** Cost Accountant with 5 Years Experience -- Job # 3212

Another strategy in creating an effective subject line would be to market a major achievement or area of experience you know an employer would be most interested in. Here are a few examples:

> **Subject:** Management Consultant to *Fortune* 500 Corporation
> **Subject:** CEO with Global Channel Development Experience
> **Subject:** Restaurant Manager for Operations with Revenues to $10 Million
> **Subject:** Executive Secretary to President and CEO
> **Subject:** Corporate Receptionist with 5 Years PBX Experience

Putting Electronic Cover Letters to Work for You

Many employers don't accept cover letters for input into electronic databases, so review all instructions at employer or online resume posting sites. Do what they say: If a letter is requested, then supply it; if you're told not to send one, then don't. When you do submit a cover letter, follow the same set of guidelines for converting it to plain text or ASCII format as you did in converting your resume.

A Word about Attaching Files to E-Mail Messages: Don't!

Most employers and resume posting sites request that you insert your resume into the body of your e-mail message rather than attaching it as a separate file. Opening an attached file often requires employers to have the same word processing program that you used to save your file. If they don't have that program, they may decide it is too much work to deal with your resume and never open or view it. So don't attach either your resume or cover letter as a file unless you are specifically asked to do so.

Conducting Your Online Job Search

Before you begin your Internet job search, or start posting your resume online, it's best to decide which type of positions you want. Then identify the geographic area where you're willing to work. Armed with this knowledge you'll then be able to search for and access job and resume posting sites that will meet your needs.

Be Careful about Confidentiality on the Internet

It's important to remember that all information contained in your resume will be available to anyone anywhere once you post it on the Internet. Many recruiters and resume posting sites have systems that allow you to maintain confidentiality by establishing a mailbox or code name. Employers can then review your resume and contact you through your mailbox or code name without having access to your name or personal information. You may also want to remove the names of current and past employers from your resume if they can be used to identify you in any way. Remember, there's always a chance that your current employer might stumble across your resume and not be happy to find out that you're job hunting. Before posting your resume, decide if there is any information that you should leave out; if so, don't include it.

Internet Job Search Strategies

If you are an Internet novice, conducting an online job search can be an overwhelming and time-consuming task. There are thousands of career resource, employer, recruitment, job, and resume posting sites to distract you. One way to simplify your electronic job search is to go to the Sites and Resources Section in my website at www.ProvenResumes.com/. It provides hundreds of links to job and resume posting sites, career resources, and online magazines, as well as links to tutorials on how to navigate the Internet.

To find even more career resources, you can perform a keyword search for topics such as "Internet job search," "career resources," "job posting sites," "resume posting sites," or "Internet tutorials" using a major search engine like Dogpile (www.dogpile.com), which allows you to search fourteen top websites, including Yahoo!, Excite, and Webcrawler. You can find additional search engines by conducting a keyword search for "search engines" on Dogpile.

Mega Career Sites That Give Fast, Broad Exposure

Mega career sites, those sites that generate millions of visitors and post anywhere from 10,000 to 500,000 jobs each year, should be your first stop. They will quickly give your resume broad exposure to thousands of employers and recruiters, free of charge. Mega sites provide forms to search job openings by job title, geographic region, and keywords. You'll also be provided instructions for copying and pasting your plain text or ASCII resume into online resume building forms or for sending your resume via e-mail. In addition, you can sign up to receive automated e-mail notifications whenever a job is posted that matches your criteria. Here are twenty mega sites to get you started:

America's Employers	www.americasemployers.com	JobHunt	www.job-hunt.org
Career City	www.careercity.com	JobServe	www.jobserve.com
CareerMosaic	www.careermosaic.com	JOBTRAK	www.jobtrak.com
CareerPath	www.careerpath.com	JobWeb	www.jobweb.org
Career Shop	www.careershop.com	The Monster Board	www.monster.com
E-Span's Job Options	www.joboptions.com	NationJob Network	www.nationjob.com
HeadHunter.Net	www.headhunter.net	Online Career Center	www.occ.com
Help Wanted.com	www.helpwanted.com	Recruiting-Links.com	www.recruiting-links.com
HotJobs	www.hotjobs.com	TOPjobs USA	www.topjobsusa.com
JobExchange	www.jobexchange.com	USA Jobs	www.usajobs.opm.gov

Targeting Industry-Specific Sites

To gain targeted, industry-specific exposure, visit sites that specialize in your career field. Below is a short list of industry-specific sites, but you'll find many more in the Sites and Resources Section at my site (www.ProvenResumes.com). You can also locate industry-specific sites by performing a search for the types of jobs you want using a major search engine. The diversity of job categories listed here illustrates how easy it can be to find jobs for any career field. Here are a few industry-specific job and resume posting sites:

Administrative	The Admin Exchange	www.adminexchange.com
Construction Jobs	Construction Education Connection	www.construction.st
Contract Jobs	Contract Employment Weekly	www.ceweekly.com
Education	Academic Employment Network	www.academploy.com
Engineering	Engineering Jobs	www.engineeringjobs.com
Federal Jobs	FedWorld	www.fedworld.gov/jobs/jobsearch.html
High-Tech Jobs	Westech Virtual Job Fair	www.vjf.com
Hospitality Jobs	Hospitality and Food Services Jobs	www.hospitalitylink.com
MBA Jobs	MBA FreeAgents.com	www.mbafreeagents.com
Medical Positions	Medzilla	www.medzilla.com
Nonprofit	National Opportunity Classifieds	www.opportunitynocs.org/home.html
Outdoor Jobs	Cool Works	www.coolworks.com
Retail Jobs	Retail JobNet	www.retailjobnet.com
Performing Arts	Career Shop	www.careershop.com
Professional	Omni Search	www.the-salesnet.com
Sales Openings	Net-Temps.com	www.net-temps.com
Social Services	Social Services.com	www.socialservices.com
Union Jobs	Union Jobs Clearinghouse	www.unionjobs.com

Targeting Specific Employers

You can go right to the source of jobs you want by visiting employer websites. Sites such as America's Employers and JOBTRAK provide links to hundreds of top U.S. employers. You can also find listings for specific employers through online yellow pages such as GTE Superpages. If you can't locate an employer through one of these lists, perform a keyword search for the company's name using a major search engine. Websites such as Yahoo! (www.yahoo.com) also provide links to thousands of employers. Yahoo! opens with a list of website categories that it contains. Click on Business/Economy/Companies and you'll be taken to an index of thousands of employer websites broken into industry categories. A handy list of major search engines and website databases is provided at Hotsheet.com. It provides links to major search sites such as Yahoo!, Excite, Webcrawler, GoTo, HotBot, Lycos, and Infoseek.

Employer websites generally provide a wealth of information about their companies, which can be helpful in refining and targeting your resumes and cover letters. ProvenResumes.com also provides links to hundreds of sites that provide employer profiles. Here are a few sites:

Big Yellow	Online yellow pages	www.bigyellow.com
Career City	Includes 27,000 employer profiles	www.careercity.com
Career Magazine	More than 100 employer profiles	www.careermag.com
Career Resource Center	More than 5,000 employer links	www.careers.org
GTE Superpages	Online yellow pages	ww.superpages.gte.net
Hoover's Online	Links and profiles of 13,500 employers	www.hoovers.com
Open Market Commercial Sites Index	Links to more than 35,000 employers	www.directory.net

National and State Employment Security Websites

America's Job Bank is provided by the United States Department of Labor and posts more than 400,000 job openings submitted by Employment Security Offices throughout the U.S. Links to state employment security office websites are also provided. Within each state's ESD site, you'll find additional links to career resources available in that state. Here are two useful sites:

America's Job Bank	www.ajb.dni.us
Washington State Employment Security	www.wa.gov/esd/employment.html

College and University Websites

Many college and university career centers post jobs, accept resumes online, and provide a wealth of resources for students. Here are several links of interest to college graduates. You'll find many more by conducting a keyword search for topics you are interested in using a major search engine. You might want to search for topics such as "college grad jobs," "college internships," "lists of universities or four-year colleges," "liberal arts jobs," or "MBA jobs."

Beyond College	www.usnews.com
College Grad Job Hunter	www.collegegrad.com
CollegeNet	www.collegenet.com
Extreme Resume Drop	www.mainquad.com
Internships	www.internships.com
JobWeb	www.jobweb.org/catapult/homepage.htm
New Grad Job Network	www.newgradjobnetwork.com
Student Now College Life	www.studentnow.com

Sites of Interest to Executives

Executives and senior management professionals generally find few high-level positions posted in mega sites or industry-specific sites. Therefore, to save time you may want to start with these sites, which specialize in openings in the $100,000 to $200,000+ range. You'll find many more sites of interest to executives by using a major search engine to search for keywords such as "executive jobs," "CEO jobs," or "senior management jobs."

Executive Jobs.com	www.executivejobs.com
Executive Recruiter Galleria	www.executive-recruiters.com
The Executive's Resume Center	www.inpursuit.com/sirc/seeker.html

What Kind of Employers Use Electronic Methods to Recruit?

The U.S. Department of Labor reports that about sixty-six percent of all U.S. companies employ up to 250 employees; about eighteen percent employ 250 to 1,000 employees; and about sixteen percent employ more than 1,000 employees. So what does this mean to your electronic job search? Overall, it means that smaller companies still generate the majority of jobs, and they are places where you might want to consider looking first. However, many smaller companies may not have websites and may not use resume tracking systems or accept scannable or electronic resumes because their hiring demand or turnover doesn't warrant expensive database systems. As you conduct your Internet job search, keep in mind that almost everyone thinks to apply with large corporations even though they only provide about thirty-four percent of all jobs. This means your competition in being hired by a large corporation is usually much greater than with a smaller firm. If you're interested in a smaller, local company, call them and ask if they have a company website or if they accept resumes by e-mail or in scannable format. You'll also want to follow the strategies for contacting employers directly, which are provided in the next chapter.

Creating Homepage Resumes

One problem with posting your resume to dozens of resume posting sites is the time it takes to revisit each site whenever you wish to edit or upgrade your resume. An effective way to get around this problem is to create a homepage resume. This will allow you to post a generic resume in all resume posting sites but include a link to your homepage resume, which you can easily update on a regular basis.

If you link to a generic resume from resume banks, be sure that it contains enough keywords to come to the top in a computer sort and creates an image that motivates employers to contact you.

Creating a homepage resume will require some computer skill on your part, and it's preferable that you know or are willing to learn simple HTML codes to format your resume. HTML—hypertext markup language—is the programming language that is used to create documents for posting on the World Wide Web. The sites for The Globe.com (www.theglobe.com), Geocities (www.geocities.com), and Free Yellow.com (www.freeyellow.com) offer homepage builder sections where you can build your own homepage resume and then post it on the Web. These free services provide HTML tutorials. The Globe.com and Free Yellow also provide systems to submit your homepage resume to major search engines and resume posting sites. Once you've posted your resume to several mega career sites and industry-specific sites, you may want to consider taking the time to create your own homepage resume. You can view my homepage resume by visiting http://www.ProvenResumes.com/myresume.html/.

Resume Posting and Resume Writing Services

There are numerous online services that will post your resume to job and resume posting sites for a fee. Many will also convert your word processing file to plain text or ASCII format, as well as create an HTML or homepage resume. They may also post it on the Web and provide you with a URL that you can include as a link in the generic resumes you post to resume banks or in resumes you send via e-mail. To find resume writing and posting services, perform a keyword search for "resume posting services" and "resume writing services" using a search engine such as Dogpile.com.

Be aware that there is a wide range of skill levels among resume writing services. Some may be secretarial or copy centers that merely type your resume but say they will spruce it up, while others say they provide full editing and writing but do not have proven success as professional resume writers. Before hiring either a certified or uncertified writer, ask how many resumes he or she has written, if the writer has experience creating resumes for your career field, and what his or her success rate has been in helping job seekers land more interviews and higher salary offers. Compare the services of several. Then rely on your intuition to guide you in selecting someone with the highest skill level that you'll feel comfortable working with. You can learn more about my resume writing services by visiting my website at www.ProvenResumes.com. The Professional Association of Resume Writers tests and certifies writers. By visiting the PARW site (www.parw.com), you can access a list of writers in your area.

What about Resume Writing Software Packages?

Although they may seem like the fastest way to get a resume done, resume writing software programs frequently result in resumes that do not work. Most of the programs do not include instructions about how to understand and control the image you present in your resume, how to develop designs that direct and control the reader's eye, or how to develop resume content that sells your strongest skills and achievements. Most programs provide standard resume formats that can't be customized. If you use a software program to create your resume, use the information in this book to develop your skill headings, modify your job titles, and create powerful resume content. Then select a resume format that you like in this book. Use the program to input your resume data and customize the standard formats as much as possible to match the one you selected. This will result in a much more effective resume—which means more interviews and higher salary offers!

14 How to Find and Land the Job You Want

You've created a great resume and launched your electronic job search. Now it's important that you supplement your online efforts with traditional job search methods in order to broaden the number of jobs you'll be able to find and apply for. In this chapter you'll learn how to uncover and cultivate job openings offline. You'll continue to present the image you want when making job contacts, whether you're making a networking contact, calling about an advertised position, or contacting an employer who hasn't advertised but that you would like to work for. You'll also learn strategies to help you find current openings at companies that have had past jobs like those you want and who may be ready to fill those positions again.

By following each section presented in this chapter, you'll be directed through a logical, step-by-step approach to find and successfully apply for the jobs you want. I've found that the only thing more fearful to most job seekers than interviewing is having to contact employers or make networking contacts to inquire about jobs. As you complete the worksheets and learn new information in this chapter, you'll see an increase in your confidence, and you'll begin to look forward to applying each new strategy.

Apply a Systematic Method to Your Job Search

You'll want to approach your job search like a salesperson. Successful salespeople know that honing and shaping their sales message until it is highly effective will inevitably lead to sales. Once their message is perfected they then look for and qualify their sales prospects—those buyers who have an interest in what they are selling and have the means to buy. By making a large volume of sales contacts, they are assured that qualified buyers will buy. Savvy salespeople also know that they can't expect to hear a "yes" every time they try to make a sale. If they expected this they would soon become demoralized. Rather, they step over the "no's" and look for the "yes's."

Throughout this chapter you'll follow these same strategies. You've already learned how to craft a written presentation of your skills and abilities that has been proven to generate higher salary offers, land more interviews, and better jobs. Now you'll learn how to shape this same message for your verbal sales presentations—those times when you'll be speaking with networking contacts or talking with employers and verbally showcasing your top qualifications.

Look for the "Yes"

If you have no expectation that you will get an interview when contacting an employer or when networking, then you won't be disappointed if you don't get one. However, if you do get an interview, you'll be pleased and excited. This is not to say that you can carelessly call employers and inquire about jobs. You want to put one hundred percent preparation and motivation into every call. You want to develop a mindset that says, "I know there are numerous employers out there that will benefit from my skills and experience. I just need to find them. When I do and it's a good fit, then I'll land an interview and potentially the job that I want."

To make this approach work, you need to develop a significant list of networking contacts and employers you are interested in. By using effective job search methods, you'll find a bounty of employers to contact. You'll then prepare a script, or sales presentation, which markets your strongest qualifications. Once you've practiced this script you'll be ready to undertake your job search campaign. If you have been selective in compiling your list of employers—those who can provide opportunities that fit your qualifications—you can feel confident that out of every hundred employers you contact you will generate up to ten interviews or more.

That means that you may receive as many as ninety rejections, but if you've adopted an attitude to look for the "yes's" you won't care. By reminding yourself that you only need one or two positive responses, all you'll care about is getting the next employer on the phone and hearing if he or she is interested in your skills and abilities. If they're not then you're ready to move on until you do hear a "yes." Each individual call or contact will be a small investment and can take as little as one minute to make. Unless you live in a very small town, there are probably enough employers in your area who will be interested in your skills and abilities to make it worthwhile for you to go out and find them. Develop a relaxed attitude about your job search and ignore the rest.

Employers Respond Well to Job Seekers Who Are Relaxed and Confident

Consider how adopting this attitude will affect your personality on the phone. When you call an employer, you will feel free to be spontaneous and relaxed because you won't feel like your life and job are hinging on that one phone call. This will give you an air of confidence and enthusiasm that employers are attracted to. No one feels especially attracted to people who sound desperate or pushy.

Learn from What Doesn't Work

Job seekers often go along in their job search haphazardly applying here and there for jobs they think they're interested in. Then they sit back and wait. They frequently become frustrated and discouraged because their efforts haven't paid off, yet they don't know what else to do. So they start the process all over, then experience failure a second, third, or fourth time.

To ensure that you're not faced with this dilemma, you'll want to track and analyze all job search contacts you make. If you make between twenty-five and fifty contacts and don't receive a positive response or land an interview, then you'll want to systematically analyze each step of your job search. This will allow you to determine where your job search is going wrong and how to correct it. Just like a successful salesperson, you'll want to evaluate the quality of contacts you're making and determine if you are reaching the appropriate decision makers. Make sure that you are applying for positions that are a correct match for your skills and salary requirements. Analyze the verbal presentation you give when introducing yourself to networking contacts or employers. Assess if you have correctly identified what each networking contact or employer is most interested in hearing about. Decide if your message sells your top qualifications in seconds.

If your job search doesn't meet with imminent success, you'll be able to use the Job Search Success Sheet found at the end of this chapter. By using this sheet, you can rest assured that if some component of your job search goes wrong, you'll be able to identify it and correct it, and ultimately achieve the results you want.

If You Dread Any Part of Your Job Search . . . You May Procrastinate

Frequently job seekers think ahead to what will happen when they contact employers, network, interview, or begin a new job. If they doubt they'll succeed in any of these areas they may procrastinate or avoid the situation entirely by never looking for a new job. Since so many job seekers have told me how their feelings negatively affect their job search success, I'd like to share Rob and Sharla's stories. Both felt totally unmotivated to look for a job but turned their feelings around and achieved job search success.

We'll start with Rob, who came bounding into my office, a big guy who was all smiles. As we talked, I asked what areas of his job search were difficult for him. It was amazing; his whole demeanor changed. His shoulders became hunched, his voice dropped, and he appeared overwhelmed as he said, "I dread looking for a job or interviewing." In an instant the sparkle had gone out of his eyes. He said, "Every time I think about calling an employer or sitting in an interview I feel terrible. My hands get sweaty and I imagine how miserably I'm going to do. I just don't want to interview. That makes me feel wimpy, and I hate that feeling. I know I have to interview but it really scares me. That's why I've put off looking for a new job for over a year."

I then said to Rob, "It's obvious you would like to do just about anything but interview for a job. But you know you've got to. So we need to find some tools to help you feel confident and capable of contacting employers and interviewing successfully. Can you remember when you gave a presentation or discussed something important at work and felt you did a good job?"

Rob replied, "Well, yeah, two months ago I recommended buying a new machine for our shop. We make surfboards and I knew this machine could increase our productivity. I did some research and ran some of our materials on it. It was so much faster. I talked with the sales rep about how much the machine cost and how long it would take to pay it off. I realized the extra work we could produce would pay for the machine in six months. So I went to our department manager and told him what I had discovered. He was really excited and bought the machine."

Within a few seconds the sparkle was back in Rob's eyes and he was feeling confident. I then said, "Rob, it looks like you're really proud of what you accomplished. Do you realize how many skills you used to get that machine placed in your shop?" Rob looked at me, shook his head, and said, "No. It doesn't seem like I used any. It was just fun." So I asked, "Don't you think you used your analytical as well as sales skills?" Rob replied, "Well, yeah, I guess so." I explained, "You came up with an idea, researched it and proved it, then sold your employer on it. Do you realize these are the same skills you'll use to interview well?"

Rob looked confused for a second. Then he smiled and said, "Yeah, I guess it is the same." I said, "You need to research a job you want, prove how you are qualified for it, then convince an employer to hire you. If you take the excitement you feel right now and use it to market yourself, you'll be amazed at how well you'll do. Now let's practice some interviewing questions. As we do, I'd like you to focus on the confidence you feel right now. Imagine that I am no different than your boss and sell me on your qualifications just like you sold your boss on that machine."

After about twenty minutes of role playing, Rob felt entirely different and had associated new, positive feelings with interviewing. As he left my office he said, "I can't wait to start researching employers and getting interviews. I know I'll be a little scared, but when I remember researching that machine and selling my ideas I will feel confident. Practicing for an interview while I'm feeling this way really motivates me."

By associating and linking positive thoughts to the interview process, Rob became excited and motivated about his job search. In a month's time he landed a new job as a materials and equipment manager responsible for workflow and production analysis with a much larger surfboard shop. The bonus was being paid four dollars more per hour for something he loved doing.

When People Worry about Failing on Their Next Job

Unlike Rob, Sharla hadn't worried about interviewing. She imagined herself accepting a job and being trained, but not understanding what she was being told. She said, "I just keep imagining how stupid and embarrassed I'm going to feel." Sharla had completed more than forty-five credits in accounting—and had a 4.0 GPA—but she discounted her skills. She confided that fear had kept her in school an extra year, because she dreaded that first day on the job and she couldn't bring herself to begin a job search. I was quite surprised when Sharla shared these feelings, because otherwise she came across as a very confident person.

Reviewing Sharla's resume, I saw that it was extremely weak—worse than the Before examples in this book. I realized that it probably represented how she viewed her skills. So I had her go through the Six Steps in Chapter 4 and worked with her to revise her resume. During this process a dramatic transformation came over Sharla. Her fidgeting disappeared as she began to say things like, "Gee, I hadn't thought about all the skills I really have developed. I can't believe it, but my new resume is stronger than anyone else's in my class and some of them have had accounting jobs before." When I asked Sharla how she felt about contacting employers or interviewing now, she said, "I feel totally different. Now that all my skills are listed, I see that I really do have them. Now I'm sure I can talk to employers. I'm also a lot more confident that I can succeed on the job. If I don't know something, then it won't be the end of the world because I know I will understand almost everything I'm told to do."

Within three weeks Sharla had landed three interviews and two job offers, and accepted a job that paid her $6,000 more per year. Like Rob and Sharla, if you are experiencing any level of anxiety about your job search, ask yourself what is really bothering you. Then focus on what you have achieved to build your confidence, and use those feelings to motivate yourself.

FEAR

Zig Ziglar, a leading motivational speaker, discusses the acronym FEAR in one of his video programs. He describes FEAR as "False Evidence Appearing Real." There's no better situation to apply this acronym to than a job search. When Rob and Sharla came to me they were both experiencing FEAR. What they imagined about themselves wasn't true at all, but it appeared very real to them.

Ask yourself if your fear is false evidence appearing real. Our imagination can often run amuck, making us feel anxious and leading us to believe we can't succeed, or that we'll fail when making job search contacts, in interviews, or on a new job. If this happens to you, ask yourself, "What strengths and skills do I already possess that will help me in my job search or in my next job?" As you remember good things about yourself, keep focusing on them. Use them as a foundation to conduct your job search. I've seen this process take hundreds of discouraged job seekers at all income levels from despair to success. Our feelings really do control not only what we're willing to put in a resume but how much effort we put into our job search. By turning fear or negative feelings into positive ones, we can succeed and obtain the job of our dreams.

Now that we've discussed how you can successfully deal with some of the feelings you may experience as you launch your job search, let's move on and discover those job search methods that are most effective.

Proven Job Search Methods

I'm sure you've heard the job search process referred to as a numbers game, and it is. The more employers you contact, the more interviews you are likely to generate. The more interviews you generate, the more job offers you will receive. To maximize your success, you must know which job search methods are most effective. In 1976 the U.S. Census Bureau published a survey of ten million job seekers that reveals the effectiveness of various job search methods. Before I give you the statistics, I'd like you to take the quiz below and rate each method on a scale of 1 to 6. Put a 1 next to the method you think generates the most jobs. Put a 6 next to the method you think generates the least jobs.

> **RATE EACH METHOD ACCORDING TO EFFECTIVENESS:**
>
> _____ Answering newspaper want ads
>
> _____ Networking with friends and relatives
>
> _____ Using unemployment offices for job leads
>
> _____ Working with employment agencies
>
> _____ Running your own "work-wanted" ad
>
> _____ Applying to an employer even if there's no job opening

Compare how you rated the list above to the survey results below, which start with the most effective job search method and end with the least effective method. Did you correctly rate each of the methods? If not, you may be surprised at the information you're about to learn and the impact it can have on your job search. As you can see, the top four methods of obtaining a job are applying directly to employers, networking, answering want ads, and working with private employment agencies, in that order.

> **OF 10 MILLION JOB SEEKERS SURVEYED, APPROXIMATELY . . .**
>
> 1. 3.1 million of 6.6 million who applied directly to employers obtained jobs.
> 2. 2.5 million of 5.1 million who networked with friends or relatives obtained jobs.
> 3. 1.1 million of 4.5 million who answered local want ads obtained jobs.
> 4. 500,000 of 2.1 million who worked with private employment agencies obtained jobs.
> 5. 460,000 of 3.3 million who worked with public unemployment offices obtained jobs.
> 6. 21,000 of 160,000 who ran work-wanted advertisements obtained jobs.

In a more recent 1991 survey of 60,000 households conducted by the Bureau of Labor Statistics, job seekers applying directly to employers achieved a 23.2 percent success rate, those networking with friends or relatives achieved a 22.6 percent success rate, and those answering ads achieved a 21.6 percent success rate. Surprisingly, this survey showed that working with private employment agencies achieved a 24.8 percent success rate. However, an additional study was referenced that suggested job search methods such as contacting employers directly or networking with friends and relatives were more likely to lead job seekers to employment. It was also noted that the likelihood of finding a job increased slightly with each additional method of job search, but declined when five or more methods were used.

This data confirms that the top four most effective job search methods haven't changed and that job seekers appear to have greater success using two to four methods, compared to using only one or more than four. As job seekers begin using five or more methods, they may experience reduced success because their efforts are being spread too thin. This new information tells us that optimum job search success, which includes landing a job more quickly, is achieved by using a combination of two to four job search methods.

Now let's discuss how you should schedule your time and get organized in order to launch an effective job search. Then we'll discuss each of the top job search methods in detail.

Maximize Your Time and Marketing Efforts

It's important that you estimate the amount of time you will devote to your job search each week. Then set goals for how much time you will spend pursuing and using each job search method. For example, it makes sense to spend

1. The greatest amount of time applying directly to employers.
2. The second greatest amount of time networking.
3. A smaller amount of time answering newspaper ads.
4. The least amount of time waiting for agencies to send you on interviews.

Create a Job Search Notebook

Conducting a job search can seem overwhelming. To minimize these feelings, you'll be wise to purchase a three-ring binder with several dividers and label them according to the activities you'll do. You can begin by making divider labels for employer lists and research, networking contacts and job leads, help-wanted ads, and employment agencies. As you move through this chapter, create additional dividers for other job search strategies you'll employ or for information you'll need to keep track of. Use your notebook as a central place to keep and track all of your job search data.

Applying Directly to Employers

As we've discussed, applying directly to employers is the most effective job search method. Therefore, you should devote the greatest amount of your time pursuing this method. You can do this in two ways, either by phone or letter. Calling by phone is quick and yields results in the shortest amount of time. Many people feel they are being pushy or presumptuous to get on the phone and call employers. However, I recommend you do just that. Within an hour's time you can make ten to fifteen calls or more. On the other hand, you may be able to write only two letters in this amount of time. Then you have to wait several days for each letter to be received before you can call and follow up. After each letter is received, you still have to muster the courage to get on the phone and follow up. So you might as well get motivated and call in the first place. Remember, you'll generate the maximum number of interviews in the shortest amount of time by calling and speaking directly with key decision makers.

Before you begin your phone calling campaign, you'll want to develop a targeted list of employers to contact. Shortly, we'll discuss how to use the library to develop a good list.

Narrow Your Focus

To develop a targeted list of employers, you must have a good idea of the type of position you want, the type of industry you want to work in, and the geographic region where you're willing to work. Otherwise, you have no way of narrowing your focus among thousands of employers. It's important to identify those positions and industries to which your skills and abilities will be the most valuable. Then find companies within the geographic areas where you're willing to work that employ staff in such positions. After I gained experience in the temporary industry I contacted several employers in that field who had locations within a twenty-mile radius of my home.

My phone calls generated a high response rate because employees who have experience in this industry are rare, which made me more valuable to prospective employers. Within two weeks I had landed over four interviews and two job offers, which resulted in my accepting a position that was within my targeted geographic area.

When I left the personnel field I knew I wanted to teach. Knowing my skills and education were a good match for vocational schools, I called a friend who worked for one. As timing would have it, her company had an opening for an instructor. I interviewed the next day and was hired three days later. By targeting specific industries and marketing skills that made me an excellent candidate for each field, I achieved excellent interview rates with a high percentage of job offers.

Just like I did, spend time thinking about the position you want and the industry you want to work in. You may decide to stay in the same industry or to make a career change. John had been a building contractor until he hurt his back and could no longer do that type of work. As a contractor he had marketed his services and had an extensive knowledge of construction procedures and materials. In mulling over his work experience, he realized he really liked the construction industry and enjoyed dealing with customers. On the basis of these insights, he decided he would like to become an inside sales representative marketing construction materials. He developed a list of twenty-five prospective employers and presented his best qualifications to them over the phone. Within two weeks he had five interviews and was offered two positions. He was amazed at how quickly his job search progressed once he became focused.

Using a sheet in your job search notebook, create a form like the one shown on the following page and place it under your divider labeled "Employer Lists and Research." In the first column, list the skills you would like to use in a job. In the second column list the types of positions that use these skills. In the third column list the type of industries that employ people in these positions. For easy reference, I've included a space to list each industry's standard industrial code (SIC). Companies are assigned four-digit standard industrial codes by the government, classified according to one or several industries they are involved in. In a moment you'll learn about library reference tools that list thousands of employers by their SICs. Once you know what the SIC is for one employer, you can use that SIC to find other employers in the same industry. As you find information on employers write down their industry codes. You may come across employers who have different SICs than you originally considered. In this way you can expand your list to include a broader range of industries.

Skills	Positions	Industries	SIC
_____	_____	_____	_____
_____	_____	_____	_____
_____	_____	_____	_____
_____	_____	_____	_____
_____	_____	_____	_____
_____	_____	_____	_____
_____	_____	_____	_____

Research to Develop Your Employer Lists

Once you've identified the type of position you want and the industry you'd like to work in, then you can begin doing research at the library or on the Internet. Here we'll discuss library research; refer to Chapter 13 for Internet research. If you've never been to the library to do job research, you may feel a little anxious about it. However, using library materials is easy and the librarians are there to help you. Next we'll discuss the types of materials you can use to learn more about employers. Knowing this information will increase your confidence and allow you to ask the librarian for assistance if it's needed.

Write Down Important Information about Each Employer

Before you begin gathering information about employers, create a form with duplicate sections like the one shown below. Make enough copies of your form to enter information for fifty to a hundred employers. Then insert them into your job search notebook under the divider labeled "Employer Lists and Research." A space is provided in the form below for you to list the SIC number of each employer. The "Notes" section provides space for you to record special information that may be helpful when speaking with an employer or in identifying what skills you possess that are a good match for that employer's needs.

EMPLOYER WORKSHEET

Person to Contact: _____   Phone: _____

Title: _____   SIC: _____

Company: _____   Number of Employees: _____

Address: _____   Years in Business: _____

_____   Products/Services Provided: _____

City: _____ Zip Code: _____   _____

Notes: _____

_____

_____

Once you've created your Employer Worksheets, you're ready to begin conducting library research and utilizing the various reference tools described below.

Business Directories

Many companies that sell business mailing lists lease them to libraries. For example, in Washington State, Inside Prospects and Contacts Influential lease business listings for more than 10,000 employers. All employers are broken into these four categories:

1. Alphabetical	3. Standard Industrial Code (SIC)
2. Zip Code	4. Key Individual

Alphabetical section: Each company has been sorted alphabetically. If you know the name of a company you are interested in, turn to the alphabetical section and locate it. You will find the address and phone number as well as other data we'll discuss below.

Zip Code section: Each company has also been sorted by zip code. This is very handy if you prefer to work in a specific geographic area. Make a list of the zip codes for the areas you wish to work in, then turn to each zip code section. Within each section you'll find an alphabetical list of businesses located within that zip code area.

SIC section: Each company has also been sorted by its standard industrial code. Look in the front of each directory and find the industry you want to work in. Next to the industry you will find a four-digit code. Then go to the volume that contains the SICs and look up the code. This section will contain an alphabetical listing of all employers classified within your industry.

Key Individual section: The Key Individual section can come in handy if you've heard someone's name and would like to contact that person but you don't know the company she or he works for. Locate the name in the Key Individual section and you'll also find the name of the company where that person is employed.

Keys to Each Listing: At the bottom of each page is a small list of keys that provide information about each company. Below is a sample of the keys:

TYPE OF OFFICE

H = Headquarters Office

B = Branch Office

S = Subsidiary Headquarters

NUMBER OF EMPLOYEES

A = 1–4	D = 20–49	G = 250–499	J = 5,000–9,999
B = 5–9	E = 50–99	H = 500–999	K = 10,000+
C = 10–19	F = 100–249	I = 1,000–4,999	

You can see how easy it is to classify employers and break down job leads by using these directories. Let's say you want to work as an office manager for a doctor's office or clinic. You prefer working in Bellevue or Mercer Island, Washington. Bellevue has five zip codes—98004, 98005, 98006, 98007, and 98008. Mercer Island is 98040. The SIC code for physicians and clinics is

8060. With this information you can turn to the 8060 SIC section and look for physicians and clinics within your six zip codes.

Or you can turn to the Zip Code section and look for the 8060 SIC codes. If you start your search by zip code, you can concentrate on those zip code areas closest to you first. Then gradually make more and more employer contacts farther away from your home. As you look at each listing, you can select or eliminate employers based on annual sales, how long they've been in business, and how many employees they have.

Other Directories and Reference Materials

There are numerous reference materials available in larger, metropolitan libraries. Below we'll discuss several and give you an idea of how you can use each of them in your job search.

Computerized periodical and newspaper indexes: These indexes provide a wealth of information about companies and current happenings within them. You'll use the computer to do a search of magazine and newspaper articles for subjects or companies you are interested in. The computer's database will give you a short synopsis of what each magazine or newspaper article is about. Many of the magazine and newspaper articles are available on microfilm, which you can read using a viewing machine. If there's an article you are interested in, the machine has the ability to photocopy it for you.

This is a fun, easy, and fast way to get information about major employers and news on industries. Before interviewing with Dunhill Temporary Systems, I used this process to get information on the temporary industry. I copied more than forty articles and learned a lot of valuable information. I was surprised to learn that this was a $12 billion industry. I took all the copies of the articles to my interview and used them as a selling tool to show how interested I was in that position. I casually pulled them out of my attaché case, spread them out about six inches, and said, "I've really enjoyed doing library research on the temporary industry. I learned that Dunhill Temporary Systems has 148 offices throughout the U.S. and Canada. One of the articles rated Dunhill fourth in sales among twenty-eight temporary agencies." Wow, was the person interviewing me surprised and impressed! Evidently no one else had gone to that much work before an interview. I was really glad I had taken the time to do the research, even though I had been nervous about doing it because it wasn't something I was used to. In addition to learning industry information, you may also uncover names of companies and employers you can contact that you had previously been unaware of. It really is fun to see all the information that's out there at your fingertips.

Newspaper clipping files: Ask if your library keeps newspaper clippings on major employers in your area. If so, you have another source of information to use.

Manufacturers' directories: There are numerous directories of manufacturing companies published by state and private publishing firms. These directories describe the goods and services produced by each manufacturer. They also provide information on the size of each company, the SIC code, and how long it has been in existence. My local library carries the *Washington State Manufacturer's Guide* and *Advanced Technology in Washington State Directory*. The latter provides information on high-tech companies involved in computer-based products and services.

Dun & Bradstreet directories: These directories provide financial information on companies with sales of two million dollars and up. If you are interested in a larger firm, Dun & Bradstreet can be one more source of information.

Standard & Poor's: This directory lists more than 30,000 corporations and provides financial data as well as biographical data for over 75,000 key officers.

Annual reports: Ask if your library keeps a file of annual reports and publicity packets for major employers in your area. These reports offer a wealth of financial information and describe the goods or services each company provides. You can learn excellent information for your interviews from these packets.

Companies with new business licenses: Many libraries receive lists of companies that have been granted business licenses within the last month or quarter. If you can verify that a start-up company will be stable, then getting in on the ground floor can be a growth opportunity. These lists are generally updated on a regular basis so it's wise to ask if there is a recent addendum.

Organizations and Associations

Chambers of commerce: Many chamber of commerce offices are interested in helping their citizens find employment. These offices can provide detailed information on companies that are members. Call and ask to speak to the chamber's manager. Tell him or her what type of work you are looking for. Ask for referrals to local employers that can provide the type of job you want. You may luck out and get several referrals. Many chambers of commerce sell lists of their business members. If this information is critical to your job search, consider buying it.

Local civic and charity organizations: These can also be a good source of information and networking leads. Talk to people involved in such organizations and send those who are interested in helping you, and that you feel comfortable with, a copy of your resume. Ask them to pass it on. You could get a job doing this alone.

Professional associations: Look for associations in your yellow pages that might be able to help you in your job search. There are hundreds of professional sales, secretarial, bookkeeping, teaching, public speaking, and business groups that meet on a regular basis to network. If one association isn't quite right for you, then ask them if they know of any other associations that might be helpful.

Church employment offices: One of my clients said she had used an employment referral office set up by the Church of Jesus Christ of Latter-Day Saints. According to her it was open for use by anyone, not just church members. She received several good job leads with employers in her local area. Check with local churches to generate referrals and to network.

Job Lines and Governmental Openings

Job lines are another resource to help broaden your employer contacts and to find openings you're interested in. Almost every employer with 200 or more employees provides a job line. All you need to do is locate the proper telephone number and call it. You'll hear a tape-recorded message that describes each position, the closing date (the last day you can apply for the position), the salary, and education and experience requirements.

If you are interested in a city, state, or federal position, ask your librarian to direct you to current job postings. Notices for these positions are often mailed to libraries on a regular basis. There are also several good books that tell you how to apply for governmental work. Ask the librarian to help you find them, and take advantage of their recommendations.

Identify Your Goal in Contacting Each Employer

Once you've developed a targeted list of fifty to a hundred employers, your next step will be to prioritize your lists and decide what your goal will be in speaking to each one. Spend the bulk of your time pursuing those employers you are most interested in. Spend less time on employers who rank lower in your list.

Your goal in contacting the employers high on your list will be to ask for an informational interview. Your goal in contacting employers you are less interested in will be to call and quickly find out if they have current openings or anticipate openings in the future.

If your skills are highly specialized you may not have a large pool of employers to contact. In this instance, you'll want to treat each employer as a top priority and conduct research on each company before requesting an informational interview. Now let's discuss how to request an informational interview and on page 258 we'll discuss how to contact employers you are less interested in.

Informational Interviews

Informational interviews are short meetings that you'll request to learn more about a particular company and possible opportunities within that firm or the industry it is involved in. As you gather such information during each informational interview, your goal will be to share details about your top skills, achievements, and qualifications. In this way you can cultivate employer interest in you rather than merely asking for a job.

When I first heard about informational interviews, I thought it was far-fetched to believe that employers would take the time to grant such interviews. However, many employers *will* set aside time to chat with you. I hadn't used this strategy until I wanted to work for a technical college. I obtained the name of the evening program director and called her. I decided before getting on the phone that I wanted a face-to-face meeting. I knew such a meeting would give me valuable information in case I was granted a "real interview." Even though I felt nervous and pushy, I called. Our conversation went something like this:

Me: Hi, my name is Regina Pontow. I am interested in teaching courses for your evening program and have experience as a computer and career development instructor for a local business college. I have also owned a personnel agency and would like to see if my experience fits any of your current programs.

Lori: *It sounds like it does. We offer computer training in MS Word, Lotus, and Excel. Do you have experience with those programs?*

Me: Yes, I am currently teaching MS Word and training in Excel.

Lori: *We also have a supervisory program. Do you have supervisory experience?*

Me:	Yes, managing my personnel agency required interviewing, hiring, and supervising all of the employees we placed.
Lori:	*Can you send me a resume and cover letter?*
Me:	Yes, however, I would like to meet with you for ten to fifteen minutes to gather a little more information before putting together a packet to send you. Is there a possibility we could meet late this week or next week?
Lori:	*Well . . . I guess so. But this wouldn't be an interview. I select applications but give them to a committee that does the interviewing. This would only be to tell you an overall idea of what the college offers.*
Me:	That would be great! It would help me target my resume and highlight more specifically how my background fits your programs.
Lori:	*Let me get my calendar. Would next Tuesday be good for you?*

Before I contacted Lori I was quite nervous. At one point during this conversation I really had to push myself to continue. Can you guess where that was? It was when Lori asked me to send a cover letter and resume. She was trying to get me off of the phone, but I knew from the tone of her voice that if I didn't get in to talk with her she would only consider me to teach computer classes. I no longer wanted to do that, so I knew it was important to meet with her and stress my qualifications to teach the supervisory class.

Pushing myself, I asked for that meeting and as a result of this conversation I met with Lori. To prepare for our meeting, I thought about what the dynamics of teaching such a course would be. Then I developed a list of ideas and selling points I could talk about that would allow me emphasize my qualifications. It worked. Two weeks after our meeting I was called to interview for the "Stepping Up to Supervision" program. Lori wouldn't have considered me for this position if I hadn't met with her.

Before you begin the process of contacting employers and requesting informational interviews, sit down and write out a phone script. Anticipate the questions you'll be asked, as well as what you'll need to say to employers to grab their interest. Here's a conversation that Seth employed to land an informational interview with a regional manager in the pharmaceutical sales field:

Seth:	Hello, Miss Fairfield. My name is Seth Grant. As a pharmaceutical territory manager I have increased my division's revenues by $6.3 million in the last six months and oversee two sales reps. Through industry literature, I've learned that you have developed a stellar career moving on a fast track from outside sales to senior management. If possible, I'd like to schedule a quick, five- to ten-minute meeting with you to seek your advice on avenues you would recommend to achieve career growth in our field. Would you be willing to meet with me for a brief meeting?
Ms. F:	*Well, I'm very booked up for the next two weeks. But I guess I can take a few minutes to chat with you if you have time to drop by my office. There were several people who assisted me in my career growth so I guess I can do the same. My schedule is open two weeks from now on Wednesday, 2:00 P.M. but I can only spare ten minutes. Will that work?*
Seth:	Yes, that time is excellent. I'll see you on Wednesday at 2:00. Thanks for giving me an opportunity to meet with you. I'll see you then.

During Seth's meeting with Ms. Fairfield, she referred him to a fellow member in the marketing association of which she was the president. Seth joined the association and after cultivating a relationship with the referral, he was hired as a senior territory manager three months later. This position increased his salary by twenty-two percent and substantially expanded his management responsibility.

How to Determine If There's an Opening

For employers you are less interested in but still want to contact, your goal will be to call and find out if they have current openings or anticipate future openings you'd be interested in. Here's how Roxanne handled this situation. She had compiled a comprehensive list of real estate employers but couldn't schedule informational interviews with all of them. For those she felt were less important, but that she still wanted to contact, she developed a script to determine if there were potential openings. As you can see by reading her phone script on the facing page, these conversations were a little different than the ones I had with Lori, or Seth had with Ms. Fairchild.

When you create a script to determine if an employer has a potential opening, be sure to identify the needs of each employer. Then incorporate your top three to five skills that match those needs into a few sentences that you can say within thirty to forty-five seconds. Read through the script to discover how Roxanne marketed her executive secretarial experience combined with her real estate bookkeeping experience to sell herself as a project manager in that industry. On page 260 is a blank phone script, like Roxanne's, that you can complete.

Before you prepare your phone scripts, read Chapter 15. It will help you think through strategies to best market your skills and to anticipate a wide array of questions employers may ask you during these initial conversations. You don't want to miss out on an interview because you weren't well prepared before calling.

Once you've reviewed Chapter 15, pull out several sheets of paper from your job search notebook and develop a phone script to request an informational interview as well as a script to find out if there are openings with a particular company. Keep them in your notebook and review them before you contact employers.

Before You Call Employers

The better prepared you are, the better response you will get from employers over the phone. Place all the information you will need in front of you and then make sure you can call employers in a quiet and uninterrupted environment. It sounds very unprofessional when dogs are barking, the kids are crying, or your spouse wants to know what's for dinner.

Gather together your note pad, resume, reference sheet, phone script, ad or job description, and your appointment calendar. Have several pens ready to take down notes. Know ahead of time when you are available for interviews so that you don't waste an employer's time. Write down all the questions you want to ask before getting on the phone. Refer to your phone script as you need to and use it to build your confidence. Having practiced it confidently several times, just looking at it will give you a positive association while you're on the phone.

Be sure to breathe normally. Speak calmly and pronounce your words fully. Use the tone of your voice to show your confidence and enthusiasm. Put your best voice forward and use it to develop a rapport with both receptionists and employers. Don't mumble your words or fumble with your paperwork. Be prepared and present a professional image.

SCRIPT TO FIND OUT IF THERE IS AN OPENING

Receptionist:	*XYZ Real Estate, how may I help you?*
Roxanne:	May I speak with Tom Galley?
Receptionist:	*Yes, may I tell him who's calling?*
Roxanne:	Yes, my name is Roxanne Woodry.
Receptionist:	*May I ask what this is regarding?*
Roxanne:	Yes, I have over five years real estate experience and would like to talk with him about employment opportunities.
Receptionist:	*Can you hold, please?*
Roxanne:	Certainly.
Tom:	*This is Tom Galley, what can I do for you?*
Roxanne:	Mr. Galley, my name is Roxanne Woodry. I have over five years experience in real estate office administration and bookkeeping. I'm looking for a comparable position and want to inquire if you have or anticipate a similar opening.
Tom:	*Well, I'm not sure. Just exactly what type of position did you have in mind?*
Roxanne:	I am interested in an office management position that will allow me to coordinate and manage projects. I managed the administrative details for real estate transactions valued in excess of $1 million.
Tom:	*Well, I'm not considering hiring an office manager, but I am considering hiring a project manager to assist my sales agents. That position would involve a lot of coordination with escrow companies. You would be out of the office quite a lot overseeing projects and completing details. Does that sound like something you'd be interested in?*
Roxanne:	It sounds perfect!
Tom:	*Are you familiar with escrow operations?*
Roxanne:	Yes, while I was with Ammes Real Estate I coordinated with numerous escrow companies to track monies being held. In this capacity, I gained a broad knowledge of escrow operations.
Tom:	*Well, how about coming in Thursday at 3:00 P.M. to discuss possibilities?*
Roxanne:	That's great! Thank you for your time. I will see you at 3:00 P.M. Thursday.

PHONE SCRIPT WORKSHEET

Receptionist:	*XYZ Company, how may I help you?*
You:	May I speak with _____?
Receptionist:	*Yes, may I tell _____ who's calling?*
You:	Yes, my name is _____.
Receptionist:	*May I ask what this is regarding?*
You:	Yes, _____ _____ _____
Receptionist:	*Can you hold, please?*
You:	Certainly.
Employer:	*This is _____, how may I help you?*
You:	My name is _____. I have over ____ years experience in _____. I am looking for a comparable position and wanted to inquire if you have or anticipate a similar opening.
Employer:	*Well, I'm not sure. Do you have _____ _____experience?*
You:	Yes, I have _____ _____ _____.
Employer:	*Well, I'm not sure what I've got coming open but it wouldn't hurt to talk with you. Can you come in at _____?*
You:	Yes, and thanks for your time. I'll see you at _____ _____

WHEN CONTACTING EMPLOYERS, DON'T ASK, "ARE YOU HIRING?"

When calling, don't ask the receptionist or employer, "Are you hiring?" or "Can you tell me if you are accepting applications?" When a receptionist or an employer is busy and harried, it's too easy for them to say "no" and get you off the phone. Quickly state your top selling points before the receptionist or employer can interrupt you. In this way, you give the listener enough information to interest them and motivate them to begin a conversation with you.

REMEMBER TO ASK FOR REFERRALS

If you are unable to schedule an informational interview, or you find out that the company is not hiring, be sure to ask for referrals. Many people will be willing to refer you to other agencies or employers that may have openings. If you approach people in a polite and friendly way you'll be surprised at their willingness to help you. Asking for referrals works.

DEALING WITH "NO"

If you receive a negative response from an employer you really want to work for, find the name of another key person within that company to contact. Then call him or her. Chad shared this success story in one of my classes. Beaming, he said, "I had contacted a company that I really wanted to work for but never got a response and was very discouraged. Following your advice I decided I would contact a key decision maker that was two levels above the position I would like.

"So, I made a list of my top sales achievements and contacted the vice president of marketing. During my conversation I mentioned that I was very familiar with some problems universal in our industry and shared my successes in dealing with them. This grabbed his attention and he asked me to interview with him the next day. I was originally interviewing for a $75,000 position, but after we met, the V.P. referred me to another division V.P. for a position at $100,000. I'm so excited I can't stand it. I'm meeting next week to discuss that position."

Like Chad, hundreds of other job seekers have told me that this type of follow-up can turn an initial "no" into a great opportunity. If you experience so many "no's" that you get discouraged, then be sure to review the Job Search Success Sheet at the end of this chapter. It can help you identify where your efforts need improvement and get your job search back on track!

Networking

As you've learned, networking is the second most successful job search method for the majority of job seekers. But for some, especially executives and professionals, it appears to be the most successful method. In the job search classes I've taught, I've been surprised at how many people say they dread networking. Some say they hate the thought of asking friends or relatives about jobs because they feel like they are groveling. It is easy to understand such feelings, yet conducting a successful job search often comes down to doing things that make us feel uncomfortable. If you happen to feel this way, you will find that these feelings dissipate or disappear entirely when you learn how to make initial contacts and share your qualifications in a way that gets results.

Networking works because many employers rely heavily on the advice and recommendations they receive from their employees or business associates when hiring new applicants. If you are introduced to an employer through a networking contact, then you are a known commodity compared to someone answering an ad whom the employer knows nothing about. So treat your networking contacts and referrals as if they are a gold mine—because they are!

Who Can You Network With?

On a sheet of paper begin developing a list of people you can network with. Studies show that networking with friends where you work can yield the highest success rates. Next comes networking with your relatives, followed by networking with teachers, professors, or guidance counselors. But this is a very small list. Also consider contacting past supervisors or employers, people in your church, acquaintances at sporting events or hobby-related activities you attend, or associations you belong to. To find associations targeted to your career field, look in the yellow pages under Associations. You can also ask your librarian to direct you to the *Encyclopedia of Associations*, which is an immense volume containing tens of thousands of associations. Your local chamber of commerce can also be an excellent resource for networking and development of job leads.

Once you've compiled a comprehensive list of fifty to a hundred people you should consider contacting, prioritize your list by groups of people whom you think will be most important to contact first. Then prepare a worksheet with duplicate sections like the one shown below. Complete a section for each networking contact you'll make. Then place your lists in your notebook under the divider labeled "Networking Contacts and Job Leads."

When you're ready to begin networking, write down additional information about each contact including their phone numbers and addresses. Later when you begin contacting your network, you'll fill in the names of people you're referred to as well as their contact information. If you feel a little anxious doing this, remember this is just an exercise. You're not ready to call or contact any of these people yet, so brainstorm and develop as large a list as you can.

NETWORKING LIST

Who You Networked With:	**Who You Were Referred To:**
Name _____	Referred to _____
Title _____	Title _____
Phone _____	Phone _____
Company _____	Company _____
Address _____	Address _____
State _____ Zip _____	State _____ Zip _____
Date Contacted _____	Date Contacted _____
Date to Follow Up If Needed _____	Date to Follow Up If Needed _____

Notes _____

_____

_____

_____

_____

Before You Make Any Networking Contacts

Before you make any networking contacts, you should be clear on what you want from each contact and what you have to offer. As mentioned before, this will require that you know the types of jobs you want or the types of skills you want to use. When networking you'll want to ask your friends, relatives, and acquaintances if they know of companies that can use your skills, or if they know anyone whom you can contact that works for a company you are interested in. You might also ask them if they know of any associations or professional organizations you should contact to learn more about companies and job openings you are interested in.

You may need to change what you'll say to each networking contact based upon the types of jobs or organizations they will be able to refer you to. For example, let's say a secretary is interested in two very different types of jobs. One goal is to move into sales and the second is to land a higher paying position as an executive assistant. She might know one contact that works in sales. When speaking with this person, she should share the skills and experience she possesses that qualify her for a sales position. When speaking with a contact who can help her cultivate leads for executive assistant positions, she should market experience that qualifies her for executive assistant positions. So her scripts will be quite different. Just like you've learned how to identify your audience, what your audience wants to hear, and what you have to tell them when writing your resume, you'll continue this same strategy when networking or contacting employers.

To stay organized, be sure to jot down notes on what will be most important to share with and ask each of your networking contacts. While all of this sounds like a lot of work, it's really quite simple if you take the time to prepare and keep your notebook organized as you move step by step through your job search.

DON'T WASTE A CONTACT'S TIME

Most people are willing to help provide you with leads to employers or people to contact if you are enthusiastic, know what you want, and know how they can help you. Many job seekers make the mistake of calling a networking contact and expecting that person to guide them in almost every aspect of their job search. Some job seekers call networking contacts and tell them how depressed they are because they're not landing interviews—this isn't a good move. Such actions result in long and time-consuming conversations that most people and employers want to avoid.

Think Ahead and Prepare What You'll Say

Below is a short networking script that shows a typical conversation you might have with a networking contact. To illustrate, I've used Sam as an example. He's a civil engineer and wants to land a job that offers him greater opportunities to manage projects and supervise other engineers with less responsibility for project design. Take a moment and read through his script. Then take several minutes to develop a rough draft of the script you'll use when making network contacts and place it in your job search notebook. Remember to practice and adapt your script before making each contact.

Sam:	Hi, Melissa, this is Sam Wilson. I wanted to ask your advice. Do you have a moment to talk?
Melissa:	*Sure, how can I help you?*
Sam:	I'm considering looking for a new job using my experience managing civil engineering projects. I've worked on projects valued up to $60 million and have supervised over thirty engineers. I'd like to move away from a job that's strictly design and into having more responsibility for project management. Do you know of any companies that might be good for me to talk with or someone that would be good for me to contact?
Melissa:	*Well, let me think. Sure. XYZ Engineering just expanded it's consulting division and may need project managers. Wait a sec. Here, why don't you give Roger Smith a call. His number is 555-555-5555.*
Sam:	Can you tell me his title?

Melissa:	Yes, it's senior project manager. I believe he oversees a staff of twelve project managers.
Sam:	That's great. Can you think of anyone else?
Melissa:	No, not really. But if I think of anything else I'll give you a call.
Sam:	Great. Would you mind if I call you back next week to see if you've thought of someone else?
Melissa:	No, that'd be fine.
Sam:	Thanks. I really appreciate your help and will let you know how things go with Roger. Can I let him know that you referred me?
Melissa:	Sure. No problem. Roger and I are old friends.
Sam:	Thanks again, and I'll talk with you next week.

This conversation is like most of the networking contacts you'll make. So if you've been worried about talking to people, there's no reason to be. By being prepared and not wasting other people's time, you'll be very pleased with the results and referrals you get. Now I'd like to share several success stories that show how networking pays off.

Networking Success Stories

My brother-in-law's networking happened in a roundabout way. Fresh out of the navy with experience in communications and electronics, he had problems being considered for jobs because he didn't have a four-year degree. My mother-in-law went into action knowing he wanted to work for Boeing. She networked with one of her neighbors who was a retired Boeing executive. She asked him if he would contact his associates at Boeing and set up interviews for my brother-in-law. After several referrals and contacts he got an interview and was hired.

In my networking classes, clients have cultivated good job leads in the most unexpected situations. Rita struck up a conversation with a person at her bus stop. He gave her a referral and she had an interview within three days. Many of my students network with one another. When Rachel received a new job, she told Felicia about her old job and set her up for an interview. In two weeks Felicia was hired. Another example was when John closed his own business and used networking to get his next job. He called several of his friends and asked them about employment opportunities that matched his background. Over the next couple of weeks his friends called to tell him about possibilities. Within two and a half weeks he was offered and accepted a new position. In each of these situations, the job seekers pursued networking in different but effective ways. Now that you've learned the diverse ways networking can pay off, let's move to the next job search method you should employ.

Answering Want Ads

Answering want ads ranks as the third most effective job search method. A big mistake that many job seekers make in using this method is relying on ads as their only, or primary, job search method. In my classes I always ask why people use this method rather than applying directly to employers or networking. Everyone quickly points out that mailing a cover letter and resume in response to an ad is nonthreatening. It doesn't require contact with people and won't result in being rejected over the phone, which many job seekers want to avoid. This is another example of how people's feelings can keep them from conducting an effective job search.

As we discussed before, job seekers experience higher success rates when they employ from two to four job search methods rather than only one. So it's important not to let your comfort zone lead you to use help-wanted ads as your only job search method.

Ways to Find Help-Wanted Ads

You can find help-wanted ads by reading a local metropolitan newspaper or by going online to search hundreds to thousands of current openings. Online, perform a keyword search for "online newspaper directories" with a major search engine such as Dogpile.com. You can also visit the Internet Public Library (www.ipl.org), which provides links to thousands of national and international online newspapers. Many online newspapers also provide direct links to employer websites either on their homepage or within the help-wanted ads you'll access. This is an excellent and fast way to conduct employer research.

Organizing and Tracking the Ads You Respond To

As you find and apply for help-wanted ads, it's important that you track them. Paste each ad you're interested in on a separate sheet of paper in your job search notebook under your divider labeled "Help-Wanted Ads." Write down the date that you responded to the ad and the date that you should follow up in case you haven't received a response. It's also good to put a copy of your cover letter with the ad so that you'll know what was in each letter in case that employer does call you for an interview. If there were any special thoughts you had as you read or responded to the ad, write them down. This could include realizing there are several other companies like this one that you should investigate.

Keep your notebook near your phone. When an employer calls you in response to an ad, ask what position you are being called about. Then flip to that ad in your notebook and quickly review it. Many times employers prescreen applicants by phone. Having immediate access to your ad will help you identify which skills and areas of experience you should market in a prescreening interview. By following the steps outlined in Chapter 15, you can prepare thoroughly for such prescreening interviews.

When you do receive a response to an ad, be sure to make a note of it on the ad, including the date each employer calls you. If you landed an interview or several interviews in response to each ad, then write this down also. Every week or so, calculate the total number of ads or companies you've contacted, how many phone interviews you've had, and how many in-person interviews you've landed. Later, if you find your job search isn't working, this information can help you analyze where problems are occurring.

As you review each week's want ads, keep an eye out for companies you would be interested in working for. Even if they advertise a position that you're not interested in, they may still have unadvertised positions that you qualify for. Be sure to cut these ads out and put them in a separate place in your notebook as potential leads.

Use Old Help-Wanted Ads to Find Employers

Another excellent strategy is to go back over help-wanted ads for the last three months to a year's time. Using this method you can compile a larger list of employers who have advertised for exactly the types of positions you want. To speed this process, select three or four job categories to look for. This way you won't have to read the entire help-wanted section. For example, I could look in the C column for "Career Counselors," the I column for "Instructors," the T column for "Trainers," or the V column for "Vocational Counselors." If it's been some time since the last ad was placed there's a good chance that one or more of these employers are in need of filling that or a similar position.

Now that we've discussed the importance of tracking the ads you'll respond to as well as using older ads to identify potential employers, let's discuss the next job search method you should consider using.

Working with Employment Agencies

Working with private employment agencies is the fourth most effective job search method. Private employment agencies include headhunters, executive search firms, and industry-specific recruiters as well as permanent, contract, and temporary placement agencies. Some job seekers use private employment agencies as their sole job search method because applying directly to employers or networking causes them too much discomfort. They find it easier and less threatening to sit back and let an agency send them on interviews. However, there is often a price to pay since many agencies charge a fee for their services. There is also a price to pay when job seekers avoid using the other top job search methods. If they don't apply directly to employers or network, they can't tap into what's known as "the hidden job market." As a result, this group of job seekers ends up looking for a job for a longer period of time and missing out on some of the best jobs, since it's estimated that from eighty-five to ninety-three percent of all jobs available each year are never advertised.

Most headhunter, executive search, and industry-specific firms that place candidates in the $60,000 to $200,000 range don't charge a fee to the applicant; the employers pick up the tab. On the other hand, the applicant pays the majority of permanent placement agencies, those placing candidates in the $20,000 to $40,000 range. This means that if you accept a position through such an agency you may be responsible for the entire fee, or at least some portion of it. With going placement fees ranging from eighteen to twenty-four percent of an applicant's annual salary, it can take an entire month's salary or more to pay such fees. My recommendation is that you avoid these fees by thoroughly applying the strategies in this book to land jobs on your own. If you are more comfortable working with an agency, it's best to deal with those agencies where the employer pays the fee.

Working with Temporary Placement Agencies

If your work experience is limited or you are being skipped over in favor of applicants with more experience, consider working as a temporary or contract employee. You can often land very good permanent positions this way. Many employers like to hire on a contract or "temp to perm" basis and see how the person works for a week to several months. If an employer then wants to hire the employee, they buy out the temp or contract staffer from the agency.

Because contract and temporary placement agencies frequently have small pools of qualified applicants, you may be sent on interviews for jobs you could never get on your own. This happened to Melissa. She wanted to use her website management skills but only had four months of experience. She found that companies advertising full-time jobs had many well-qualified candidates with extensive experience. Melissa appeared unqualified in comparison and couldn't land interviews. Being persistent in wanting to use her Web skills, she then found three temporary agencies that specialized in the field of new media. All of the temporary agencies were impressed with her skills.

Within three weeks of signing up with these agencies, Melissa was set up for an interview with Microsoft. Since Microsoft is known throughout the world, competition for jobs with this mega corporation is fierce. If Melissa had competed with a large pool of applicants applying directly to Microsoft, her chances of being hired would have decreased substantially. This was a great opportunity, as Melissa was offered a thirty-five percent salary increase.

There should never be a fee to you when you accept contract or temporary assignment. So be sure to read carefully any contracts and confirm this before putting your signature to them.

Working with State Employment Agencies

Working with state employment agencies is the fifth most effective job search method. However, many people avoid working with state agencies because they believe it is too time consuming and that their job listings are out of date. In the last few years, the Employment Security System in all the states has been revamped and streamlined. These offices now provide new strategies in workforce training and placement. Since this method was ranked fifth, we won't discuss it further in this chapter, but do consider reviewing what services your local employment security office provides before ruling it out of your job search plan.

Running a Work-Wanted Ad

Running a work-wanted ad is the least effective of the top six job search methods. Few people use this method, and subsequently very few employers look for work-wanted ads. As a result, they generate little response from employers. We won't discuss this method further and it is recommended that you concentrate your efforts on the top four job search methods listed above.

Develop a Job Search Plan That Meets Your Needs

Now that you've learned about the top four job search methods I'd like to briefly discuss a few additional methods that have been proven effective for specific groups of job seekers. Several university placement surveys have shown that college grads often experience the highest job search success rates by networking, the second highest by applying for positions posted through their college career placement offices or online, the third highest by responding to classified ads, and the fourth highest by contacting employers directly. These results reveal that college grads may benefit by using networking, their college placement office, and the Internet over other job search methods.

Executive outplacement agencies—those firms that teach job-search techniques to executives and professionals in the $80,000 to $150,000+ salary range—report that thirty-nine to sixty-seven percent of their clients who network extensively land positions via this method. Applying directly to employers is the second most effective job search method. Few help-wanted ads are placed in newspapers for positions at this income level; therefore, answering want ads results in low success rates for this group of job seekers. Positions in this income range are turned over to executive recruiting and headhunting agencies to fill. Nationwide, it's estimated that these agencies handle up to four times the number of executive and professional positions than are advertised. This shows that networking, applying directly to employers, and working with employment agencies can be the most beneficial for executives and professionals.

These strategies also work well for technical personnel in a narrow career field. For example, there will be fewer ads placed for an HVAC design engineer (heating/ventilating/air conditioning) than for a computer network administrator who may find many advertised openings. Job seekers with highly specialized skills in a narrow job market may benefit most by employing the same strategies as those that are most successful for executives and professionals.

Online job searching is the hot trend in finding and landing jobs, particularly for those in high-tech, management, sales, and executive positions. So this job search method is also resulting in high success rates for select groups of job seekers. If you haven't launched an online job search, you can determine if you should conduct one by using the strategies outlined in the previous chapter. Begin by visiting sites that post thousands of jobs for a wide range of career fields where you can search for job openings that meet your needs. Then go directly to employer websites that interest you to review employment opportunities. Then visit sites specifically targeted to your career field. After visiting several, you should be able to determine if the types of jobs you want are in high demand via the Internet. This research will allow you to decide if an online job search meets your needs, is a good investment of your time, and could be a top job search method for you.

So what do all these different job search methods mean to you? To be the most effective, you need to ascertain which job search methods meet your needs, as well as those you will be most motivated to use and apply. For example, if you truly hate the prospect of marketing yourself and know that you won't actively look for a job on your own, then you may want to consider using an employment agency. But be willing to stretch your comfort zone and supplement this method by networking, applying directly to employers, and answering want ads.

A Blueprint for Maximizing Your Time and Launching Your Job Search

Here's a short outline of how you might want to begin your job search and expand it to encompass the top four job search methods we've discussed. Revise this blueprint to fit the types of jobs and industries you'll be applying for. Here we're merely outlining those beginning job search items that make the most sense for the average job seeker.

1. Review Help-Wanted Ads to Quickly Locate Openings

Begin your job search by spending a few hours each Sunday reviewing help-wanted ads in a major newspaper or go online to review them. Even though this job search method is ranked the third most successful, it makes sense to start your job search here since you can apply for immediate openings. Your time investment to find jobs that fit your needs is minimal. However, plan on spending only a small portion of your time answering ads.

2. Sign Up with Several Employment Agencies

While you are perusing help-wanted ads, you will probably find many ads that are placed by private employment agencies. If you find positions that match your needs and are fee-paid, then consider signing up with several agencies at the start of your job search. This makes sense because it can often take several weeks to a month, or more, for employment agencies to set you up for interviews and help negotiate job offers that you may wish to accept. During this waiting period, you should be busy pursuing the top job search methods that meet your needs. Don't spend more than a few days applying with employment agencies. Don't spend any time idly waiting for agencies to send you on interviews. It often seems like agencies will set you up for lots of interviews, but many job seekers working with agencies report never being sent out on even one interview. If you feel that working with employment agencies is a good investment of your time then do so, but spend a small portion of your time on this job search method.

3. Make a List of Networking Contacts

Once you've started Steps 1 and 2, then begin developing and exploiting your networking contacts. Ask all of your contacts if they know anyone employed at the firms you are most interested in working for. If they do, then your next step should be to use your referrals to contact those companies. Such introductions can speed the process and increase the receptiveness of an employer in taking your call or speaking with you.

4. Apply Directly to Companies You Are Interested In but Don't Have Referrals To

Once you've exhausted all referrals and leads from friends and associates, then select those companies you are most interested in working for, but do not have leads for. Conduct library or Internet research to learn what type of products, services, problems, or issues each company faces and how you can help. If the company provides a website, then visit it to learn all you can about that company. Decide what level of person, or key decision maker, it would be best for you to contact to inquire about potential employment. Call that person, briefly hit your top qualifications, and ask if you can meet with him or her for five to ten minutes to learn more about the company.

Negotiating When You Receive Multiple Offers

Within the first week of your job search, you should be able to apply for a wide range of openings, as well as sign up with several agencies. Then over the next two to six weeks you'll concentrate your efforts and time pursuing the top two job search methods: applying directly to employers and networking. This four-step approach gives most job seekers a sense of direction and makes the process of looking for a job less overwhelming. By employing all four of the top job search methods, you will be able to generate a maximum number of interviews in the shortest amount of time. This should result in several job offers that come in quick succession to one another. By having two or more job offers in the air at any one time, you can substantially boost your negotiating power with employers. This also allows you to compare the offers and determine which one is best for you. When you receive multiple job offers, your confidence will shoot up and you'll have a much better feel for what your true value is in the employment market. If you put little effort into your job search and spread your efforts out over a long time period, then you'll have fewer interviews and may only receive one job offer during any time frame. You may then feel you have to take that offer since it's the only one you've landed.

You're Now Ready to Launch Your Job Search!

By following the methods you've been learning in this chapter, you should achieve substantially higher success rates than your competitors. However, if you don't get the results you want, take the time to go through the Job Search Success Sheet below. It can help you analyze each component of your job search and identify any areas that need improvement. Good luck. Like my job search class participants, get out there, have fun networking, meeting employers, and landing the job of your dreams!

The Job Search Success Sheet

If you're not getting the job search results you want, take the time to thoroughly review the suggestions listed below. You'll see how every facet of your job search affects the results you achieve. Any problem you face will involve analyzing several of the steps you've completed while reading this book. These can range from reviewing the effectiveness of your resume and cover letters to refining your interviewing skills to doing more follow-up or expanding the type of jobs or industries you will pursue. This worksheet is not meant to be exhaustive; rather it covers the top six situations I've seen job seekers experience when their job search goes wrong. Some of these situations may occur after you have already gone on interviews. If you've gotten a poor response after interviewing, these tips can help you pinpoint where you're having problems and help you apply what you'll learn in the next chapter in order to bring your interviews back on track.

If you find that you haven't followed through correctly on any of the items listed below, take the time to go back and do them correctly. Then start the process of applying for jobs again, and track your response rates so that you can see what does and doesn't work for you. This will enable you to take control of your job search and ensure that you do get the results you want.

If You Don't Get a Response to the Resumes and Cover Letters You Mail . . .

If you have sent out twenty-five to fifty cover letters and resumes for advertised positions but haven't landed interviews or gotten the response you want, then consider these issues:

1. Are you selecting and applying for help-wanted ads or positions that match your qualifications and salary requirements? If you are sending cold call letters, have you followed the tips provided on pages 225 to 226?

2. Are you taking the time to carefully analyze ads or job openings and make sure that your cover letters and resumes address each employer's needs and market at least two of the top skill requirements each employer requests?

3. Do your cover letters and resumes market the bottom-line benefits of why an employer should hire you? Do they show how you've helped improve sales, cut costs, increase productivity, improve morale, or in other ways improved an employer's work environment?

4. Are you submitting your cover letters and resumes to employers the day or next day after you find them?

5. Do you avoid including salary information in your cover letters as much as possible? If it is included, do you give a range that includes the advertised or estimated salary for the job you want?

6. If you have gaps in employment or have relocated from out of state, have you used the strategies in Chapter 9 that de-emphasize negative employment issues?

7. Have you asked other people to critique your resume and cover letter as described on pages 137 and 221? Do your cover letters and resumes use design elements that direct and control the eye path? Do they sell your top skills in seconds? Do they create an image of you as being well qualified for the jobs and salary you want?

8. Do you call to follow up on the cover letters and resumes you mail? Do you ask to speak to the person your letters were addressed to? Do you then engage the person in a conversation in an effort to learn more about the position and to sell your qualifications for it?

If You Don't Get a Positive Response When You Network or Call Employers . . .

If you have made at least twenty-five to fifty networking and employer contacts but haven't gotten a positive response, then consider these issues:

1. Have you carefully thought out how each networking contact might be able to help you and do you share this with each networking contact? Have you honed your networking and phone scripts until you can tell each networking contact what type of job you are looking for and what your top qualifications are within a one- to two-minute conversation?

2. Before contacting employers, have you identified the correct level of decision maker to contact? Generally, you should contact hiring officials or managers that are one to two levels above the type of position you want.

3. Before contacting employers (particularly those that you really want to work for), have you researched the company or department you'd like to work in? Have you identified the types of products, services, or problem areas the company or department faces? Are you ready to share how you have successfully dealt with these products, services, or problems? Are the stories you share as dynamic as the information presented in your resume—do you use numbers to show your accomplishments when speaking with networking contacts and employers?

If You Land Initial Interviews but Aren't Asked to Return for Second Interviews. . .

If you are landing a good percentage of interviews but aren't being asked back for second interviews, then consider these issues:

1. As you review each interview, is there a point in the interview when the employer finds a weakness in your background? Does this occur when the interviewer is looking at your resume or cover letter? If so, then determine what is causing employers to notice this weakness and correct your cover letters and resumes before going to another interview.

2. Do problems occur as you're being asked questions? If this is the case then review each interview and make a list of the questions you've been asked that cause you problems. Then review Chapter 15 again and put more work into anticipating and effectively answering difficult questions before going to another interview.

3. Are you making sure that your attire and accessories match the level of position you want? Do you look as well dressed as other employees in the company? Are

you arriving on time and presenting yourself as someone who is confident and well composed? Do you maintain good eye contact and shake hands firmly? Have you put a total effort into your grooming?

4. Before leaving each interview, do you ask if you are a top candidate? Do you probe to find out what each employer might think your weaknesses are so that you can address them and turn them into strengths before leaving the interview? Do you summarize your top qualifications for the job as you are leaving each interview?

5. Before leaving each interview, do you ask when second interviews will be conducted if the employer doesn't schedule you for one? Do you inquire as to when a hiring decision will be made? Then do you follow up the day or day after the hiring decision was to be made so that you present yourself as being interested in the position?

6. Are you sending thank-you letters the same day or next day after your interviews? Do your letters remind the interviewer of your top qualifications and expand on skills you possess that may not have been mentioned during the interview? Does the tone of your letter present an enthusiastic interest in the job and state that you would like to be considered a top candidate?

7. Have you checked in with your references and inquired if they've been contacted by any of the employers you've referred to them? If your reference is a past supervisor or employer, did you inquire as to what type of information each supervisor or employer is relaying about you? If you feel any former employer may be sharing negative information, then consider taking that company or reference off your reference list.

If You Are Offered Jobs Beneath Your Salary Level . . .

If you find you are consistently landing interviews but are offered low-paying jobs, then consider these issues:

1. If you're not getting salary offers at the level you want, then your resume and letters may present you as underqualified for the jobs you want. To correct this, review page 137.

2. Did the resume you created by using this book elevate your image substantially? However, are you still applying for jobs at a lower level? If so, it's important that you begin applying for jobs at a level that matches your resume.

3. Are employers excited when they first meet you as a result of reviewing your resume and letter, but are less excited as the interview proceeds? Do they offer you the job anyway but at a lower salary than you'd like? In this instance, review Chapter 15.

If You've Exhausted All Networking Leads and Employer Contacts and Don't Know What Else to Do . . .

If you feel as though you have exhausted every networking lead and employer contact available to you but haven't landed a solid job offer, then consider these issues:

1. Have you made direct contacts with people who could have the power to hire you that are at least one level, preferably two levels, above you within the companies you've already contacted? This will often require making new contacts with individuals other than those you originally contacted.

2. Have you focused on marketing only one area of your expertise? If so, consider broadening the full range of skills and reasons why each employer would want to hire you. Then share this information as you make each new contact.

3. Have you developed a list of companies or firms outside of your industry or target area that may also need your skills and abilities? If not, develop this list and contact them.

4. In doing such research, have you identified the types of products, services, or problem areas the company or department faces? Are you ready to share examples that show your experience in dealing with these products, services, or problems? Are the stories you share as dynamic as the information presented in your resume—do use numbers to show your accomplishments?

If You Want to Make a Career Change but Are Told You're Not Qualified . . .

If you are changing careers, or trying to move into a management or technical position, but employers seem to feel you don't have the proper qualifications, then consider these issues:

1. Have you carefully thought out how each networking contact might be able to help you? Have you then honed your networking script until you can tell each networking contact what type of job you are looking for and what your top qualifications are within a one- to two-minute conversation?

2. Do your cover letter and resume devote a large amount of space to specific skills that match the career you wish to change to? Do they devote a large amount of space to skills that match the level of management jobs you want? Or do they provide significant details about the technical skills you possess that match the jobs you want? If not, go back and review the Six Steps in Chapter 4. Then answer the Twelve Questions in Chapter 6, keeping the type of job you want in mind as you do so.

3. When networking or interviewing are you ready for questions like "You don't have any experience in this career field. What skills do you have that make you qualified?" or "You've never managed the size of staff needed for this job. What management skills do you possess that qualify you for this job?" or "Explain your knowledge of this technical area (such as a software program, piece of technical equipment, or troubleshooting skills)"? If you stumble when answering these questions, then it's important that you take the time to thoroughly prepare for tough interview questions by studying and applying each strategy in Chapter 15.

15 Winning Interview Strategies

Every business and organization needs to maximize profits and productivity—and those two factors are uppermost in an interviewer's mind when hiring new employees. To get hired over other candidates, you must first identify each employer's needs, then clearly understand and explain how your knowledge, skills, and experience will meet those needs and result in increased profits and productivity.

Keep in mind that interviewers face a certain level of risk when they hire a new employee. If that person doesn't perform well on the job or must be terminated, they can lose thousands of dollars and many hours of time, and then they must hire again. Employers know this all too well, so they enter each interview with the goal of preventing such losses. Employers gauge the potential risk they face in hiring you based on the way you present yourself physically and verbally throughout the interview process. When you show employers how well you meet their needs, you eliminate or significantly reduce such risks. If an area of risk does come up during the interview, you must be prepared to deal with it effectively.

As employers move through the interview process, they gauge how candidates present themselves, from the very first word they speak to how often they make eye-to-eye contact to how they shake hands. Interviewers pay close attention to how well prepared applicants are for the interview and how they answer questions. Employers are also busy assessing how closely each candidate's experience, skills, and education match specific job requirements. Interviewers may not show it, but they react to your every verbal and nonverbal communication. Since applicants can't readily gauge an employer's reactions during an interview, many job seekers misunderstand or view interviews as a mysterious and overwhelming process.

Most resume and job search books add to this sense of confusion because they present lots of ideas, questions, and answers for conducting stronger interviews, but they don't provide a systematic method to help job seekers understand what is really happening throughout the interviewing cycle. This chapter is designed to demystify the interview process and give you the skills to accurately assess how you will be perceived. When you have a solid understanding of how interviews work, you'll be much better equipped to shape and control them.

How Employers Judge Applicants

As you prepare for each interview, imagine that you are the employer and are hiring someone for the position you want. How could this new employee help your firm maximize profits or productivity? What traits and skills would you look for in such an employee? What criteria would you establish and use to judge each candidate? Here's a list of the thirteen most common requirements or standards that many employers judge applicants by:

1. Is the person's appearance and dress appropriate for our work environment and the level of this position?

2. Does the applicant present him- or herself confidently? Can he or she communicate effectively?

3. Does the applicant demonstrate a thorough understanding of the job and his or her ability to do the job?

4. Does the person possess the primary, secondary, and supportive skills needed for the job?

5. Can the applicant make bottom-line contributions such as cutting costs or increasing profitability?

6. Do the person's past work history and current demeanor demonstrate reliability and trustworthiness?

7. Does the applicant's past behavior indicate he or she will be successful in the job?

8. Does the candidate have a proven history of initiative and an ability to work independently and to be a team player?

9. Can the applicant handle stressful or demanding situations that may occur in this job?

10. Does the person have the intelligence and/or alertness this job demands?

11. Does the candidate's educational background or training match the job's requirements?

12. When we review these factors, how quickly will this applicant be productive on the job? What level of productivity will he or she be capable of?

13. How does this applicant stack up in terms of the combination of experience, skills, personal traits, and potential productivity compared to other applicants? Do this applicant's skills and experience justify the salary we are offering or negotiating about?

Use Graphing to Understand and Control Your Interviews

Graphing is a great way to analyze how employers respond to you and the statements you make during every phase of your interview. We've used graphing with resumes and cover letters, and you can apply the same strategy to analyze the image you present during interviews. This will give you a better sense of where you stand during and at the end of each interview. It also helps you to identify any answers or comments you might make that could damage your image. Being aware will help you take immediate action to prevent or repair such damage by strengthening your answer or focusing the employer's attention on skills he or she is interested in. On the next pages we'll use a graph like the one that follows to plot an interview that didn't land Cynthia a job offer. Then we'll plot an interview that landed Cynthia a great job. We'll use the list of thirteen requirements or standards shown above to assess how employers will rate Cynthia as being overqualified, qualified, or underqualified.

Cynthia had been an inside sales representative making $35,000, but wanted to become a call center manager and boost her salary to the $45,000+ range. Cynthia had trained new sales reps, helped to create a very successful telemarketing and lead development program, and managed a call center employing thirty-five sales staff during her manager's absence. To assess how Cynthia performed during her interviews, we need to develop a picture of typical call center managers. They dress in corporate attire, present themselves confidently, must be able to manage diverse staff and multiple activities, and be able to guide sales reps in making thousands of daily sales contacts. The call center manager is responsible for generating a high percentage of qualified leads that can be turned into sales by outside sales staff. Let's gauge how employers will perceive Cynthia as she moves through her interview.

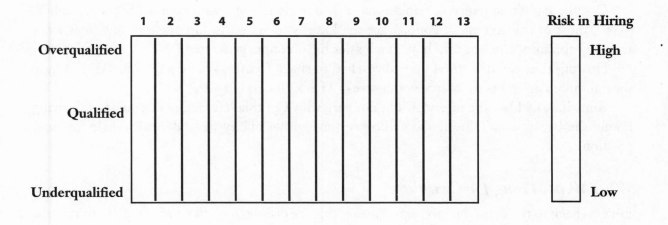

Cynthia's First Interview

Even though Cynthia had landed an interview for a call center manager position, she hadn't spent any time thinking about her skills, how they matched the job, or how she could contribute to a call center's profitability or productivity. She wore slacks and a blouse to her interview. On the day of the interview it was windy and Cynthia was running a few minutes late, so she didn't stop to brush her hair. Kendall, who had been selected to interview her, had just come into the reception area to see if his next appointment was going to show up. Cynthia immediately realized that Kendall, dressed immaculately in a dark suit, seemed like a no-nonsense person. As he introduced himself and shook hands with Cynthia, Kendall noticed she glanced away. He wondered whether she had the confidence she would need as a call center manager.

Once in Kendall's office, Cynthia put her purse on the floor and began rummaging through it to take out her resume. After a moment, she straightened up and asked Kendall if he needed her resume. He said, "No, I have a copy," and pointed to her resume already on his desk. Kendall leaned back in his chair and said, "To start, why don't you give me an overview of your skills and why you feel you are qualified for the call center manager position."

Surprised her interview was starting so quickly, Cynthia replied, "Well, I'm currently an inside sales representative for a call center and have helped to train other sales representatives. My supervisor has been very open in complementing me on my sales skills and has said that in the future she will consider me for a management position."

Kendall then asked, "How long have you been in this position?"

Realizing her experience was short and a big weakness, Cynthia shifted uncomfortably in her seat. She then replied, "I've only been in this position for about two years but have progressed rapidly, moving from sales assistant to inside sales within six months of being hired."

Realizing Cynthia only had eighteen months of call center experience, Kendall then said, "Well, I'm afraid we're looking for someone with at least three years of call center experience. Looking at your resume, I saw that you had been with this company for three years, so I assumed it was all in the call center. Why don't you tell me a little about your education."

Feeling the interview slipping away, Cynthia replied, "I have a bachelor's degree with a major in marketing from the University of Michigan. I pursued marketing because I love working with people and wanted to combine that interest with my minor in advertising."

Kendall then leaned even farther back in his chair and said, "Can you give me an idea of the type and size of accounts you've handled in the call center?"

Cynthia hadn't anticipated being asked this question. She stammered a little and replied, "Well, most of the accounts I contact are the lower-end accounts, although I sometimes assist with key accounts. I'm not sure how much sales the accounts generated."

Hearing this, Kendall stood up and reached to shake Cynthia's hand and said, "Well, I have several more applicants to interview this week. Thanks for coming in."

Knowing she blew the interview but not sure why, Cynthia left feeling discouraged. Driving home, she began wondering if she had overestimated her ability to land a call center manager position.

What Went Wrong for Cynthia?

Let's go back to the common job requirements that we discussed earlier and use them to rate the image Cynthia presented in her interview (they've been condensed and listed below). Reading the description of Cynthia's interview and how Cynthia was dressed, would you rate her as presenting an image that makes her seem overqualified, qualified, or underqualified as a call center manager making $45,000? See if you agree with how I ranked my impression of Cynthia's dress and appearance in the first column of the graph on the facing page. Then continue on and rank Cynthia in each of the thirteen requirements.

Cynthia's Image: Overqualified, Qualified, or Underqualified?

1. Appearance and dress matches level of position

2. Presentation of self and communication skills match needs of positions

3. Understands job and possesses the ability to perform the job

4. Has all, or many, of the skills required for the job

5. Can make bottom-line contributions

6. Past work history and current demeanor demonstrate reliability and trustworthiness

7. Past behavior indicates ability to be successful in the job

8. Has initiative, is able to work independently, and can be a team player

9. Can handle stressful, demanding situations

10. Has the intelligence and alertness required for the position

11. Educational background is close to or matches job requirements

12. How quickly will Cynthia be productive? How productive will she be?

13. Do Cynthia's experience, skills, personal traits, and potential productivity match and justify the salary offered?

When we graph our responses to the common job requirements we've listed, we see that Cynthia seems consistently underqualified. How would you rate the employer's risk in hiring Cynthia for a call center manager position? As you can see, I rated the risk an employer would face as high. This helps to illustrate the image Kendall had formed of Cynthia and why he dismissed her so quickly.

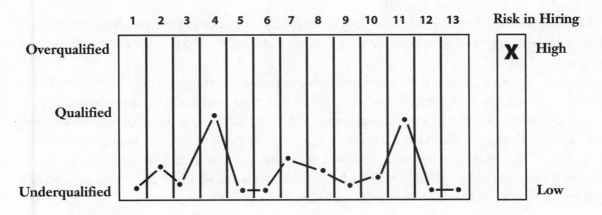

Bottom-Line Contributions Make a Difference

A few days after her first interview, Cynthia contacted me to help her revise her resume and coach her on her interviewing skills. Analyzing several ads for call center managers, Cynthia identified the top skills required for such positions. She then determined how her skills would contribute to increased sales, profitability, and productivity. Using this information, she created a resume that matched her skills to employers' needs and highlighted her bottom-line achievements. Cynthia also realized that she needed to present a polished corporate image, so she purchased several new suits that matched the image of a call center manager making $45,000.

On her second interview, Cynthia made sure she arrived ten minutes early and carried only a briefcase with her. This time her interview was with Frances, who had been promoted from the position of call center manager to department manager. Following Frances into her office, Cynthia noticed several sales awards that Frances had been given. Cynthia said, "It looks as though you've been very effective as a call center manager, having received so many top awards."

Francis smiled and answered, "Yes, I have worked many long hours to earn those awards. Tell me, have you received any sales awards?"

Cynthia replied, "Yes. I received performance awards for generating the highest number of leads competing with over thirty other sales representatives in our call center. I also received a commendation and bonus for training approximately half of our sales staff, which increased the production of leads from our department by more than ten percent."

Leaning forward and seeming very interested, Frances replied, "That sounds like just the kind of initiative that helped me become the call center manager. Can you describe the type of accounts and volume of sales generated from the leads your department developed?"

Feeling confident, Cynthia answered, "I managed up to thirty-five staff, overseeing initial sales contacts to more than 2,000 accounts per week for accounts such as IBM, Microsoft, UPS, and Hewlett-Packard. I served in this capacity whenever our call center manager was out of the office, which could be up to fifty percent of the time. Our staff was responsible for identifying buyers and key decision makers, and for qualifying customer interest. We then prepared a detailed summary of each account, equipment needs, and potential sales products. This information was forwarded to our district sales manager, whom I often communicated with on a daily basis. His staff then contacted each company and followed up. He documented the fact that the training I provided increased our leads to sales ratio by more than thirty percent, which resulted in an increase of over a quarter million dollars in annual sales. Key account sales ranged anywhere from $50,000 up to $125,000 annually."

Looking pleased, Frances then asked, "Looking at your resume, I see you have a bachelor's degree in marketing. Our minimum requirement is a B.A. degree. Do you have any other education that is relevant?"

Cynthia answered, "Yes, I have a minor in advertising that was a great asset in helping me to identify customer needs and market our products, which also increased lead development."

Looking even more interested, Frances stood up and said, "Great. Our call center also employs between thirty and thirty-five sales staff. It sounds like you're familiar with accounts similar in size to the ones we deal with and you seem to be comfortable overseeing call center activities. I'm in a rush today but want to give you a short tour. Then I'd like to set up a second interview so that we can discuss your sales experience in depth."

What Went Right This Time?

Again, consider each of the job requirements listed below and use them to rate the image Cynthia presented in her second interview. See if you agree with how I ranked Cynthia's interview using the graph on the facing page.

Cynthia's Image: Is She Overqualified, Qualified, or Underqualified?

1. Appearance and dress matches level of position
2. Presentation of self and communication skills match needs of positions
3. Understands job and possesses the ability to perform the job
4. Has all of many of the skills required for the job
5. Can make bottom-line contributions
6. Past work history and current demeanor demonstrate reliability and trustworthiness
7. Past behavior indicates ability to be successful in the job
8. Has initiative, is able to work independently, and can be a team player
9. Can handle stressful, demanding situations
10. Has the intelligence and alertness required for the position
11. Educational background is close to or matches job requirements
12. How quickly will Cynthia be productive? How productive will she be?
13. Do Cynthia's experience, skills, personal traits, and potential productivity match and justify the salary offered?

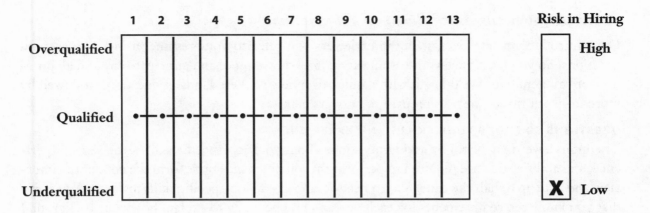

In her second interview, the professional image Cynthia presented along with answers that demonstrated her ability to increase call center profitability and productivity made her look well qualified. As a result, Frances felt little or no risk in hiring Cynthia. This case is an excellent example of how proper appearance, effective communication, and interview preparation can turn unsuccessful interviews into job offers.

The Interviewing Cycle

Like Cynthia, the biggest mistake job seekers make before going on interviews is lack of preparation. Most interviews last from fifteen minutes to an hour or more. Considering it can take only one to two minutes to answer a question, you could be asked anywhere from seven to thirty questions or more during each interview. Getting caught off guard by an unexpected question can leave us feeling like we've fallen into the great interviewing pit. We may stammer, blush, look confused, shift nervously in our seats, and ultimately give a weak answer to an important question. Interviewers are trained to look for such nonverbal cues and use them as red flags to identify problems and find weaknesses that can eliminate us as viable candidates.

To prevent raising such red flags, you must understand and anticipate each phase of the interviewing cycle and the questions it may generate. I've categorized the interviewing cycle into three phases—from introductions to questioning to closure—that occur sometime during each interview. My goal is to teach you how to analyze each position you'll interview for and the unique questions it will generate. The next step is to prepare answers tailored to market the best of your skills for that particular position. This is much more effective than memorizing a group of general questions and answers that are not designed to match the jobs you want.

Phase I: Introductions and First Impressions

Most interviewers spend a few minutes making chitchat to build rapport and put the applicant at ease at the opening of each interview. This includes asking conversational questions like "How was your drive?" Substantial interview questions are not asked during this introductory phase but the interviewer is already assessing handshake, eye contact, appearance, confidence, poise, vocabulary, and nonverbal communication.

Phase II: Questions Asked Based on Your Resume

Once introductions are over, many interviewers will refer to your resume, using it to ask you questions. So you must view your resume as an interviewing tool and anticipate any and all questions it will generate. We'll begin with a quick overview of these kinds of questions, followed by more in-depth tips on how to prepare to answer them.

QUESTIONS TO JUDGE YOUR SKILLS AND EXPERIENCE

The interviewer may begin by asking questions about your job-specific skills—the skills, experience, and abilities that are required to perform the job. Such questions form the core of the interview and take up to half the time. Such a heavy emphasis on job-specific skills makes it imperative that you know the requirements for each position and be ready to explain how your background matches each requirement.

QUESTIONS ABOUT YOUR BOTTOM-LINE CONTRIBUTIONS

As employers gather information about your skills and experience they assess the degree to which you can contribute to their bottom line and determine if you provide enough value to justify your salary. To promote yourself as the top candidate, you must anticipate questions you'll be asked and prepare answers that demonstrate your ability to cut costs, maximize profits, increase sales, and enhance productivity. This strategy alone can put you in the top five or ten percent of applicants who are interviewed.

QUESTIONS TO ASSESS PERSONALITY, VALUES, AND COPING STYLE

In the long run, your personality, values, and coping style may weigh more heavily in helping you get hired than your job-specific skills. Consider two applicants with equal skills. One has a very distant personality and the other is very friendly and outgoing. The friendly, outgoing person will probably be the one that's hired because that person will be seen as more of a team player. As a result, employers will ask questions to uncover your personality, values, and work habits, and how you handle stressful or demanding situations.

QUESTIONS ABOUT YOUR WORK HISTORY

As interviewers gather information about your skills and achievements they will review the work history presented in your resume or application. You should also review your work history in order to anticipate any questions employers may have about problem areas such as gaps in employment or an erratic work history.

QUESTIONS ABOUT EDUCATION AND TRAINING

When interviewers ask questions about education, they are most interested in how your training and involvement in college activities has resulted in skills or knowledge that in some way enhances your ability to do the job. Therefore, it's important that you be able to articulate how your education will assist you in performing the position being sought.

QUESTIONS ABOUT YOUR REFERENCES

Many employers ask that you bring a list of references or several letters of recommendation with you to the interview. Employers are looking for feedback and verification from others that the information you present during an interview is accurate, that you are reliable, and that you possess key skills and personality traits that indicate you will be a successful employee.

QUESTIONS ABOUT SALARY REQUIREMENTS

Toward the end of each interview, many employers will ask you what salary you desire so that they can determine if your needs fall within their salary range. They will also use this figure and balance it against their assessment of you in order to determine if you are worth the salary you request.

QUESTIONS YOU CAN ASK TO DIRECT AND CONTROL THE INTERVIEW

Employers control and direct interviews by asking questions. You can also take part in directing and controlling each interview by asking leading questions. This strategy gives you an opportunity to sell those skills that the interviewer may fail to ask about or that you wish to emphasize.

Phase III: Interview Closure

Once an employer feels he or she has gathered enough information from each phase of the interview cycle, the interview will be drawn to a close. If the interviewer feels you are a good candidate, he or she may discuss a second interview. If the interviewer feels you are not a viable candidate, second interviews will not be discussed and you will be sent on your way. Before leaving an interview, you should identify any negative assumptions an employer may have made about you so that you have an opportunity to address them and turn them into a positive impression.

After the Interview: Follow-Up and Thank-You Letters

Follow-up and thank-you letters are a must in generating second and third interviews and solid job offers. Many employees are hired because they pull ahead of the pack by writing strong thank-you letters (see examples on pages 307 and 308).

The Interviewing Cycle in Detail

On the following pages we'll discuss each phase of the interviewing cycle in more detail. After that discussion, I've provided key strategies to help you answer questions along with tips that allow you to introduce and emphasize your top skills. Then, at the end of this chapter you'll be provided a checklist that will guide you in preparing for each phase of the interviewing cycle.

Phase I: Introductions and First Impressions

I'm not sure why people don't pay closer attention to their grooming, dress, handshake, eye contact, and other nonverbal signals during interviews, especially when first greeting an employer. Perhaps they think employers really won't care if an applicant's hair is a little windblown, that shoes are scuffed, or that clothes are not freshly pressed. It's not so much that any one of these things in itself will cause you not to be hired; it's the underlying assumptions that employers make about you when they see such behaviors that will prevent you from being hired.

For example, an employer may assume that windblown hair, scuffed shoes, and unpressed clothing means the person is careless about his or her appearance; may be on the edge financially and can't afford new shoes or clothing; or just doesn't go the extra mile to present a good image.

These assumptions can make an employer believe the applicant will also be careless on the job, won't care about doing the best job possible, or if facing financial difficulties, that the candidate may not be reliable. A weak handshake, poor eye contact, fidgeting, getting embarrassed, or becoming flustered can also result in an impression that leads to negative assumptions. Let's say an employer needs to hire someone to support high-level staff, work independently, and deal with the public in stressful situations. These kinds of awkward behaviors can lead an employer to assume that the applicant is not confident, may be intimidated by senior staff, and therefore not be effective in supporting them. Employers might also assume that this person would be unable to work independently without a lot of direction, or cannot deal with difficult customers or challenging situations.

It's these underlying assumptions that an applicant with poor grooming or awkward physical presence must really battle against and prevent. My recommendation is that you identify the level of dress, demeanor, and communication style—including handshake and eye contact—portrayed by those doing the job you want, then mimic them as closely as possible. This greatly increases interview success.

Phase II: Questions Asked Based on Your Resume

Even though interviewers often use the resume as a guide to ask questions, many job seekers are not familiar with the information in their own resumes and get caught off guard when employers question them. Therefore, it's important that you become familiar with every line of your resume. You must anticipate questions that employers are likely to ask about every item in your resume and then prepare effective answers. This preparation can help you catch a negative conclusion that an employer might make about you or to prepare for a negative question. In this case, you'll have a chance to revamp your resume before submitting it so that you can prevent negative questions. Below is a statement from a resume along with a question an employer might ask about the statement. It is then followed by an effective answer. Use this as an example to anticipate questions you may be asked about every item in your resume.

Resume Statement

- Increased departmental productivity by 15% by preordering short-term inventory.

Employer's Question

"Can you tell me more about what you did to increase your department's productivity?"

Applicant's Answer

"I analyzed operations and found that many departments were waiting for parts that often came several days behind schedule. I then planned our monthly parts requirements and ordered just enough parts so that we had them at least one week prior to production deadlines. This enabled us to bring over six production lines back on track and increased our production by fifteen percent."

USE STORIES THAT PROVE YOUR QUALIFICATIONS

Many applicants do poorly during interviews because they have not selected stories from their backgrounds that prove they are qualified. As a result, their answers are too long or not direct and to the point. Another weakness is that most job seekers are not aware of the full range of their skills and falter when trying to explain how their skills match each employer's needs. I normally spend from one to two hours with each client when writing a resume. The bulk of that time is spent talking about each person's background and then paring down descriptions of their achievements and skills for a concise resume. This same preparation is mandatory for maximizing interview success. In the same way, you need to pare down verbal descriptions of skills and achievements into stories that take only one to two minutes to share.

I remember working with Tony, a furniture designer. He was upset because he was landing many interviews but receiving salary offers in the $32,000 range, although he had left a position making $40,000. Coaching him on his interviewing skills, I asked Tony what skill was requested the most in ads he applied for. He replied, "Problem-solving skills are almost always mentioned." I then asked Tony to describe a work situation that demonstrated his problem-solving skills as a furniture designer. After thinking a moment, he spent about ten minutes recounting a situation that saved his company from losing a big order. It took us another five minutes to pare his story down to a verbal description that he could share in one to two minutes during an interview. Then it took us five more minutes to pare it down and create a written statement for his resume. As we went through this paring-down process, Tony kept remembering more and more examples of work situations where he had used his problem-solving skills—yet none of them were in his resume. Just like thousands of job seekers' resumes, Tony's was a reflection of how he viewed his skills and how ill prepared he was for interviews. If Tony had gone on another interview without learning how to prepare such success stories, he would have continued to receive low salary offers.

The key to preparing for interviews is to review each statement in your resume and anticipate the questions it may generate, as the example above illustrates. Then select stories from your work history that you can use to answer each question and explain why you are well qualified. Write down each story, then practice saying it aloud until you can share it within one to two minutes. This is a lot of work, but will increase your confidence and impress employers.

TONY'S ANSWER TO QUESTIONS ABOUT HIS PROBLEM-SOLVING SKILLS

"During my second week at XYZ Furniture we received an order from the Bon Marche for 200 display units to be delivered within three days. Production had already started when I was given the project. Our company had been told that if we couldn't meet the deadline, the order would be canceled. I quickly estimated how long it would take to finish the order and realized it would take over five days. I gathered together all of our gluing clamps so I'd know how many units we could glue at one time. Then I designed a customized jig to speed the set-up of each unit. By designing the jig and using all our clamps, we cut our production time from five days to three days, and were able to meet the Bon's requirements. My being able to step in and solve both the design and production problems resulted in our keeping a $400,000 order."

Statement Written for Tony's Resume

- Designed a customized jig and set up a gluing schedule, which cut production time from 5 days to 3, allowing us to meet Bon Marche project deadlines and retain a $400,000 order.

QUESTIONS TO JUDGE YOUR SKILLS AND EXPERIENCE

Employers also use want ads and job descriptions to guide them in asking questions because ads provide a quick review of the required skills, experience, and education needed for each position. This makes it important that you also analyze ads or job descriptions. This knowledge will allow you to accurately anticipate questions employers may ask you and will allow you to prepare answers that present you in the best possible light. Below, I've broken down an ad for a division assistant into numbered items such as the job title, skill, and educational requirements. Compare each of the numbered items to the numbered questions below. This example shows how each skill or requirement in an ad can be used to anticipate questions.

<u>**1. Ad for Division Assistant**</u>

2. Leading engineering consulting firm requires 3 years administrative experience.

3. Will provide staff support to Division Managers and Project Teams.

4. Prepare and approve correspondence.

5. Process invoices, coordinate meetings, travel arrangements, client visits, and presentations.

6. Prepare technical documents, proposals, budgets, and spreadsheets.

7. Set up new files and maintain them.

8. MS Word, WordPerfect, and Excel.

9. Able to work with large, diverse workgroups.

10. B.A. degree preferred.

11. $16.79 to $20.59 per hour.

Questions That May Be Asked about This Ad

1. Can you describe your experience as a division assistant or as an executive assistant for me?

2. Please tell me about any experience you have with engineering or consulting firms.

3. Can you tell me how many staff you support in your current position and what their titles are?

4. What type of correspondence have you been responsible for preparing or approving?

5. Do you have experience preparing invoices and other billing functions?

6. Have you been responsible for coordinating presentations, meetings, and travel arrangements?

7. This position requires heavy contact with clients. What type of client interaction have you been responsible for?

8. Have you been responsible for preparing technical documents such as proposals, budgets, and spreadsheets?

9. You will be responsible for file setup and maintenance. Have you been responsible for such systems?

10. This position requires heavy Word, WordPerfect, and Excel use. What is your experience using these programs?

11. You will coordinate with large, diverse workgroups. Do you have similar experience?

12. Our entry requirement is a bachelor's degree. Do you have such a degree?

13. The salary is quite high for this position. What skills do you possess that qualify you for this salary?

ANOTHER EXAMPLE

Here's another example to show that analyzing ads to anticipate employer questions works for any position at any salary level. The following ad is for a branch manager, which is a higher-level position. Yet analyzing the ad works equally well to anticipate employer questions. Use ads and job descriptions to help you develop a good understanding of what each job entails, who you will work with, and the types of problems you will be responsible for solving. Preparing in this way will increase your confidence prior to interviews. The more confident and prepared you are, the better presentation you will make during every phase of the interviewing cycle.

1. Ad for Branch Manager

2. Take-charge, executive-level manager to open new office furniture distribution center.

3. Extensive experience acquiring major accounts with sales of up to $5 million annually.

4. Proven history of managing multiple branch functions including the following:

5. Marketing, advertising, training, and supervision of up to 20 sales staff.

6. Overseeing contract negotiation, vendor scheduling, and customer relations.

7. Hiring and supervising office staff. Managing accounting, budgeting, and sales reporting.

8. Proven ability to minimize bad debts and implement credit /collections procedures.

9. Coordinate warehouse and fulfillment operations to service a 3-state customer region.

10. MBA preferred but can substitute the right combination of experience and education.

11. $45,000 to $60,000 DOE (depending on experience).

Questions That May Be Asked about This Ad

1. Can you give me an overview of your branch or departmental management experience?

2. Can you describe your experience opening and managing office furniture or related distribution centers?

3. Tell me about your background managing major accounts and the sales volume your branch generated.

4. Have you been responsible for managing multiple locations and internal functions?

5. Marketing management includes all phases of advertising. Do you have related experience?

6. This position will train and supervise up to twenty sales staff. What size of staff have you managed in the past?

7. What experience do you have overseeing contract negotiation, vendor scheduling, and customer relations?

8. Have you hired and supervised office staff? If so, what were their job functions and the size of your staff?

9. We demand an exceptionally low bad-debt ratio. Can you describe your experience in this area?

10. You will direct credit and collections functions for multiple sites. Give me a review of your credit background.

11. Have you managed warehouse and fulfillment operations to support accounts in multiple states?

12. We prefer an MBA but will consider other alternatives. Tell me how your education fits our needs.

13. The salary range is from $45,000 to $60,000. Where do you fall in this range and why?

QUESTIONS ABOUT MODIFIED TITLES OR SKILL HEADINGS

If you've modified your job title by using an interchangeable and truthful title or used skill headings that are different from your title, employers may ask you questions to determine how you gained such experience. Sandy used the title of executive assistant, which is truthful but different from her actual job title of secretary. In Sandy's situation it's not likely an employer would question the difference between these two titles since they are often used interchangeably. By inserting your actual title into your work history and writing a short statement describing how you gained the experience, most employers will understand why you've used a particular title and won't question you. However, if there is a dramatic difference between your real title and the modified title you've used, then you might be questioned about that difference. For example, Dan replaced his actual title of returns authorization clerk with test technician. Seeing these differences, an employer might ask Dan the following questions, which are followed by his answers.

> *I see that you performed work as a test technician. Was your real job title returns authorization clerk? How do I know that you actually performed the work of a test technician?*

My actual title was returns authorization clerk and in that position I was responsible for all areas of electronics testing. To be sure that I was really performing the work of a test technician, I reviewed about twenty want ads and job descriptions for test technicians, including the ad for the position with your firm. I've brought them with me if you'd like to see them and have put check marks next to each duty for which I've been responsible. As you can see, I have almost every skill or responsibility required.

I knew it was important to use the title of test technician because everyone that hears the title of returns authorization clerk automatically thinks I handle merchandise returns for a retail store, although I actually authorize the return of electronic computer parts, test, and then repair them. I was concerned that employers viewing my resume would also react this way and would think I wasn't an experienced test technician. However, as you can see from reading my resume and these ads, I am a well-qualified test technician.

By following Dan's example, you will be able to present yourself as a highly qualified and truthful candidate.

BEYOND THE OBVIOUS: QUESTIONS ABOUT THE EMPLOYER'S HIDDEN NEEDS

Although ads are a good way to anticipate many of the questions that employers will ask you during an interview, they are only snapshots that provide a small amount of information about each position. There are many more hidden needs that each employer must deal with beyond those mentioned in an ad or job description. Such hidden needs can include additional skills, abilities, or problems that an employer may be concerned about and ask about during your interview.

You will increase the success of your interviews if you analyze the hidden needs each employer faces and determine how your skills, experience, and knowledge allow you to solve those needs. You can do this by analyzing and then making assumptions about the needs or problems each employer faces. To illustrate we'll use the division assistant ad again, shown below. Read through it and imagine what other skills or abilities someone will need to do this job. Consider the types of problems and situations this person will face on a daily basis. See if the skills or problems you thought of are in the left-hand column of hidden needs I listed below. In the right-hand column are questions I developed that employers will be likely to ask about each of these hidden needs.

Ad for Division Assistant

Leading engineering consulting firm requires 3 years administrative experience.

Will provide staff support to Division Managers and Project Teams.

Prepare and approve correspondence.

Process invoices, coordinate meetings, travel arrangements, client visits, and presentations.

Prepare technical documents, proposals, budgets, and spreadsheets.

Set up new files and maintain them.

MS Word, WordPerfect, and Excel.

Able to work with large, diverse workgroups.

B.A. degree preferred.

$16.79 to $20.59 per hour.

Hidden Needs

- Strong typing/10-key skills
- Can catch errors in data
- Good writing/editing skills
- Has good follow-through
- Strong attention to detail
- Good organizational skills
- Adept at problem solving
- Requires minimum instruction
- Must work independently
- Can meet deadlines
- Can handle pressure
- Is a team player

Questions about Hidden Needs

1. How fast do you type? Can you use a 10-key by touch? How accurate are you?
2. Can you describe your ability to proof contracts and verify project data?
3. What type of documents have you been responsible for writing and editing?
4. Can you describe your experience following through on work projects?
5. How would you describe your attention to detail and accuracy?
6. Tell me about your experience organizing tasks to support multiple departments.
7. Tell me about some of the most important problems you've solved.
8. Describe your ability to initiate and complete tasks with little instruction.
9. Give me an example of when you worked independently on a major task.
10. Describe two instances in which you had to meet important deadlines.
11. Tell me about your ability to handle pressure.
12. Describe a time when you served as part of a team and what you accomplished.

QUESTIONS ABOUT BOTTOM-LINE CONTRIBUTIONS

Throughout the interviewing cycle, employers will ask a variety of questions to determine whether and how you can contribute to their firm's bottom line. As the example to follow illustrates, it's wise to make a list of ways an employee performing the job you want can contribute to increased profitability and productivity. Anticipate questions you may be asked about each of the areas you identify and then prepare answers that show how your past experience, skills, and current abilities allow you to positively impact the employer's bottom line.

Some Ways Employees Contribute to the Bottom Line:

1. Cutting costs, streamlining operations, and maximizing productivity
2. Increasing sales and profitability or generating new and repeat business
3. Inventing new products or procedures
4. Improving employee morale or customer relations
5. Cutting costs by researching and negotiating lower vendor and supplier prices

Questions Employers May Ask:

1. Have you helped your department cut costs, streamline operations, or maximize productivity?
2. How have you contributed to increased sales or profitability, new or repeat business?
3. Have you assisted in the creation of new products or procedures?
4. What is your history of success in improving employee morale or customer relations?
5. How have you helped cut purchasing costs?

QUESTIONS TO ASSESS YOUR PERSONALITY, VALUES, AND COPING STYLE

Most employers will hire employees who might require training or development—if they are enthusiastic, have the right personality, and can cope with the job—over employees who can step right into the job but that no one will like. That's why interviewers ask questions to see how you would react in a particular situation. They want to predict how well you get along with others, can handle pressure, or deal with problems. Here's a short list of questions used to reveal personality traits, values, and coping styles.

Questions to Reveal Personality Traits:

1. What supervisor have you disliked the most and why?
2. What kind of boss and working situation do you prefer?
3. Are you more of an optimist or a pessimist?
4. Do you like to work as part of a team or to spend most of your time working alone?

Questions to Reveal Values:

1. What is more important to you, your pay or your job satisfaction?
2. How do you spend your spare time?
3. Which is more important to you, getting along with everyone or doing things right?

Questions to Reveal Coping Style:

1. What would you do if you saw a co-worker steal from the company?
2. What would you do if a supervisor severely criticized your work without good reason?
3. How would you prioritize answering a busy phone, a customer emergency, and preparing an extremely important package that must go out the door in five minutes?
4. If you were asked to falsify a document, what would you do?

Take a moment and select one of the questions shown above and imagine what you would say in answer to it. If you're like most people, the answer probably doesn't roll right off your tongue. Our first tendency when answering questions like these, unless we are professional interviewers, is to be honest. That may sound like what we should do, but in fact we just tend to blurt out things that don't help us. Being too honest often knocks many job seekers out of the running by revealing weaknesses or problem areas. For example, if a supervisor severely criticized me with no good reason, I would be angry, or if I really liked the person, I might feel like crying. But that would not be an appropriate answer to give and would probably keep me from being hired. A better reply would be this:

"I would take some time to review what I did and try to determine if I had made a mistake. If so, while it's always hard to be criticized, I would review what my supervisor told me and see how I could correct the mistake. If I reviewed what I had done and found that I had not made a mistake, I would wait for an appropriate time and then ask my supervisor to explain in more detail what he or she felt I had done improperly. Then we could work on improving the situation together."

Tip: There are hundreds of questions like these that you can read and try to remember answers to. Rather than trying to answer so many different questions, you may find it most helpful to list several of your strongest personality traits, values, and coping skills that lead you to be a top worker. Develop a short story of how you used your best personality traits, personal values, and coping skills successfully on the job. Then use these stories to answer questions like those shown above.

QUESTIONS ABOUT WORK HISTORY

Work history questions can sometimes be the hardest to answer. To prepare for them, review the work history you have listed in your resume and in your application. Then anticipate any questions that may come up during your interviews. Be sure to provide reasons for gaps in employment or having held too many jobs. An effective formula is to agree with the problem and then provide an example that shows why you experienced the problem and ways in which you have overcome or successfully solved it.

For example, if you worked while attending college, you might be asked, "Why have you held so many jobs?" To which you could say, "My employment has been somewhat erratic because I worked part-time while going to school full-time. My top priority was completing my education and my work schedule often didn't fit my college schedule. As a result, I frequently had to find positions that fit the time schedule of important classes. Unlike many students who don't put themselves through school, I demonstrated my ability to set and achieve goals and pay my own way—all while maintaining a 3.5 GPA. Now that I've graduated I can devote all that energy to being a top employee on a full-time basis." The following list shows additional situations that may prompt concern about your work history and the questions an employer may ask about each one.

Questions about Work History Problems:

- **Gaps in employment between jobs.**
  I see you were unemployed for some length of time between the last positions you held. Can you tell me why?

- **Too many jobs.**
  You've held a lot of jobs in the last five years. Tell me why you would change your pattern of employment now.

- **No industry experience related to the job you want.**

  You haven't worked in this industry. Why do you think you are a good fit for this job?

- **Only temporary or contract positions.**

  Why have you held only temporary or contract positions?

- **Only volunteer experience.**

  I see your background comes solely from volunteer experience. Why do you feel that qualifies you for this job?

- **Haven't worked in several years, reentering the workforce.**

  It's been several years since you've worked. How current are your skills and how do they match this position?

- **Self-employed.**

  Most people who have been self-employed have a hard time working for someone else again. Why won't you?

- **Previously employed at a much higher level.**

  This position is at a much lower level than the positions you've held. Why do you think you'd be happy in this job?

- **Employed in one job for a long period of time.**

  You've been in your current position for over ten years. Tell me why you've stayed so long with one company.

- **Fired, downsized, or laid off.**

  Have you ever been fired, downsized, or laid off? If so, why?

QUESTIONS ABOUT EDUCATION, TRAINING, AND EXTRACURRICULAR ACTIVITIES

When employers ask questions about education and training, they are most interested in how the education you've received can enable you to perform the job you are seeking. When inquiring about extracurricular activities such as being involved in sports, clubs, or associations, interviewers want to assess leadership skills, areas of interest, initiative, or community involvement. So in preparing to answer these questions, first ask yourself what skills are required to do the job you want. Then select matching skills, knowledge, or achievements from your educational background to discuss during your interviews. For example, an employer hiring a management trainee will be interested in supervisory, leadership, communication, and problem-solving skills. A hospital hiring a registered nurse will be interested in clinical training that matches the position being filled. Reading the two examples below, you'll see how these concerns were addressed in each answer. I've also provided several more questions that employers may ask about your educational background.

How can your education benefit you in performing this job?

Management Trainee: "While completing my accounting degree, I served as the Secretary-Treasurer for Student Activities and managed an annual budget of $60,000, which involved writing report summaries to the board. Completing an internship, I trained ten staff in the use of computerized accounting applications. Both required strong communication and accounting skills, which are needed for this position."

Registered Nurse: "To obtain my B.S.N. degree, I completed eight clinical rotations in obstetrics, pediatrics, geriatrics, telemetry and surgery, medical, surgical, cardiac, and oncology units, working with staffs of up to fifty physicians and interdisciplinary team members. My clinical experience is quite broad and proves my ability to move between medical specialties, as the RN float position requires."

Some Questions about Education and Extracurricular Activities:

1. What was the major and minor you completed to obtain your degree?

2. How many hours of study did you complete to obtain a community college degree or a technical certificate?

3. Did you complete an internship or an externship? If so, where and what did it entail?

4. Were you a member in any associations or organizations? If so, what was your role?

5. How was your college education funded?

6. What were your grades like? Were you ever on the honor roll?

7. What were your study habits and attendance like?

8. How would your teachers describe you?

9. Do you plan to pursue additional education? If so, how will you balance that with working full-time?

10. What was your favorite subject or class? Why?

QUESTIONS ABOUT YOUR REFERENCES

Before going to an interview, prepare a list of three professional and three personal references and bring it with you to each interview. Always ask permission to use someone as a reference and let him or her know the types of positions you will be interviewing for and the skills needed in those positions. Then ask your references to point out your best traits and abilities that match the positions you'll interview for. Also, bring any letters of recommendations from instructors, employers, or other business professionals that you have received. If you feel a particular supervisor or instructor can give an employer great feedback about you, then ask for a letter of recommendation. Here is a short list of questions employers may ask about your references.

Some Questions about Your References:

1. Do your references know I will be calling? What will they say about you?

2. Which reference will know the most about your work performance skills?

3. Which reference will give you the best recommendation? The least enthusiastic recommendation? Why?

4. Can you tell me in what capacity each of these references knew you and why they are recommending you?

5. Can I contact every reference on this sheet? Are their addresses and phone numbers current?

QUESTIONS ABOUT YOUR SALARY

Wait for the employer to bring up the issue of pay so that you can put yourself in the best bargaining position. If the employer believes that he has to sell himself to you, he will consider a higher pay rate than if you bring up salary on the first interview. It's also important to learn what salary range employers are considering before stating your salary requirement. The employer's range may be higher, but if you state a lower range that's usually what you'll be offered. When an employer asks, "What pay rate or salary level are you looking for?" answer with either of these statements:

> "I am flexible. At this time, my primary concern is obtaining a position that offers stability and career potential. Can you tell me the salary range for this position?"

OR

> "I am much more interested in working for the right organization and obtaining a position that will fully utilize my skills. I am flexible regarding my pay and am sure your firm offers competitive rates. I would prefer to discuss pay after I've learned more about the position and how I can meet your needs."

To make either strategy work, you must confidently look the employer straight in the eye and speak in a friendly, relaxed manner. If you mumble, avoid eye contract, or act nervous, many employers will push you to tell them the salary you expect. You may feel intimidated by the thought of using either of these statements, so plan to practice what you'll say until it feels like second nature to you, and you can say it without stumbling or feeling self-conscious. These strategies work. I've been told numerous stories where these strategies helped individuals receive from $2,000 to $20,000 or more per year. It's like getting a raise before you're hired!

WHAT'S YOUR BOTTOM LINE?

Before going on an interview, determine what your rock-bottom salary requirement is. Make sure that this is the least you would be willing to take, even if your dream job came along. By being sure of this amount, you will know where you stand on salary issues when employers ask you. You don't want to lose a great opportunity and regret it later because you weren't ready to negotiate. When considering what your bottom line is, take into account other factors such as healthcare, sick leave benefits, vacation allowances, bonuses, and stock options.

ASK QUESTIONS TO DIRECT AND CONTROL YOUR INTERVIEWS

Asking questions allows you to direct the interviewer's attention to your strongest qualifications. Begin by creating a list of your top five to ten skills. Then develop a question you can ask that will allow you to sell each skill. The sample questions below introduce fund-raising and executive support skills into the interview. Another great question to ask early in an interview is "Can you tell me your top concerns or needs in hiring someone for this position?" This question elicits a wealth of information from employers that you can use as a guide to match and market your skills to their needs. Asking questions in this way creates a dynamic image of you as someone actively taking part in each interview.

Question to Sell Your Skill:

- Does your agency have an ongoing need to procure funding in addition to grants?

Employer's Answer:

"Yes, like every agency we are solely dependent upon grants and corporate donations. What is your experience in fund-raising?"

Your Response:

"As a program director, I obtained over $60,000 from donating corporations as well as receiving annual grant approval each year that I managed the fund-raising program."

Question to Sell Your Skill:

- Does this position support executive staff?

Employer's Answer:

"Yes, it requires working closely with the president and vice president of marketing."

Your Response:

"Great, in my last position I served as an administrative assistant to the president, CEO, and department heads who were responsible for sales staff in three states."

Phase III: Interview Closure

As you talk with employers, keep track of which of your skills and experience most interest them. Then summarize this information when closing your interview. For example, an employer was very interested in Randy's ability to develop new accounts. As he shook hands with the interviewer, Randy summarized his skills by saying, "Having pioneered a new territory and developed over 200 new accounts in only nine months, I've acquired the skills to step in and assist you in quickly meeting your sales quotas. I'm very excited about this opportunity and look forward to a second interview." Summarizing your skills in this way presents you as dynamic and purposeful and ends the interview with your strongest selling points.

BEFORE YOU LEAVE, ASK IF YOU'RE A TOP CANDIDATE

If the interviewer doesn't state that you are a top candidate at the end of your interview, be sure to ask, "Do you feel my skills and experience qualify me as one of your top candidates?" This gives you an opportunity to hear the employer's concerns about hiring you before you leave her or his office. Once you've heard her or his concerns, you can then deal with them. For example, an employer might reply, "I'm not sure you have enough direct customer experience." You might then ask, "Can you tell me what you mean by direct customer service experience?" The employer might reply, "Well, we generally need someone who has dealt with customers in person rather than by phone." You reply, "Great, at XYZ Company I managed front counter sales dealing in person with more than 40 customers a day to process orders valued up to $7,000. This required strong problem-solving, organizational, and prioritization skills. Is this the type of experience you prefer?" Looking interested, the employer might then answer, "Yes, let me ask you a few more questions. . . ."

Salespeople use this tactic all the time. If customers hesitate to buy a product, it's their job to find out why. Once customer concerns are identified, the salesperson can then explain how their product meets customer needs. This tactic substantially increases sales. Do the same thing when you interview. Practice asking, "Do you feel my skills and experience qualify me as one of your top candidates?" until you can do so confidently. Then anticipate and practice overcoming any concerns an employer may have about hiring you.

ASK WHEN SECOND INTERVIEWS WILL BE CONDUCTED

Before you leave an interview, find out when the employer will conduct second interviews or make a hiring decision. You might ask, "Do you know when you'll be conducting second interviews?" Employers will generally tell you when you can expect to hear from them. If they don't, ask, "May I follow up with you on such-and-such date if I haven't heard from you?" By following up on a specific date, you'll be able to determine where you stand and won't be left wondering what has happened to the job. Both this strategy and the previous one make many people uncomfortable. It's normal if you feel that way, but don't let your discomfort keep you from practicing and using these techniques.

Now that we've discussed the three phases of the interviewing cycle, let's talk about how you can strengthen your image even further and address specific questions you may be asked during interviews.

More Tips to Strengthen Your Image

To add more power to your interviews, this section includes tips to help you strengthen your image even further. For example, providing specific details about your industry knowledge and ability to perform a particular job task convinces employers of the depth of your skills and experience. The first example below shows the depth of knowledge this person has of family law; the second one shows an in-depth knowledge of MS Word and advanced word processing functions; and the third example shows depth of experience supervising a broad range of electronics production personnel. Be sure to use specific examples and relevant industry language to market any experience you have that matches the position you want.

Q: Tell me about your experience scheduling family law court cases.

A: Overseeing court calendaring required a knowledge of all legal cases being scheduled including dissolutions, modifications, paternity, adoption, custody and support, prenuptial agreements, property division, will, and estate planning.

Q: Describe your advanced word processing skills using MS Word to prepare contracts.

A: Over five years of experience using Word includes preparing and formatting contracts and proposals with page numbering, table of contents, tables and columns, style sheets, templates, mathematical calculations, and the importing and placement of graphics.

Q: How many electronics production staff have you supervised at any one time?

A: In my current position, I supervise up to forty-five staff including eight production leads, six electronic technicians, ten wave flow solder specialists, ten manual solder assemblers, nine electronic component and circuit board assemblers, and two electronics inventory control clerks.

DE-EMPHASIZE YOUR WEAKNESSES

To increase your success in landing interviews, it's important to identify your weaknesses and turn them into strengths. If you can't turn a weakness into a strength, then you must deflect an employer's attention away from it. Sherry wanted to become an accounting clerk but didn't have experience. As you can see from the Before example shown below, Sherry ran into problems when asked about her bookkeeping experience. As a result, Sherry was disillusioned and worried. However, Sherry did have experience that was bookkeeping related and was able to focus the employer's attention on that experience—which took her response rate from zero to one hundred percent. Take a moment and read the After example below. In only two weeks of using this new approach Sherry landed three interviews and two job offers.

BEFORE

Employer: *Tell me about your bookkeeping experience.*

Sherry: "I recently completed a course in bookkeeping and received a ninety-five percent average. Using this training I want to move into the accounting field."

Employer: *"Well that's nice, but we need someone with experience. Send your resume and we'll keep it on file."*

AFTER

Employer: *Tell me about your bookkeeping experience.*

Sherry: "While I was with Frederick and Nelson I handled over $60,000 in cash and receipts for my department. In addition, I have a certificate in bookkeeping and office automation."

Employer: *"Great, that sounds just like the experience we need. Can you come in for an interview tomorrow?"*

As you can see, Sherry drew upon a related skill to offset her lack of bookkeeping experience. This focused the employer's attention on her strength, not on a possible weakness. As you list the skills required for each position, ask yourself how your background relates. Even if there is only a small thread in your experience that relates, take that thread and expand upon it. Focus your answers on that experience and minimize or eliminate what you don't have. Remember, many qualified applicants are never hired, but those who market themselves most effectively are, even if they don't have all the skills an employer is looking for. Maximize what you do have. It will get you a job.

ANTICIPATE AND ANSWER QUESTIONS YOU'RE WORRIED ABOUT

It seems we all have one or two questions we worry about being asked in an interview. It might be a question about our education, experience, or work history. Sherry had worried most about being asked to describe her bookkeeping experience. Believing she didn't have a good answer, she felt unqualified. Her mind would go blank and she'd begin imagining how terrible she would do in her interviews. Then she'd become even more anxious and dread going on interviews. However, we came up with a terrific answer that landed Sherry several interviews and two great jobs offers. By practicing how she was going to answer that question, she slowly built her confidence. After several role-playing sessions, her whole demeanor changed and she left feeling motivated, excited, and proud of herself. That's exactly what you want to do. You want to identify any questions you're afraid of being asked and then write and practice answers that boost your confidence.

Overcoming your fears puts you in control of your emotions. Rather than letting fears run wild in your mind, face your fears, deal with them, and move on. If you don't face your fears and gain control of them, they will have a negative impact upon your interviews. Studies show that public speaking is a number one fear for many people. Interviewing must rank a close second. Fear of interviewing can cause you to procrastinate in your job search, or botch an interview, so it's very important to identify your fears and overcome them.

DEMONSTRATE YOUR KNOWLEDGE OF THE JOB, COMPANY, OR INDUSTRY

An incredibly strong interviewing technique is to subtly mention important facts you've learned about a job, company, or the industry you are pursuing. This worked for me. I had gathered about forty articles on the temporary industry and took them to my first interview. The position was for a personnel coordinator with a leading placement agency. Since I had never worked in this field, the employer was concerned and asked me the question shown below. While answering it, I casually fanned out the articles. This strategy made a strong statement about my motivation and desire to work in this field. The employer later told me he was impressed by my research, and even though he had already selected someone else, he changed his mind and hired me. I hadn't really believed that doing such research would help and I had also felt very anxious doing it. Yet, it worked! Just like I did, think of creative ways you can share information you learn as a natural part of your conversations during each interview.

Employer's Question

> "I see you haven't worked in this industry; why have you chosen it and why do you think it's a good fit?"

Applicant's Answer

> "Prior to finding your advertisement, I had already planned on going into the personnel field so I began conducting research. I was very surprised to find that temporary placement is a $12 billion industry and that it includes many specialty areas such as technical, administrative, and legal placement. Knowing my administrative and business management skills are a good fit for administrative placement, I then began researching firms and found over forty articles on this industry including several on Dunhill. Reviewing this information I realized that this field is growing and will offer me many opportunities."

USE POWER WORDS AND QUANTIFY YOUR QUALIFICATIONS

While writing your resume, you learned how to quantify and use action or "power words." You'll also want to quantify and use power words when answering interview questions. Using them can have a tremendous impact on the image that an employer develops of your skills. Controlling and elevating the image you present will generate a greater number and higher quality of job offers. Below, you'll see two sets of examples that illustrate how important it is to use power words and numbers.

Can you tell me about your outside sales and account management experience?

BEFORE "Well, I set up and handled key accounts. I also increased the sales to my accounts substantially."

AFTER "While managing key accounts such as Key Bank, Nordstrom, and Microsoft, I increased sales by over thirty-five percent, or $170,000, annually."

Can you tell me about your customer service skills?

BEFORE "While driving trucks, I dealt with customers dropping off goods and having them sign their paperwork."

AFTER "With XYZ Company I provided customer service to a client base of over 2,000 accounts. Delivering products from $1,000 to over $10,000 per order often required strong problem-solving skills. If there was a problem with an order, I had to resolve it to the customer's satisfaction as quickly as possible. Because I had become so good at dealing with customers, over one-third of our client base had requested that I be assigned to service their accounts."

EMPLOYERS HIRE ENTHUSIASTIC APPLICANTS

When interviewing for each and every position, be sure to show your enthusiasm for that position. Hiring officials who have conducted a lot of interviews will tell you that many applicants hardly ever smile or act genuinely interested in the position for which they're applying. Even though you may really want the position, if you don't show your enthusiasm, an interviewer will probably assume that you can take or leave the job. So why would he or she hire you?

I once interviewed someone for an office position that required a lot of record keeping and paperwork. During the interview, the applicant said he didn't like bookkeeping and wouldn't really be happy dealing with paperwork all day. When I reminded him that the position required a lot of paperwork, he tried to backtrack and said, "Well, I don't really like doing it, but I'm good at it." The impression he gave me was that he'd take the job and as soon as something better came along he'd be gone. Of course I didn't hire him.

I almost didn't land a teaching position because I hadn't determined what I wanted before the interview. After closing my personnel agency, I had planned to take a couple of months off before going back to work. However, when I contacted a friend she set me up for an interview the next day. During the interview the employer kept asking when I would be available and I kept giving a vague answer because I hadn't really made up my mind about going back to work.

After I left the interview I went to the library and called several vocational schools to see if I could find similar positions. During this process I discovered there were very few teaching positions I would qualify for without a master's degree. After that my attitude changed. The job was suddenly exactly what I wanted, even though it meant having to go back to work sooner than I wanted. I wrote a thank-you letter knowing that I had to use it to overcome the lukewarm response I had given during my interview.

In my letter I stated the following: "This position is an excellent opportunity for me. Being able to use my business management and computer skills combined with my teaching and motivational skills will provide me with a tremendous amount of job satisfaction. I would like to accept this position, if I am selected, and will be available in two weeks. I look forward to talking with you on Monday."

I wouldn't have been hired if I hadn't rescued my interview with that thank-you letter. This experience shows how important it is to cover all your bases when interviewing, even if you're not sold on the job one hundred percent. I ended up staying in that position for two years and would have been very upset with myself if I had lost that opportunity because of my lack of enthusiasm. Make a list of all the reasons you are excited about the position you are applying for. It could be that the job is close to your home, that it will allow you increased career growth, or that you excel in a particular skill that this position uses. Each of these reasons can be turned into a selling point during your interviews and can be used to convince an employer to hire you. Be creative and show your enthusiasm.

USE PROPS

Another great selling tool to use in an interview is what I call a prop or visual aid. The articles I took into my interview with Dunhill Temps were a prop. Having them in hand was much more impressive and convincing than just saying I had done a lot of research. Other props can include

- Letters of recommendation
- Great performance evaluations
- Awards
- Examples of work you've done.

Using them allows you to be actively involved in your interview and helps to draw attention to your selling points. I also consider attaché cases and nice folders as props. Using a nice case or folder helps me feel more professional and confident.

Carefully plan what props you are going to use. You'll want to make sure that they are easy to use and that you understand them thoroughly. One of my clients took a report he had prepared into an interview. The employer seemed impressed until he asked my client several questions about the report that my client couldn't answer. He had been doing great up until that point, but then lost control of the interview. If he had practiced using this prop and had anticipated questions about it, he would have been prepared and felt that he would have been hired. I like to use an attaché case that holds my keys and all the items I normally carry in a purse. Fumbling with both a purse and a case makes me feel awkward. In a similar way I also consider clothes and shoes as props. Just like an actor or actress going into wardrobe to select clothes and props for a big scene, you'll want to select props that help you put on the best show, increase your confidence, and sell your top skills.

The Most Common Questions and How to Answer Them

We've already covered many of the questions interviewers ask, but let's take another look at the most common questions to further strengthen your interviewing skills. In general, there are two types of questions that applicants find difficult: open-ended questions or questions intended to create stress.

OPEN-ENDED QUESTIONS

Open-ended questions generally get people in the most trouble. For example, "Tell me about yourself," is an open-ended question. Many people have no idea how to answer this question properly and as a result feel themselves falling into the great interviewing pit—they begin rambling. In one interview I conducted, a woman told me she was getting a divorce and then proceeded to tell me about her marital problems. I felt she was going through some very difficult times and assumed it might be hard for her to concentrate on work. I also assumed she might have a hard time making it to work. As a result, I excluded her as a candidate.

To answer open-ended questions effectively, you must be prepared for them. Use them as an opportunity to sell your professional skills and abilities rather than talk about your hobbies or where you're from. While some interviewers may want to know about your personal history, most employers want to know about your skills and experience.

Many employers interview dozens of people in a day, so it's important to keep your answers short, to the point, and related to the position you are applying for. As you answer each question your ability to communicate and think on your feet will be judged. That's another reason why it's important to have anticipated the questions you'll be asked and to have practiced your answers. You'll want to come across as smoothly and confidently as possible. Watching award-winning actors, we often forget how much work they've put into being so polished and convincing. As a result, we marvel at their talent. However, their talent is in large part hard work and rehearsal.

STRESS QUESTIONS

Angie came back from an interview feeling rather miffed. She said the person interviewing her had asked, "Don't you think you are just a little too confident and overqualified for this position?" in a snooty tone of voice. Angie replied firmly but pleasantly, "No, ma'am, my qualifications match this position. It requires someone who has good problem-solving skills and is confident, and these are two of my strongest skills." When she went back to her second interview she was told she had answered that question very well. The employer was looking for someone who could think on his or her feet and handle tough situations. Having anticipated such questions, Angie presented a confident image and was hired.

The Ten Common Interview Questions

Here's a quick summary of the most common interview questions, followed by tips and examples of effective answers. These answers are just guidelines—you can be creative. Write answers that sell you and your unique skills. Ask yourself what kind of assumptions the employer will make about you based on each answer you give. Make sure that your answers create the type of assumptions you want employers to have about you, and that such assumptions match the image you want to present. If they don't, then change your answers.

1. Tell me about yourself.

Keep your answer short, to the point, and related to the position you are applying for. Spend one to two minutes answering this question.

ANSWER: "I have over five years experience in office administration, which includes bookkeeping and supervision of clerical personnel. I enjoy a fast-paced environment and like a challenge. Having a variety of duties to perform each day such as coordinating projects and solving problems makes a job fun for me. Your office seems busy and challenging, just the type of environment I thrive on."

2. What are your three greatest strengths?

When answering this question, provide answers that match your strengths to the skills or abilities needed for the job you want. For example, consider a machinist deciding to apply for a customer service position. When asked this question, he says, "I like designing mechanical parts, using my hands to make things, and solving problems to make my designs work. These are three of my greatest strengths."

This answer would be fine if the machinist were continuing as a machinist, but it isn't effective in selling him for a customer service position because it doesn't match the employer's needs. The interviewer will probably assume the machinist prefers working alone and with objects rather than with people and wouldn't hire him. Be sure to give answers that illustrate how your strengths match the job for which you are interviewing. Here's an example of how to answer this question when applying for a customer service position.

ANSWER: "Dealing with up to 200 customers per day requires that I be patient and enjoy working with customers. I'm a good listener and problem solver with the ability to put people at ease and diffuse tense situations. All three are strengths that have contributed to my being promoted in customer service positions."

3. What is your greatest weakness?

When answering this question, be sure to select a weakness that you can talk about confidently and can turn into a selling point. Many people feel guilty if they don't pick their worst weakness. Don't fall into that trap. Pick a weakness that you're not embarrassed to talk about and then explain how you deal with it effectively. This is a good example of how to answer this question:

ANSWER: "I tend to be creative and used to get sidetracked coming up with new ideas rather than sticking with systems that were already in place. Unless something is causing a problem, or I can see how improving it will increase productivity or profitability, I've learned not to waste time trying to improve it. Now I actually enjoy seeing if I can continually improve the quantity and quality of my daily production."

4. Why should I hire you over other candidates?

As you watch the person interviewing you, be aware of subtle buying signals. If the person leans forward during your interview and seems more interested in a particular skill, be sure to talk about that skill when answering this question. If the interviewer seems overly concerned about the habits, skills, or traits he or she desires in an employee, then be sure to give an answer that demonstrates how your skills and abilities meet those needs.

ANSWER: "It seems you need someone who is reliable and trustworthy in this position. While working at XYZ Company, I demonstrated these traits. Handling up to $10,000 a day in sales and receipts, I consistently balanced each till to the penny. This position also required someone with excellent attendance and reliability. With my proven abilities I believe I fit what you are looking for in an employee."

5. Where would you like to be with this company in a year?

Keep your answer tied to the position you are interviewing for. Make sure you present an image that you will be happy in this position for quite some time. Many people make the mistake of saying they want rapid growth and promotion, which conflicts with the needs of many employers.

Employers want employees to stay in a new position for a good length of time, so it's important to let the employer know you will do your best to excel in the position for which you've applied. Let him or her know that after a substantial period of time in that position, and after you have proven yourself, that you would like to be considered for promotion and growth.

ANSWER: "I am very interested in this position and plan to achieve top sales as an account manager. My goal is to grow within this position for as long as possible. After I've proven my abilities over time, I would then like to be considered for growth opportunities as they become available."

6. Why are you looking for a new position?

This is another one of those questions that causes many people to fall into the great interviewing pit. It's tempting to unload on past and current employers, but avoid it. Instead, say that you feel the position you are interviewing for is a growth opportunity and sounds challenging. If the company you are leaving is experiencing turnover or isn't stable, mention these facts, but do so without showing anger or irritation. Avoid painting a negative picture of any of your employers because most interviewers will assume you are the problem, not the employer.

ANSWER: "After having been with XYZ Company for over two years, I wasn't actively seeking a new position. However, a friend gave me your advertisement and your ad intrigued me. This position seems to be a perfect match for my career goals."

7. Why are you interested in our company?

If you're asked this question and you haven't done any research, you will feel very foolish. So it's a good idea to gather information on each company before your interview. However, you may not be able to find literature regarding smaller firms. In this instance, ask the receptionist if you can look over the company's brochures as you wait for your interview. Pick out information that will help you sound knowledgeable. If you can't get information about the company, then describe the job requirements that make you want the position you're applying for.

ANSWER: "I am very interested in working for XYZ company because the accounting position will use and expand my cost accounting and contract administration experience. Also, I noticed that your office seems to be relaxed yet very busy and your employees seem to be happy and interact well. Altogether, this makes the position and your company very attractive to me."

8. How would you describe your last supervisor?

Never say anything negative about your supervisor. If you had a poor relationship with your supervisor or thought he or she was incompetent, be aware of your body language as you answer this question. You may say pleasant things but if your foot begins to twitch or you get an irritated look on your face, the employer's intuition will kick in and a warning signal may go off about you. Find something positive to say about your supervisor that you actually believe. If you believe it, then you won't have a problem between what your mouth is saying and what your body is doing.

ANSWER: "My last supervisor has excellent organizational skills. She plans ahead and has an innate ability to delegate projects to the right employee for each job. I learned a lot by working with her."

9. Why were you fired?

Don't become defensive, embarrassed, or sad when answering this question. Be honest yet slant your answers so that they put you in the best light. One student I worked with had been accused of stealing $30,000. She was fired and the case was taken to court, but she was not convicted due to lack of evidence. Our staff was convinced that she had not taken the money and left her in charge of the front office, where she handled money being paid by new students. After six months, there were no problems and she received an excellent letter of recommendation from the director. She was then able to share her letter of recommendation with prospective employers. No matter why you were fired, use role-playing to practice your responses to this question until you can do so confidently and give examples that show how you have overcome the problem.

ANSWER: "I was let go for poor attendance. Since leaving that company, I have completed a two-year college program and have three letters of recommendation with me [you pull them out] from my instructors. During this time I missed only one class. Would you like to read my recommendation letters?"

10. Why have you held so many jobs?

Be ready for this question if you have had a sporadic work history. Be honest, yet have answers prepared that put you in the best light. It may be that you've gotten bored, been fired, or had car problems. Don't mention any of these reasons if you can avoid it. If you left one job for another one, say that you were offered a position with better pay or better growth opportunities. If you worked while going to school then be sure to point this out. Role-play until you have an answer that presents you as reliable.

ANSWER: "After I relocated here, I accepted my first position out of financial necessity but moved to a higher position in only three months. Two of the firms I worked for went out of business so I had no control over leaving them. If you exclude them, I have left only one company by choice over the last five years."

And the List Goes On: More Interview Questions

If it seems as though we've exhausted every possible question that interviewers can ask, we haven't yet. Given what's at stake in hiring new employees, interviewers want to make sure they've covered every base. You want to take the same approach as you prepare. Below, you'll find a list of additional questions that you may wish to practice answering. Read through the list and pick out at least ten more that you feel you will be asked. Use role-playing to answer each one until you can do so confidently and smoothly. To project a dynamic image, be sure to quantify your achievements, use action words, and give examples of what you have accomplished. Keep your answers short and to the point, using them to build a case for your qualifications.

If you prepare for each phase of the interviewing cycle and the questions it may generate, you'll be amazed at how much more confident you will feel before and during your interviews. Practice your questions and answers until they seem like second nature to you. I usually spend from one to three hours preparing for interviews. The more nervous or concerned I am about my qualifications, the more time I spend preparing. Even though it's stressful and makes me feel anxious, I do it. I achieved a one hundred percent interview and hire rate for the last three jobs I held by using these strategies. My clients also report very high hire rates when they prepare thoroughly for each phase of the interviewing cycle.

Practice Interview Questions

1. What will previous employers tell me about your performance on the job?
2. What are your long-term career goals with our company and into the future?
3. Describe your perfect job.
4. Why do you want to change career fields?
5. Why have you been unemployed for so long?
6. How long do you plan on staying with our company?
7. Describe your organizational skills for me.
8. Describe your ability to handle stress.
9. Describe your problem-solving skills.
10. What do you find most frustrating in a job?
11. What type of people do you dislike working with?
12. What do you think makes a good employee?
13. Do you feel you are a good employee? Why?
14. How can you contribute to our company?
15. How would you handle a problem with a co-worker?
16. Can I contact your references? If not, why not?
17. What has your attendance on the job been like?
18. How do you feel about working overtime?

19. Are you willing to take work home if needed?

20. When changes are needed, how do you react?

21. How much sick leave did you take last year?

22. What do you feel your top qualifications are for this job?

23. How do you feel about being trained for multiple jobs?

24. If I verify your punctuality, what will past employers tell me about you?

25. If we need to change your work schedule and hours, is that acceptable?

26. This job sometimes requires travel. How often can you travel?

27. Do you smoke? How long has it been since you've stopped smoking?

28. Our company policy requires drug testing. Is that acceptable to you?

29. This position requires the ability to lift fifty pounds. Can you do that?

30. This job is repetitive and may be boring. How do you feel about that?

31. We were looking for someone with more experience. Why should I hire you?

32. Tell me about a time that you handled a very difficult work situation.

33. Do you prefer working with customers or working alone?

34. Give me an example of how quickly you learn new things on the job.

35. How would your co-workers describe you?

After the Interview: Writing Successful Thank-You Letters

Thank-you letters are an opportunity to remind employers who you are and to finish selling yourself as a top candidate. After your interviews, take notes on which of your skills and abilities seemed of greatest interest to interviewers. You'll know this by their body language, such as if they lean forward and smile when you talk about one of your skills. You'll also be able to gauge what they are particularly interested in by thinking about the detailed questions they asked. Use this information to write a powerful thank-you letter. Compare the thank-you letter on the facing page to the one on page 308. Which letter has the best design and content? Which one could have been written by anyone? Which one is unique and sells the candidate most strongly? Of these two people, whom would you call for a second interview? Use these examples to guide you in writing effective thank-you letters. Send your thank-you letter the day of or the day after your interview to ensure that employers receive it before they make a hiring decision.

Don't Hesitate to Follow Up

If you know the employer will make a hiring decision on a certain date and you do not hear on that day, get your courage up and call the following day. If the employer has not yet decided whom to hire, your call may put you in the forefront. Dorothy had been told a hiring decision would be made on a Tuesday but wasn't contacted. Wednesday morning she called the employer. He told her he had been wavering between hiring her and someone else but that her phone call, coupled with the thank-you letter she had sent, made the decision for him and he offered her the job. Her competitor had not sent a thank-you letter and had not followed up. Follow-up can land you a job. It can also let you know if you're not in the running so that you free up your energy and focus on your next job lead.

Rex VanderHolm
1414 50th Street
Sacramento, Arizona 37374
(555) 555-5555

Date

National Customer Service Corporation
57483 Lillyington Lane
Sacramento, Arizona 37374

Dear Mr. Parfitt:

Thank you for interviewing me yesterday for the Customer Service Representative
position.

I am confident that I have the skills needed for this position and look forward to a
second interview. I am very excited about your expansion and the opportunities
for growth that it would provide me.

Again, thanks for your time and consideration. I can be contacted at (555) 555-5555.

Sincerely,

Rex VanderHolm

Rex VanderHolm
1414 50th Street
Sacramento, Arizona 37374
(555) 555-5555

Date

National Customer Service Corporation
57483 Lillyington Lane
Sacramento, Arizona 37374

Re: Thank-You for Yesterday's Interview

Dear Mr. Parfitt:

Thank you for interviewing me for the Customer Service Representative position. Your plans for expansion are very exciting. My knowledge of customer satisfaction measurement and service recovery methods will allow me to implement your new programs and train staff as needed. I'd like to summarize additional points of my background that are relevant but which we did not discuss:

Customer Service Administration
Dealing with up to 200 customers and accounting for over $ 1/4 million in sales per month required strong troubleshooting and liaison skills. As a Customer Service Lead, I trained and supervised 12 staff in all areas of service and sales.

Professional and Corporate Customer Service Training
The 1,400-hour certificate program I completed at Sacramento College focused on increasing corporate profitability and gave me a hands-on knowledge of customer retention, marketing, invoicing, and collections techniques.

Computerized Customer Service Applications
My use of computerized systems includes running cash, sales, and expense reports; MS Word, Excel, and Access; and customer account processing, and automated billing programs.

Again, I would like to thank you for speaking with me. As we discussed, I will contact you next Tuesday regarding a second interview. Please call me at (555) 555-5555 if I can provide additional information regarding my qualifications.

Sincerely,

Rex VanderHolm

A Final Word about Preparing for Interviews

Finally, you've landed an interview for your dream job! To guide you through each phase of the interviewing cycle, I've provided the checklist below. Before you begin, take a note pad and use several pieces of paper to prepare questions and answers for each phase of the interviewing cycle. On the first page tape several ads or job descriptions for the job(s) you want. Then go through the checklist step by step, identifying potential questions, and writing answers that sell your best skills. Then role-play each question until you can say your answers smoothly, confidently, and quickly.

Graph each of your answers and the image you present as well as the risk employers will face in hiring you. Improve any answers that make you appear over- or underqualified. Don't let the graphs intimidate you. They're only meant to help you identify where your weaknesses are and where you need to spend time practicing. Even if you think you're weak in some areas, you'll still come across as a top candidate if you follow the strategies in this chapter. This is true because the majority of job seekers do not prepare for interviews. Your preparation is what will set you apart, even if you do have some weaknesses (although they may not be apparent to employers). Remember, the more time you put into pre-interview practice, the bigger payoff you will receive by landing more second interviews and better job offers.

INTERVIEWING CHECKLIST

Phase I: Introductions and First Impressions

- Do your clothing and accessories present an image appropriate to the position and salary you are seeking?
- Are you ready to maintain confident eye contact and offer a firm, friendly handshake?
- Have you prepared enough so that you feel confident and ready to answer any question you're asked?

Phase II: Questions Generated from Your Resume

- Have you reviewed each statement in your resume to anticipate any questions it may generate?

Questions to Judge Your Skills and Experience

- Have you compiled between five and ten ads or job descriptions for the jobs you want?
- Have you made a list of the job requirements necessary for the positions you want?
- Have you made a list of questions employers may ask along with appropriate answers regarding each requirement?

Questions about Your Bottom-Line Contributions

- Have you identified each employer's bottom-line needs and questions they may ask about them?
- Have you prepared answers that demonstrate how you can contribute to profitability and productivity?
- Have you created a list of questions you can ask that allow you to market your bottom-line contributions and skills?

Questions about Personality, Values, and Coping Style

- Have you written at least nine questions you will be asked about your personality, values, and coping style?
- Have you prepared answers that you can use in response to such questions?

Questions about Your Work History

- Have you reviewed your work history and created a list of questions it may generate?
- Have you prepared answers that present your background in the best possible light?

Questions about Your Education and Extracurricular Activities

- Have you made a list of questions that you are likely to be asked about your education?
- Have you assessed the skills gained from your education or extracurricular activities?
- Can you explain how your education or activities have provided skills that match the job you want?

Questions about Your References

- Have you asked your references for permission to use them? Did you prepare a reference sheet?
- Have you prepared a list of questions you may be asked about your references?
- Have you developed answers that present you in the best light?

Questions about Your Salary History and Requirements

- Do you know the average pay rate for the job you want?
- Have you role-played how you will answer or delay salary questions?
- Do you know your minimum salary requirement?

Phase III: Interview Closure

- Have you practiced how you will close your interviews and what you will say?
- Are you prepared to ask if you are a top candidate?
- Are you prepared to ask when second interviews will be conducted?

RATE HOW YOU'LL BE PERCEIVED BY EMPLOYERS

Your Image: Overqualified, Qualified, or Underqualified?

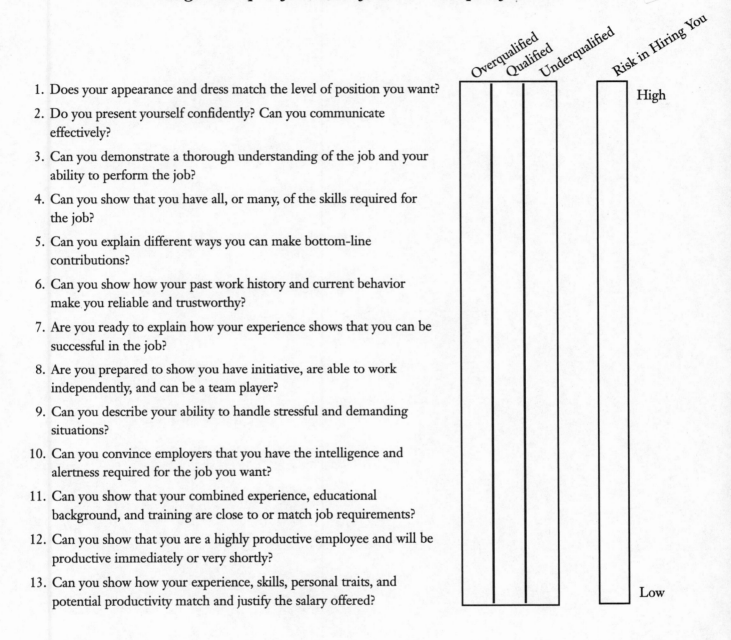

1. Does your appearance and dress match the level of position you want?

2. Do you present yourself confidently? Can you communicate effectively?

3. Can you demonstrate a thorough understanding of the job and your ability to perform the job?

4. Can you show that you have all, or many, of the skills required for the job?

5. Can you explain different ways you can make bottom-line contributions?

6. Can you show how your past work history and current behavior make you reliable and trustworthy?

7. Are you ready to explain how your experience shows that you can be successful in the job?

8. Are you prepared to show you have initiative, are able to work independently, and can be a team player?

9. Can you describe your ability to handle stressful and demanding situations?

10. Can you convince employers that you have the intelligence and alertness required for the job you want?

11. Can you show that your combined experience, educational background, and training are close to or match job requirements?

12. Can you show that you are a highly productive employee and will be productive immediately or very shortly?

13. Can you show how your experience, skills, personal traits, and potential productivity match and justify the salary offered?

CONCLUSION

All phases of looking for a job require effectively marketing yourself, whether you're writing your resume, networking, or interviewing. The most important job search tool to learn is how to control and elevate your image so that it matches the job and salary level you want. This helps you understand how employers perceive and judge you, and what you have to offer them. This understanding paves the way for accelerated career and salary growth. By correctly positioning your image, you will not only be able to achieve current job search goals, but will have a head start when seeking promotions or changing jobs throughout the rest of your career.

Writing your resume is the foundation of learning how to control and elevate your image and requires that you complete a wide range of steps. These include identifying all of your skills, using powerful language to show the depth of your achievements, analyzing employer needs and showing how you can meet them, and learning how to convey quickly why an employer should listen to you, want to interview you, and ultimately hire you.

As you move forward in your career, write a new resume for each of your career goals. Come back to this book and complete the steps listed above so that you gain fresh perspective on new skills you have developed and should market, as well as to determine how your image should be altered in order to look well qualified for each promotion or job you want. In this way, your resume will guide you in successfully competing for future promotions and jobs.

By taking control of the image you present in all areas of your job search, you will consistently market yourself as a top candidate. Good luck! With a proven resume, you will achieve the job and salary of your dreams!

APPENDIX: Action Verbs

ACCEPTING
_Accepted
_Adopted
_Received

ACCOUNTING FOR
_Accounted
_Audited
_Balanced
_Budgeted
_Calculated
_Computed
_Credited
_Detailed
_Documented
_Estimated
_Inventoried
_Measured
_Posted
_Reconciled
_Recorded
_Registered
_Reimbursed
_Scanned
_Scored
_Screened
_Selected
_Tabulated
_Tracked
_Validated
_Verified

ACHIEVING
_Accomplished
_Achieved
_Advanced
_Attained
_Championed
_Earned
_Excelled
_Promoted
_Succeeded
_Surpassed
_Won

ACQUIRING
_Accrued

_Accumulated
_Acquired
_Brought
_Captured
_Obtained
_Recaptured

ADVISING
_Advised
_Advocated
_Affirmed
_Consulted
_Counseled
_Helped
_Prescribed

ANALYZING
_Analyzed
_Appraised
_Ascertained
_Assessed
_Compared
_Considered
_Critiqued
_Deciphered
_Diagnosed
_Evaluated
_Examined
_Explored
_Graded
_Impacted
_Inspected
_Investigated
_Proofed
_Proofread
_Researched
_Reviewed
_Studied
_Surveyed
_Tested

ANTICIPATING
_Anticipated
_Forecast
_Perceived
_Predicted
_Projected

APPROVING
_Approved
_Authorized
_Awarded
_Certified
_Commended
_Elected
_Nominated
_Recommended
_Recognized
_Referred
_Sponsored

ASSEMBLING
_Arranged
_Assembled
_Built
_Compiled
_Constructed

ASSISTING
_Accommodated
_Assisted
_Enabled
_Served
_Supported

CATEGORIZING
_Catalogued
_Categorized
_Charted
_Coded
_Correlated
_Departmentalized
_Indexed
_Logged
_Mapped
_Ranked
_Rated
_Related
_Rendered
_Specialized
_Specified

COLLECTING
_Collected
_Intercepted
_Reclaimed

_Recouped
_Recovered
_Retained
_Retrieved

COMBINING
_Assimilated
_Attached
_Collaborated
_Combined
_Compounded
_Included
_Incorporated
_Integrated
_Linked
_Loaded
_Networked
_Synthesized

COMMUNICATING
_Communicated
_Dialogued
_Discussed
_Interacted
_Interfaced
_Joined
_Merged
_Responded
_Translated

COMPLETING
_Closed
_Completed
_Finalized
_Finished
_Formalized
_Furnished
_Operated
_Performed
_Prepared
_Processed
_Produced
_Provided
_Submitted
_Supplied
_Terminated
_Transacted

CONDENSING
_Concentrated
_Condensed
_Conserved
_Consolidated
_Cut
_Deleted
_Derived
_Downsized
_Economized
_Eliminated
_Extracted
_Lessened
_Narrowed
_Reduced
_Released
_Removed
_Retired
_Saved
_Summarized

COORDINATING
_Contributed
_Cooperated
_Coordinated
_Dealt
_Facilitated
_Followed
_Orchestrated
_Participated
_Scheduled

CREATING
_Conceived
_Conceptualized
_Configured
_Created
_Designed
_Developed
_Devised
_Engineered
_Established
_Fabricated
_Formed
_Formulated
_Founded

_Generated
_Innovated
_Installed
_Invented
_Modeled
_Molded
_Originated
_Programmed
_Rendered
_Styled
_Visualized

DELEGATING
_Appointed
_Assigned
_Delegated
_Designated
_Devoted
_Issued
_Notified
_Required

EMPHASIZING
_Emphasized
_Focused
_Underscored

EXPANDING
_Deregulated
_Diversified
_Divested
_Enlarged
_Expanded
_Extended
_Grew
_Increased
_Multiplied
_Syndicated

EXPLAINING
_Clarified
_Defined
_Described
_Elaborated
_Illustrated

FINDING
_Located
_Sought

_Sourced
_Traced

GUARANTEEING
_Ensured
_Guaranteed
_Insured

HIRING
_Employed
_Enlisted
_Hired
_Interviewed
_Recruited
_Rehired
_Restaffed
_Staffed

IDENTIFYING
_Decided
_Detected
_Determined
_Discovered
_Identified
_Pinpointed

IMPACTING
_Affected
_Effected
_Impacted

IMPLEMENTING
_Activated
_Actualized
_Administered
_Applied
_Executed
_Implemented
_Initialized
_Initiated

IMPROVING
_Accelerated
_Adapted
_Adjusted
_Altered
_Augmented
_Automated
_Centralized
_Changed
_Converted
_Corrected
_Debugged
_Energized

_Enhanced
_Exchanged
_Expedited
_Improved
_Modernized
_Modified
_Normalized
_Overhauled
_Perfected
_Progressed
_Realigned
_Rebuilt
_Reconstructed
_Recreated
_Rectified
_Recycled
_Redesigned
_Reengineered
_Reinforced
_Remodeled
_Renewed
_Reorganized
_Repaired
_Replaced
_Replenished
_Resequenced
_Reshaped
_Restored
_Restructured
_Retooled
_Returned
_Revamped
_Revised
_Revitalized
_Rewired
_Shaped
_Simplified
_Solidified
_Solved
_Stabilized
_Standardized
_Stimulated
_Streamlined

_INSTITUTING
_Introduced
_Launched
_Opened
_Piloted
_Pioneered

_Raised
_Reignited
_Reinvented
_Set Up
_Sparked
_Spearheaded
_Started

MANAGING
_Acted
_Allocated
_Assumed
_Chaired
_Comanaged
_Commanded
_Conducted
_Controlled
_Directed
_Enforced
_Exercised
_Governed
_Guided
_Handled
_Headed
_Held
_Led
_Maintained
_Managed
_Manipulated
_Monitored
_Oversaw
_Presided
_Protected
_Regulated
_Represented
_Supervised
_Sustained

MARKETING
_Advertised
_Brokered
_Displayed
_Exhibited
_Lobbied
_Marketed
_Merchandised
_Penetrated
_Positioned
_Publicized
_Sold

_Solicited

MAXIMIZING
_Capitalized
_Maximized
_Optimized

MOTIVATING
_Convinced
_Encouraged
_Engaged
_Entertained
_Influenced
_Inspired
_Interested
_Involved
_Motivated
_Persuaded

MOVING
_Drove
_Emerged
_Moved
_Navigated
_Placed
_Pushed
_Relocated
_Returned
_Transitioned

NEGOTIATING
_Agreed
_Arbitrated
_Challenged
_Conciliated
_Concurred
_Confronted
_Contracted
_Mediated
_Negotiated
_Proposed
_Reasoned
_Renegotiated
_Subcontracted

ORGANIZING
_Grouped
_Organized
_Planned
_Prioritized
_Sorted
_Strategized
_Structured

PREVENTING
_Circumvented
_Deferred
_Deflected
_Diverted
_Preempted
_Prevented
_Thwarted

PURCHASING
_Bid
_Bought
_Collateralized
_Funded
_Invested
_Leased
_Ordered
_Procured
_Purchased
_Requisitioned

SENDING
_Delivered
_Dispatched
_Dispensed
_Dispersed
_Distributed
_Exported
_Forwarded
_Outsourced
_Routed
_Transferred
_Transmitted

SOLVING
_Neutralized
_Resolved
_Treated
_Troubleshot
_Turned

SPEAKING
_Addressed
_Announced
_Moderated
_Narrated
_Presented
_Quoted
_Reported
_Spoke

_STRENGTHENING
_Systematized

_Transformed
_Updated
_Upgraded
_Vitalized

TEACHING
_Coached
_Cross-Trained
_Debriefed
_Demonstrated
_Disproved
_Educated
_Enlightened
_Illustrated
_Indoctrinated
_Informed
_Instructed
_Lectured
_Mentored
_Proved
_Retrained
_Showed
_Taught
_Trained

UNDERSTANDING
_Construed
_Familiarized
_Interpreted
_Learned
_Mastered
_Practiced
_Realized

USING
_Exploited
_Used
_Utilized

WRITING
_Authored
_Coauthored
_Composed
_Corresponded
_Drafted
_Drew Up
_Edited
_Published
_Rewrote
_Transcribed
_Wrote

INDEX

A

Accomplishments
   accurately describing, 20–21, 22–23
   maximizing, 19–26
Accounting/bookkeeping
   resumes, 53, 143–46, 174
   skill lists and sample sentences for, 67
Action verbs, 108, 314–15. *See also* Power words
Administrative/clerical
   resumes, 147–50, 163
   website, 241
Ads. *See* Help-wanted ads; Work-wanted ads
Annual reports, 255
Applicants, standards for judging, 275–76
ASCII format, 238–39
Assembly. *See* Production/parts/assembly
Associations
   professional, 127–28, 255
   religious, 131
Automotive
   resumes, 195
   skill lists and sample sentences for, 69
Awards, 101

B

Bookkeeping. *See* Accounting/bookkeeping
Bottom-line contributions
   importance of, 279–80
   interview questions about, 282, 289–90
Business directories, 253–54

C

Career changes, 24, 273
Cashiering. *See* Customer service/retail
Certificates, 101
Chambers of commerce, 255

Chronological resumes
   creating, in six steps, 50–64
   skill-based vs., 28–29, 33
Computer industry
   resumes, 167–68
   skill lists and sample sentences for, 71, 72
Confidence
   importance of, 246
   increasing self-, 23–24
Confidentiality, maintaining, 129, 138, 240
Construction/general labor
   resumes, 145, 196, 199–200
   skill lists and sample sentences for, 73
   website, 241
Consultants
   resumes, 177
   skill lists and sample sentences for, 84
Contact information, 138
Coping style, interview questions about, 282, 290–91
Coursework, 125
Cover letters, 203–26
   addressing to specific person, 216–17
   analyzing ads for, 204, 207
   body of, 217–18
   closing paragraph of, 218
   critiquing, 221
   designing to save time for employer, 203
   electronic, 240
   examples, 205–6, 208, 210, 220
   following up on, 223–24
   generic, 219–20
   gimmicks in, 215–16
   graphing, 212–14
   highlighting important skills in, 203, 211
   introductory paragraph, 217
   making content powerful, 204
   no response to, 270–71
   P.S. in, 218–19
   redundancy in, 215

Cover letters, continued
    resume's relationship to, 211
    salary history in, 216
    targeting correct decision maker, 226
    worksheet, 222

Curriculum vitae (CV), 153–54

Customer service/retail
    resumes, 13, 37, 155–56, 236, 237
    skill lists and sample sentences for, 70
    website, 241

CV. *See* Curriculum vitae

D

Dates, 120–21

Directories
    business, 253–54
    Dun & Bradstreet, 255
    manufacturers', 254
    Standard & Poor's, 255

Drafting
    resumes, 165
    skill lists and sample sentences for, 75

Driving/shipping
    resumes, 105, 198
    skill lists and sample sentences for, 74

Dun & Bradstreet directories, 255

E

Educational history, 43, 48, 58, 63, 123–27
    dates in, 120
    interview questions about, 282, 292–93

Education/teaching
    resumes, 153–54, 157–58
    skill lists and sample sentences for, 86
    website, 241

Electronic resumes. *See also* E-mail
    converting keyword resume to, 234–39
    example, 237
    homepage, 243
    keywords in, 228–34
    posting and writing services, 244
    visual resume vs., 227

Electronics engineering technician resumes, 166

E-mail
    attaching files to, 240
    resumes by, 225
    subject lines for, 239

Employers
    contacting, without advertised positions, 225,
        250–61
    determining if there are openings at, 258–61
    hidden needs of, 288–89
    hiring decisions by, 25–26
    large vs. small, 243
    looking for growth and promotion potential, 3
    lowering risk to, 3
    researching, 252–56
    screening by, 3
    standards for judging applicants, 275–76
    using electronic recruiting methods, 243
    websites of, 242

Employment agencies. *See also* Temporary place-
    ment agencies
    private, 266–67
    state, 267

Employment history
    addresses in, 128
    in chronological resumes, 58, 63
    dates in, 120–21
    gaps in, 121
    interview questions about, 282, 291–92,
        304–5
    with many employers, 304–5
    number of years in, 120
    with only one employer, 121–22
    out-of-state, 130
    reasons for leaving position, 129, 304
    several positions with one employer, 121
    in skill-based resumes, 43, 48
    with temporary agencies, 122

Employment Security, 242

Engineering
    resumes, 176
    skill lists and sample sentences for, 75
    website, 241

Enthusiasm, importance of, 246, 299–300

Executive/management
    resumes, 138, 189–92
    skill lists and sample sentences for, 81
    websites, 243

Executive secretary. *See* Office
    management/executive secretary

Extracurricular activities, 292–93

F

Facilities maintenance/janitorial, 77

Failure, fear of, 248

Fax, resumes by, 225

FEAR (False Evidence Appearing Real), 248

Following up, 223–24, 306

G

Governmental openings, 241, 255–56

Grade point average, 127

Graphing
cover letters, 212–14
interviews, 276–81, 311
resumes, 11–18

H

Hard skills, 39, 54

Healthcare/medical
resumes, 159–62, 175
skill lists and sample sentences for, 78
website, 241

Help-wanted ads
analyzing, for cover letters, 204, 207
analyzing, for keywords, 229–33
analyzing, for resumes, 39, 46, 54, 61
answering, 224, 264–66
finding, 265
interview questions based on, 286–88
organizing and tracking, 265
quick response to, 224
using old, 265–66

Hiring decisions, 25–26

Homepage resume, 243

Hospitality
resumes, 169–70
website, 241

Human resources
resumes, 171–72
skill lists and sample sentences for, 79

Human services. *See* Social/human services

I

Image
controlling with Twelve Questions, 89–102
conveyed by resume, 1–2, 10–18, 32
importance of, 313
strengthening in interviews, 296–301

Informational interviews, 256–58

Internet. *See* Electronic resumes; E-mail; Job search, online; Websites

Internships, 125, 151

Interviews, 275–311
checklist, 309–10
closure, 295–96
common questions in, 301–6
demonstrating knowledge of employer at, 298
directing and controlling, 283, 294–95
first impressions, 281, 283–84
following up, 306
graphing, 276–81, 311
increasing number of, 10
informational, 256–58
not being asked back for second, 271–72
phases of, 281–96
power words in, 299
props for, 300–301
strengthening image in, 296–301
thank-you letters after, 306, 307–8
writing resumes as preparation for, 4

J

Job lines, 255–56

Job search, 245–73
applying directly to employers, 225, 250–61
developing plan for, 245, 267–69
effectiveness of methods, 249–50, 267–68
fear of failure and, 248
importance of confidence and enthusiasm in, 246, 299–300
negotiating with multiple offers, 269
networking, 261–64
notebook, 250
online, 227–28, 240–44, 268
problems with, 270–73
procrastination and, 247–48
tracking and analyzing, 246, 250

Job titles
customized, 106
describing, 47, 56, 62, 90–102
interview questions about, 288
meaninglessness of many, 20–21
military, 130–31
number of, on resume, 106
repetitive, 32
salary level and, 21

Job titles, continued
    skill headings vs., 18, 21
    targeted, 103, 106
    upgrading, 20–21, 30–32, 288
Journalism
    resumes, 201–2
    skill lists and sample sentences for, 87

K

Keywords, 228–34

L

Labor. *See* Construction/general labor
Legal resumes, 147, 175

M

Machine shop
    resumes, 197, 200
    skill lists and sample sentences for, 69
Management. *See* Executive/management;
    Supervision
Manufacturers' directories, 254
Military service, 130–31, 177–78
Multiple offers, 269

N

Network administration resumes, 167
Networking, 261–64, 271, 272–73
Newspapers. *See also* Journalism
    clipping files, 254
    indexes, 254
"No," dealing with, 261

O

Objective statements, 109–17
Office management/executive secretary. *See also*
    Reception/general office
    resumes, 143, 149, 150
    skill lists and sample sentences for, 76

P

Parts. *See* Production/parts/assembly
Periodical indexes, 254
Personal information, 128–29
Personality, interview questions about, 282,
    290–91

Plain text format, 238–39
Power words, 299. *See also* Action verbs
Procrastination, 247–48
Production/parts/assembly
    resumes, 179–82
    skill lists and sample sentences for, 68
Professionals, licensed
    associations, 127–28, 255
    resumes, 173–76
    website, 241
Promotions
    avoiding, 23–24
    describing, on resume, 100
    potential for, 3
Property management resumes, 183

R

Real estate resumes, 183–84
Reception/general office. *See also* Office manage-
    ment/executive secretary
    resumes, 148, 150
    skill lists and sample sentences for, 82
References, 132–33, 282, 293
Referrals, asking for, 261
Rejection, dealing with, 261
Religious affiliations, 131
Relocating, 130
Response rates, boosting, 10
Restaurant/food service
    resumes, 164, 169–70
    skill lists and sample sentences for, 83
Resume posting services, 244
Resumes. *See also* Electronic resumes; *specific fields
    and parts*
    choosing format of, 27–33
    chronological, 28–29, 33, 50–64
    creating, in six steps, 35–64
    designing and printing, 135–38
    determining audience for, 11
    difficulty of writing, 21–22
    effects of negative feelings on, 19–20
    employer screening of, 3
    graphing, 11–18
    importance of, 1–8, 26
    length of, 119–20
    no response to, 270–71
    omitting data from, 119–33

as preparation for interviews, 4
scannable, 228, 234–36
skill-based, 27–28, 33, 35–49
strengthening content in, 103–8

Resume writing services, 244

Resume writing software, 244

Retail. *See* Customer service/retail

S

Salary
cover letters and, 216
determining your bottom line for, 294
history, 129
interview questions about, 282, 294
offers too low, 272
weak titles controlling, 21

Sales and marketing
resumes, 17, 105, 185–88
skill lists and sample sentences for, 80
website, 241

Scanning, 228, 234–36

Search engines, 240

Secretarial. *See* Office management/executive
secretary; Reception/general office

Self-employed, 84

Skill-based resumes
chronological vs., 27–28, 33
creating, in six steps, 35–49

Skill headings
customized, 106
describing, 41, 47, 56, 62, 90–102
interview questions about, 288
job titles vs., 18, 21
number of, on resume, 106
relabeling skills with, 38–39, 44, 51, 59
selecting, 40, 46, 55, 61
targeted, 103, 106

Skills
hard vs. soft, 39, 54, 234
interview questions about, 282, 284–88
lacking some, 25
listing, for previous jobs, 38, 44, 51, 59
list of, by fields, 65–87
marketing full range of, 4–6
relabeling, with skill headings, 38–39, 44,
51, 59
requested in ads, 39, 46, 54
summarizing strongest, 23

technical, 98
transferable, 66, 88

Social/human services
resumes, 193–94
skill lists and sample sentences for, 85
website, 241

Soft skills, 39, 54, 234

Software, 244

Special projects, 96

Standard & Poor's, 255

Statements. *See also* Objective statements
action verbs in, 108
bulleted, 138
creating strong, 107
prioritizing, 108
sample, by fields, 65–87

Students
college, 151–52
high school, 163–64

Supervision
describing experience in, 99
skill lists and sample sentences for, 81

T

Teaching. *See* Education/teaching

Temporary placement agencies
on resumes, 122
working with, 266–67

Thank-you letters, 306, 307–8

Trades
resumes, 195–200
skill lists and sample sentences for, 69

Training
describing experience in, 99
interview questions about, 282, 292–93
on resumes, 127

Transferable skills, 66, 88

"Twelve Questions," 42, 57, 89–102

V

Values, interview questions about, 282, 290–91

Visual resume, 227

Volunteer experience, 122–23

W

Warehouse
    resumes, 179–82
    skill lists and sample sentences for, 74

Weaknesses, de-emphasizing, 297

Web development resumes, 168

Websites
    author's, 240
    college and university, 242
    employers', 242
    Employment Security, 242
    executive/management, 243
    industry-specific, 241
    mega career, 241

Work history. *See* Employment history

Work-wanted ads, 267

Writing
    resumes, 201–2
    skill lists and sample sentences for, 87

NOTES